The Bengal Artillery

The Bengal Artillery
Development & Campaigns in India, 1749-1849

ILLUSTRATED

Captain E. Buckle

The Bengal Artillery
Development & Campaigns in India, 1749-1849
by Captain E. Buckle

ILLUSTRATED

First published under the title
Memoir of the Services of the Bengal Artillery

Leonaur is an imprint of Oakpast Ltd

Copyright in this form © 2021 Oakpast Ltd

ISBN: 978-1-78282-946-1 (hardcover)
ISBN: 978-1-78282-947-8 (softcover)

http://www.leonaur.com

Publisher's Notes

The views expressed in this book are not necessarily those of the publisher.

Contents

Introduction	9
Destruction of 1st Company in Black Hole	12
Reduction in Establishment	38
War in the Carnatic	66
Guns and Carriages	95
Introduction of Horse Artillery	117
Augmentation by Adding Golundaz	143
Rocket Troop Raised	174
Establishment of Retiring Fund	215
Reorganisation of the Regiment	246
Battles of Aliwal and Sobraon	253
Chillianwallah and the Close of the Sikh War	278

To
Lieut.-Gen. Sir George Pollock, G.C.B.
Of the Bengal Artillery,
This Memoir
Of the Services of a Corps
Of Which He is so Distinguished a Member,
Is Affectionately Inscribed by
His Sincere Friend and Admirer,
J. W. Kaye,
Late Lieut. Bengal Artillery

Introduction
By J. W. Kaye

The circumstances under which the greater portion of this *Memoir* was written, are set forth so truthfully in the following passages, taken from an Indian periodical, that I cannot do better than transcribe them:—

It was well known for some years before Captain Buckle, driven homewards by the pressure of ill health, resigned the important regimental office which he had held so creditably to himself and so advantageously to his corps, that he had long been collecting materials for a *Memoir of the Bengal Artillery,* and had been engaged, in brief intervals of leisure, in their arrangement and reproduction in the form of an elaborate work of military history.

In the immediate circle of his own private friends it was known, moreover, how deep was the interest that he took in the progress of this work; how laboriously he pursued his investigations into the past history of his regiment; and what gratification it afforded him, in the midst of much that was necessarily dull and thankless, to exhume, out of a mass of long-buried records, or a heap of printed volumes with the damp of years upon them, some neglected historical fact, some forgotten statistics, or some illustrative anecdote which had never reached the ears of the present generation.

It was emphatically a labour of love. It was the recreation, after hours of office drudgery, of the last few years of his sojourn in India—of the last few years of his life. His health had been for some time perceptibly failing; and for many months before he finally determined to turn his back upon Dum-Dum, he had suffered under one of the most distressing and most fatal disorders of the country. Like many others, who have been buoyed up by such delusive hopes, he thought that he could weather it out a little longer. Intervals of seeming convalescence gave him new confidence and courage; and he was disinclined to anticipate the date at which he had originally designed to visit Great Britain.

But the hot weather of 1846 tried him severely; his disorder was aggravated; and at last he reluctantly determined to strike his tent, and to seek renewed health beneath the milder sun of his native country. He embarked on board the steamer leaving Calcutta in September; and it was hoped that the sea-breeze would check the progress of his malady; but as the vessel steamed down the bay, he grew worse and worse, and on the 19th of that month, off the island of Ceylon, he rendered back his soul to his Maker.

It was, we believe, one of his last expressions of earthly solicitude, that the manuscript of the *Memoir of the Bengal Artillery*, on which he had been so long and anxiously employed, should be given over to his executor, an old brother officer and most esteemed friend, to be dealt with as might seem best to him. It was the known wish of the deceased, that the work should be published: indeed, the thought of laying before the world a fitting memoir of the distinguished regiment to which he was attached, had often, in hours of sickness and weariness, been a solace and a stimulant to him. It is an ambition worthy of any soldier, to be the historian of his corps. (*Calcutta Review.*)

The manuscript was placed in my hands by Captain Buckle's executor, and I undertook to see it safely through the press. The *Memoir* was brought down by the author to the close of the Afghan war; but during the interval which had elapsed since he laid down the pen, the Sikhs had crossed the Sutlej, and the battles of Moodkhee, Ferozshuhur, Aliwal, and Sobraon had been fought. It seemed desirable that some record of these engagements should be added to the *Memoir*, and I attempted to supply what was wanting to complete the work.

But whilst the sheets containing the annals of this campaign were passing through the press, the second Sikh war broke out, and the further necessity of bringing down the chronicle to the close of that memorable campaign which resulted in the annexation of the Punjab, was imposed upon the editor.

Others would have done this more effectively and more expeditiously. My qualifications for the due performance of the work intrusted to me were mainly the cheerfulness with which, both from respect for the memory of the deceased author and affection for the regiment of which I was once a member, I undertook the labours it entailed; and such aptitude as may be supposed to result from a life spent in literary pursuits. For the three last chapters I alone am responsible. I am indebted to others for the information they contain; but if any errors should appear in them, they must be laid to the account of my misuse of the materials placed at my disposal.

That, valuable and interesting as are many of the details of this *Memoir*, it would have been more interesting and more valuable if Captain Buckle had lived to complete it, is no mere conjecture of mine. The marginal pencil notes which appear on the face of the manuscript, indicate the writer's intention of furnishing fuller information on many important points already touched upon, and of supplying many additional details which in the progress of the work had escaped his notice, but which subsequent inquiries, or, in some instances, the suggestions of friends, had enabled him to introduce, and which would have been introduced had he lived to superintend the passage of his *Memoir* through the press. It is certain, too, that the details in the concluding chapters would have been more accurate and more complete.

I have followed the original manuscript, as far as it went, with scarcely the alteration of a word; and I have endeavoured, in the concluding chapters, as nearly as possible to retain the manner of the original work.

Some apology is due for the delay which has occurred in placing the *Memoir* before the public. This has been occasioned partly by the necessity of obtaining original information relative to the events of the Sikh campaign, and partly by the pressure of other literary engagements which have absorbed the editor's time. In the record of the great victory of Goojrat, the history of the achievements of the Bengal Artillery has a fitting termination; and I can hardly regret the delay which has enabled me to chronicle, however inefficiently, the services of so many of my distinguished cotemporaries in the course of the last few memorable years.

J. W. K.

Chapter 1

Destruction of 1st Company in Black Hole

Adepts in natural history, from a few fossil bones and teeth, are able to delineate the animal to which they belonged, and from comparing the analogy of the parts, to clothe their skeleton with appropriate covering, thus making, as it were, the animal kingdom of by-gone ages pass in review before the present generation.

A similar talent would be necessary, effectively to rake up the early history of a regiment. Old records preserved in public offices form the fossil bones; and the "fleshy tenement" with which these are to be clothed must be culled from many a quarter ere the " animal" can be completed; and when this is done, there still remains the difficult task of giving him life and spirit, or, to drop the metaphor, of rendering the record useful and entertaining.

Much difficulty besets the undertaking; and, though we are conscious of our want of ability to do full justice to the present task, yet, as we believe that a good deal of information not generally known, and collected from sources inaccessible to the majority, is contained in the following pages, and which will be acceptable for its own sake, without reference to the form in which it appears, we have been induced to give publicity to our rough notes.

The first company of Bengal Artillery was raised in 1749; the orders were received, it is believed, from Bombay, then the chief presidency. A company was ordered, at the same time, at each presidency, in the Court of Directors' general letter of 17th June, 1748. A copy of the warrant for that at Madras will be found in the *Artillery Records* for October, 1843, and for Bombay in one of a series of papers entitled "Three Years' Gleanings," which appeared in the *E. I. United Service Journal* in 1838, and some extracts from which are made hereafter in these pages: the entire warrants are too voluminous for insertion. A similar one was most probably sent to Bengal, but all records perished when Calcutta was taken.

Admiral Boscawen was requested to supply such aid in raising the companies as he could spare from the fleet, for gunners; and the master gunner was appointed to the Bombay company. The companies were to be completed as early as possible, and all the gun-room's crew, who were qualified, were to be included.

The "gun-room's crew" appears to have been the denomination given to a certain number of men set apart for the duties of the artillery; their officers were called gunners, gunners' mates, &c., and combined the magazine duties with the more properly-called duties of artillerymen.

The new company was to consist of one captain, one second captain, one captain-lieutenant, and three lieutenant fireworkers; four sergeants, four corporals, three drummers, and one hundred gunners; the established pay was as noted:—

Captain and chief engineer	£200 per annum.
2nd captain and 2nd engineer	150 ,,
Captain-lieutenant, and director of laboratory	100 ,,
1st lieutenant fireworker	75 ,,
2nd ditto ditto	60 ,,
3rd ditto ditto	50* ,,
Serjeant	2s. per diem.
Corporal	1s. 6d. ,,
Gunner	1s. ,,

*There were probably some perquisites or other sources of emolument.

The want of artillery during the wars on the coast from 1746 to 1754, and the impossibility of forming a sufficient number on the spot, induced the Court of Directors to obtain and send out two companies of Royal Artillery to Bombay; and, when the war broke out in 1756, three companies more were sent, with the reinforcements under Clive, to Bombay, and were afterwards distributed among the presidencies.

With Colonel Aldereron's regiment (39th Foot—"*primus in Indis*") at Madras, there were also forty artillerymen, on its arrival in 1754; these he considered part of his regiment, and they were most probably borne on its rolls, and allotted to the duties of the field-pieces attached.

At Madras, attention seems to have been earlier paid to the military establishment than in Bengal. A field train had been organised in 1755, to which Lieutenant Jennings was appointed adjutant (this officer was afterwards transferred to the Bengal presidency), but in Bengal in 1756, on the war with France breaking out, the whole force amounted to only 300 European troops, including the company of artillery raised in 1749.

In 1756 the company of artillery was commanded by Captain Witherington, and stationed in Fort William, with detachments at the smaller factories, such as Dacca, Balasore, Cossimbazar, Patna, &c. On the siege of Fort William by Sooraj-ul-Dowlah, only forty-five artillerymen were in the garrison, and these, with their commanding officer, perished in the Black Hole.

The character of Capt. Witherington is sketched in Mr. Holwell's interesting *Narrative* as:

> A laborious active officer, but confused. There would have been few objections to his character, diligence, or conduct, had he been fortunate in having any commander-in-chief to have a proper eye over him, and take care that he did his duty.

One point, however, is clear—that whatever his talents or character may have been, he perished at his post, whilst others deserted theirs.

An instance of devotion highly honourable is also recorded by Mr. Holwell of a man named Leech, an artificer, most probably of the artillery:

> And clerk of the parish, who had made his escape when the Moors entered the fort, and returned just as it was dark to tell me he had provided a boat, and would insure my escape if I would follow him through a passage few were acquainted with, and by which he had entered. I thanked him in the best terms I could, but told him it was a step I could not prevail on myself to take, as I thereby should very ill repay the attachment the gentlemen and garrison had shewn me; that I was resolved to share their fate, be it what it would, but pressed him to secure his escape without loss of time, to which he gallantly replied that 'then he was resolved to share mine, and would not leave me.'

★★★★★★

The following was copied from an inscription in charcoal, on the wall of a small mosque on the declivity of a hill, about a mile from Chunar, and the same distance from the Ganges, in October, 1780:—

"This is the place of confinement of Ann Wood, wife to Lieutenant John Wood, taken prisoner by Jaffir Beg, *Commandant* to Sir Roger Dowler, taken out of the house at Calcutta where so many unhappy gentlemen suffered; the said Jaffir Beg obtained promotion of Segour Dowler for his long service, Fouzdar of Chunar Gur."

"I, Alexander Campbell, was taken, along with the unfortunate lady, at eleven years old, by the same persons who afterwards made me an eunuch; my only employment was to attend this lady, which I did in this place four years. 1762, May 3rd, the said Jaffir Beg sent to acquaint the lady that if she did not consent to live with him the 4th of the said month, she should be strangled, and by my hands. The 3rd, at midnight, we jumped out of this window and got to the river side, where I hired boat for fifty gold *rupees*, to carry us safe to Chinsurah, where we arrived on the 11th. The first news we heard was that Lieutenant Wood died for grief; soon as she heard this, she fell sick, and died the 27th of the month."

"Mr. Drake behaved with the greatest imprudence, he did deserve to be shot! shot! shot!"

"Alexander Campbell, I am now in Dowlah's service."

"*N.B.*—Mrs. Wood's apartment, and which is all the house consists of, is 9 feet 5 inches by 8 feet 9 inches, and 7 feet 9 inches high; the window, 18 inches."

"Mrs. Bowers was a young woman, and inhabitant of Calcutta when it was taken by the Moors in the year ——, where upwards of —— British subjects were confined in the dungeon; she concealed herself until night in one of the warehouses in the factory, from whence she made her escape on board a small vessel lying in the river opposite the old fort."—*Hickey's Gazette*, 1780.

Neither of these names is mentioned by Holwell.

★★★★★★

The remnants of the company were probably collected together at Fultah, and joined the force with which Clive afterwards avenged our disgrace on its reaching the Hooghly. In the arrangements made for retaking Calcutta, it was intended that the guns sent from Madras on the *Marlborough* should have been worked by the artillerymen of Aldereron's regiment. This plan was, however, frustrated by the colonel refusing to allow them to go, unless he accompanied with his regiment, or, in other words, unless the command of the expedition was vested in him. The want of artillerymen was therefore supplied by a detail from the Madras company under Lieutenant Jennings.

The actual strength is not known; but as in February 1757, in the attack on the *nawab's* troops near Omichund's garden, we find from Orme that Clive mustered about 100 artillerymen, and as not more than 20 or 30 of the old company can be supposed to have escaped, it must have been at least half a company.

The expedition reached Fultah on the 20th December, 1756, and met with but little opposition (a night attack on the troops landed near Fort Marlborough being the chief) in the progress to Calcutta, which was retaken, after a short cannonade from the shipping, on the 2nd January, 1757.

To protect Calcutta from the incursions of the *nawab's* army, Clive formed a fortified camp, with outposts around it, about a mile north of the town, and half a mile from the river, on the spot now called Chitpore. This situation was well chosen, as it was impossible for the enemy, when coming from the northward, to enter Calcutta without passing between the camp and salt-water lake (then more extensive than at present), within sight of the camp. Towards the end of January, the field artillery was completed by the arrival of the *Marlborough*, which had the greatest part on board.

******

It is probable that Captain (afterwards Sir R.) Barker was in this vessel; he was transferred from the Royal to the Bengal Artillery, but appears to have been employed in line commands, and never to have joined the regiment.

******

On the 3rd February the *nawab's* army passed along the Dum-Dum road, leaving it near the turning at the Puckah-bridges, and spreading irregularly over the plain to the eastward of the Mahratta ditch, the *nawab's* own camp being pitched in Omichund's garden, the ground now called "Nunden Bagh."

Surrounded by so numerous an enemy, Clive would soon have been straitened for provisions. To prevent this inconvenience, and to alarm a timorous enemy, he resolved to surprise their camp before daylight, and for this purpose he marched out from his camp—the artillery, 100 men, and six 6-pounder guns in the rear; the ammunition on *lascars'* heads, guarded by sailors; the *sipahis* and European battalion, leading.

At dawn, they came upon the enemy's advanced posts, placed in the ditches of the Dum-Dum road, whom they easily dispersed, and continued their march parallel to the Mahratta ditch until they came opposite Omichund's garden, when the fog, usual at that season, came on and obscured everything before them; they proceeded onwards, however, the field-pieces in the rear firing round shot obliquely outwards, until they reached a causeway which ran from the ditch towards the lake, and on which was a barrier; mounting the causeway, the troops wheeled and marched along it, which brought them under the fire of their own guns, and caused considerable confusion.

In order to avoid this, Clive ordered all the troops to cross the causeway and lie down till the firing from the rear could be stopped. Some guns from the ramparts of the Mahratta ditch also opened on them, and made great havoc, so that Clive was forced to continue his march until he reached the Bally-a-ghat road, when, turning to his right, he marched up the Boitaconnah and Salt Bazaar to the old fort, abandoning two of his guns, whose carriages broke down, and in the evening regained his camp by the road along the river.

This expedition, though ill-planned, produced the desired effect on the *nawab*, who eagerly desired to enter into terms of accommodation with the British, whose activity he feared.

In March, the reinforcements arrived from Bombay, and an attack on the French settlement of Chandernagore was resolved on; it was attacked both by land and from the river, the chief attack being made by the ships of war; the artillery had but a comparatively small part to play.

The political events which followed, and the intrigues which led to our subsequent hostilities with Sooraj-ul-Dowlah, it is not our province to detail. We purpose only to relate events with which the corps is connected, and accordingly we next join Clive on the 21st June at Cutwah. With his little army, we find 100 artillerymen, eight 6-pounder guns, and two howitzers, commanded by Captain Jennings. In the council of war which sat. Captain Jennings's vote was given for an immediate attack (as recorded in the Life of Clive, while in Sir Eyre Coote's evidence before the Secret Committee, the names and votes of the members are found very differently recorded. Sir Eyre Coote's is more probably the correct list, as he spoke from memoranda); the majority were for delay, but Clive, after dissolving the council, followed the dictates of his own bold spirit, and directed the army to cross the river, which was done, and by midnight of the 22nd, the army had reached Plassey.

The next day the battle took place; it was chiefly a distant cannonade. The guns were placed three on each flank of the Europeans, and the remainder about 200 yards in advance of the left division of *sipahis*, sheltered by some brick-kilns, to check the fire of the enemy's guns, manned by the French party, and posted at a tank in front. The shot from the British guns which missed those opposed to them, took effect on the bodies of cavalry and infantry in the rear. The cannonade was sustained till noon, when rain falling damaged the enemy's ammunition, and forced them to slacken their fire. The English fire continued, and Major Kirkpatrick, advancing with a party, drove the French from the tank, and the English guns were pushed on.

Meer Jaffar, with his troops, at this time advanced, intending to join the British, but was opposed and driven back by a party and the fire of a field gun, under Mr. Johnston, a volunteer.

The whole of the guns now cannonaded the enemy's camp from the high banks of the tank; the enemy came out, and Clive advanced, posting half his troops and guns at a smaller tank in advance, and the rest on a rising ground about 200 yards to their left; the French field-pieces renewed their fire, and the enemy's cavalry prepared to charge, but were always driven back by the quick firing of the English field artillery; the enemy beginning to draw off, the whole British Army advanced, and driving them from a redoubt and mound, part of the intrenchment of their camp, about five in the afternoon completed the victory which laid the foundation of our Eastern empire.

The volunteer, Mr. Johnston, above noticed, was one of the fugitives collected at Fultah. His name is mentioned among those saved at Dacca; he not improbably belonged to the artillery, and was employed as a clerk in some confidential office, for, in a letter dated in 1765, from himself to Lord Clive, he endeavours to exculpate himself from a charge of disclosing: confidential transactions from his office, preferred against him by Governor Drake. In this letter, he mentions his having been "remanded to the artillery, his former" occupation, and serving with the army till 1765, when he returned to Calcutta; the date of his removal is, however, uncertain. (This man was afterwards a member of council, and a bitter opponent of Clive.)

A detachment was sent forwards towards Patna, under Major Coote, consisting of 230 Europeans, 800 *sipahis*, 50 *lascars*, and two 6-pounders, but much delay occurred in starting, owing to the debaucheries ensuing on the plunder gained at Plassey. It was protracted by a mutinous spirit on the way, so that the French party had, by the time they arrived, rendered their position at Patna too strong, and the detachment returned to Cossimbazaar in September. The remainder of the army was removed to Chandernagore.

Towards the close of the year 1757, a second advance, with a stronger party, and Clive at its head, was made, and an arrangement satisfactory to the British having been concluded, he returned to Moorshedabad in May, 1758.

His first care was to organise the army, and in doing this, the coast army was taken as a model; a company of artillery was raised in Fort William, 29th June, from the men who had served at Plassey. Lieutenant Jennings was promoted to its captaincy, and this may be considered as the first company of the present establishment, and bears at present, after many changes of numbers in the successive formations of the regiment, the denomination of 1st company, 4th battalion.

A second company was raised at Cossimbazaar on the 19th September, the party mentioned above as being left there most probably having been incorporated in it: Captain Broadbridge or Broadburn, from the Royal Artillery, was its captain.

The company of Royal Artillery which came from Bombay accompanied Colonel Forde's detachment to Masulipatam in April, 1759, and aided in that brilliant operation, but did not return with the detachment after the campaign. (This was rather a detachment of Royal, Bombay, and Bengal Artillery; Lieutenants Winwood and Kinch, of the Bengal Artillery, seem to have been with it, but nothing very distinct can be ascertained.)

Since that period no Royal Artillery have served in Bengal, except in 1798, when a company was in Fort William; but this probably was a temporary arrangement, the company coming to Bengal *en route* to Ceylon.

In 1759, a combination having been entered into against the British, the English troops, aided by Meer Jaffar, marched towards Patna, against the *Shahzadah*; Patna was taken, a garrison left, and Clive returned to Calcutta, Colonel Calliaud having joined him first at Berhampoor, with 300 Europeans, 1,000 *sipahis*, 50 artillerymen, and 6 guns. The artillerymen, there is reason to suppose, belonged to the 2nd company.

The battalion of *sipahis* left at Patna with two 6-pounders and 70 Europeans, under Lieutenant Cochrane, was defeated in an engagement into which they were forced, in assisting our ally Ramnarain against the emperor's forces, in January, 1760.

The conduct of the European troops is spoken of as highly creditable. The European officers of the *sipahis* all fell, and the *sipahis* were cut to pieces or dispersed. The English who remained fought their way back to the city under Doctor Fullerton.

The author of the *Siyar-ul-Mutakherin* says:

> Other English officers may have been present, whose names I know not, who ranged them in order, and as one of their guns

was to be left behind on the field of battle, they found means to render it of no avail, by thrusting a large needle of iron into its eye; the other being in good condition, they took it with them, together with its ammunition; and that handful of men had the courage to retire in the face of a victorious army, without once shrinking from their ranks; during their journey, the car of ammunition chanced to receive some injury, the doctor stopped unconcernedly, and after having put it in order, he bravely pursued his route again.

Lieutenant Buck, of the artillery, was killed in this action.

Calliaud's advance having been delayed by his allies, he did not engage the enemy till the 22nd February, near Sooraj, and the same cause prevented his following up the advantage.

The 50 artillerymen of the 2nd company were engaged in this action, and the carriages of four of their guns broke down during the engagement, causing some delay in repairing them.

After his defeat, the emperor fled, and endeavoured to double back and surprise Moorshedabad ere Calliaud could overtake him. In this, however, he failed; the British pursued in boats, and coming up with him, he struck across the Currukpoor hills. The British disembarked and followed him. After a difficult march, the emperor emerged from the hills, about 30 miles from Moorshedabad. The English and Jaffier had, however, joined, and on their attacking him, he set fire to his camp and fled.

To secure Patna, a detachment of 200 Europeans, a battalion of *sipahis*, and four field-pieces, marched from Moorshedabad, under Captain Knox, in May, 1760, and, marching with the utmost rapidity, reached it in thirteen days. Crossing the river, this little band attacked and defeated the army of the *Naib* of Purneah, who had come to the emperor's assistance, near Mozufferpore, on the 27th May.

A third company of artillery was formed on the 26th May, 1760, (This date is doubtful), in Fort William, promoting Captain-Lieutenant Kinch; but there is reason to believe he remained with the second company, until Captain Broadbridge's death, in 1761, gave him the command.

Colonel Calliaud having been succeeded by Major Carnac, returned to Calcutta; the latter pursued the emperor's forces to Gyah Maunpoor, where he overtook and completely routed him in January, 1761. Mr. Law, the head of the French party, was captured in this engagement.

The 2nd company of artillery, under Captain Broadbridge and Captain-Lieutenant Kinch, shared in these transactions, and remained as part of the garrison of Patna.

It forms no part of our plan to enter into the history of such occurrences as those which led to the dismissal of the members of council from the Company's service, and placed Mr. Ellis in charge of the factory at Patna; or to examine whether our subsequent misfortunes are attributable to his mismanagement. For information on such points we must refer the reader to the histories of the times.

Many points of difference arose with the *nawab*, Meer Cossim, which led to various misunderstandings; they were brought to a crisis by the British, on Mr. Ellis's order, surprising and seizing Patna, on the 26th June, 1763. Mr. Amyatt was attacked and killed near Moorshedabad, by order of Cossim Ali, whom he had left only two days before, having been deputed to him at Monghyr by the Council, and this brought on open war.

The energy shewn at first was, however, suffered to die away, and the troops in Patna dispersing for plunder, the late governor of the city rallied his men, and, being joined by a reinforcement from Monghyr, attacked and drove out the British, who, spiking their guns, retired to Bankipore, and afterwards fled in boats to their factory at Manjee, near Chuprah; where the whole, and among them the company of artillery, were taken prisoners.

The prisoners taken were sent to Monghyr, and there confined with others captured at Cossimbazar, which factory was plundered about the same time.

On the news of these disasters, the English Army, under Major Adams, moved from their cantonments at Ghyrettee early in July. The first company of artillery was with this force, under the command of Captain Jennings.

In the present day (as at 1852) it would scarcely be deemed possible to march a force at the season in which this army moved through Bengal—in the middle of the rains, when the whole land is a swamp, and every stream full to overflowing; yet, in spite of the difficulties presented, this gallant band, about 800 Europeans (including the artillery) and 2,000 *sipahis*, forced its way, and came in contact with Meer Cossim's troops at Gheriah, near Sooty, on the 2nd August.

A severe action was fought, lasting nearly four hours, and at one time two of the British guns were taken possession of by the enemy;

victory at length decided in favour of the British.

The artillery lost one officer, killed during the action, Lieutenant Kaylor.

Undaunted by his defeat, Meer Cossim again disputed the advance of the British at the pass of Oudenullah, a little to the south of Rajmahl, where the road is confined between the river and spurs of hills. This pass had been intrenched with walls and towers at short distances, and several strong posts raised on eminences along its front. The army was detained before these intrenchments for nearly a month. At length, by an attack on the hill forming the right of the lines, and a feint on the river end, they were carried with severe loss on 5th September, Captain-Lieutenant Green, of the artillery, acting as field engineer. Meer Cossim left his troops the next night, and retired to Monghyr in haste, thence carrying his prisoners with him to Patna.

In October Monghyr was invested, breached, and capitulated. Meer Cossim, driven into a paroxysm of rage by this event, directed the massacre of all his English prisoners. In this horrid act he found a ready tool in Sumroo, the German, whose widow, the Begum Sumroo, has rendered his name notorious in history.

******

His real name was Walter Reinhart, but he was called Sombre from the darkness of his countenance, and this was easily changed into Sumroo. Franklyn says:—"Major Polier, at Delhi, to Colonel Ironside, at Belgaum, in May, 1776, writes—'His name is Balthazar ——; the rest I have forgot. Sombre is *son nomme de guerre*. He is a deserter of ours; he enlisted at Calcutta before the taking of the place, I think, in one of the Swiss companies, commanded by a young officer, I suppose Vussarot or Ziegler, and deserted shortly after. This anecdote is not generally known, and might serve, should he ever fall into our hands, for a valid plea to hang him, which could not well be done otherwise without straining a point, as he certainly only executed the commands of his infamous master, and his life might have been endangered by non-compliance.'"

******

All were massacred save Mr. Fullerton, the surgeon, who, in the exercise of his profession, appears to have gained a place in the esteem and affections of Meer Cossim.

Whether Captain Kinch and his subalterns perished in the attack on Patna or in this massacre we are unable to say, but in one or other he fell. The bodies of all were thrown into a large well, over which a tomb has been since built, but no record of the names of those who perished exists on it. (Six subalterns of artillery, including a commissary and adjutant, appear to have perished: Lieutenants Hockler, J. Brown, Deckers, Perry, Adamson, and J. Read.)

After avenging the fate of their comrades by the reduction of Patna, the army followed Meer Cossim, who threw himself on the protection of the *Nawab* of Oude, as far as the banks of the Carumnassa. Here Major Adams left them, and the command devolved on Major Jennings, of the artillery. The force was cantoned on the frontier of the *nawab's* territories, in the expectation that he would give up Meer Cossim, and also to watch the emperor's troops, which, under the pretence of preparing an expedition against the Boondelas, remained in the vicinity of Allahabad.

In the month of December, 1763, a fourth company of artillery was raised in the field, probably at Patna.

In February, 1764, an alarming state of dissatisfaction shewed itself in the English Army, still in its cantonments at Sant. The troops were dissatisfied with the rewards bestowed upon them for having regained the provinces from Meer Cossim. The English battalion seized the park and marched towards the Carumnassa. The *sipahis* were also in motion; but by the exertions of Major Jennings and the other officers, the English and *sipahis* were nearly all induced to return. The French and foreigners, to the number of 150, went off, under Sergeant Delamar, to Allahabad. Few of the artillery joined in this affair.

The seeds of this mutinous disposition still remained when Major Carnac arrived in March and assumed the command. Provisions were scarce; and though the government instructions were to carry the war into the *nawab's* territories (whose hostility was now open), he agreed with his officers, that, in the then temper of the troops, it would not be safe to proceed.

On the enemy's forces crossing the river, the English fell back and encamped under Patna, where, on the 3rd May, 1764, they were attacked. Sumroo, with a large body of the *nawab's* cavalry and infantry, assailed the front. The engagement lasted till sunset, when the enemy withdrew with a heavy loss; and although he hung about the neighbourhood till the end of the month, did not venture on another action.

A detachment, under Colonel Munro (whose army had joined Major Carnac's at Patna), marched after one of the *sipahi* battalions, which had deserted, with four guns. Colonel Munro sent on 100 Europeans, one *sipahi* battalion, and two guns. This force overtook them at Chuprah, and coming on them while asleep, took them all prisoners. Colonel Munro, on receiving them, considered that strong measures were necessary to check the spirit of insubordination which had arisen, and accordingly selected fifty of the worst for execution. Twenty-four were blown from the guns at Patna and other stations. On this occasion it was that the grenadiers claimed precedence in death—an anecdote familiar to all acquainted with the early history of our Indian Army.

The whole army now advanced towards the Soane. The advance was covered by Colonel Champion with a detachment and four guns, who was attacked by large bodies of the enemy's horse near Mooneah, at the junction of the Soane and Ganges, whom they beat off, and Colonel Munro coming up crossed the river immediately. The march to Arrah was a good deal harassed, and the guns frequently called into play to keep off the enemy's horse.

At Buxar, on the 22nd October, they came up with the enemy, and on the following morning, about 8 o'clock, the enemy marched out to attack them. The British were drawn up in line with their guns, twenty field-pieces and seventy-one artillerymen of the 1st company, on the flanks of battalions. The enemy were repulsed, and about 12 o'clock they retired slowly, blowing up their tumbrils of ammunition. One hundred and thirty-three pieces of artillery, mostly with English carriages, and among them twenty-seven which had been lost the previous year at Patna, were the trophies on this occasion.

In the acknowledgment of this victory, written by Mr. Vansittart and his council, 16th November, 1764, to Munro, he was requested:

> To return thanks to the field-officers and commandant of artillery (Major Jennings) for their care and diligence in preserving the disposition for attack, and taking every advantage over the enemy.

Captain Winwood and Lieutenant Duff of the artillery are mentioned "as meriting particular notice, and having gained great honour."

A detachment of two battalions failed in November, in an attempt to take the fortress of Chunar; in January, 1765, however, Sir Robert

Fletcher succeeded in gaining possession of it, and in February he breached Allahabad, when the garrison evacuated it. On the 3rd May a battle was fought near Korah, against the *vizier*, aided by the Mahrattas; these latter were quickly dispersed by the fire of the artillery, and they separated from the *vizier* and retired towards the Jumna with precipitation. These events placed the southern part of the Dooab under British rule. (This was *not* the Battle of *Korah*, for which the 1st and 10th regiments of N. I. wear an honorary distinction; that took place in 1778, between the English and some of the *nawab's* troops, on their being disbanded.)

The army was this year (1765) divided into three brigades, and the companies of artillery attached one to each, while the remaining company was stationed in Fort William.

  1st Brigade ..... 1st Company .... Monghyr.
  2nd ditto .... 2nd ditto.. .... Allahabad.
  3rd ditto .... 4th ditto........... . Bankipore.
  Ditto .... 3rd ditto............ Fort William.

In addition to the guns with the park, each battalion of infantry was equipped with two six-pounders or three-pounders, worked by the men of the regiment, assisted by native officers and *lascars* from the artillery.

	Major.	Captain.	Capt.-Lieut.	1st Lieut.	2nd Lieut.	Lieut. Fireworkers.	Serjeants.	Corporals.	Drummers.	Bombardiers.	Gunners.	Matrosses.	Adjut. & Qr. Master.	Deputy Comr.	Conductors.	Serj.-Major.	Qr.-Mast. Serjt.
* Per Comp.	–	1	1	1	1	3	6	6	3	8	24	53	1	1	2	1	1†
Total	1	4	4	4	4	12	24	24	12	32	96	212	4	4	8	4	4

 † Non-effective—1 pay serjeant, 1 drill serjeant, 1 major serjeant, 1 park serjeant, 1 drill corporal, 3 camp colour-men, a bullock serjeant, and overseer of bildars in time of service.

 The ordnance with each company appears to have consisted of six light 6-pounders and two howitzers; to assist in working these and the field-pieces with sipahi battalions, a large body of lascars were attached to each company.

 Heavy guns and mortars were supplied from magazines at the head-quarters of brigades to the extent available and required for any particular service.

A major was this year allowed to the artillery, to command the corps, and a practice-ground formed at Sulkeah.

In 1766 the alarming mutiny on the part of the officers of the army, caused by the reduction of allowances, broke out, and was only suppressed by the firmness and decision of Lord Clive and Colonel Smith. The part taken in this by artillery officers cannot now be fully traced; but Captain Duff, Captain-Lieutenant Clifton, and Lieutenant Black, appear to have taken prominent parts. Many, we learn from the army-list, were dismissed about that time, most probably on account of the mutiny; others resigned. Nearly all, in every branch of the army, were, however, restored to the service, and placed in the position they would have held, had they remained in it.

Insubordinate as the conduct of a large portion of the officers of the army was on this occasion, and deservedly as it has been stigmatized, yet it must be borne in mind that they failed of success by conscientiously not admitting the soldiery to a knowledge of or participation in the measures they had taken to secure the *batta*, though solicited by the latter to accept of their support, as soon as it was known that government had resolved to persist in enforcing their resolution to deprive them of their allowance.

In 1768 a lieutenant-colonel and a major were added to the regiment, and, in consequence of the Court of Directors being desirous of obtaining, not only cadets but officers from Woolwich, Major Pearse was nominated to command the corps, with the rank of lieutenant-colonel. He was, however, superseded by Captain Martin, to whom the command was given by the Indian Government, and again by Major Kindersley, whose commission as major was antedated by the local government, on the vacancy being caused by Captain Fleming's removal to the engineers, from which he came. On the death, however, of Major Kindersley, which occurred in 1769, he succeeded to the command of the regiment.

The application for a supply of officers and cadets from the Royal Artillery originated in a difficulty of finding candidates, the artillery service being neither so lucrative, nor holding out the same prospects, as the infantry. In the Secret Committee's letter of 30th September, 1765, to the Court of Directors, it is stated that:

> It would be of the utmost benefit to our plan that you should send out, every year, six or seven gentlemen from the academy at Woolwich for artillery officers; this being a service which suffers extremely for want of persons properly instructed in the business, since no officer who knows the benefit of the infantry service here will choose to quit it for any advantages the artillery offers.

★★★★★★

In consequence of this want, the recent mutiny and perhaps the inefficiency of some of the officers of the corps. Russell, Baillie, and Thelwall came into the corps from Madras; Rosat and Burnett from H.M.S. *Folly*, from Bencoolen.

★★★★★★

On the death of Major Kindersley, 28th October, 1769, Lieutenant-Colonel Pearse succeeded to the command of the regiment, and, as its organisation is much indebted to that officer, it is fortunate that we are able to quote from letters to his early friends his record of the state in which he found it:—

> When I first came into command of the corps, I was astonished at the ignorance of all who composed it. It was a common practice to make any midshipman who was discontented with the India ships an officer of artillery, from a strange idea that a knowledge of navigation would perfect an officer of that corps in the knowledge of artillery. They were almost all of this class, and their ideas consonant to the elegant military education which they had received. But, thank God! I have got rid of them all but seven.

The strange idea above referred to appears to have affected the Home Government at a still earlier period, as, on the first formation of artillery companies, "such assistance as the fleet could spare" was given. To this idea are we indebted for many terms which have hung about the corps till the present day, (1852): our *tindals, lascars, serangs, cossibs,* all came from the naval nomenclature, and their etymology would most probably be found in the Portuguese dialect, which has retained its influence on shipboard; from the same fountain of "English (not) undefiled" must have been drawn the "banks-hall," a name by which our gun-sheds are known throughout the regiment, but a term of considerable mystification to the uninitiated.

In March, 1770, a fifth company of artillery was raised in Fort William, and in May the companies were formed into a battalion, to which an adjutant was allowed. In September the *lascars* were divided into 28 companies, of which seven (consisting of 2 *serangs*, 2 *tindals*, and *100 lascars* each) were attached to each of the three companies, with the brigades, and to one of those in Fort William.

The embodying the companies of artillery into one battalion must have increased the efficiency of the army, by introducing uniformity of system into their management, and a more effectual supervision than could have existed in their scattered state.

The regiment at this time, supposing no change had occurred in the strength of companies, would have consisted of—

	Lieut.-Col. Commandant	Major	Adjutant	Captains	2nd Captains	1st Lieutenants	2nd Lieutenants	Fireworkers	Serjeants	Corporals	Drummers	Bombardiers	Gunners	Matrosses	Lascars Serangs	Lascars Tindals	Privates
By calculation	1	1	1	5	5	5	5	20	20	20	40	120	300	56	56		2800
* By returns of 1772	1	1	-	4	4	16	16	11†	30	20	18	340	-	48	200		2350

    * With a staff of 1 surveyor of stores, 1 regimental adjutant, 5 adjutants and quarter-masters, and 12 conductors.
    † Cadets.

Of the officers of the corps a description was given in Colonel Pearse's letter, above quoted. It was written in 1775, and refers to the period now described. An extract from one written in 1772 contains a very graphic picture of a *fast* man of those days, specimens of whom long continued:—

> To be a gentleman you must learn to drink by all means—a man is honoured in proportion to the number of bottles he can drink: keep a dozen dogs, but in particular if you have not the least use for them and hate hunting and shooting. Four horses may barely suffice; but if you have eight, and seven of them are too vicious for the *syce* to feed, it will be much better.
>
> By no means let the horses be paid for; and have a *palanquin* covered with silver trappings—get 10,000 *rupees* in debt, but 20,000 would make you an honester man, especially if you are convinced that you will never have the power to pay. Endeavour to forget whatever you have learnt—ridicule learning of all sorts—despise all military knowledge—call duty a bore—encourage your men to laugh at orders—obey such as you like—make a joke of your commanding officer for giving those orders you do not like, and, if you obey them, let it be seen that it is merely to serve yourself. These few rules will make you an officer and a gentleman, and they are the first lessons which young men take when they arrive in this country.

With officers of this stamp, and the class of men from whom the Company's European troops were then recruited, we cannot suppose that much discipline existed. Drunkenness—the bane of the European soldier in India—was rife, and its natural consequences, disease and death, followed. To this cause, too, must be added the want of good barracks and internal economy, which of late years have gone far to remove the idea of the climates of India being deadly to the European constitution.

The *lascars* were employed in dragging and assisting the Europeans to work the guns; a detail also was detached with each infantry regiment, to assist in working the guns attached to it, for two 6-pounders formed part of the equipment of each battalion, and thirty *sipahis* were set apart for their service. These duties, with those of the park, would account for the number of *lascars* being so large in comparison with the establishment of the present day. They were in many respects native artillerymen, and in the subsequent successive changes from *lascars* to *golundaz* and back again, the change was often rather in name, and increase and decrease of pay, than of the men themselves.

They were a most efficient and useful body—a class on whom, perhaps, more of the hard work of the service and fewer of its substantial rewards have fallen than any other of the Native Army. At all times accompanying the European artillery, they have borne a part in every expedition which has left the shores of India. On land and on board ship, hard service has been their lot, and all who have been brought into contact with them join in testifying to the willingness, courage, and patience they have exhibited.

A large body of artificers was also at this time attached to the corps; these, with the quartermaster's establishment, completed the regiment as to its *personnel*.

The *matériel* appears to have been as bad as possible. At this time Colonel Pearse complains that:

> The fusees burnt from nineteen to forty-eight seconds, though of the same nature; the portfires were continually going out; the tubes would not burn; the powder was infamous; the cartridges were made conical, and, when necessary to prime with loose powder, a great quantity was required to fill the vacant cavity round the cartridge; the carriages flew to pieces with common firing in a week.

The contractor who furnished the carriages, and the laboratory in which the fusees were made, appear to have been beyond his control: "I have no more to do with it than his Holiness at Rome," are his words. The iron guns were all very indifferent:

> Two 12-pounders burst on the ramparts in 1770 in firing the morning and evening gun, and one 12-pounder on a rejoicing day, in firing salutes.

It was under such circumstances that Colonel Pearse took command, and set himself to work to improve the state of the regiment. To weed the inefficient from the officers; to teach the remainder and the new-comers their duty; to introduce an efficient internal economy and discipline into the ranks, and to obtain a proper control over the *matériel* of the regiment, were his first duties. That his endeavours were in some degree successful may be gathered from his correspondence, for in 1772 he writes:—

> Now I have got all the laboratory implements with me at practice, and am going to teach my officers what they never saw.

Steadily he pursued his object through difficulties and disappointments, and was rewarded, ere his death, by seeing the corps raised to a high state of discipline and efficiency. At a review of it by General Clavering in November, 1774, he expressed himself as delighted with the corps, and astonished at its performance, being superior to anything he could have expected in India, and so much to his satisfaction, that Colonel Pearse, in a letter to an old friend, writes:

> The performances at the review would not have been a disgrace to dear old Woolwich.

The years 1771-2 afforded leisure to attend to the discipline of the corps, for it seems not to have been called on for any field service. In 1773 the expedition under Captain Jones proceeded against the hill fort of Delamcotta, situated on the pass by which the Durla River, which runs into the Teestah, emerges from the mountains, and not far from the present sanatorium, Darjeeling. Lieutenant R. Bruce, of the artillery, was present at the attack, but with what portion of the corps is unknown.

This year the army was again called into the field to check the Mahrattas, but after a cannonade across the Jumna at Ramghat, near Delhi, they retired, and our army went into cantonments at Sultanpoor, Oude.

In 1774 a portion of the army under Colonel Champion was sent to assist the *vizier* in his attack on the Rohillas. An action was fought on the 23rd April, in which the 2nd company of artillery was present.

In his report Colonel Champion says:

> The Rohillas made repeated attempts to charge; but our guns being so much better served than theirs, kept so constant and galling a fire, that they could not advance, and where they were closest was the greatest slaughter.

Captain W. A. Baillie was wounded in this action. Lieutenant G. Deare, Lieutenant B. Doxat, and Lieutenant W. W. Hussey were also present.

The action was followed by much severe marching and exposure in the hot and rainy season, in the jungles of the Pillibeet district. While encamped near Pillibeet, a report reached Colonel Champion of four *crores* of *rupees* being concealed in the fort; and in a letter to government he suggests "the propriety of examining into the truth of the report, in duty both to the Company and to the army:" a naïve suggestion, which, considering the British were there as allies of the *vizier*, the government negatived. However, as a compensation to the army, the *vizier* granted a donation of 10½ *lacs*, which was divided among the 2nd brigade in August, 1779, agreeably to a scale laid down by a committee of officers. This scale gave a *sipahi* two-thirds of a European soldier's share—a proportion which has been adhered to ever since in distributing prize-money. The scale there fixed is here given:—

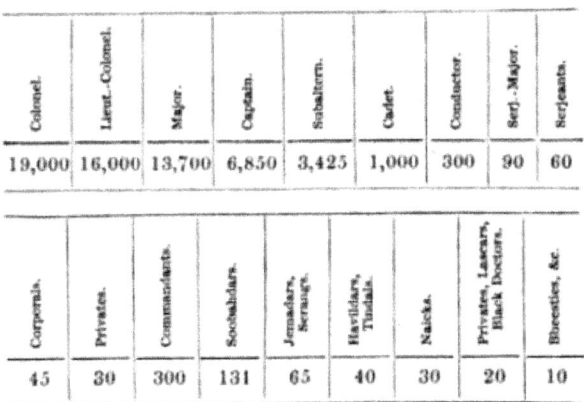

Colonel	Lieut.-Colonel	Major	Captain	Subaltern	Cadet	Conductor	Serj.-Major	Serjeants
19,000	16,000	13,700	6,850	3,425	1,000	300	90	60

Corporals	Privates	Commandants	Soobahdars	Jemadars, Serraugs	Havildars, Tindals	Naicks	Privates, Lascars, Black Doctors	Bheesties, &c.
45	30	300	131	65	40	30	20	10

In 1775 an alteration took place in the arrangements for the *matériel* of the army; a Board of Ordnance was formed, and magazines established, at the principal fixed stations of the army.

The board consisted of:

The Governor-General as president, the Commander of the

Forces, the members of the Supreme Council, the Commissary-General of Comptrol; the Commandant of Artillery; the Chief Engineer; the Commissary of Stores, and the Military Store-keeper, as members; with a secretary, and such assistants as might be found necessary.

To this board returns of all ordnance and military stores were to be made by commanding officers of garrisons and cantonments, artillery officers, and all others in charge; all contracts for the supply of stores, proofs of ordnance and powder, plans for new construction of ordnance, reports of powder-works, laboratory and arsenal, were to be submitted: in short, the general control of the stores for the army was vested in this board.

Magazines were established at the fixed stations of Berhampore, Dinapore, and Chunar; a commissary, a deputy-commissary, and two conductors were appointed to them, and placed under the control of the board; they were to be paid by the board-office, and receive instructions for carrying on their duties and office from the board, independent of any other control but that consistent with the general regulations of the army, which required that they should be subordinate to the commanding officer in the field or fixed stations, and the commanding officer of the artillery under whose immediate control they were placed.

To the commissaries were intrusted the ordnance stores, camp equipage, &c., for the use of corps; and an officer of the department was to accompany the army, when moving on service, to superintend their issues. A return was to be made monthly of all receipts and issues; and no issue was to be made without the orders of the Board, or commanding officer.

Carriages for the ordnance were to be constructed in Fort William by the military storekeeper. No repairs of magnitude involving large contingent bills were to be made in the field, but the articles required supplied on indent.

The establishments for the magazines were furnished by a reduction of the artificers and *lascars* attached to the artillery; the *lascars* were reduced to a small number, and the surplus applied to the magazines.

2 Serangs, 4 Tindals, 100 Lascars,	on the peace establishment ;	7 Serangs, 16 Tindals, 400 Lascars,	on the war establishment ;

were the number retained with the regiment.

The appointment of this board appears to have interfered with the control which the commandant of artillery had previously exercised over his department, and Colonel Pearse attributed its formation to a personal motive, on the part of General Clavering, to lower him. In writing to an old friend, after other complaints he goes on to say:

> General Clavering instituted a Board of Ordnance, and made me a member of it; took all my authority away, and made me a cipher. I was hurt, and complained, as he had put into the Board a Lieutenant-Colonel Dow, the translator of a miserable history of Hindustan, and the author of two wretched plays. This man is commissary-general, and, as such, controller of military accounts. He uniformly attacked me and my department, and I defended myself and officers. This created disputes, and, as I was wounded, I was warm; and thus, because my opinions were always contrary to Dow's (and D—— is the general's tongue, brains, head, and heart), it was as bad as attacking the general himself.

Of the working of the cumbrous machinery of the Board of Ordnance, in its original formation and in the successive changes which have been made from time to time, in the vain attempts to obtain energy and celerity from a body of men without individual power or responsibility, it will often, in the course of these pages, be necessary to speak, for to the want of arrangement on their part must be attributed, in many instances, the inefficient state of the siege-trains with the armies.

At this time the headquarters of the regiment were quartered in Fort William, moving out during the cold months to a practice-ground at Sulkeah, nearly opposite the western mouth of the Circular Canal: the powder-works were between the canal and Cossipoor. The dress of the regiment consisted of a blue coat, faced with scarlet, and cut away in the fashion of the time; white cloth waistcoat and breeches, with buckles at the knees; and gaiters, or half-spatterdashes, as they were called; red leathern belt, with swivels; black silk stock; buff gloves, and regimental hat, supposed to be a plain cocked, in the fashion of George the Second's time. The hair was worn greased, powdered, and tied in a *queue*, false hair being substituted when the natural was not long enough.

The hours for parades, and, in fact, for everything, were early: parades were before gun-fire in the cold season; dinners were in the middle of the day, not only in private houses, but on public occasions; and invitations were given on a scale of hospitality only practicable in a small society. The orderly book was the common channel of invitation used by the governor-general and officer commanding the garrison. Many such entries as the following will be found in it:—

> The Honourable the Governor-General requests to be favoured with the company of officers and gentlemen belonging to the army now in the garrison of Fort William and the Chitpoor cantonment and the presidency on Monday next to dinner, at the Court House, and in the evening to a ball and supper. The governor-general requests that gentlemen will not bring any servants to dinner, nor their hookahs to the ball at night.

Or:

> Lieutenant-Colonel Wilding presents his compliments to all the officers in Fort William, staff of the garrison, and surgeons, and requests their company to breakfast, and dinner at half-past two o'clock.

A good account of the manners and habits of the people at this period would be interesting, and probably materials for the purpose could be found, were a qualified person to undertake the task: they are only noticed above incidentally, as likely to affect the discipline of the regiment. (Since writing the above, the want is being supplied by some spirited articles in the *Calcutta Quarterly Review*.) The early dinner was too much followed by a long sederunt over the bottle, and the absence of ladies' society gave a tone of grossness to the habits, which are happily much improved in modern days.

This year a number of memorials were presented to the Board by artillery officers, as to the relative rank of cadets; and it was decided that those appointed expressly to the artillery should have the full benefit of the Court of Directors' order, that all cadets appointed in India were to rank below those of the same year appointed in England, but that the time of service was to date from arrival in Bengal; and all those who were in the infantry, and entered as cadets in the artillery, were to rank above all who were cadets in the artillery at the same time. This, and the circumstance of several who resigned in the mutiny of 1766 being allowed to return to their original standing, will partly account for the supersessions which will appear on consulting the gradation list.

At the conclusion of the year 1775 three companies of artillery, to be commanded by European officers, were ordered to be raised for the *Nawab* of Oude and attached to the brigade of disciplined troops raised for his service; officers were nominated to them, and struck off the strength of the regiment; but whether the companies were ever raised seems doubtful. In the following year they were directed to be formed into a battalion, under command of Major Patrick Duff, and then to be transferred to the regular army, and fresh ones raised of native artillery in August, 1777. If the companies first ordered had been European, it is difficult to say what became of them, because the sixth, seventh, and eighth companies were raised by minutes of council, July 13th and 24th, 1778; the two former, however, may have been raised from the men of the Oude companies.

The artillery, in 1775, appear first to have used Dum-Dum as a practice-ground, and to have been encamped there, when, their tents being wanted for the use of a brigade marching to Patna, they were ordered into Fort William, and their practice cut short with one fortnight instead of two months. In the following year, however, in December, they marched out with their tents and stores, and began the practice (as the orders record) by firing "a royal salute, and after that one of 19 guns, for the Company."

It is not easy to ascertain what Dum-Dum was previous to its occupation by the artillery. The first mention made of it is by Orme, in the account of the action near Omichund's garden, in 1757. He speaks of Clive crossing "the Dum-Dum road:" this road, however, was only a *cutcha-bund* leading to Dum-Dum, the name of the place now occupied by Dum-Dum House, the origin of which building is enveloped in mystery. (The Cutcha road was formed, of its present breadth, in 1782–3.—Colonel Green's Letter, 21st October, 1801.) It is said to have been built by a Mr. or Colonel Home, (was there not a member of council of that name?) but who he was, or the date, cannot be ascertained. Supernatural aid has been called into play, and the mound on which it stands is reported to have been raised by some spirit of the ring or camp, in the course of a single night, and to this day visions of ghosts haunt the grounds.

At the practice season the officers inhabited the house, and the men's tents were pitched in the compound, and the natives in the "Montague lines," the ground now occupied by the Nya Bazaar, called after Lieutenant Montague, the adjutant who marked them out. The name is known to the present day.

It was not until 1783 that the cantonment was marked out by Colonel Duff, who is said to have made, or rather widened, the road from Shambazar to Barasut, (in all probability this formed the regular road to Berhampore) and to have planted the avenue of *mulseery* trees now running along the southern end of the small exercising-ground.

Many villages were scattered over the ground occupied by the cantonment; their sites were purchased up, from time to time, by government; the last, that of Deiglah, in 1820.

From 1775 to 1778 the corps does not appear to have been called into the field, and Colonel Pearse occupied himself in improving its internal economy. A regimental school for the instruction of the native officers and gunners was established in 1775—an institution which, with all the faults which still exist in it, has been of much use, both in teaching the elements of knowledge and affording a rational employment to some of the many hours which hang heavily on the soldier.

That the corps had attained a respectable proficiency in its peculiar duties we may believe from an extract of one of his letters, dated March, 1777:

> I have had my corps reviewed twice; first by the governor, who was excessively pleased, and thanked us in orders; and next by the general, who also thanked us. It was our good performance forced the general's thanks; he would have been better pleased to have found fault—first, because we pleased the governor; and next, because I commanded and had disciplined them myself." Not one circumstance had I to lessen the pleasure I received from the good performance of my corps, as a battalion of infantry, as a battalion of artillery with sixteen cannons, and as a body of artillery on service in their batteries; for we went through all these exercises equally well. The Saturday following, General Clavering reviewed us, and what gave me most satisfaction was, to hear that he had said in private he had reviewed most of the King's regiments, and never saw any perform better.

In May, 1778, General Leslie's force marched from Culpee, on its expedition to assist the Bombay Government; it consisted of six infantry and one cavalry corps, some European artillery, and the 1st company of *golundaz*, raised for the *nawab's* service. A short account of this detachment will be given when we come to speak of its return, in 1784.

The formation of the three native or *golundaz* companies for the

Oude service was most probably recommended by Colonel Pearse, and the experiment answered so well that in August, 1778, a new organisation of the artillery was ordered, in which the *golundaz* were to form a considerable part.

Hitherto, as want dictated, company after company of artillery had been added to the establishment; but the artillery was now formed into an independent brigade of one European regiment and three native battalions. The European consisted of seven field and one mounted, or garrison, company, and the native battalions of eight companies each: the former was to be completed by drafts of fifty men from each of the three European infantry regiments (and possibly the Oude companies), and the latter by all fit for the service who might volunteer from the two native companies, with the temporary (Oude) brigade and their *lascars*, from the *lascars* of European companies and with the guns of infantry regiments, and from the eight companies of *lascars* at the Presidency.

The *lascars* were all reduced.

The European regiment, exclusive of garrison company, consisted of seven companies:—

Lieut.-Colonel.	Majors.	Captains.	Capt.-Lieutenants.	Lieutenants.	Lieut. Fireworkers.	Adjutant.	Quarter-Master	Surgeon.	Assist.-Surgeons.	Serjt.-Major.	Qr.-Master Serjt.	Drill Serjeant.	Drill Corporals.	Drum Major.	Fife-Major.	Serjeants.	Corporals.	Drummers.	Bombardiers.	Gunners.	Matrosses.
1	2	7	7	21	21	1	1	1	3	1	1	1	2	1	1	42	42	21	56	168	361

The three *golundaz* battalions consisted of eight companies each, in all—

Major	Captains.	Lieutenants.	Jemadars.	Havildars.	Naicks.	Drummers.	Fifers.	Golundaz.	Seebahdars Commt.	Ditto Adjutant.	Havildars Major	Adjutant	Quarter-Master	Surgeon.	Assist.-Surgeons.	Serjt.-Major	Qr. Master Serjt.	Native Doctors.	Sircars.	Armourers, Master.	Ditto Workmen.	Chucklers.	Watermen.
1	3	24	48	192	192	24	24	2400	3	3	3	1	1	1	3	1	1	9	24	3	9	3	24

The European commissioned officers of the artillery brigade were—

Lt.-Col. Comot.	Lieut.-Colonel.	Majors.	Captains.	Capt.-Lieutenants.	Lieutenants.	Lieut.-Fireworkers.	Major of Brigade.	Aide-de-Camp.	Adjutants.	Quarter-Masters.	Head Surgeon.	Surgeons.	Assist.-Surgeons.	Paymaster.
1	1	3	10	7	45	21	1	1	2	2	1	2	6	1

The staff and artificers of the field-train will be referred to shortly, when another formation of the corps renders it necessary to advert to the subject.

In the above formation we find the great error which has pervaded the service ever since—the supposition that companies of Native do not require as many officers as companies of European artillery; and while the establishment of officers of the latter was fixed at a proportion which shews that the wants of the branch were then better understood than they have been in later times, the former was left ridiculously unprovided with officers.

The officers of a company of artillery should be proportioned to the number of guns it is intended to man. No officer can do justice to more than two pieces; and as the companies were then adapted to eight field-pieces, four officers, with a fifth to command the whole, is the number which ought to have been *present* in the field. On this subject, however, it will be necessary to dwell more, as the successive changes pass under review.

Chapter 2

Reduction in Establishment

The formation detailed in the preceding chapter was not destined to remain, for in March, 1779, Lieutenant-General Sir Eyre Coote arrived from England with the commission of commander-in-chief, and soon after his arrival it was rumoured that he had brought authority to disband the *golundaz*.

From representations grounded in error and party views, alarm had been taken by the Court of Directors and the government at the supposed danger of teaching the natives the use of artillery, and in August the *golundaz* were ordered to be disbanded, the men having the option allowed them of entering infantry regiments or joining the *lascars*.

To this corps, having been raised at his suggestion and disciplined by himself, Colonel Pearse was much attached, and, both on public grounds and private feelings, was averse to its being broken up. He unfortunately had many enemies in high rank in Calcutta;—the consequence of the feelings of rancour which had so long disturbed the settlement, and which were still kept up by Mr. Francis's and General Clavering's faction and Warren Hastings's adherents. Among these was Colonel Watson, commanding the engineers, who vowed the overthrow of the *golundaz*, and, having considerable influence, urged Sir Eyre Coote to proceed in this ill-judged measure.

Those readers, who may recollect the *golundaz* at Cawnpore under Major Hay, may well conceive how deeply it must have wounded Colonel Pearse to see a similar corps sacrificed to jealousy and party views; and there is every reason to suppose that Colonel Pearse's *golundaz* were equal to Major Hay's, which is saying everything, for there never was a corps better disciplined than the latter.

Colonel Pearse determined that the *golundaz* should not be reduced, if any exertions on his part could save them; and accordingly, as soon as the rumours reached him, addressed a letter to the commander-in-chief, in which he urged the necessity of employing native artillery, from the impossibility of keeping up sufficient European artillery for the service of our extended empire, liable to be attacked at both extremities, and at such a distance as to preclude the possibility of assistance.

He combated the argument of danger from native artillerymen deserting and teaching their art to the *golundaz* of native powers, by proving that, at that time and previously, the native states had artillerymen not inferior to ours in the mere gun exercise and preparation of common stores, and that, were this not the case, the desertion of a few European artillerymen would render all precautions useless; that in reality for many years past there were thirty men nominally infantry, but in reality artillerymen attached to each battalion, for the service of the two field guns, which arrangement entailed the possibility of all the evils now feared, though without the advantages which a regular corps of native artillery would give.

He deprecated the system of battalion guns as useless, the guns being without officers to manage them so as to produce the best effect, by attending to the advantages of ground and selection of ammunition best adapted to the occasion; the two European artillerymen detached with each battalion for this purpose being ignorant of the higher—the more scientific parts of the profession, which knowledge is confined in general to the officers; that it ruined the discipline of these men, who, though they went out good men, returned, in general, drunken vagabonds; that the *lascars* sent, though of the artillery, were only employed in dragging the guns, and were unarmed and undisciplined, but that they served for menial offices, which made them desirable to captains commanding the infantry battalions.

He recommended that the guns should be collected in small brigades, or batteries, and brought to the points wanted, instead of being frittered away along the line; that the discipline of the men working them, from being under their own officers, would be better preserved, and that cannon would be better looked after, and their fire produce more effect in action, by being under the exclusive command of an officer bred up to the profession.

He concluded by urging that, even should the artillery desert and take service with native powers, there was in reality little to fear, for though the country powers have infantry formed like ours, they are inferior in every respect: their irregularity of pay is the grand foundation of it; their want of sufficient instruction and of the essential knowledge of our discipline, will long keep them so; and such as their *sipahis* are to ours their artillery will be to our artillery, though the men should desert in equal proportion, which he did not think would occur, particularly if the *golundaz* had a small increase of pay over the infantry, which was the case in all other services.

On the receipt of the order, Colonel Pearse again attempted to prevent this ill-judged measure, by a respectful representation to government, in which he pointed out that the European artillery numbered but 370 in all, of whom only 150 were at the presidency; that two ships of the season had come in without a single recruit; that it would therefore be impossible to complete the corps till the next year, and that, even, was doubtful, from the scarcity of recruits, His Majesty's regiments being filled by pressing; that if an attack was made, the European artillery were insufficient even for the defence of Fort William, much more were they unable to furnish the detachments which would be necessary; that the *golundaz* were good artillerymen; the name and service the highest in repute among the natives; and that they would not, even if the pay were equal, enter the ranks of the *lascars*; so that raw and ignorant men must be enlisted for that class, who would require instruction, and, till they were taught, the presidency would be almost destitute of artillery. He submitted that, under these circumstances, the execution of the order should be delayed until the commander-in-chief could be consulted, lest any ill consequences should follow the immediate execution of it.

Colonel Pearse's endeavours were, however, looked upon by Sir Eyre Coote as arising from a spirit of insubordination, which never had a place in his breast; and they drew forth a severe and cutting letter from the commander-in-chief, taxing him with unmilitary and unprecedented conduct, tending to sap subordination and obedience to its foundation, and telling him that he was called upon for obedience and not for an opinion, and that he was in nowise answerable for the results.

It must, however, be stated, in justice to Colonel Pearse, that, during the command of General Stibbert, several important military transactions occurred, and General Stibbert being absent in the field, Colonel Pearse obtained permission from him, as commander-in-chief, to address the government direct on urgent occasions; and it was in the spirit of this permission, considering the disbanding the *golundaz* as a measure fraught with danger, that Colonel Pearse addressed the representation to government.

To the commander-in-chief's letter Colonel Pearse replied, regretting he had fallen under his displeasure, and detailing circumstances, such as the rumour of a body of Mahrattas being in the neighbourhood of Burdwan; the arrival of the ships without any recruits, of which he believed the commander-in-chief to have been in ignorance when the order was dictated, and which seemed to call for the exercise of some discretion on his part, in carrying into execution an order which would cramp the means of defence; that he had, in the exercise of what he deemed a sound discretion, stated the facts to government, who could at once determine whether orders might with safety be instantly carried into execution, or whether they should be delayed until the commander-in-chief could be consulted; he deprecated any unguarded expressions, if such there were, in his former letter, being construed into a want of respect; and concluded by begging that the step he had taken might be considered as founded in error of judgment, and not in want of obedience; and entreated the commander-in-chief to overlook his error, and entertain a more favourable opinion of him than that expressed in the letter with which he had been honoured.

The appeal to government was ineffectual, and the minutes of Council of 23rd November, 1779, ordered that:

The native officers of the *golundaz* corps, at the presidency, be paid up to the end of this month and immediately discharged from the service; that the commandant of artillery be directed to repeat the offers already made to the men, and those who still decline to accept of them be immediately discharged.

Those who feared the native powers training up good artillerymen by means of deserters from the British service, do not appear to have considered that without the material which is provided and kept up at a heavy expense, the best artillerymen would be useless; and that, although artillerymen are *taught* the preparation of stores, still very few have that intimate knowledge which only results from constantly handling and making them up; and which is, in reality, found in a much greater degree in the magazine workmen—a class who come and go at their pleasure, and appear to be little thought of, although the practical information they could carry to an enemy would be worth more than hundreds of mere well drilled artillerymen.

The Court of Directors, however, must be excepted, for in their warrant (17th June, 1748) they direct that:

> No Indian, black, or person of a mixed breed, nor any Roman Catholic, of what nation soever, shall, on any pretence, be admitted to set foot in the laboratory, or any of the military magazines, either out of curiosity, or to be employed in them, or to come near them, so as to see what is doing or contained therein.

And to such an extent did this fear then carry them, that another paragraph runs:

> And if any person belonging to the company of artillery marry a Roman Catholic, or his wife become a Roman Catholic after marriage, such person shall immediately be dismissed from the company of artillery, and be obliged to serve the remainder of his time in one of the other companies, or be removed to another of the Company's settlements, to serve it out there, if the Council think fit, &c.

And again, in their military letter to Bombay (6th April, 1770), they say:

> As it is very essential that the natives should be kept as ignorant as possible, both of the theory and practice of the artillery

branch of the art of war, we esteem it a very pernicious practice to employ the people of the country in working the guns; and, if such practice is in use with you, we direct that in future you attach European artillerymen to the service of the guns which may belong to *sipahi* corps, and that no native be trusted with any part of this important service, unless absolute necessity should require it.

With these views it is not to be wondered at that the Home Government should have directed the *golundaz* to be reduced; but Indian experience might even then have taught that no more dangerous ally can be found for a native army than a large and imperfectly-equipped artillery. A native power will hardly bear the heavy *continued* expense required to keep it efficient; or, if the state should supply the means, the want of integrity in its agents will divert them from their proper course; and consequently, in the hour of emergency, the army is forced to fight a pitched battle to protect the unwieldy train of cannon, which becomes an incumbrance instead of a support: so it had been at Plassey and Buxar, and so it has been in every general action since. Assye, Argaum, Laswaree, Mahidpoor, would have been avoided, had there been no artillery in the native armies; unencumbered, they could have evaded the British; but the necessity of protecting their trains, and, perhaps, the confidence which their presence inspired, induced them to try the result of a battle.

Instead of discouraging native powers from organising large parks of artillery, our policy should have been the reverse, resting confident that native parsimony and dishonesty would insure inefficiency in that branch.

In the new organisation of the artillery now ordered, it was formed into two European battalions of five companies each, and to each company was attached a battalion of six companies of *lascars*, under the command of the same officer; they were to perform the whole duty dependent on the corps of artillery, and to be instructed in the usual services of artillery, with the exception "of pointing and loading guns and mortars." They were dressed in uniform, and armed with a light pike, so constructed as to form a *cheveux-de-frise*.

The regiment was to be commanded by a colonel, and Lieutenant-Colonel Pearse was to hold the rank of lieutenant-colonel commandant, "until the lieutenant-colonel in the army next above him was disposed of by promotion or otherwise; and then, in conformity with

ORGANIZATION of 1779.

		per Company	per Battalion	Total	On returns 1 Feb. 1780	
EUROPEAN	Colonel Commandant	-	-	1		
	Lieutenant-Colonel	-	1	2	2	1
	Major	-	1	2	2	1
	Captains	1	5	10	10	1
	Captain-Lieutenants	1	5	10	9	-
	Lieutenants	3	15	30	29-30	2
	Lieut. Fireworkers	3	15	15	4	-
	Adjutants	-	1	3	4	-
	Aides-de-Camp	-	1	1	-	-
	Serjeant-Majors	-	1	2	-	-
	Qr. Master Serjeants	-	1	2	-	-
	Drill Serjeants	-	1	2	-	-
	Drill Corporals	-	2	4	-	-
	Pay Serjeants	1	5	10	-	-
	Serjeants	6	30	60	44	17
	Corporals	6	30	60	41	10
	Drummers	3	15	30	31	-
	Bombardiers	8	40	80		
	Gunners	24	120	240	529	43
	Mattrosses	53	265	530		
LASCARS	Serangs Commandant	-	1	10	10	-
	Serangs	1	6	60	53	-
	Tindals	2	12	120	106	-
	Coolies	2	12	120	87	-
	Lascars	50	300	3000	2272	-
	Bivors	1	1	10	8	-
	Native Doctors	2	10	20	16	-
	Doolies	2	15	30	-	-
	Havildars	2	11	10		
	Bheesties	1	6	30	8	-
					Effective	Invalids

44

the custom in Bengal, and the concurrence of the Court of Directors, to be promoted to the rank of colonel;" the promotion of the additional lieutenant-colonel and major, to complete the new establishment, to take place on the arrival of the recruits of the season.

The brigade-majorship was abolished, and his duties performed by a regimental adjutant.

These changes were not completed until April, 1780, as far as relates to the European portion. The *golundaz* were discharged in December, 1779, very few taking service in the ranks of the *lascars*.

The *golundaz* considered themselves belonging to the most honourable branch of the army, and were unwilling to enter an inferior service; the difference of pay was another, and a stronger reason, and we accordingly find, that from 2,438 *golundaz* of all ranks who were on the rolls of the regiment in November, 1779, in December 1,783 took their discharge. The returns for the next months are incomplete, and it therefore cannot now be ascertained what became of the remaining 650 men; but it is probable some were those who were entertained from the *lascars* in 1778, and had less objection to return.

It has been said before, that a company of *golundaz* from the Oude Brigade accompanied General Leslie's detachment. The force marched from Culpee in May, 1778, on what appeared to many the wild expedition of crossing India and effecting a diversion in favour of the Bombay Government, heavily pressed by the Mahrattas.

After crossing the Jumna, the force was soon brought into contact with the enemy; the Boondeelas met them at M'how, near Chatterpoor, but they were beaten, with the loss of their guns; all of which that were serviceable were taken on by General Leslie, who found his own train of four 12-pounders, twelve 6-pounders, and two howitzers insufficient.

Leslie remained in Bundelcund until October, when his death devolved the command on Colonel Goddard, who pushed on to Hoshungabad, which place he reached on 30th November, and remained at until the middle of January, awaiting a reply from Bombay.

That the *sipahis* looked on this service with some dread and dislike we may conclude from the desertions which took place, and which called forth strong reprehension from Colonel Goddard in the orders of 1st November; after pointing out the ingratitude for all the former indulgences they had received, and the unmilitary nature of their conduct, in quitting their colours in their present situation, with the daily expectation of being engaged with an enemy, he concluded with the following high compliment to the *golundaz*:—

> The commanding officer, with much pleasure, excepts the corps of artillery in the foregoing observations. Their steadiness, fidelity, and military conduct claim his particular thanks; and he desires the commanding officer will assure himself that he will make proper mention of their merits to the Honourable the Governor-General in Council.

Leaving Hoshungabad on 16th January, this gallant band continued their route through an unknown country until, on the 9th February, 1780, Colonel Goddard received a letter from the Bombay field deputies, directing his return to Bengal, in consequence of a treaty they had negotiated with the Mahrattas. This mandate he declined obeying, urging that his orders were from the Supreme Government, and he continued his march to Surat, which he reached on the 25th February.

The following are the artillery officers who served with the force:—

Major ... W. A. Baillie, on the returns till April, 1781—retired in 1802.

Captain ... — Sears, joined detachment in March, 1781—returned in 1784.

Lieutenant R. Bruce, promoted to Captain in 1781 and joined Major Popham's detachment.

„ A. Forbes, died in 1779.

„ L. Kempt, returned in 1784.

„ — Hamilton, ditto.

„ J. Harris, died October 15, 1780.

„ W. Rattray, returned in 1784.

„ H. Cotes, died in 1782 in China, whither he must have gone sick.

„ A. Rattray, joined detachment October, 1779—died at sea 1782.

Lieut. Fireworker McLean, joined detachment March, 1781—returned in 1784.

„ „ Boyce, joined detachment December, 1782—returned sick in March, 1783.

In January, 1780, this force took the field again, and, crossing the Taptee, attacked the fortress of Dubhoy, in Guzerat, on the 19th, and took possession of the province; on the 10th February the army was before Ahmedabad, and stormed it on the 15th, and it was intended to have attacked the combined camps of Holkar and Scindia at night; but intimation that the Mahrattas were willing to treat prevented its being carried into execution; evasion followed, and all attempts to bring them to action were fruitless, till on the 3rd April, marching at 2 a.m., Colonel Goddard, with four European companies, four grenadier *sipahi* battalions, and twelve field-pieces, entered the camp at dawn, and quickly threw the Mahrattas into confusion; they attempted to take up a position near, but on being again attacked, fled and dispersed. In this attack Lieutenant-Colonel Baillie, of the artillery, led the first line.

The detachment returned to Surat, and in October, 1780, moved against Bassein, a fort on the mainland opposite the northern extremity of Bombay Island. The detachment was increased by a body of Europeans from Madras. A battery was opened on the 16th November of six guns and six mortars, at 900 yards, and a second of nine heavy guns at 500 yards on 9th December, together with twenty mortars to bombard the works; on the 10th, the breach being practicable, the enemy offered to surrender, but some demur taking place, the fire was renewed, and on the 11th they yielded at discretion.

From Bassein, in the middle of January, 1781, the detachment marched for the Bore Ghat, and reached it on the 8th February. Holkar and the Poonah armies were encamped on the top, but Goddard struck awe into them by storming the pass the night of his arrival, and by 5 a.m. the next day gained complete possession. It was not deemed advisable to carry the war further into the Mahrattas' territories, so the detachment remained holding the *ghats* until the middle of April, when they descended without disturbance, but were a little harassed by the enemy in the three days' march to the coast, during which Lieutenant W. Rattray, of the artillery, was wounded.

The detachment continued in the Bombay Presidency until the cold weather, 1783, when it set out on its return to Bengal, under Colonel Charles Morgan (Brigadier-General Goddard having sailed sick for England), and reached Caunpoor in April, 1784.

The European artillerymen who returned with it were posted to the company at Caunpoor, and the *golundaz* were also cantoned at that station. All the *lascars* entertained previous to 1783 were retained in the service, the worst from the battalions being discharged to make room for them. The remainder were discharged.

The orders which were issued by government, on this occasion, will be noticed when the return of Colonel Pearse's detachment is mentioned, and in the meantime, it is necessary to look back a little, to relate the part the regiment took in other operations then going on.

With the detachment under Captain Popham, collected in 1779, for the purpose of reinforcing Colonel Goddard, was a portion of the 2nd company 1st battalion, being under the command of Captain Mayaffre, Lieutenants Legertwood and Vernon. The original destination of this force being changed, it was employed in aiding the *Ranee* of Gohud against the Mahrattas. In February, 1780, it crossed the Scind, and in April besieged Lahar. From want of a sufficient battering train, the breach made was imperfect, and on this, as on many future occasions, the want of *matériel* was supplied by the spirit of the troops. Lahar was successfully stormed on the 21st April. To this succeeded, on the 3rd August, the dazzling enterprise of the escalade of Gwalior. In this attack the advance of two companies of *sipahis* was followed by twenty Europeans, artillerymen of Captain Mayaffre's detachment.

Captain Popham's detachment was replaced towards the end of the year by one under Colonel Carnac, with which was the 1st company 2nd battalion of artillery, with the officers noted in the margin. (Captain Macklewaine, Captain-Lieutenant Scott, Lieutenants Legertwood, Hart, Glass, and Baillie.) The detachment pushed on to Seronje, where, surrounded by a powerful enemy, and their supplies cut off, they were reduced to great distress, and would have perished, had not the bold resolution of attacking Scindia's camp by night, on 24th March, 1781, been taken and successfully carried out, rewarding the victors with guns, elephants, and grain, the "*spolia opima*" of an Indian camp.

The difficulties being removed, the detachment fell back towards Gwalior, and met Colonel Muir's brigade coming to their assistance at Antree, on 4th April. The detachments then moved into cantonments.

When Captain Popham's detachment was broken up, Captain Mayaffre with his company (2nd company 1st battalion) was stationed at Mirzapoor, and on the massacre of the force placed by Warren Hastings over the *Rajah* of Benares, on the 16th August, 1781, an order was sent to him, as senior officer at Mirzapoor, to march, with the company of artillery, remaining four companies of Popham's battalion, and the French Rangers (sending his guns and stores by water to Chunar), upon Ramnagur, *viâ* Chunar, and wait further orders; and also by Major Popham, with a caution to avoid hostilities, and attend to the safety of the whole party until Major Popham should arrive.

On receiving the order from Warren Hastings, on 17th August, Captain Mayaffre immediately set out, replying, that he would march, "observing his directions in every respect, and otherwise acting to the best of his judgment for the good of the service."

Colonel Blair, commanding at Chunar, was also directed to send four 6-pounders, two tumbrils of ammunition, an 8- and 10-inch mortar with 100 shells and 200 fuses each, with powder, &c. to Chota Mirzapoor on the 20th, where Captain Mayaffre was expected to be. These were intended to have been used from an open space on the shore opposite, selected by Major Popham to bombard Ramnagur, and there is little doubt that a place so particularly ill-adapted for defence against such a mode of attack would have proved an easy conquest.

On reaching Ramnagur, however, without waiting for the arrival of Major Popham or further orders, without plan, without inquiry, and contrary to the advice of the officers with him, Captain Mayaffre, on the morning of the 20th August, marched precipitately into the narrow streets, where, in an instant, the leading party was annihilated. Captain Mayaffre, and Captain-Lieut. Doxat, with thirty-three of the Rangers, fell at once, and the detachment was forced to retreat with a loss of 107 killed and 72 wounded, two field-pieces and a howitzer remaining in the enemy's possession.

It is most probable that Captain Mayaffre was urged to his precipitate and rash attack by the recollection of the successful enterprise against Gwalior, in which he had shared the preceding year; the hope of acquiring reputation led him to disregard the maxims of prudence, forgetting that, although he staked his own life upon the issue, he also hazarded his government's safety unnecessarily.

This failure raised the whole country in arms, and rendered Mr. Hastings's flight to Chunar imperative—a flight which gave rise to the memorable but oft misquoted distich—

Ghora per howdah, hat'hee per zeen,
Juldee bagh gee'a, Warren Hasteen.

Lieuts. F. W. Grand and Sand, doing duty with Major Popham's detachment, accompanied W. Hastings to Chunar.

★★★★★★

Lieutenant F. W. Grand was a younger brother of the Mr. Grand whose name is connected with Sir Philip Francis, from the latter having seduced his wife, who afterwards was married to Talleyrand. Lieut. G. commanded two 6-pounders attached to the two companies of Popham's regiment acting as a bodyguard to Hastings.

Lieutenant Sand probably commanded two guns with the remaining companies of the wing of the regiment.

******

Active measures were taken to collect troops, and on the 3rd September a party was sent out to surprise the enemy's camp, which was formed at Pateeta (about seven miles from Chunar), but being retarded by the bad bullocks and drivers with the two 6-pounders which accompanied it, at daylight it found the enemy, to the number of 4,000 infantry and 400 cavalry and six guns, drawn up; the fire of our artillery and infantry was, however, so quick and effective, that the enemy fled, leaving four guns, among which was the one left by Captain Mayaffre at Ramnagur, in our possession.

With the enemy's guns, was all the usual apparatus of artillery, such as portfires, tubes, chain-shot, quilted grape, equal or nearly equal to the production of an European laboratory; the artillery, however, was not equal to the stores: one gun, a modern cast, was pretty good; the others old and indifferent; the carriages of all much worn and bad.

The conduct and activity of Lieut. Baillie, of the artillery, was particularly acknowledged by the commanding officer.

On the 10th September, a brigade from Caunpoor, under Major Crabb, arrived, with which were thirty European artillerymen (1st company 2nd battalion), four 6-pounders and 1 howitzer, under Captain Hill.

The enemy had collected in force at the strong holds of Pateeta and Luteefpoor, the former seven miles, the latter fourteen miles from Chunar, and from information received, it was deemed advisable to drive them from those positions, rather than attack Ramnagur; two detachments were therefore got ready, one under Major Crabb, and the other under Major Popham; the former, accompanied by four 6-pounders and one howitzer, under Lieut. Baillie, with the ammunition, carried on bullocks, marched, on the night of 15th September, by a route through the hills, to take Luteefpoor in reverse, under the guidance of a native, named Bandoo Khan, who had proposed the plan of attack; and as the chief difficulties of this march were caused by the guns, it will not be out of place to give an abstract of Major Crabb's interesting journal of the expedition:—

15th.—The stores and ammunition being ready by ten p.m., the detachment marched at that hour, but was very shortly brought up at a *nullah*, the water in which was deep, and the limber ammunition-boxes forced to be taken off and carried over on the *lascars'* heads: a delay of two hours. The road led along a plain through low jungle, a *ghat* with sharp turnings caused a long delay, and it was sunrise ere the guns reached the top. A low thick jungle continued for about a *coss*, and was succeeded by an extensive plain, slightly cultivated and with two small villages. About a *coss* in advance, two hours' delay was caused by a narrow deep *nullah*, and three-fourths of a *coss* further, a second, with rocky beds and banks, occupied an hour and a half in crossing. The road led along the bank under a high hill, for about a mile, full of rocks.

Recrossed the river with more difficulty than before; the banks very high, and forced to cut a road for the guns, and it was two p.m. ere all were over; the jungle thick, ground broken, hills on both sides. Came upon a small *nullah*, its bed full of rocks and the opposite sides a steep pass; the cattle were knocked up, and the *sipahis* were put on to the drag-ropes to aid them; over by four p.m., and then no water to be found nearer than a lake three miles in front, which they reached by sunset and halted, after twenty hours' marching and about six *coss* from Chunar.

17th.—Under arms at four a.m.; marched through a thick jungle, crossed a small river by a steep and narrow road, up a long steep pass with a deep gully on the right, the ascent very difficult from large smooth stones, on which the cattle could not retain their footing; the *sipahis* again at the drag-ropes, and by ten a.m. the top was gained. A large level but rocky plain, studded with large trees, now opened; about a mile further a river, bed full of large rocks, and the guns were moved with much labour.—One p.m.; after moving over rocky ground, the country opened, and about a *coss* from the river, an extensive plain near the village of Korada; several villages scattered over the plain, whose inhabitants fled. The country was cultivated, chiefly rice *khets*. At sunset encamped: computed distance, six *coss*.

18th.—Started three a.m., over a plain full of deep holes, difficult and dangerous for the cattle; before daylight, entered a thick jungle with many deep dry *nullahs*—forced to cut roads for guns; no trace of a road. About two p.m., entered a large plain with several small villages, whose inhabitants fled. At three p.m., encamped by a large lake, and set smiths and carpenters to mend yokes and pintles of two guns, broken: distance, five *coss*.

19th.—Marched at four a.m., at first over a plain, then through swamps and rice-fields; the high banks retarded the detachment much.

Passed a large deserted village, Muddoopoor; had the intelligence that the *rajah's* troops were in front, with guns, at the village of Loorah; encamped: day's march, three *coss*.

20th.—Moved at daylight, for one *coss* through jungle, in parts thick; by sunrise, the advance guard was clear of jungle, and saw the enemy drawn up, about 2,000 in number, in a good situation, guns on their right, immediately opposite the road out of the jungle, on a rising ground, and with a small bank thrown up in front. *Tope* and village of Loora on their left, and a deep morass in front. The enemy's guns opened on the troops emerging into the plain, and fired briskly until all had cleared the jungle and formed, the advanced guard returning it from one gun. When formed, the detachment advanced as quickly as the ground would admit, firing the 6-pounder until near enough for small-arms.

A party was detached to the (enemy's) right, under Lieut. Polhill, to carry the guns, and the enemy fled, leaving their guns, 150 dead, and 20 wounded, and made for Luteefpoor, distant about four *coss*, through the jungle. The ammunition was destroyed and the guns spiked and buried, there being no means to carry them off. The road to Luteefpoor ran through the jungle, rugged and steep, and no water; pursued them to the pass of Succroot, about a *coss* from Loora, and halted to bury the dead and collect the wounded, amounting to thirty-four; two and a half *coss*.

21st.—Marched at four a.m., road good but jungly for two *coss*; a dry *nullah*, descent rugged and ascent still more so; road narrow and winding, full of large stones and rocks; the guns were lifted over these, and gained the summit with much labour. The fort visible about three miles off; the road now along the side of hill was worse than ever; from the bottom of hill to fort very narrow though level, through thick jungle; at noon, entered town of Luteefpoor, which had been evacuated and plundered by the *rajah's* people while the detachment was getting down the hill; six pieces of cannon and a quantity of ammunition were found; three pieces were taken on the hills, intended to defend the entrance from Pateeta.

The fort of Luteefpoor stands in a bottom, surrounded on three sides by high steep hills, with thick jungle close up to the ditch, which is deep on the Pateeta side, where, too, the wall is of stone with loopholes; on the other sides it is part stone and part mud; the guns, on wooden swivels in the centre of bastions; the citadel has a high stone wall, with deep ditch and loopholes, in many places much cracked.

In concluding his report, Major Crabb says:

> Lieut. Fireworker Baillie, of artillery, in particular I beg leave to recommend to your notice, for the very great attention he shewed in his particular department.

The other detachment under Major Popham marched against Pateeta on the 16th, but on arriving, he found it so strong, that he sent back for the two battering-guns and one mortar, originally intended for Ramnagur; these reached him, and Captain Hill either accompanied these or was with the original detachment. After five days' firing, he made no impression; he ordered a storm, which took place successfully on the 20th, about the same time that Major Crabb defeated the enemy at Loora Succroot.

After these defeats the *rajah* fled to Bidjegurh, through the hills, and was followed by Major Popham.

******

The governor-general noticed Lieutenant Baillie's conduct in general orders of 8th September and 19th October, 1781; on the latter occasion the order says: "The strong recommendation which Major Crabb has given Lieutenant Fw. Baillie for his distinguished attention and activity in the management of the artillery under his charge, affords the governor-general a second occasion of acknowledging the services of that officer on the same campaign, and publishing his thanks for it."

******

On the 4th November, a battery of two 18-pounders opened against the fort, but probably from the rapidity of the firing, one of the guns burst, and it became necessary to send back to Chunar for others; in the meantime a mine was opened, which it was hoped would be ready to be sprung on the 6th.

On the 11th the place was taken, and the spoil divided among the captors on the spot, giving a large amount of prize-money to officers of all ranks—a proceeding highly disapproved of by the governor-general, though not unwarranted by his instructions. All attempts, and there were several subsequently made to recover the amount for the use of government, were ineffectual.

The total value of the prize was estimated at twenty-five *lacs*. (Major Popham received 2,94,000; major, 44,956; captain, 22,478; subaltern, 11,239; sergeant, 200; *soobadar*, 300; *jemadar*, 140; *havildar*, 100;

naick, 80; *sipahi*, 50.)

The officers, Captains Mayaffre and J. Hill took a part in these exciting proceedings, and the following, Lieutenants Gillespie and B. Bruce, Lieutenant Fireworkers E. F. Baillie, H. Balfour, W. Shipton, J. E. Grand, R. Sands shared in the prize-money of Bidjegurh. Lieut. Balfour claimed a share for bringing up the heavy ordnance, but they probably arrived too late, and his claim was not allowed.

The misfortunes which had occurred in the Madras Presidency in the war with Hyder Ali, and particularly by the defeat of Colonel Baillie's detachment and retreat of Colonel Munroe, rendered assistance from the Supreme Government necessary: a detachment, consisting of two European companies of artillery (5th company 1st battalion, and 4th company 2nd battalion), with their battalions of *lascars*, and 350 European infantry, was prepared, and sailed in October, 1780, under the command of Sir Eyre Coote.

The detachment reached Madras early in November, and shared in the relief of Wandewash and Cuddalore in January and February, 1781, in the unsuccessful attack on the fortified pagoda at Chillambram, and the victory near Porto Novo.

Another detachment, under the command of Colonel Pearse, of the artillery, consisting of one European (5th company 2nd battalion), and one Native (2nd *golundaz*) company of artillery, with their *lascars*, and three additional companies raised for the service, one company of gentlemen volunteers, about forty or fifty, and six battalions of native infantry, and 16 field-pieces, followed by land.

The *golundaz* company raised for this service was most probably formed from the remnants of the old *golundaz* battalions, reduced in the preceding year; so soon had the inexpediency of that measure forced itself into notice.

Much delay occurred in preparing camp equipage, and it was not until the middle of January, 1781, that Colonel Pearse joined the detachment at Midnapoor.

Before starting, he complained of the inadequacy of his artillery (twelve 6-pounders, two 12-pounders, and two howitzers), and indented for six more 6-pounders; but whether these were furnished is not known.

Soon after the detachment started, we find Colonel Pearse complaining of the absurdity of the Board of Ordnance expecting regular and minute returns of all articles expended in a train while on service with the same punctuality as within a settled cantonment; and pointing out that all stores issued to a train on service should be struck off the board's books, and an account rendered when the service was over.

The detachment reached Ganjam in March, where it suffered severely from cholera, then a new disease, and which gave an impression that the water had been poisoned.

In April they had reached Vizianagram, Ellore on 20th May, Pulicat on 1st August, and joined Sir E. Coote's army at St. Thomas's Mount on the 3rd August, 1781.

Immediately after their arrival, the Bengal division was broken up and divided among the other brigades; an ill-judged and rash measure, causing much desertion, which resulted from ill-feeling on the part of Sir Eyre Coote towards Colonel Pearse.

This was partly, perhaps, on account of the correspondence regarding the *golundaz*, but chiefly, no doubt, from Colonel Pearse's being a friend of Warren Hastings, against whom he expressed himself very strongly in a letter to the Supreme Government in March, 1781, objecting to Colonel Pearse's detachment accounts being kept separate, as likely to cause expense and unnecessary staff appointments; to his being entrusted with permanent authority in any shape, as unjust to himself, and assuming a privilege (on the governor-general's part) in military details, which cannot be vindicated; and complaining that the instructions given Colonel Pearse were a direct indignity offered to his authority. He concludes by observing that:

> He sees the newspapers are replete with promotions and arrangements in the military department in Bengal, without any reference to him as commander-in-chief: he protests against the whole as irregular, unmilitary, and entailing enormous unnecessary expense, and has the satisfaction of committing to record in this place, that he ascribes these encroachments on the authority of the commander-in-chief to the governor-general, who now unites in his person the whole powers of government.

The officers and companies of the regiment employed in this service were as follows, as well as can be gleaned from the records. Unfortunately, from July, 1780, to April, 1781, the returns are left blank, and these companies are not included in the returns until their rejoining in 1785.

No. 2.

4th Company 2nd Battalion.

Captain	...	... Elliott, rejoined May, 1784.
Lieutenant	...	... Woodburn, rejoined May, 1784.
,,	...	... Wilkinson, rejoined May, 1784.
,,	...	... Holland, rejoined May, 1784.
,,	...	... Groat, rejoined April, 1784.
Lieutenant Fireworker		Turton, rejoined May, 1784.
,,	,,	Dunn, rejoined May, 1784.
,,	,,	McDonald, rejoined May, 1784.
,,	,,	Neish, rejoined May, 1784.

No. 5.

5th Company 1st Battalion.

Captain	...	... Hussey, rejoined April, 1784.
Lieutenant	...	... Carnegie, rejoined April, 1784.
,,	...	... Maud, died August, 1783.
Lieutenant Fireworker		Douglas, rejoined June, 1784.
,,	,,	Exshaw, rejoined June, 1784.
,,	,,	J. Green, rejoined June, 1784.
Lieutenant	...	... Robinson, rejoined June, 1784.

The above sailed with Sir Eyre Coote's detachment.

No. 10.

5th Company 2nd Battalion and 2nd Golundaz.

Captain	...	... C. R. Deare, rejoined June, 1784.
Captain-Lieutenant	...	E. Montague, rejoined April, 1784.
Lieutenant	...	... Horsburgh, rejoined June, 1784.
,,	...	... Blundel, rejoined June, 1784.
,,	...	... W. Bruce, rejoined June, 1784.
,,	...	... Tomkyns, rejoined June, 1784.
,,	...	... J. Walker, rejoined June, 1784.
Lieutenant Fireworker		McDermott, rejoined June, 1784.
,,	,,	Hardwicke, rejoined November, 1783.
,,	,,	Nelly, rejoined June, 1784.
,,	,,	Barton, rejoined December, 1783.
,,	,,	Macbeagh, died August, 1781.

Commandant's Company of Volunteers.

Captain-Lieutenant ... W. Harris, rejoined June, 1784.

Staff to Colonel Pearse.

Captain-Lieutenant	...	C. Green, Aide-de-Camp, rejoined June, 1784.
Lieutenant	...	Herbert, Quarter-Master, died December, 1781.
,,		Brown, Adjutant, rejoined May, 1784.

Joined Detachment at Madras.

Lieutenant	...	Constable, December, 1783, went on sick leave and joined detachment.
Lieutenant	...	Addison, March, 1783.
,,	...	Flemyng, March, 1783, returned June, 1784, with 5th company 1st battalion.
,,	...	Nash, November, 1781, returned June, 1784, with 5th company 1st battalion.
Lieutenant Fireworker Hollingsbury, 1782.		
Lieutenant	...	Syme, died June, 1784.

On the 16th August, 1781, the army marched from the Mount, and reached Tripassore on the 18th, and took possession of it after only three days' siege. 27th—Engaged Hyder Ali's army on the spot where Baillie had been defeated, and were forced to retire to the Mount from want of provisions. On the 19th September the army again took the field, and on the 23rd the Fort of Pollom surrendered to it. Hyder's army was in sight; the two next days were spent in collecting grain, and on the 27th, Sir E. Coote went out to reconnoitre, and found the enemy's whole force in camp near Cuppoor, about five miles off. He then advanced to attack them, Colonel Pearse commanding the left wing, which, from having to pass through much broken ground, bore the heaviest part of the action.

Hyder endeavoured to turn it, but his attempts were frustrated by Colonel Pearse's movements, and his cavalry driven back by discharges of grape. The two wings were much separated, and Colonel Pearse was at one time nearly captured, from his horse taking fright and running away with some of Hyder's horsemen, who charged through an interval in the line; in endeavouring to get back, he was followed by a horseman, whom his *aide-de-camp* shot. The action lasted from three till dark, and it was eleven p.m. before the army had encamped at Cuppoor, on Hyder's ground.

In October, the army marched into the Pollams, and a detachment of six battalions with two 6-pounders from the artillery, the whole under the command of Captain Owen, were sent to secure provisions and intercept a convoy of Hyder's. Captain Owen conceived the quixotic design of storming the fort of Chittoor, but, unluckily, Hyder marched suddenly and attacked him, on the 23rd October, in his camp, and drove him back with heavy loss. One of the guns fell into the enemy's hands, but was retaken by a gallant effort made by Captain Moore, with forty Bengal grenadiers, whom an artilleryman informed of the loss.

After this, the whole army moved against Chittoor, on the 7th November. On the 8th, a battery of two guns and two howitzers fired from a hill against the fort, but without effect. On the 19th, a battery of two 18-pounders was formed on the banks of an artificial lake, within three hundred yards of a ruinous round tower, in which a breach was made before night, and the enemy offered to capitulate. Their terms were refused, and firing renewed, and the next day, the troops being ready to storm, the fort surrendered.

Hyder had, in the meantime, taken Poloor, in which were four 18-pounders, and surprised Polipett, where the baggage was left under charge of a battalion with three 6-pounders, and carried off all, and moved against Tripassore.

The army marched to relieve Tripassore, and arrived just in time, as a breach was just made. After destroying the works, they moved into Poonamalee on the 30th November.

Early in January, 1782, the army marched to the relief of Vellore, and on the 9th, encamped near Hyder's troops. On the 10th, Hyder attacked the rear, while the main body was moving through the dry bed of a lake. Beyond this was a wet one, and the main body crossed this also, but the carts and followers were in the swamp when Hyder reached the bank of the dry lake. Colonel Pearse, who was commanding the rear, formed up three battalions, and his guns, consisting of one 12-pounder, one howitzer, and six 6-pounders, which checked the enemy, who opened a cannonade from upwards of twenty heavy guns, but, with little effect. The position was held for upwards of an hour, until the baggage had all crossed, when Colonel Pearse crossed also, and joined Sir Eyre Coote, and after a little desultory firing Hyder withdrew.

Having thrown his convoy into Vellore, Sir Eyre Coote returned on the 13th, and on reaching his old ground, at the swamp, was again attacked. The passage was covered by a heavy cannonade from the 12 and 18–pounders, and when across, Hyder fell back, but made another attempt at sunset, which was beaten off. The succeeding days were spent in manoeuvres on both sides, without coming to an action.

The detachment was engaged in no further service of any consequence until the unsuccessful and mismanaged attack on Cuddalore, in June, 1783, in which Colonel Pearse was wounded, whence they returned to Madras, and remained encamped till April of the next year,—the death of Hyder Ali, and conclusion of a peace with Tippoo, rendering their further services unnecessary.

On the 22nd April the detachment made their first march homewards, and the European artillery accompanied them as far as Musulipatam, where, about the middle of May, they embarked with guns and stores, and reached Calcutta in June, 1784. The strength of each company on its return is annexed.

******

No.	Company.	Battalion.	Serjeants.	Corporals.	Drummers.	Gunners, &c.
2	4	2	6	6	2	61
5	5	1	6	7	2	55
10	5	2	7	6	3	56

******

There must, however, have been some recruits sent during the service; but as from the day of their quitting Bengal, the companies were struck off the strength of the regiment, it is impossible to trace their actual loss. Captain Hussey and Lieutenant Brown appear to have suffered from wounds, for in Mem. C. 19th July, 1784, on Lieutenant Browns promotion to Captain-Lieut.:

> The board observes that this promotion occasions the number of artillery officers to exceed the establishment, which they have been induced to admit, in consequence of the peculiar situations of Captain Hussey and Lieutenant Brown, by the wounds they received while on service in the Carnatic.

The following order was issued by government the 5th July, 1784:—

> The board having received ample testimony from the late Sir Eyre Coote, from Colonel Pearse, and from the President and Council of Fort St. George, of the uniform good conduct of

Lieutenant-Colonel Elliot, and the officers and men of the artillery, who have served under his command in the Carnatic, have much pleasure in expressing to this part of the Bengal detachment, the high sense they entertain of their gallant behaviour, and the important service which they have rendered to the Company, during the course of the war.

The board trust that this special mark of their approbation will be remembered as an animating example to the Bengal troops, whenever the public service may call for similar exertions.

The *golundaz* company, when the Europeans embarked, continued its march with the detachment, and the whole reached Ghyretti in January, 1785, where Warren Hastings honoured them with a visit, and testified the approbation of government, in general orders, which after expressing thanks to the commander and troops, for "their gallant behaviour, and useful services in the defence of the Company's territories," direct that:

As a lasting mark of their approbation, a pair of honorary standards be bestowed on each *sipahi* regiment; on each *soobadar* a gold, and on each of the *jemadars*, a silver medal, with such device, motto, and description as shall be judged applicable to the occasion; and medals of the same sort to the officers of the *golundaz* company; also similar badges of inferior value, to such of the men, warrant officers and privates, as have served with the detachment from the commencement of the expedition until its return to the provinces.

The governor-general and council further direct, that in acknowledgment of the services of the two great detachments, which have served in the Carnatic, and the West of India, an additional pay of two *rupees* per month be granted to each non-commissioned officer and private of the European corps, and one *rupee* per month to each non-warrant officer and *sipahi* of the native corps, composing those detachments, who were originally attached to the same, on the march to their respective destinations, and returned with them.

The governor-general likewise issued an order on the occasion of his visiting the detachment, and one of the last acts of his government was a proposal in council that:

A sword should be given to Col. Pearse and the two officers next in command; that all officers holding commands in the detachment of infantry battalions should be confirmed in them, notwithstanding the general rules of appointment, and that the names of all the officers be entered on record, for such future marks of the favour of government as the rules of the service may admit.

And to these propositions the council readily agreed.

It was also ordered, that the *lascars* of the artillery who were with these detachments should receive medals, in like manner as the *sipahi* regiments.

We are not sure whether medals for these services can now be found; we have been able to obtain a medal, the reverse of which is illegible, which we are induced to believe was given to one of these detachments, probably Colonel Goddard's, and the fort in the distance, representing Ahmedabad: a drawing of it is shown.

We have also been informed by an old native officer, that the medal was of the same pattern for both detachments.

The 1st *golundaz* company, which marched with Colonel Leslie's detachment, was raised in 1777; the 2nd, which marched with Colonel Pearse, in 1780; and the 3rd, 4th, and 5th were raised in 1782, at the Presidency, Chunar, and Dinapore. But the same feeling, before spoken of, prevented their retention, and accordingly, in August, 1784, the 3rd and 4th *golundaz* companies were reduced, with the option to the men of the former of entering the *lascars*, and the latter, the 9th or 14th regiments, which were at the same station. In March, 1785, the 5th company followed, the native officers being allowed the option of half-pay at Chunar, or three months' gratuity and discharge, and the men, after completing the 2nd company, of enlisting in the infantry.

In 1779, the necessity of a train of draught-bullocks for the artillery was pressed on the government by Sir Eyre Coote, and 4,000 were directed to be kept at certain stations for this purpose: they were to be from four to six years old, of fifty inches high, and to be condemned at twelve years old, and able to draw ordnance, as in annexed statement.

★★★★★

24-pounder	....	12 pair	8-inch Howitzer	......	7 pair
18 ,,	....	9 ,,	5½ ,,	,, ...	5 ,,
12 ,,	....	6 ,,	4½ ,,	,, ...	3 ,,
6 ,,	....	3 ,,	Wagon	....	7 ,,
3 ,,	....	2 ,,	Tumbril	....	5 ,,

★★★★★★

The commanding officers of artillery and of trains were to be inspectors of all bullocks received into the service, and responsible that none but proper cattle were admitted, and they were to be marked in the presence of an artillery officer. They were reduced to 600 at Caunpoor, 400 at Futteygurh, and 250 at Chunar, by Mem. of Council, 14th February, 1785, and the contract given to Sir Charles Blunt.

A gun-foundry existed at this time, for, in 1781, we find that:

> Two 12-pounders and ten 6-pounders were ordered to be cast (if none available) for the use of the ship *Betsey*, Captain Giddes, going with opium to China.

It was probably under the commissary of stores.

Powder-works also existed on the banks of the river, near Cossipoor. The gun-carriages were all constructed by the commissary of stores at Fort William.

On the reduction of the artillery brigade, Captain C. R. Deare, the major of brigade, was appointed regimental adjutant, but the brigade-majorship was restored in April, 1781, to be again, however, reduced to a regimental adjutant in 1785. Captain G. Deare resigned it in October, 1784, and Captain C. R. Deare was appointed.

In July, 1784, the adjutancy to the train in the field was abolished, but each company in the field appears to have had an adjutant and quartermaster attached to it.

In March, 1785, at the recommendation of Colonel Ironside, commanding at Caunpoor, tatties were first allowed to the European troops at Caunpoor.

Colonel Pearse at this time resumed command of the corps, Colonel Duff having temporarily held it while he was employed with the army on the coast; and earned the acknowledgments of the council and general orders, for the state of discipline it was in.

In this year many reductions were made in the army, by abolishing staff appointments, fixing the rate of pay and allowances to all classes, and laying the foundation of a code of regulations to guide all.

The commissaries of ordnance were reduced from five to two, and the deputies from eight to four; the brigade-majorship of artillery was altered to an adjutancy; the general command of artillery in the field was given to Lieutenant-Colonel Duff; his station was not fixed, but he was to move as his judgment prompted, was to inspect the field magazines and report on their state, but in these tours he was to exercise no command (though entitled by seniority) in the stations which he visited.

The following was the rate of pay allowed to all classes of the regiment:—

	Full Batta.	Half Batta.	Offreckonings.	Table Allowance.	Writers, &c.	Pay.	House-Rent.	Total.
Colonel Commdt.	750	—	150	1,200	645	310	120	3,175
Lieut.-Colonel ...	—	300	150	—	105	248	120	923
Major	—	225	150	—	—	186	120	681
Captain...........	—	90	36	—	—	140	90	356
Captain-Lieut. ...	—	90	36	—	—	90	90	306

	Lieutenant.	Lieutenant Fireworker.
Half Batta	60	45
Gratuity	24	24
Pay	101	91
House-rent	60	60
	245	220

* When quarters were not furnished.

Serjeant	20	Serang	21	0	0
Corporal	17	1st Tindal	14	5	3
Bombardier	16	2nd Tindal	11	5	3
Drummer	15	Lascar	5	12	0
Gunner	15	Serang Commandant	51	0	0
Matross	10				

Jemadar 20/8, Drummer 11, Havildar 14, Naick 11/4, Golundaz 7 rupees.

The scale of pay differs but little from the present day; but the subject will more properly be touched on when the effect of placing the army in certain stations on half *batta* in 1828 comes to be noticed.

In conjunction with the reductions above noticed, on the 30th January, 1786, it was resolved in council to incorporate the two battalions of artillery into one, of ten companies; but that the establishment of commissioned and non-commissioned officers attached to them should remain as at present until vacancies and casualties reduced them to the necessary establishment; but afterwards (March), all in excess to the latter were permitted to reside wherever they pleased within the Company's territories, drawing the pay and half *batta* of their ranks, and, such as were entitled to them, the gratuity and additional allowance.

	Colonel	Lieut.-Col. Commdt.	Majors	Captains	Capt.-Lieutenants	Lieutenants	Lieut.-Fireworkers	Serjeants	Corporals	Drummers	Bombardiers	Gunners	Matrosses	Adjutant	Quarter Master	Asst. Surgeon	Serjeant Major	Qr. Master Serjeant	Drum Major	Fife Major	Pay-Serjeants	Drill Serjeant	Drill Corporals
Necessary	-	1	1	10	10	20	30	60	60	30	80	240	530	1	1	2	6	1	1	1	1	10	1	2
Temporary	1	1	2	10	10	30	30	60	60	30	80	240	530	1	1	2	6	1	1	1	1	10	1	2

In making these arrangements, the original numbering was restored to companies. *Lascars* were to be attached to each company; in the field, 1 *serang*, 6 *tindals*, 6 *cossibs*, and 156 *lascars*; and in the provinces, 1 *serang* and half the number of *tindals* and *lascars*. The battalions of *lascars* were broken up. Two six-pounders were attached to each infantry regiment, with 5 European artillerymen, and 24 *lascars* to point and work them. The remainder of the *lascars* were paid up and discharged, and grants of waste land in the Rhotas district given to all who would settle on them.

A slight alteration was made in two months, *viz.* substituting *golundaz*, 1 *havildar* or *naik*, and 6 *golundaz* in lieu of the European artillerymen, who were in the first instance furnished by reducing the 1st and 2nd *golundaz* companies, the companies which marched with Goddard and Pearse, and the sole remnants of the *golundaz* battalions; the men were divided among the regiments, and in April directed to be enrolled as privates; the commissioned officers were retained in the service, and stationed, 1 *soobodar* at Caunpoor, and 1 *jemadar* at Futteygurh, Chunar, Dinapoor, Berhampoor, and Barrackpoor, to be employed at the discretion of the commanding officer.

As, however, in the case of the organisation in 1779, the Home authorities appear to have entered upon the same subject at the same time as the Indian, and in consequence, the above arrangement was hardly completed when the order of the Court of Directors (sess. 85) was received, and published in *Minutes of Council,* 2nd June, 1786, reforming the whole military establishment, and directing the artillery to be formed into three battalions of five companies each; each company to consist of 1 captain, 2 lieutenants, 2 lieutenant-fireworkers; 4 sergeants, 4 corporals, 8 gunners, 56 *matrosses*, 2 drummers, 2 *puckalies*. The *lascars* to consist of 30 companies, each having 1 *serang*, 2 first *tindals*, 2 second *tindals*, 56 *lascars*, 1 *puckalie*.

Each infantry regiment, when in the field, to be equipped with 1 European non-commissioned officer, and 8 privates, for pointing the guns, and 2 *tindals* and 28 *lascars*, to work them, while with each brigade there were to be, in addition to the battalion guns, 4 guns attached to the grenadiers, making a total of 16 guns, exclusive of the field train, and one company of European artillery and four of *lascars*.

An additional company of artillery was raised for service at Fort Marlborough, but not brought on the establishment.

Colonel Pearse, although a colonel and the officer next in seniority in the Company's service to the commander-in-chief, was declared available to command a battalion, thus lowering him from the command of a brigade, which the artillery had hitherto been, to that of a battalion, a command below what his rank entitled him to. This indignity was not, however, long continued, for in August he was appointed to the general command of the artillery stationed at the Presidency, and allowed an *aide-de-camp*.

The *lascars* lately broken up and dispersed among the regiments were withdrawn, to reform the companies, the first 6 of which were stationed at Caunpoor, the next 4 at Futteygurh, next 4 at Dinapoor, next 4 at Berhampoor, 6 with first battalion, and 6 with third battalion, at the Presidency; the *tindals* lately discharged were re-entertained; all *lascars* in excess of the establishment were discharged, and none in future were to be entertained, except such as were *seamen* or *boatmen* by profession; and in March, 1787, 5 feet 6 inches was the standard fixed for them.

The artillery companies were stationed, 10 at the Presidency, 1 at Berhampoor, 1 at Dinapoor, 2 at Caunpoor, and 1 at Futteygurh, and the companies were enrolled in the battalions according to the seniority of their captains at first; this, however, was shortly altered, by making the first and second battalions change numbers.

The regiment now stood, according to this arrangement—

Colonel.	Lieut.-Colonels.	Majors.	Captains.	Capt.-Lieutenants, Lieutenants.	Lieut.-Fireworkers.	Adjutants.	Quarter-Masters.	Serj. Major.	Qr.-Master Serj.	Drill-Serjeants.	Drill-Corporals.	Drum-Major.	Fife-Major.	Serjeants.	Corporals.	Gunners.	Matrosses.	Drummers.	Syrangs.	1st Tindals.	2nd Tindals.	Lascars.
-	3	3	15	30	30	3	3	3	3	3	5	3	3	60	60	120	840	30	30	60	60	1680
1	2	3	15	30	30	3	3	3	3	non-effect.		2	1	71	59	825		32	27	60	54	1679

The lower line line is actual strength, taken from the returns of the regiment for August, 1786.

CHAPTER 3

War in the Carnatic

Although so recent, the formation with which the last chapter closed was soon modified. In April, 1787, the artillery was constituted one of the brigades of the army—a change made probably with the view of placing Colonel Pearse on an equality with other officers of his rank, though junior to him in standing. But a curious circumstance is connected with this formation, in the nomination of an infantry officer:

> Lieutenant Peter Cullen, brigade-major to Colonel MacLeod, to act as brigade-major to the artillery, with the rank of captain, conformably to the orders of the Court of Directors, until a vacancy happens in that staff-line in the infantry to which he is to succeed.

The reason of this appointment is, however, clearly shewn in a subsequent order:

> The Honourable Captain T. Maitland, H. M.'s 72nd regiment, is appointed major of brigade, to do duty under Colonel MacLeod *vice* Lieutenant Cullen.

In March, 1788, however, Captain Grace, of the artillery, succeeded to this appointment.

Several changes took place at this period in the army, at which we need only glance. The colonels were detached from their brigades, and placed in a situation similar to that of general officers of divisions and brigades in the present day; tent allowance was given to officers in all situations; fusils and spontoons were superseded with infantry officers by swords; the dress of the army was altered, as was that of the artillery, and it is amusing to find that what is ordered in 1844 should be little more than reverting to the orders of 1786; for what is the order directing white covers to be worn on caps, but the principle of "White hats may be worn on the line of march, or black hats with white linen folded round them?" though, in truth, there may be little doubt whether the round hat so prepared was not a far preferable head-dress to the present shako.

The formation of a regimental school was an object of much interest with Colonel Pearse; as early as 1770 some orders were issued on the subject; but we learn from subsequent orders, in 1778, that these had "for various causes been neglected and forgotten, but that the commanding officer now resolves to carry them into execution;" and accordingly, rules are laid down for conducting the school duties,—the amount each man is to pay for being taught, what stoppages are to be carried to the school fund, and, finally, that any deficiency is to be borne, half by the commanding officer, and half by the captains. Again, in the year 1787:

> Colonel Pearse, having the welfare of his soldiers at heart, and being desirous to do for their benefit anything that lies in his power, has thought proper to establish a school for their instruction; that, by teaching them to read, he may enable them to learn their duty as Christians from books of their religion, and as soldiers, from the orders and regulations laid down for their guidance. It is his intention to visit it from time to time, and by his authority, to make it seriously a matter of attention.

Then follow some rules for the school, and as an encouragement to the non-commissioned officers to qualify themselves, he directs that:

> Every sergeant employing a man to write and read for him shall pay him 6 *rupees* a month, or to write for him, 4 *rupees* a month, and he shall not read on parade, or be excused his duties.

The number allowed to attend the school from each company

was limited, and the order has remained so nominally till late years, although, in reality, none wishing for instruction have been refused; but of late years the recruits for the regiment have been from a better class, and a very large proportion are able to read and write when they join the regiment. This may be partly caused by the more general diffusion of education in all classes, or from the crowded state of all lines in England, impelling a class to enlist who formerly found occupation in other professions.

As another instance of the interest which Colonel Pearse took in the welfare of his corps may be quoted the following order; it shews, too, how just were his views on questions of duty and discipline: "The rules of duty, as laid down, may seem extremely rigorous to those who do not properly consider the consequence; Colonel Pearse hopes that there are not any; but lest there should be, he desires that they will carefully remember that military discipline can only be really made easy by being enforced with precision in every part, however minute it may appear; that strictness with mildness will make the soldiers love their officers as their parents, and create in their minds a desire to be highest in esteem, and an emulation to deserve the preference, and the fear of losing it; then it will habituate the officers to regard the soldiers as the object of their attention, and lead them to watch over their morals with that pleasing anxiety which naturally arises from the desire to produce superior excellence in those who are immediately under them; and lastly, that in the corps in which these principles are most conspicuous, courts-martial and punishments are very rare; the lash is only heard when it falls on the really worthless and abandoned, whom the rest shun and detest for having brought disgrace upon them, and who are, of course, discharged soon after."

Vaccination had not at this time been introduced, but to lessen the danger from smallpox, inoculation on a large scale appears to have been first tried on Europeans in India this year. In February, 1787, 1 officer, 20 artillery, 26 infantry, and 53 children of artillerymen and *lascars*, were admitted into the artillery hospital at Dum-Dum, and inoculated; the party were left under the charge of Captain Rattray when the regiment marched into Fort William, and a report of the result was published in orders in April, from which it appeared that 90 took the infection and recovered; of the remainder who did not take it, some had been previously inoculated in England, but without such effect as to induce the supposition that they had had the small-pox; from the result above detailed, there is, however, little doubt but that they must have taken it.

In September, a general order having been issued directing the companies of artillery to be numbered in the different battalions, Colonel Pearse searched into the records of the corps as far back as 1770, at which time only 5 companies existed, and ascertained the exact seniority of each company; he laid a plan before Lord Cornwallis, which was approved of and published. Hitherto, the companies had stood on the returns agreeably to the seniority of their captains, or the order for field duty; this led to constant changes, for on the promotion, for instance, of a captain to a majority, his company would be given to the captain just promoted, and the company would be moved from the first to the last in the battalion.

In the accompanying tabular arrangement these successive changes could not all be shewn, though it is believed that it will be found essentially correct; however, from this period there can be no doubt of the identity of the different portions of the regiment, and for the valuable materials from which it has been arranged, the author is indebted to Lieutenant-Colonel Tennant, for many years assistant adjutant-general of artillery, and at a time when documents, which have since crumbled away, were accessible.

In March, 1789, Lord Cornwallis attended at Dum-Dum, to witness the results of some experiments carried on by Lieutenant Hill, with a view to ensure the ignition of the powder in a shell on the moment of its touching the ground; the success seems to have been complete, for:

> Lord Cornwallis has been pleased to desire Colonel Pearse to communicate to Lieutenant Hill, that his lordship has received the utmost satisfaction from the experiments this day carried on before him, and from the successful endeavours of Lieutenant Hill to fire the powder within shells the instant they touch the ground. Colonel Pearse adds his own hearty congratulations on this success, and feels the utmost pleasure that what has so long been sought for by artillerists, has at length been discovered by an officer of the Bengal Artillery under his command.

Lieutenant Hill's plan, from an incidental notice in the third number of the *East-India Military Repository*, seems to have been the same as that of an Englishman named W. Wilton, which was tried at Woolwich in 1784. The wood of a common fusee is partly cut away to about half its thickness on both sides, and the space filled up by two small wedges of brass; a washer of leather being placed under them, a hole is drilled through them and the fusee, a brass or copper wire is inserted, and riveted firmly on both sides. The wire, when heated, becomes as brittle as glass, and the shock of the shell touching the ground breaks it off; the little wedges fall into the shell, and the fire finds two lateral vents into the powder.

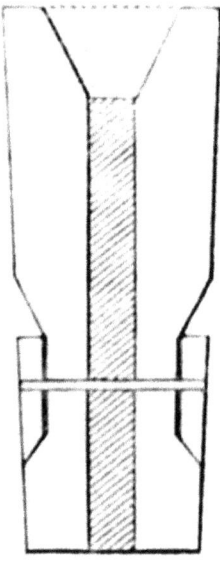

A fusee similar to Mr. Wilton's (*East-India Military Repository*), with the *leaden pins* (four small ones to give additional security to the brass wedges), was produced by the conductor of the *Expense Magazine, amongst several other kinds* said to have been invented by the late Colonel Hill, of the Bengal Artillery. These specimens are now in the model-room at Dum-Dum, but we have never seen any invention for the purpose more simple or more perfect than Mr. Wilton's fusee.

Of eight shells fired with the fusees at Woolwich, in 1784, six ignited at the moment of the shell touching the ground.

At the beginning of this month a fire broke out in the Arsenal, at night, consuming the workshops, and all they contained, "except a number of carriages of different kinds, which, by the unparalleled efforts of the officers and soldiers, were preserved from the flames." Colonel Pearse was present, and his presence stimulated their exertions to the utmost, but there is reason to believe that his own end was hastened by the exposure to this night, under the influence of mercury, as we find was the case from his own correspondence. Early in April he gave over the command of the garrison to the next senior officer, and proceeded down the river for a change of air, in the hope of restoring himself to health, but without the desired effect, and on the 15th June he ended his life; a garrison order by the governor-general thus announces it:—

> It is with the utmost concern that Earl Cornwallis has occasion to prepare the mournful duties of a last tribute of military honour to the remains of Colonel Pearse, in whose demise the army has lost a zealous and most respectable officer.
> On the corpse being brought into garrison the colours are to be lowered half-staff, and to remain so until the corpse is interred.
> The brigade of artillery is to furnish the funeral party, which is to consist of such part of the late Colonel Pearse's own battalion as is in the garrison, completed to the strength of a battalion, and commanded by Lieutenant-Colonel Deare; the remainder of the brigade, with the 4th battalion European infantry, are to attend the interment with their side-arms, in such disposition as the senior officer present may direct.

He was buried in the great burial-ground of Calcutta, and a handsome pillar of the Corinthian order raised to his memory at Dum-Dum.

The inscription given below is cut on a tablet let into the base of the pillar:—

TO THE MEMORY OF
THOMAS DEANE PEARSE,
COLONEL COMMANDANT OF ARTILLERY,
THIS COLUMN IS
ERECTED BY THE OFFICERS OF THE BRIGADE
IN TESTIMONY OF THEIR RESPECT,
MDCCXC.

In Colonel Pearse the regiment lost a commandant devoted to its welfare; of a high order of talent, fitted, in no common degree, for command, fond of his profession, and anxious for distinction in it, his whole energies were directed to the performance of his duties; his

Colonel Pearse's Monument

intercourse with his officers and men was marked by an earnest desire for their happiness and comfort, and an endeavour to raise the tone of manners and habits to be found existing in both ranks. Although a personal friend of Warren Hastings, his influence never seems to have been used for any private end; the good of the service was emphatically his guide; from his duty he never swerved, and in it he was influenced always by high-souled and chivalrous feelings. That he would have won for himself high honours, had an opportunity been afforded, who can doubt who has carefully considered his conduct when in command of the detachment to the coast; and that he had not opportunity must be in part attributed to the prejudice or jealousy of Coote.

For twenty years he commanded the regiment, and under his eye it grew from infancy to maturity, and passed through many trials, yet always winning for itself thanks and praises; to his exertions in instructing all parties in the details of their duties, it owed its excellence, and long as the regiment may last, and high as its fame may rise, the name of Pearse ought always to be gratefully associated with it.

The command of the artillery brigade now devolved upon Lieutenant-Colonel G. Deare (who joined the corps as a 2nd lieutenant when Pearse commanded it); he was at this time at Cawnpoor, commanding a battalion, and the duties of the brigade were carried on till he could join by "the brigade-major, Captain Grace, referring for advice to Lieutenant-Colonel C. R. Deare, commissary of stores, and brother to the commandant."

There being a paucity of artillery officers, such officers as chose to volunteer from the line and were approved of by the commandant of artillery were appointed. The following, this year, joined the corps from the infantry:—Lieutenants Drummond, Jones, H. Green, Clements Brown, Winbolt, Matthews, and Hopper; others joined in a similar manner previously, but their names have not been ascertained, though from a correspondence three years afterwards, we find Lieutenants Macalister and R. Browne were among them.

From the return of the two great detachments from Western India and the coast in 1785, the corps does not appear to have been called on to take the field; but this calm was soon to be at an end, and the Carnatic once again became the field of battle. Tippoo inherited with his dominions all his father's hatred and jealousy of the British, and from the time of his succession it was evident that he would take the earliest favourable opportunity to renew the war; with such feelings on his part, and jealousy and fear on the part of the British, peace could not long remain.

The war having recommenced with Tippoo in the Carnatic, assistance was called for from the Bengal Government, and in January, 1790, the whole of the second battalion of artillery was directed to be in readiness to embark for Madras on the shortest notice; and to economize the store of gunpowder, its issue was prohibited, save for service and artillery practice; country powder was ordered to be purchased by agents, and supplied for all other purposes.

The men of the 2nd battalion, unequal to the fatigues of field service, were removed to the 1st and 3rd battalions, and their places supplied by volunteers from them; twelve companies of *lascars* were attached, and the whole marched from Dum-Dum on the 5th February, and embarked on the 16th on the *Houghton* and *Chesterfield* Indiamen, and sloop *Lucnow*, except a detachment of one-half of the 2nd company, which marched with the infantry of the detachment under Lieutenant-Colonel Cockerell, and which was afterwards joined at Masulipatam by a complete company in addition, from the 1st battalion.

Lieutenant-Colonel Deare was at this time commissary of stores in Fort William, but giving over charge of the arsenal to Lieutenant Humphries, secretary to the Military Board, he took command of his battalion.

Lieutenant-Colonel C. R. Deare, commandant; Lieutenant Johnson, adjutant; Lieutenant Balfour, quartermaster; and Conductor Johnson.

Lascar Companies	Company	Battalion	Captains	Lieutenants	Lieutenant-Fireworkers	Non-com. Officers and Men
1, 7	1	2	Ellwood	Horsburgh / Macpherson	Butler / C. Brown	74
—	2	2	—	Nash	Feade	37
3, 4, 13	3	2	Horsford	Tomkyns / Nelly	Winbolt / H.Greene	74
2, 5	4	2	Smith	Wittit / Clarke	Dowell / Matthews	74
6, 15, 16	5	2	Sampson	Hardwicke / Cranch	Dunn / Jones	71

The 2nd battalion was probably selected for this service from its being complete at the presidency; but the officers of the other battalions seem to have thought they had been wronged by a departure from the regular roster, and accordingly Major Greene, 5 captains, and 20 subalterns appealed to Lord Cornwallis, that their juniors, or others out of turn, should not be sent. Lord Cornwallis, in general orders, commented on their proceedings, exculpating the subalterns on the plea of inexperience, but blaming the seniors for attempting to dictate to government on such a point.

Lieutenant-Colonel Deare, his staff the 1st, 5th, and a quarter of the 2nd company, under Lieutenant Nash; the 2nd, 6th, 7th, 13th, and 16th companies of *lascars*, with one-half the magazine and quartermaster's establishment, embarked on board the *Houghton*, while Major Woodburn, with the 3rd, 4th, and a quarter of the 2nd company, under Lieutenant-Fireworker Feade; the 1st, 3rd, 4th, 5th, and 15th companies of *lascars*, with the remainder of the magazine and quartermaster's establishment, embarked on the *Chesterfield*; a party, however, of 150 *lascars* from 2nd and 5th companies, with Lieutenants Horsburgh and Wittit, proceeded in the *Lucnow*.

The former ships had a fair passage for that season, and reached Madras before the end of March; the companies landed, and the headquarters, with 1st, 3rd, and 5th companies, immediately marched for Conjeveram, where, on the 30th March, they joined Colonel Musgrave's detachment, *en route* to Trichinopoly, the rendezvous of the grand army, and arrived there on the 29th April; the 4th company remained at Conjeveram.

The *Lucnow* was delayed in the river till 6th March, and did not leave the pilot till the 10th; their passage was so slow, that on the 3rd April it became necessary to reduce the allowance of water to each man; however, on the 19th April she reached Madras; the detachment of the 2nd company was landed and marched to the Mount, where it joined the part under Lieutenants Nash and Feade; Lieutenant Horsford marched for Trichinopoly, to join his company, and Lieutenant Wittit, with the *lascars*, set out for Wallajabad, where he arrived on the 2nd May, and gave them over to Captain Smith, commanding the Bengal artillery, with the force at that station, under Colonel Kelly.

The king's ships being all withdrawn, an armament, consisting of four Company's ships and two coasting vessels, was fitted out under command of Commodore Mitchell, who was knighted for his conduct in this expedition, succeeded in capturing two privateers, equal in size to small frigates, and in engaging and beating off two large frigates and another stout ship.

At this time a circumstance occurred which caused the relative precedence of the different arms of the service in the King's and Company's service to be set at rest by general orders.

Lieutenant Wittit, being for picket duty with a party of artillerymen, was proceeding to take the right of the party from H. M.'s 74th regiment, when the adjutant on duty directed him to parade on the left; to this he objected, but on being told it was Colonel Kelly's positive order, he reluctantly obeyed, and reported the circumstance to his commanding officer, Captain Smith, and Captain Speediman, commanding the artillery at the station. In forwarding the statement, Captain Smith mentioned a case having occurred in Bengal, between Captain Montague and Colonel MacLeod, of H.M.'s 73rd regiment, and requested that it might be referred to Earl Cornwallis, the commander-in-chief, which was done, and his lordship decided that:

> H.M.'s cavalry takes post of the Company's cavalry, H.M.'s artillery of the Company's artillery, and H.M.'s infantry of the Company's infantry; but the artillery takes post of the infantry, without considering the service to which they belong.

The relative precedence of the troops of the three presidencies was also decided at the same time: the Bengal troops are always to be on the right; the Madras and Bombay to take the right of each other in their own presidency, but to draw lots for the post when they meet on neutral ground.

The main body of the army was now assembled, to the number of 15,000 fighting men, at Trichinopoly; to each European battalion were attached two 12-pounders, and to each native battalion two 6-pounder guns, while a park of four iron and four brass 18-pounders, and four howitzers, for field service, accompanied, together with a large train of battering guns.

General Meadows arrived and reviewed the army on the 24th May, and on the 26th it commenced its march, the plan of the campaign being to enter Mysore by the Guzelhutty Pass, securing a communication by occupying, as a line of posts and depots, Tanjore, Trichinopoly, Carrore, Erroad, and Sattimungulum.

On the 15th June, the army reached Carrore, which they found evacuated, and, to lighten their march, deposited the iron and two of the brass 18–pounders, two of the howitzers, and about 1,200 sick in the fort.

Daropooram was taken; Coimbatore evacuated by the end of July; Erroad was taken early in August, but want of carriage was even thus early felt; officers were all directed to double up in their tents, and the battering guns, stores, and convalescents were left in Coimbatore. In the attack on Erroad the Bengal Artillery was employed under Colonel Deare. Dindigul and Palacatcherry were taken, and Sattimungulum surrendered to a detachment under Colonel Lloyd, with which was Captain Sampson's company of artillery; in the two former, the artillery of the coast were employed, and at Dindigul Colonel Moorhouse, an officer much respected, met his death.

It has been said that a detachment of the 2nd company 2nd battalion marched with Colonel Cockerell's division from Bengal; they joined the division at Balasore on the 24th March, and a complete company, in addition, from the 1st battalion, was sent by sea, and overtook them on the 20th June at Masulipatam; the officers were as follows:—

Lascar Companies.	Company.	Battalion.	Captains.	Lieutenants.	Lieutenant-Fireworkers.	No. of Privates.
11, 12	2	2	Montagu	Douglas	Briscoe	37
23, 29, 30	5	1	Barton	Hinde Toppin	Tulloh Hill	74

With the former were four 6-pounders and eight tumbrils, with spare carriages, and with the latter were ten 6-pounders and two 12-pounders.

The division reached Conjeveram on the 1st August. The 2nd company 2nd battalion, now completed by the other half joining, was attached, to the 1st brigade; the 5th company 1st battalion to the 2nd brigade, and a Madras company to the 3rd or reserve, Major Woodburn commanding the artillery. (Four 18-pounders, eight 12-pounders, twenty 6-pounders, two 3-pounders, and two 5½-inch howitzers.) This division marched under Colonel Kelly, by Wandiwash to Arnee, which place they had reached by the end of August, and were thus ready to penetrate the valley of Baramahl.

Thus far the campaign had been successful; a line of communication had been established, and the main body and centre division were ready to fall on Tippoo's dominions from two points—the Baramahl Valley and the Guzelhutty Pass.

The advanced division, under Colonel Lloyd, with which were the 1st, 3rd, and 5th companies of the 2nd battalion artillery was at Sattimungulum, the main body, under General Meadows, at Coimbatore, 60 miles in rear, and the rear division under Colonel Stewart at Palacatcherry, 30 miles in rear of the main body, while Colonel Kelly's with the centre army was at Baramahl.

Such were the positions of the British Army, when, on the 11th September, Tippoo with his whole force descended by the Guzelhutty Pass. His movements had been unknown; want of intelligence, partly caused by the numbers of cavalry who enveloped Tippoo's movements, and partly from want of arrangements, was a prevailing misfortune in these campaigns, and the first intelligence of this movement was received by Colonel Lloyd on the 12th from some battalions sent out to collect grain.

On the 13th, a cavalry party sent out to reconnoitre, fell in with the advance of Tippoo's army, and falling back on their supports, kept the enemy at bay till he drew off, and then returned to camp. Tippoo soon followed, but Colonel Floyd took up a position which confined his attack to a cannonade, commencing with three pieces, which he advanced under cover of the hedges, and which, from being at a distance, and the supply of ammunition with the British being short, were not at first molested, he gradually increased them until, by 2 o'clock, there was a semicircle of 15 pieces playing with much execution on the British line; but it may be as well to extract, from a letter of Lieutenant Hardwicke, who was in the action with Captain Sampson's company, to Lieutenant Wittit:—

> The enemy advanced so fast, that the camp was struck a second time, and all baggage thrown into a place of security. The line formed and advanced, and about 10 o'clock the enemy's guns opened upon us, and by 11 o'clock we had taken our position and returned the fire. The enemy extended his line so as to form a crescent, and opened guns to bear upon us in every situation, and so well were they served that every shot did execution.
>
> On the right of our line an 18, two 12, and two 6-pounders kept up a smart fire, against which the enemy returned a most galling one. About 12 o'clock our commandant, Lieutenant-Colonel Charles Deare, received a shot in his breast, and expired immediately. Half an hour afterwards, Captain Sampson, our second in command, while speaking to me, received a very dangerous wound in the head, from a stone which a shot, that at this moment killed my horse, had raised; whole files of the grenadiers were swept away; half our gun bullocks fell; and the desertion of all the drivers increased the confusion.
>
> The cannonade continued till the close of day, and before it was quite dark we could perceive they were drawing off their

guns. The two 12-pounders were rendered useless very early in the day by the axletrees giving way; the 18-pounder limber received a shot and blew up; both my 6-pounders were so damaged by shot that one only could travel; except the left of the line, every part of the ordnance suffered much, and it appeared impossible to bear such a cannonade till relief could come from the grand army; to stand another day seemed likely to lessen our means of getting off, and while we had guns to defend ourselves in a retreat, that measure was thought most advisable.

★★★★★★

In the Calcutta burying-ground is a tomb to the memory of Lieut.-Colonel and Mrs. Deare. She died a few days before him. The inscription on the tomb is as follows:—

HERE REST THE REMAINS OF
MRS CATHERINE DEARE,
WHO DIED AT CALCUTTA 6TH SEPT. 1791,
AGED XXXIV YEARS:
IN MEMORY OF HER AND HER HUSBAND,
LIEUT.-COLONEL CHARLES RUSSELL DEARE,
WHO FELL BY A CANNON-SHOT
ON THE 13TH OF THE SAME MONTH,
WHILE COMMANDING THE BENGAL ARTILLERY,
IN AN ACTION FOUGHT
BETWEEN A DETACHMENT OF THE BRITISH FORCES
AND THOSE OF TIPPOO SULTAN,
NEAR SATTIMUNGULUM,
AGED XL YEARS.
THIS MONUMENT WAS ERECTED BY HIS BROTHER,
COLONEL GEORGE DEARE

★★★★★★

The day had been disastrous, many killed and wounded, and three guns disabled, but Colonel Floyd reported that:

The rest of the guns fired with excellent aim, but sparingly, for the stock of ammunition was not great. H. M.'s regiments and the artillery did themselves justice with their accustomed valour.

A council of war followed at night, and, as might be expected (for when did a council of war ever recommend an energetic plan?), a retreat to Coimbatore, sacrificing baggage and followers, was resolved on. It certainly does appear strange, with a fort at hand and the main army within 60 miles, the resolution of holding the fort till help arrived was not determined on.

The intention of abandoning the followers got abroad, and they all fled, so that no artificers could be found to repair the damaged carriages; however, the experience of the officers, with the aid of the Europeans, supplied the deficiency, and by 1 a.m. of the 14th they were in a serviceable state; by 4 a.m. the army was in retreat, but from the loss of bullocks one 18, two 12, and three 6-pounders were left behind.

Crossing the "Bavani" in basket-boats, the retreat commenced unmolested, but, and here we again quote Lieutenant Hardwicke's letter:

> About 10 o'clock, we could discern the enemy's line of march, and at 1 o'clock they opened their guns upon us, moving parallel with our line and taking advantage of every situation which gave them a view of the line. About 3 o'clock their infantry and horse crowded on the rear, an advantage the nature of the country or badness of the road gave them; they enfiladed us from behind hedges, buildings, &c., and at 5 o'clock they appeared in all quarters and advanced with a 'ding' in crowds. The battalions reserved their fire, and gave it almost on the point of the bayonet with surprising effect; some faced to the rear and resisted the attacks there. A 6-pounder and two tumbrils were, however, here lost, but it was astonishing the havoc the remaining 6-pounder in that quarter made at this time; so severe did they feel our fire, that theirs slackened, and a charge made by the whole of our cavalry gave a turn to the fate of the day.
>
> Night closed on the bloody scene, and we continued our march till 9 o'clock. By the lights in the enemy's camp we could tell they were not far off, and it was thought prudent, weakened as we were by two such days' fatigue, to continue our march; we accordingly set off again at 3 o'clock, and directed our route towards the hills, expecting to meet a reinforcement from the general; we crept along all the day, suffering almost as much from fatigue, heat, and want of sustenance, as we had before from the enemy. We lost in all six guns and the greatest part of our baggage. Lieutenant Horsborough was slightly wounded in the head, and Lieutenant Winbolt in the arm.

The artillery lost in these actions—1 lieutenant-colonel, 1 corporal, 6 *lascars* killed, 2 captains, 2 lieutenants, 10 Europeans, and 15 *lascars* wounded.

The whole army was now collected at Coimbatore, and on it moving forwards, Tippoo made an unsuccessful attempt on the place.

On Colonel Kelly's death, on the 24th September, the centre army fell under Colonel Maxwell's command, and entered the Baramahl valley; but the operations of this division only once brought them into contact with the enemy, on the 12th of November, on which occasion the good position taken up, and the correct fire of a gun, prevented an attack by the overwhelming numbers opposed.

A junction took place with the main army on the 10th November, and both armies followed Tippoo, to relieve Trichinopoly, and after some desultory operations, the campaign concluded.

In November and December Lieutenants Jones and Nash, of the artillery, died, and Lieutenants T. Green, Exshaw, MacLeod, Drummond, and Buchan came round from Bengal to join the battalion.

By Lieutenant-Colonel Deare's death, Captain Montague was promoted to a majority, but directed to remain with the 2nd battalion; Lieutenant Glass to a company, and joined; Colonel Duff was ordered round to command the Bengal Artillery, and arrived about the middle of December. These promotions were made subject to the Court of Directors' approval, because Colonel Duff had memorialised to be allowed to command the artillery brigade as senior officer. The regimental formation having taken place, his claim was not allowed by the Indian Government, but referred home, where it was finally negatived, and these promotions confirmed, in the Court's letter, 4th August, 1791.

On the 12th December Lord Cornwallis arrived, and assumed command of the army; fresh energy was instilled into every department, and by the 5th February the march commenced.

The park consisted of eleven 18-pounders, six 12-pounders, and eight mortars, with an ample supply of ammunition and stores. Lieutenant-Colonel Giels (Madras artillery) commanded artillery of right wing; Major Moorhouse, left wing; Major Woodburn, heavy park; Major Montague, of the advance.

The plan of the campaign was to penetrate Mysore by the line of Vellore, Ambore, and Bangalore; and to meet the British, Tippoo moved off from Pondicherry (where he had been intriguing with the French), and was ready to oppose them by the usual routes; but Lord Cornwallis, marching in the direction of Ambore, turned suddenly to the north, and gained the foot of the Mooglee pass on the 17th February, and by the 21st the whole army had ascended, and were encamped in Mysore before Tippoo could oppose them; the *ghat* presented but few difficulties; the heavy guns, with the aid of men and elephants, gave little trouble.

On the 24th marched for Bangalore, in three columns: the artillery on the right, infantry in the centre, and cavalry on the left; to keep the enemy's cavalry at a distance, the European regiments were equipped with the iron 12-pounders from the park, and on several occasions their services were found very useful on the march to Bangalore, before which the army took up their position on the 5th March. On the next day the cavalry went out on a *reconnaisance*, in which they were worsted by Tippoo's troops, and but for the opportune arrival of Major Gowdie and Major Montague, with assistance, and contrary to orders, our loss would have been severe.

On the 7th the *pettah* was attacked and carried, and Tippoo's endeavour to retake it repulsed; the fort was now attacked; on the 12th, a 10-gun, a 2-gun, a mortar battery, and a 9-gun battery in the ditch of the *pettah* were commenced, and opened on the 15th; on the 16th a breach appeared, but two guns, an 18-pounder and a 24-pounder, were disabled. On the night of the 17th a 4-gun battery was erected against the gateway. Major Dirom says:

> So just was the aim of our artillery, that on the 18th, notwithstanding the strength of the wall, the breach was considered practicable by several qualified to judge from the experience of several years' service; another parallel, however, was laid out and completed within 200 yards, and its batteries armed.
> On the 19th, the 4-gun battery opened; this and the others kept up a constant cannonade on the breach and neighbouring towers, replied to sharply by musketry from covert way and outworks; to keep which down, additional batteries were erected in the advanced parallel, and were ready by daylight.
> On the 20th the fire widened the breach, and rendered it easier of access, although its defences were still numerous, and at dusk a working party opened a sap from the advanced battery to the crest of the glacis; the enemy employed in attempting to stockade the breach.

On the 21st the enemy meditated an attack on the British camp, but, being met, retreated; they however advanced again in the evening.

At 11 o'clock at night the storming party prepared to move forward, and for about an hour previous a heavy cannonade was kept up on the breach, and as this intimidated the defenders from remaining there, it was kept up with blank cartridges while the storming party advanced; the party gained the top of the breach without very much opposition, and wheeled off to the right and left, overcoming a considerable resistance at different points. The whole of the Bengal artillery (six companies) it is believed were employed in this service. The casualties, from 7th to 21st March, amounted to only 8 Europeans and 2 gun *lascars* killed; and the following extract from the general orders of the 22nd March records the satisfaction they gave.

> The judicious arrangements made by Colonel Duff, in the artillery department, his exertions and those of the other officers and soldiers of that corps in general, in the service of the batteries, are entitled to his lordship's perfect approbation; to which he desires to add, that he thinks himself much obliged to Lieutenant-Colonel Giels (Madras establishment) for the able manner in which he conducted the fire during the day of the 21st.

The army remained in Bangalore till the 4th May, during which time every exertion was used to collect carriage,—every expedient that could be suggested was tried: private cattle were obtained by leaving behind camp equipage and every necessary; a reward was given to camp-followers of 1½ *rupees* for every 24-pounder, and 1 *rupee* for every 18-pounder shot they would carry to Seringapatam; every nerve was strained, that an attack might be made at once upon the capital; the train was put in order, but beyond bullocks for 52 field-pieces and a few howitzers, sufficient for only 15 battering-guns could be collected.

Thus equipped, on the 4th the army marched, and after much difficulty, from the state of the carriage cattle, reached Arakerry, on the River Cavery, a few miles below Seringapatam, on the 13th May; the river was found unfordable, and no place nearer than Caniambaddy, eight miles above the fort, could be found. Tippoo, with his army, was encamped about six miles off, with his right to the river, and left to a rugged mountain. While attempting to render the ford passable, on the 14th, the army halted, and Lord Cornwallis conceived the idea of attacking Tippoo by a night march, and cutting him off from a retreat on Seringapatam.

The attempt was made, but a heavy storm overtaking the army

soon after it started, the way was lost, and the troops got entangled, so that they were forced to halt till daylight; the effect of a surprise was lost; the enemy, however, were defeated with loss. The artillery had Lieutenant Macpherson, one European, and four *lascars* wounded; but the chief part were probably left behind, under Colonel Duff, with the camp, heavy guns, and stores. Lieutenant Macpherson died of his wounds on the 21st May.

On the 20th the army had reached the ford at Caniambaddy, but in such a state, from deficiency of food, carriage, and material, and the state of the weather, that Lord Cornwallis found it would be impossible to move the battering-train from where it was, and that he must give up the hope of taking Seringapatam for the present.

On the 22nd, three 24-pounders and eight 18-pounders were burst, all the stores were buried or destroyed, and the whole of the public grain distributed among the troops, and the whole army were in motion on their melancholy retreat on the 26th May; they moved slowly back to Bangalore, which they reached on the 11th July, putting all their spare tumbrils and stores into Bangalore (Lieutenant Douglas was appointed commissary of ordnance). The army moved lightly on the 15th, to cover the passage of a convoy from below the *ghats*. Ossoor surrendered and Captain Glass's (2nd company 2nd battalion) company of artillery was thrown into it, with a battalion of Bengal volunteers as a garrison. This company, with heavy guns, was employed in September in escorting a convoy to Bangalore.

In September, a detachment under Major Gowdie was sent against Nundydroog, a hill fort, which, if left in the enemy's possession, would have given trouble to the army on their advance to Seringapatam, for which everything was now nearly ready. With Major Gowdie's detachment was a detachment of artillery under Major Montague, four iron 12-pounders and two small mortars. This detail was probably from the 5th company 1st battalion, as Lieutenant T. Hill's name is mentioned during the subsequent operations, and to that company he belonged.

On the road to Nundydroog the hill fortress of Raymanghur was taken. "The indefatigable exertion of Major Montague in getting four 6-pounders and two mortars on a rock which completely flanked the proposed point of attack, his firing with great effect, and throwing shells with much judgment," are acknowledged by Major Gowdie, as contributing to the early capture of the place.

From Raymanghur the division proceeded against Nundydroog,

a hill fortress of great strength, situated on ground most difficult of approach, where, on the 29th, they were joined by two 24–pounder guns and four mortars, with a quantity of stores.

With astonishing labour and exertion, Major Montague, on the night of the 2nd October, got two 24-pounders into the battery by means of ropes fastened round posts driven into the ground, and trees, and all the resources which an artillery officer must bring into play in such circumstances; and on the 4th, this and a mortar battery from the *pettah* opened, but the height was too great, for the mortars, and the guns were unable to make any impression on the solid blocks of stone of which the walls were formed; regular approaches were resolved on, and an 8-gun battery (18-pounders) got ready up the hill, into which, on the 11th October, the guns were drawn by two elephants each, aided by four drag-ropes and crowds of men.

On the 12th this battery opened with excellent effect, and soon silenced all the guns in its direction, except one on the south-east angle, which did much mischief; a traverse was raised against this, and an advanced battery for two 6-pounders; into this, with infinite labour, a 12-pounder was also conveyed, and the angle gave way to a few well-directed shots by Major Montague, and the troublesome gun came tumbling down the rock. The ammunition running short, the fire was slack until the 16th, when a fresh supply arrived from Bangalore.

The breach being now practicable, on the 18th the army moved up, and on that evening the assault took place. An artillery officer, with a party of men and a small mortar, to be used as a petard for blowing open the gate of the inner wall, accompanied the storming party. The resistance, though great at first, was not continued, and the place was won without a heavy loss.

Lieutenant T. Hill, of the artillery, was wounded, during the siege, in the thigh by the bursting of a shell, and Lieutenant Cranch slightly in the shoulder.

Lieutenant-Colonel Stewart's division now proceeded against Savendroog, a hill fortress on a rocky mountain, half a mile high, and eight or ten miles in circumference; on the 10th December, the division was within three miles of it, the commander-in-chief covering the siege with the main army; the hill was surrounded by a deep belt of jungle, composed of bamboos and trees, interspersed with large masses of rock; a narrow path was the only road, and this was rendered difficult from barriers.

A road for the guns was with great labour formed through this forest, and they were transported with much difficulty through; the enemy offered little or no interruption, confident in the strength of their post and the fearful ally, malaria, which haunted the jungle, and, which Tippoo affirmed, would destroy one-half of the army, while he would slaughter the other. On the 17th December, two batteries opened, one of three 18-pounders, at 800 yards, at an elevation of 23°, and the other of three 12-pounders and two 18-pounders, at 700 yards; the artillery was under Major Montague, but we are unable to ascertain what company.

The wall being formed of solid slabs of stone fastened together by iron rivets, and the guns firing at an elevation, the effect of the 12-pounders did not at first answer the expectations formed. Two 2-gun batteries were pushed on to within 250 yards, and the 12-pounders were replaced by 18-pounders drawn from the main army, and their continued fire soon opened a breach in the upper wall. On the 20th, the breach was reconnoitred, and Major Montague not considering it sufficiently open, kept up an incessant and well-directed fire upon it all day, and before dark the breach was widened, and the outer wall shattered to its foundation.

On the 21st the storm took place; the signal was to be given when the fogs, which daily rise from the low ground and ascend the hill, should wrap the fortress in their sombre mantle, hiding from the besieged the besiegers' intentions. At about 11 o'clock a.m. the signal-guns were fired, and the enemy moved down to defend the breach, but the batteries opened a deadly fire of grape, under cover of which the storming party advanced, and rapidly drove the enemy back, entering the citadel with them, and gaining possession of the place. Major Montague's successful exertions in bringing his guns into battery, and his professional skill in directing their fire, again earned the praises of the commander-in-chief in government orders.

Other fortresses fell—Ramghurry, Sheriaghurry, and Outredroog, with little resistance; Lieutenant Shipton, Lieutenant-Fireworkers Charles Brown and Butler, were present at their taking; but now all attention was turned to the main object of the campaign, the siege of Seringapatam.

During the operations above detailed, convoys of stores and ordnance had been arriving, and every care taken to put the *matériel* of the army on the best possible footing; everything was collected in Bangalore, and the train under Colonel Duff arrived there on the 12th January, 1792, in high order; "the draught cattle were in such high order" (to quote from a letter of that period), "that they literally came in with the heavy guns on a gallop."

The train consisted of—

4	24-pounders,	
24	18 ,,	
4	12 ,,	
60	6 ,,	
3	8-inch howitzers,	
4	5½ ,, ..	
6	5½ and 4½ mortars,	
1	8-inch mortar,	
60	6-pounder tumbrils,	
206	store tumbrils,	
9	spare carriages,	
225	carts.	

The Bengal Artillery during the last few months had been weakened by the loss of officers: Captain Smith and Lieutenant Horsborough died in October, 1791, at Bangalore, and Captain Sampson early in January, 1792; but Captains Howell and Burnett supplied their vacancies.

On the 1st February, the army marched from Bangalore, the troops on the right, the battering-train in the centre, and the baggage on the left; the cattle and the carriages were so good that the train moved without difficulty, and on the 5th February, the army came in sight of Seringapatam. Tippoo had drawn his army into a fortified camp on the north side of the Cavery; Lord Cornwallis, on the 6th, reached Seringapatam, and resolved to attack the enemy that night. The army marched at 7 o'clock in the evening, in three divisions, for this purpose, leaving their artillery in camp, protected by the cavalry, quarter, and rear-guards, under the command of Colonel Duff.

No guns accompanied the army; but with Lord Cornwallis's division were Major Montague (Captain Ross, Royal Artillery), and subalterns, and 50 European artillerymen; with General Meadows, Captain Howell, 2 subalterns, and 50 European artillerymen; 150 *lascars* went with each division to carry the scaling-ladders; and with Lieutenant-Colonel Maxwell were 2 subalterns, 30 European artillerymen, and 50 *lascars*. In spite of the opposition and the difficulties the nature of the ground presented, the intentions of the commander-in-chief were carried out, and the morning of the 7th found the British Army in possession of the camp; but several attempts were made by Tippoo to dislodge them from some of the redoubts they had taken, particularly the one called, hitherto, the *Sultan's* redoubt, but from this day Sibbald's, in compliment to the gallant man who, with a very small force, held it this day against Tippoo's repeated attacks.

In this defence, the life of a valuable officer of the Bengal Artillery, Lieutenant Buchan, was lost, one to whose resources in the hour of emergency its successful defence was indebted.

The detachment with Major Montague was actively employed in securing the field-artillery in the enemy's camp; instead of spiking the guns, Major Montague directed that they should be thrown off their carriages and the wheels rolled different ways, by which means the guns taken were secured without being damaged, and the parts afterwards easily collected: upwards of sixty guns were thus taken. (Among them two brass 6-pounders which had been lost at Sattimungalum.) The chief loss fell on the *lascars*, of whom eight were killed and twenty-two wounded or missing.

The fortress was now invested by the combined armies, and preparations made for the siege; in this Lieutenant Hind, of the Bengal Artillery, with 300 *lascars* assisted, collecting and preparing materials for gabions and fascines; but a treaty formed with Tippoo rendered these useless, and in May the army broke up.

The artillery marched to the coast, where Colonel Duff left them, and sailed for England in the *Dutton*, Indiaman, with General Meadows: the rest embarked in the *Ardesir, Mary, Hero,* and *Juliana Maria,* and reached Bengal early in July.

The tabular statement following, compiled from the Prize-Money Distribution Statements, will shew more clearly the officers who were present in these campaigns, as each officer had not been mentioned at the time of his joining.

Rank.	Name.	Proportion of Shares for Companies.			Remarks.
		90	91	91½	
Colonel	P. Duff ...... Staff	—	full	full	killed at Sattimungalum.
Lieut.-Col.	C. R. Deare do.	¾	—	—	
Major	W. Woodburn do.	full	full	full	
,,	E. Montague do.	,,	,,	,,	
Captain	P. Cranell do.	,,	,,	,,	died at Madras.
,,	T. Hardwicke do.	,,	,,	,,	
Captain	T. Ellwood	full	full	full	
,,	G. Howell	—	¾	,,	
,,	A. Glass	—	full	,,	
,,	J. Horsford	full	,,	,,	
,,	J. Smith	—	,,	—	
,,	G. F. Sampson	full	,,	—	
,,	J. Burnett	—	—	full	
,,	C. Wittit	—	full	,,	

Rank	Name	Proportion of Shares for Companies.			Remarks.
		90	91	91½	
Lieutenant	J. Horsborough	full	,,	—	
,,	D. McPherson	,,	¼	—	
,,	H. Douglas	—	¼	full	
,,	J. R. Exshaw	—	full	,,	
,,	T. Greene	—	,,	,,	
,,	J. Tomkyns	full	,,	,,	
,,	J. Nelly	,,	,,	,,	
,,	E. Clarke	—	,,	,,	
,,	T. Hardwicke	full	,,	,,	
,,	H. Balfour	,,	,,	—	
Lieutenant	W. Shipton	—	—	full	
,,	T. Hill	—	—	,,	
,,	J. P. Drummond	—	—	,,	
,,	T. Dowell	—	full	,,	
,,	R. Tulloh	—	—	,,	
Lt.-Firewk.	A. Dunn	¼	full	,,	
,,	A. McLeod	—	,,	,,	
,,	A. Buchan	—	,,	,,	
,,	A. Mathews	—	,,	,,	
,,	W. Winbolt	full	,,	,,	
,,	H. Green	,,	,,	,,	
,,	W. Feade	—	,,	,,	
,,	E. Butler	full	,,	,,	
,,	Charles Brown	,,	,,	,,	
,,	J. J. Briscoe	,,	,,	,,	
Cadet	J. P. Keeble	—	—	,,	{ Inf. Invalided { Lt. Co. 1820.
,,	P. Fortnham	—	—	,,	{ resigned Aug. { 1800.
,,	J. Gore	—	—	,,	{ Inf., died at { sea 97-8.

During these campaigns the following officers lost their lives, either in action or from disease:—Lieutenant-Colonel C. R. Deare, killed; Captains Smith and Sampson; Lieutenants Macpherson and Buchan, killed. Lieutenants Horsborough, Nash, and Jones, and several others, were forced to seek health in a sea-voyage.

The services of the native troops, including the artillery *lascars*, on this occasion, were rewarded by a medal, and six months' *batta* was given to all the officers and troops.

It will not be uninteresting at this period to examine the casualties of the regiment, with a view to ascertaining the relative health enjoyed in those days and at present: fortunately, the long rolls of the regiment are tolerably perfect at this period, and the following is an abstract, giving an average of 138 casualties *per annum* to a strength of 1,016, or about 13 *per cent. per annum*—almost the same proportion of casualties as have taken place from the same causes during the last three years: their amount is 368, and the strength of the regiment in Europeans maybe taken as 3,000.

	1788	1789	1790	1791	1792	1793	1794	1795
Strength on 1st Nov.	969	980	1176	1155	1162	1083	844	755
Died	51	80	133	146	102	83	65	65
Deserted	3	6	7	11	14	10	10	8
Discharged	25	30	9	7	10	11	5	7
Invalided	26	15	21	25	35	31	15	37
Total	105	131	170	189	161	135	95	117

The average, however, of a longer period will be more favourable to modern times, as the losses during the Afghanistan war, the destruction of the 1st troop, and the mortality from disease at Sukkhur, all tend to swell these years beyond their predecessors; but this subject will be adverted to hereafter, when abstracts of longer periods have been made.

In August, 1793, five companies of artillery, the 2nd and 4th of 1st battalion, the 1st of 2nd battalion, and the 4th and 5th of 3rd battalion, under command of Major Bruce, sailed for the coast, forming part of an expedition against Pondicherry. The troops do not appear to have been employed, and the artillery returned in October.

The allowances of officers of similar rank and in similar commands, at this time and fifty years later, form a contrast much in favour of the liberality of the old scale.

The allowances to Major Bruce in 1793 were fixed at				The allowances to a Major similarly placed in 1843 would be			
Pay as Major	Rs. 180	0	0	Pay as Major	Rs. 182	10	0
Batta as Colonel	1,200	0	0	Batta as Major	456	9	0
¼ Table allowance	600	0	0	Tentage as Major	120	0	0
Field allowance	120	0	0	Horse allowance	30	0	0
				Command allow.	300	0	0
Total	2,100	0	0	Total	1,089	3	0

But it must be allowed that the juniors of the army are in much better circumstances than they were then.

The whole of the officers employed were to receive full *batta* at Madras, and the difference of full and double full *batta* to be audited to them in Bengal.

A detachment of 105 Europeans and 230 *lascars*, under Captain Frazer, (Lieutenants Douglas, Hinde, Dowell, Tulloh, and Humphrays), embarked in October on board Commodore Mitchell's fleet as marines, and served for nearly a year. Their good conduct, and the unanimity which prevailed between them and the crews of the different ships, were eulogised by the commander-in-chief in general orders on their return.

The regiment was inspected by the commander-in-chief, Sir Robert Abercrombie, in February, and by the governor-general, Sir John Shore, in March, 1794, and elicited, on both occasions, praises for its appearance, discipline, and performance of exercises and evolutions.

From the general orders of 9th June of this year, we learn that:

> At the recommendation of the commandant of artillery and chief engineer, the Rev. W. Paul Limerick, chaplain, was appointed teacher of mathematics to the corps of artillery and engineers, with the allowance of 500 *rupees per mensem*, formerly received by W. Burroughs in a similar situation.

A detail under Captain Carnegie accompanied the force commanded by Lieutenant-Colonel Erskine, which proceeded to Chittagong in February and returned in June; and a detachment of 36 *matrosses* proceeded in June, under Captain Howell to Bencoolen, and were lost on the passage. Another detachment of the 2nd, 3rd, and 4th companies, 2nd battalion, proceeded to the coast, under Lieutenant-Colonel Hussey, returning, however, in October.

The only portion of the regiment which was engaged in active service this year, 1794, was the 3rd battalion, three companies of which were employed with the army under Sir R. Abercrombie, in Rohilcund, in the short campaign against Gholam Mohummud, who had murdered his brother, and usurped the government of the district of Rampoor.

The following are the companies and officers employed:—

Major C. Green, Commanding.

Lascar Companies.	Company.	Battalion.	Captains.	Lieutenants.	Lieutenant-Fireworkers.
1, 9, 20	1	3	Hardwicke	Watkins & Macleod	C. Brown
8, 17, 28	2	3	Mordaunt	Baker, A. Dunn ...	Hoffer, Tilfer
18, 19, 25	3	3	Macintyre	W. Shipton	
				Lt.-Firew. Clem. Brown was Adj.	F. Maynard (doubtful).

On the 26th October, the line (consisting of one European regiment, ten native, two weak regiments of native cavalry, and the artillery above mentioned and 28 pieces of ordnance) was under arms before daylight. The commander-in-chief and staff rode forwards to reconnoitre the enemy, whom they found some miles in advance, near Bittowrah. The line came up, the artillery in the intervals, and the Rohillas pressing forwards, the reserve was brought up into line; they moved so fast, that the artillery attached to the reserve were unable to keep up, and fell into the rear.

The enemy at this time were in the jungle on the front and flanks, and some lamentable error committed by Captain Ramsay, commanding the cavalry on the right, wheeled it to the left, and brought it upon the infantry, throwing both into confusion, which was instantly taken advantage of by the enemy, who charged in a most daring and gallant manner (though suffering severely from the fire of grape, which was well directed, and caused great havoc), cutting up the regiments on the right fearfully. Lieutenant Tilfer and the artillerymen and *lascars* at the guns were cut down to a man. The confusion was great for a time; and the enemy in part reached the centre and rear.

However, by strenuous exertions, the tide of victory was stayed, and turned in favour of the British, but not without a heavy loss, as is attested by a monument at the village of Futteygunge, erected by the order of the governor-general in council to the memory of Colonel Burrington and fourteen British officers who fell in the action, among whom were Captain Mordaunt, Lieutenant Baker, and Lieutenant-Fireworker Tilfer, of the artillery.

One sergeant, 2 gunners, and 20 *matrosses*, and 27 *lascars* also fell; and from the casualties being all in the same company (2nd company 3rd battalion), it was probably on the right where the confusion occurred.

The officers of the army considered that Rampoor ought to have been plundered, and probably made their opinion known, for in this case, as in the similar one of 1774, as a sort of compensation for plunder, the *nawab* presented to the governor-general for distribution among the troops engaged 11 *lacs* of *rupees*, and one *lac* for the families of the officers who fell. The division was made on a scale drawn up by the junior auditor-general, giving each person engaged a sum equal to 328 days' *batta* of his rank; the amount of the shares is annexed.

Colonels...	Rs. 16,400	0	0	Conductors... Rs. 1,312		0	0
Lieut.-Colonels	13,120	0	0	Serjeants	218	10	8
Majors	9,840	0	0	Gunners	109	0	0
Captains	3,936	0	0	Serangs	54	10	8
Lieutenants	2,624	0	0	Tindals	43	11	0
Lt.-Fireworkers	1,968	0	0	Lascars	21	13	10

The *lac* of *rupees* devoted to the families of deceased officers was divided—40,000 to Colonel Burrington's; 20,000 to Captain Bolton's widow; and 10,000 to Captain Mawbey's children; the remainder was reserved for such purpose as the governor-general might determine hereafter.

In September, 1795, a complete company of European artillery (5th company 1st battalion), with two companies (29th and 30th) of *lascars*, attached under command of Captain Barton, embarked for Madras, and a second (5th company 2nd battalion), under Captain Clark, soon followed. The following officers joined the force under General Stewart in the expedition against the Dutch possessions in Ceylon:—

Fifth company 1st battalion, Captain Barton, Lieutenants Humphries and Winbolt, Lieutenant-Fireworkers Clarke and Graham.

Fifth company 2nd battalion, Captain Clark.

The first service they were engaged in was the siege of Trincomalee, in January, 1796, in which the artillery suffered both from climate and fatigue, and from a daring, and for a time successful attack the enemy made on the batteries, spiking the guns, and killing some of the artillerymen. The fort capitulated after a siege of three weeks.

Jaffna next surrendered, and the troops then proceeded to Negumbo, where they landed in February, 1796, and meeting no resistance, General Stewart marched on towards Colombo, a portion of the artillery accompanying his force. During this march, though the road ran through a jungle, and was intersected by many rivers, the army was unmolested by the Dutch. Not even at the Matwal River, a strong natural position which they had taken up, did they offer any resistance, but retired in the night, alleging afterwards as a reason their fear of a landing being effected from the shipping in their rear.

The English passed the river without opposition; but the following morning were attacked unexpectedly before daylight by a party of Malays, under Colonel Raymond, a Frenchman in the Dutch service thoroughly ashamed of his associates: the attack was beaten off, and Colombo in a day or two capitulated.

The Indian Government granted medals to the native troops employed in this service, probably more as a reward for embarking on service beyond seas, than for the arduousness of its nature. A sketch of the medal is given.

The year 1796 is a memorable one in the annals of the Indian Army, its constitution having been entirely remodelled, and many advantages granted it at that time, placing it on a footing of respectability which it had not held before; but the subject will be reverted to in a future chapter.

The artillery was converted into a regiment of three battalions, of five companies each, with thirty companies of *lascars* attached.

The command of the regiment was vested in the senior colonel, and a brigade-major was allowed as his staff officer.

The chief alteration from the organisation of 1786 consists in the addition of three colonels and fifteen captain-lieutenants, and the reduction of fifteen lieutenant-fireworkers. The allowance of officers per company was five, and the rank of captain-lieutenant was a compensation for the necessarily slower promotion in a large than a small seniority regiment, thus keeping the artillery on a level with the infantry of the army.

Colonels	Lieut.-Colonels	Majors	Captains	Capt.-Lieutenants	Lieutenants	Lieut.-Fireworkers	Serjeants	Corporals	Bombrs.	Gunners	Matrosses	Serangs	1st Tindals	2nd Tindals	Lascars	
			1	1	2	1	4	4	2	8	56	1	2	2	56	per Company.
1	1	1	5	5	10	5	20	20	10	40	280	10	20	20	560	per Battalion.
3	3	3	15	15	30	15	60	60	30	120	840	30	60	60	1680	Total.
2	3	3	15	15	29	14	50	59	30	120	512	30	60	60	1733	{ Returns Dec. 1796.

CHAPTER 4

Guns and Carriages

Having traced the *personnel* of the regiment up to this point, let us take a retrospective survey and endeavour to track out the *matériel*; this cannot be satisfactorily done in the early stage; the absence of records and drawings renders it almost impossible; little more than a general idea can be given, and in this even there must be some guesswork; occasionally restoring (as the geologists say) a carriage from a few points found scattered in the reports of committees, or incidentally alluded to in other documents.

During Clive's early wars, 6-pounder guns seem to have been generally in use, mixed occasionally with howitzers and 3-pounders, and when battalion guns a few years later became the system, two

3-pounders were with most native battalions. In his organisation of the army in 1765, this became the establishment, and with the European companies of artillery there were six 6-pounders and two (probably 5½ inch) howitzers: 12-pounders as field-guns were introduced later.

The carriages at this time were probably of a double-cheek pattern, and from the histories of the actions, we find they were weak and often breaking down. When Colonel Pearse came into the command of the regiment, it will be recollected that he found great fault with them:

"They flew to pieces with common firing in a week;" and his sweeping condemnation was probably quite just.

About 1770, it is believed that Colonel Pearse succeeded in introducing the carriage then in use in England, adapting its limber to bullock-draught (Sketch No. 1). It is clumsy and ugly certainly, and with its wooden axle not very strong, (a bar of iron was however let into the axle); doubtless it was an improvement on the old one. This appears to have been the pattern till the beginning of this century; minor improvements and alterations were made from time to time as experience pointed out their necessity, but no radical change. An iron was probably substituted for the wooden axletree, during or at the close of the war with Hyder. Iron axles first appear on the ledgers of the arsenal of Fort William in 1782-3; the ledger of the preceding year is missing, and in the antecedent years they are not mentioned.

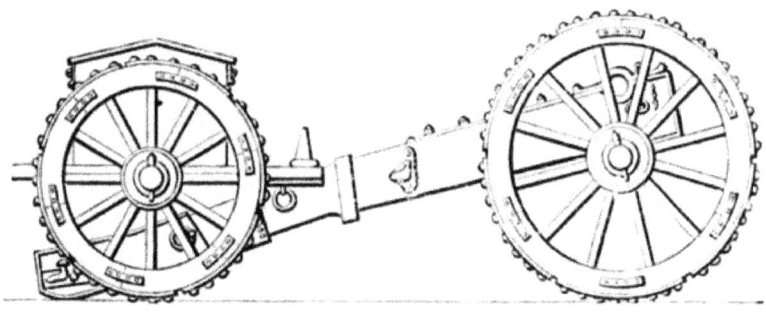

SKETCH NO. 1

At this time too the number is so small (2) as to lead to the supposition that the introduction was an experiment just being tried. The entry in the ledger is not sufficiently detailed to determine whether the axletrees in question are for siege or field-carriages; but as we find Colonel Deare alluding to four siege-carriages with iron axles sent round to Bangalore as having stood well, it is probable that about this time they became generally in use.

During the wars with Hyder, the Bengal artillery was brought into contact with that of the Madras Presidency, and comparisons were of course made as to the relative efficiency of the *matériel* of the two corps, which doubtless led to the adoption of some improvements by both.

The campaigns with Tippoo in 1790-1-2 again took a large portion of Bengal artillery into the field with the Madras regiment, and the general superiority of the Madras carriages for light field-pieces was admitted by our most experienced officers. A committee, composed of Majors Woodburne and Montague, Captains Horsford, Howell, and Glass, all officers who had served during these campaigns, was appointed in 1793, (Major Woodburne and Captain Howell going away, were succeeded by Captains Barton and Rattray), and continued sitting until 1796, to report on, and suggest improvements to, the ordnance carriages and equipments.

This committee declared that the Bengal 6–pounder carriages were much too heavy and unwieldy for field service, but that the weight and construction of the limber was by far the most objectionable part. The extension of the pintle behind the axletree lengthened the draught nearly three feet between the wheels; the height of the wheels threw the weight nearly all on the rear axletree, increasing the draught, and frequently rendering it impossible to turn the carriage without unlimbering the gun. The pintle being fixed, tore the trail-transom to pieces in travelling over rough ground; and the position of the elevating screw-boxes in the centre transom weakened it: these objections rendered it often impossible to keep up with infantry in cases of emergency when guns would have been of the greatest use; this happened frequently in the late war, when guns, mounted on the Madras pattern carriage did not meet the same difficulties.

The committee therefore without hesitation proposed the introduction of the Madras carriage, with exception to the wheels and elevating-screw, the Bengal wheels and the royal 3-pounder screw being considered better.

The Military Board, on the suggestion of the commandant of artillery (Colonel Deare), recommended that the Madras Government should be requested to send round musters of their 6-pounders, and 5½-inch howitzer-carriages, and Lord Cornwallis approved of the plan. Colonel Deare was also requested to correspond with Colonel Giels (who had commanded the Madras Artillery in the campaign) on the subject of any defects which he might consider to exist in the carriages in question. This correspondence has not fallen in our way, and it seems doubtful whether the Madras carriage was at this time introduced. Up to 1801 no pattern seems to have been permanently fixed on, or else the Madras pattern had intermediately fallen into disrepute, for, as will be hereafter noticed, some modification of the Bengal pattern was at this time preferred.

The Madras pattern alluded to is believed to have been a block trail—the trail divided in two pieces, with the cheeks on each cut out from the solid timber; the trail was very long and the limber had a projection with a limbering-hook at the end (Sketch No. 2). The chief faults in this construction were the waste of timber in cutting out the trail and cheeks; the unnecessary length of the trail, which, although it rendered the recoil easier, yet made the draught heavier; and this was again increased by the projection in rear of the limber. Another, and a serious evil, arose from the lever with which the weight of the carriage acted on the cattle in draught, the axle of the limber being the fulcrum. This pattern, however, considerably modified, became the galloper or horse-artillery carriage in Bengal.

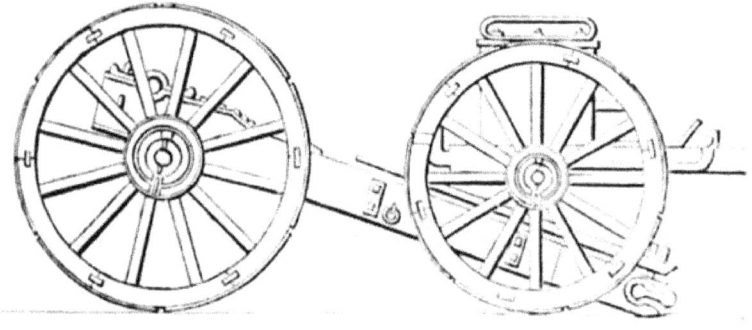

SKETCH No. 2

It is, however, worthy of notice, how nearly the principle of this carriage corresponds with that of the royal pattern introduced twenty years later, and now the standard of all India; had the fantail been cut off, and the limbering-hook attached to the axle-bed, there would have been little difference; and it is strange that this was not done, for the objection had been seen and noticed in the siege-carriages, and a remedy adopted, not indeed by giving the hook to the axle-bed, but by lowering the limber-wheels and fixing a moveable pintle on the bolster.

The *matériel* equipment was again submitted to the consideration of a committee early in 1801; Lieutenant-Colonel MacIntyre was the president, and Major Gordon, Captains Grace, Wittit, and Johnson, members. By this time a muster-carriage for the horse artillery had been made up on the general principle of the Madras pattern, by Major Glass, and in Colonel Greene's letter of instructions to the committee, he says it is "well adapted for the purpose, and can be used with equal efficacy with a line of infantry;" its particular construction was recommended to the committee's consideration, "but at the same time, as many field-carriages are wanted immediately, and cannot be delayed so long as required to complete carriages on that pattern," he advised "the adoption of the 6-pounder as altered by Colonel Duff, in preference to the present field-carriage, for the service in the line of infantry, it being much lighter, and having been found on trial sufficiently strong."

The committee gave the preference to the pattern then in use, that is, apparently, the old one with a few alterations, such as making the axletree equally thick all through, the cheek-bolts through the axle-bed, the elevating screw-box being removed from the centre transom and placed a little in front, and its shoulders working in gudgeons fitted to the cheeks; and their recommendation was adopted by the board, who ordered the 6-pounder carriages then wanted to be made of this construction.

An experiment was also made at this time with iron cheeks for a horse artillery gun-carriage; the wooden ones were, however, preferred, but unfortunately no record appears of the reasons on which the iron cheeks were disapproved; it would be interesting, now that the question of iron carriages has been agitated; it is one of the many instances which a research into the history of artillery shews perhaps more than any other science, "the thing that hath been, it is that which shall be; and that which is done is that which shall be done; and there is no new thing under the sun."

★★★★★★

A letter from Colonel Green to the Secretary of the Military Board, July, 1801, says, "As the two 6-pounders, with brass cheeks, the board were pleased to direct the agent to make up for the service of the horse artillery experiment, carrying on under my control, to replace those sent to Egypt, will take some time, &c." These carriages were proved by Major Wittit, when ready, and some alterations suggested. It is probable some mistake between brass and iron has crept into the report from which the extract was taken, or else both brass and iron were tried.

★★★★★★

Another instance may be given. In 1840, Major Timbrell made a pair of flat twisted chain traces for pole-horses, and being found very convenient, the experiment was tried on a larger scale. Captain Brind's troop was equipped with them, as also was another on the march to join the Army of Reserve in 1842, but they failed from the difficulty of insuring perfectly good workmanship. In December, 1800, "the commissary of stores is ordered to have a set of flat chains made up in the arsenal as soon as possible, for the traces of the (experimental horse artillery) harness."

At this time then there were two patterns of light field-carriages in use—one a beam-trail with the galloper-guns; the other a double-cheek with the foot artillery and battalion guns. In the accompanying sketches, Sketch No. 3 represents the galloper-carriage, while the foot artillery retained a double-cheek pattern, modified from No. 1.

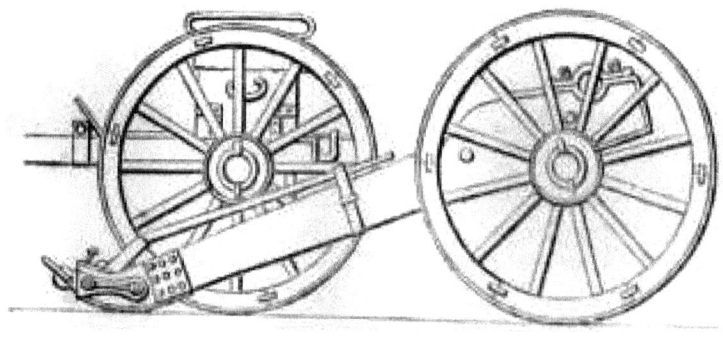

SKETCH No. 3

We must now follow the ammunition-carriages up to the same point, and in so doing less difficulty exists, as the changes which have taken place are more marked.

The earliest record we have shews us Clive carrying his ammunition on *lascars'* heads, their fidelity and steadiness insured by a detachment of Europeans with their muskets in the rear, to shoot deserters. This plan, of course, could only be adopted when the distance intended to be gone over was very small.

Tumbrils are early mentioned, both in our armies and those of native powers, and there is reason to believe that they differed but slightly from those which are now found in magazines, and generally used in the transport of treasure; they were larger and more unwieldy, and required many bullocks to draw them.

The committee in 1793 condemned them as too high, too heavy, liable to overturn, and the ammunition in them, from the absence of partitions, was shaken and broken on rough ground, (at this time serge had not been introduced it is supposed, and cartridges were made of paper—that now called cannon-cartridge, or packing); they were also unnecessarily large for the quantity of ammunition intended to be carried in them.

They recommended the introduction of one which was built under their orders, and which corresponds very nearly in measurement with that still existing (Sketch No. 4), subdivided for the reception of the ammunition, and capable of containing 90 rounds of 12-pounder, or 150 of 6-pounder ammunition; the box was easily removable, and fitted with a seat in front for the driver and his bundle; to counterbalance his weight, the centre of gravity of the box was a little thrown back; and probably this very precaution has caused the chief fault which can be found with this carriage, a tendency to fall back in going up hills; it travels lightly and easily to the cattle, and is well adapted for bullock-draught.

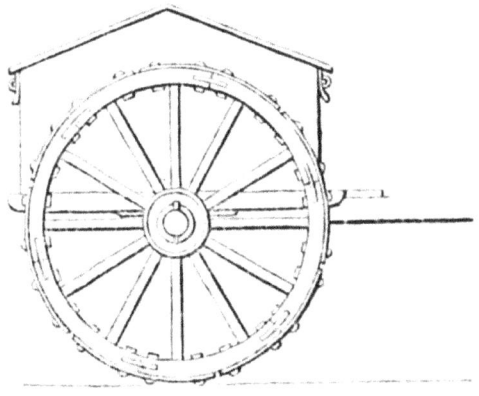

SKETCH No. 4

During the last war with Tippoo, the heavy tumbril, drawn by many bullocks—five to eight pair, was found very inconvenient with the galloper-guns, either keeping the guns in the rear, or leaving them without ammunition if they kept up with their corps. As a remedy, Colonel Blaquiere, of H.M.'s 25th Dragoons, proposed a carriage "consisting of a sort of double limber, with four wheels of equal height, drawn by four horses, and driven by two men riding the near horses." Its advantages were:

The means of carrying six additional men, the power of substituting the limber for that of the gun, if the latter was wounded, or to avoid the necessity of shifting the ammunition when the supply in the gun limber was expended.

This ammunition-carriage was adopted for the Bengal Horse Artillery and galloper-guns, and is represented in the sketch (Sketch No. 5). We must here again remark how nearly the present principle was approached, the gun and ammunition limbers similar, and the ammunition divided into several boxes; but still the fault already noticed in the gun-carriage, the unnecessarily long projection to which the limbering-hook was attached, was continued. This fault probably caused this pattern, both gun and ammunition-carriage, to be discarded, and it was not until twenty years had passed that the simple alterations necessary were introduced.

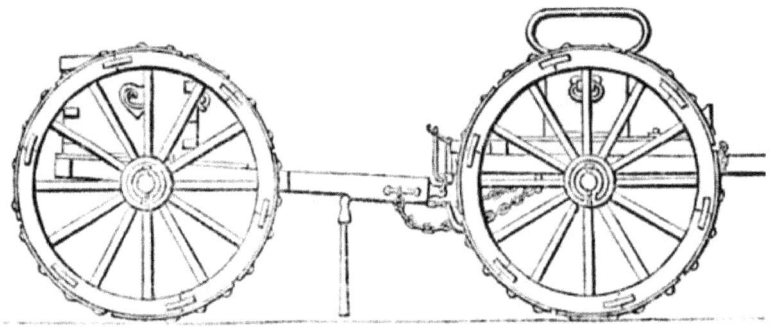

SKETCH No. 5

The light field-carriages then at this period (end of 1801), were the beam-trail gun and ammunition-carriage with limber for the gallopers, and the double-cheek carriage and ammunition-tumbril for the foot artillery.

As the elevating-screw is an important item in a carriage, a few lines to trace its progress will not be amiss. The earliest screw was fixed horizontally, and ran through a quoin, which, by its action, was forced in or out, depressing or elevating the gun; it was a cumbrous machine, and could scarcely have worked smoothly. This must have fallen into disuse between 1780 and 1790. At this latter date, a capstan-headed screw fixed in the centre transom had superseded it.

A good deal of attention was given to the elevating-screw about this period, and many plans appear to have been proposed, among other officers, by Lieutenants Toppin and Taylor, as we learn from a minute by Colonel Deare; but what they were, it is not easy to say.

The action of the screw was found to injure the centre transoms, and it was therefore placed a little in advance, the trunnions of the plate in which the screw worked resting on gudgeons fixed in each cheek; this gave the screw a power of self-adjustment to the movement of the gun, and most probably contemporary with this was the introduction of screws fixed to the neck of the cascabel of the gun.

Another pattern, and which probably followed, was one placing the screw under an elevating-board on which the gun rested. (Another was a crutch in which to receive the needle.)

In the sketch (Sketch No. 6) the general character of the screws is shewn.

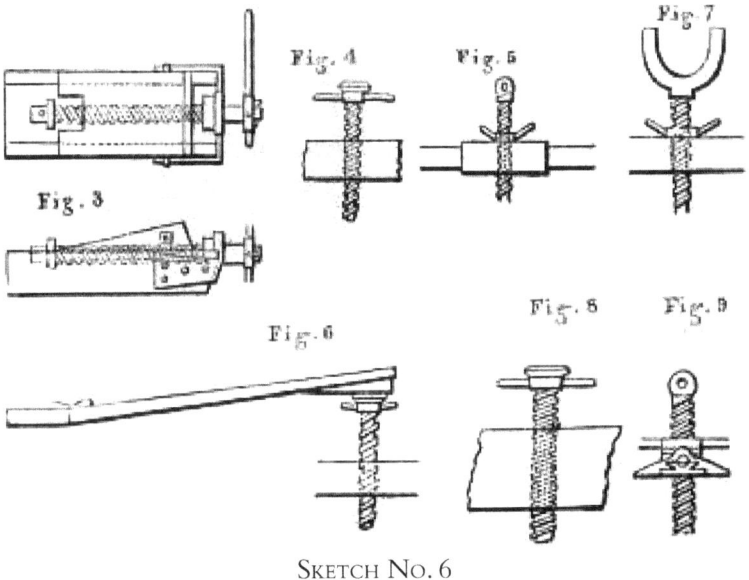

SKETCH NO. 6

A cursory notice must now be taken of the ordnance in use with the regiment. In the early times, 6-pounders were chiefly used; they were afterwards mixed with 3-pounders with the native corps, and 6-pounders with the artillery companies; the former most probably of 3¾, and the latter of 4¾ cwt. A heavier 6-pounder (6½ cwt.) superseded this light gun, and was in general use to the end of the century. This gun Major Woodburne's committee proposed replacing again by a lighter one.

During the wars with Hyder and Tippoo, brass 18-pounders constantly accompanied the armies, and were used in all the actions; and in the campaigns of 1791-2, iron 12-pounders were attached to the European regiments, and found very useful in keeping the hordes of cavalry at a respectful distance; brass 12-pounders had previously been attached to the artillery and to European regiments.

The relative merits of light and heavy guns has been a *vexata quæstio* from the earliest date, nor is it entirely set at rest up to the present day, though general opinion has decided in favour of a *via media*, rejecting both extremes. Still some members of the profession maintain that, by a judicious disposition of metal, a light gun may be made as effective as a heavy, while others, on the contrary, run into the other extreme, and would introduce guns heavier even than those at present in use. Late experiments at Woolwich on a 9-pounder of 10 cwt., nearly similar to the Bengal pattern, strengthen the opinion that the two extremes should be avoided.

A curious experiment was tried at Dum-Dum in 1787, with a view to deciding the point at issue; and it furnishes some data which, combined with practical experience, would tend to prove that a medium gun will give a range so slightly below that of a heavier one, that the increase would be dearly purchased by the increased difficulty of draught.

A 6-pounder was cast, weighing 10 cwt. and 24 lbs., and fired a certain number of rounds, after which a portion equal to a calibre in length was cut off, and the firing continued; this process was carried on, diminishing the gun, calibre by calibre, until it weighed only 3 cwt. 3 qrs. and 2 lbs., the elevation and charge of powder being in all cases the same. The result was, that of the first sixteen lengths, the seventh carried the furthest,—2,305 yards, the gun weighing 8 cwt. 2 qrs. 20 lbs.; at the fourteenth length the gun threw 2,098 yards, the gun weighing 6 cwt. 1 qr. 3 lbs.; and at the seventeenth length, 2,106 yards, the gun weighing 4 cwt. 3 qrs. 23 lbs.

It would have been more satisfactory had the first graze, as well as the extreme range, as has been the case, been given; however, it appears that 200 yards are gained by nearly doubling the weight of the gun, and the conclusion would be in favour of the very light gun, were it not that experience shews that a light gun shakes its carriage very much, and therefore that what is gained in metal is lost in strengthening the carriage to bear the shock; it is also found that a gun giving a long point-blank range does not give a proportional extreme range; and the result has been to make 6-pounders of the present day 6 cwt. in weight. The best test perhaps is a range of 800 yards, with the least elevation for a field-gun.

One other point now only remains to be noticed to bring up the *matériel* to the end of the last century—the pattern of siege-carriages. From the faults found with it by the committee in 1793, we can make a tolerable guess at it; the lowness and narrowness of the wheels, the projection of the pintle behind, to make room for a large store-box, and the height of the limber-wheels are complained of; and it therefore must have been something similar to that represented in Sketch No. 7; in all probability, up to this time little alteration had taken place in the pattern in use.

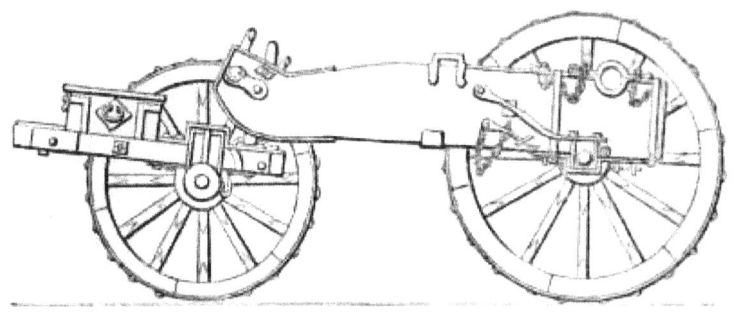

SKETCH NO. 7

While preparing the siege-train for Seringapatam, at Bangalore, in 1792, Colonel Duff made considerable alterations in the siege-carriages; he cut off the projection from the limbers, and placed a pintle on a bolster on the axle-bed, carried the draught-chain back to the gun-carriage, and cut travelling trunnion-beds in the cheeks, to divide the weight better on the axles, and make the carriage travel easier; in fact, rendered the carriages very nearly what are now known as the "old pattern."

All the alterations were continued by the committee, and they directed that the carriage should be five, and the limber-wheels three feet high, to enable them to turn under the cheeks when limbered up. Minor improvements were added: the draught-chain was made in pieces, so as to allow of a portion of the cattle being taken off in sharp turnings, or on ground where all could not act; and a carriage was then built, which, with slight changes (reducing the gun-wheels two inches) in 1801 by Colonel MacIntyre's committee, became the standard, and remained so till 1823.

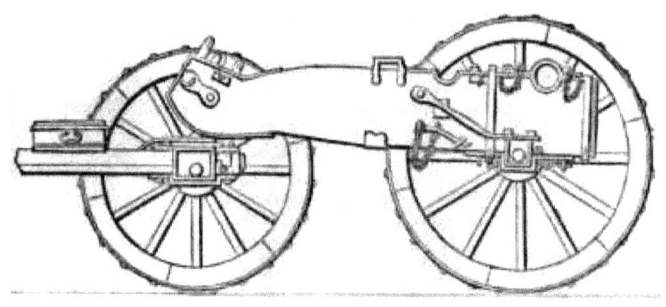

Colonel Duff's Pattern

A fancy existed to obtain the use of a mortar from an howitzer, by fitting its carriage with a sliding transom, on withdrawing which, the howitzer could be elevated to 45°, its cascabel resting on an additional transom fixed underneath. Major Green constructed a carriage of this kind in 1796, which was experimented on at Dum-Dum, and spoken favourably of, but eventually not found to answer, and therefore discarded.

Whether the result of imitation, or of half-informed mechanical taste, we find Lena Sing Majeetiah, commandant of the Punjab artillery, indulging in a similar fantasy: a carriage adapted for the double purpose. It is scarcely possible that such a one could be useful; the shock acting vertically on the axle, would be too severe for any moderate dimensions to bear; this was found in Major Green's carriage, and the proposed remedy was shortening the axle, which would, while strengthening, have rendered it very likely to overturn.

To preserve the connection of the subject, it may be as well here to notice the successive changes of ordnance and carriages up to about the present time, instead of referring to each as the record of the regiment reaches the date of its occurrence. The object is rather to give a general idea of the carriages and guns in use at different eras, and to mark the strong, rather than to note the more minute and trifling, changes which are always taking place. To do the latter would require more space than can be afforded, and after all the reader might rise from the perusal, his mind crowded with a heap of *minutiæ*, leaving no other impression than that at different times a carriage had been shortened in one direction and lengthened in another, the wheels heightened or lowered—now all of the same height, and then those of the limber reduced—a hook added from the front or taken from the rear. This is not our object, we wish to shew the principal features of the subject, so as to point out the stages through which our present excellent *matériel* has been attained.

The galloper-gun and ammunition-carriages, as well as those in use with the foot artillery at the beginning of the century, were destined to be superseded by the Gribeauval pattern, about 1810, one carriage answering for horse and foot, with the exception of some difference in the limber. The carriage was a double-cheek one, limbered up on a moveable pintle on the bottom of a limber, with two low wheels; the foot artillery limber had an arched axle with the pintle on the top. (Sketches Nos. 9 and 10.)

SKETCHES 9 & 10

These carriages had a tendency to overturn, on any but the smoothest ground; the low wheels made the draught heavy, and were also difficult to keep in order; yet this pattern held its position as the standard until 1823, when a thorough reform in the ordnance department took place.

Early in the century, the French "caisson" was introduced as the ammunition-carriage, and continued with slight changes until superseded by the royal pattern. It was a long waggon with low wheels in front, on the axle of which a pintle was fixed, working in a socket in a compartment of the body of the carriage, and enabling the front wheels to turn. This formation caused many accidents; the powder getting shaken out of the cartridges, came in contact with the pintle, and an explosion ensued; the construction was therefore altered by fixing the pintle to the carriage and the socket on the axle-bed. (Sketch No. 11.)

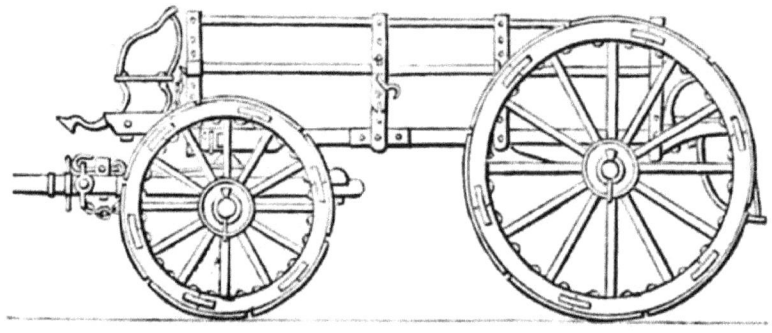

SKETCH No. 11

The faults of this carriage were the liability to overturn; the danger from explosion, the whole ammunition being in one large box; and the inconvenience, when embarking on board ship or crossing rivers, of having to unpack it all.

An attempt to remedy this was made in 1801 by the partial introduction of "Hardwicke's pattern" ammunition-carriage, consisting of two tumbrils connected by a bent iron perch. It proved, however, a perfect failure, and never came into general use, so that the caisson continued as the standard until superseded by the royal pattern; the last, probably, which existed in use was in Captain Wood's troop, 1st company 3rd battalion, at Meerut, as late as 1828.

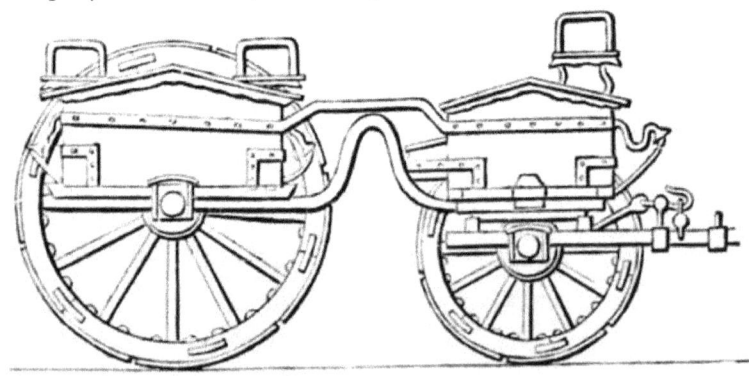

In 1801, on its formation, the experimental horse artillery was armed with two 3-pounders and four 6-pounders; the 3-pounders in 1806 gave place to two 5½-inch howitzers, and two of the 6-pounders were at a later period (when the number of troops had been increased) withdrawn, and their place supplied by 12-pounders of a pattern proposed by General Horsford of 8¾ cwt. The lines of this gun were drawn at Woolwich, but, at the same time, it was said that a gun of such light metal must prove insufficient.

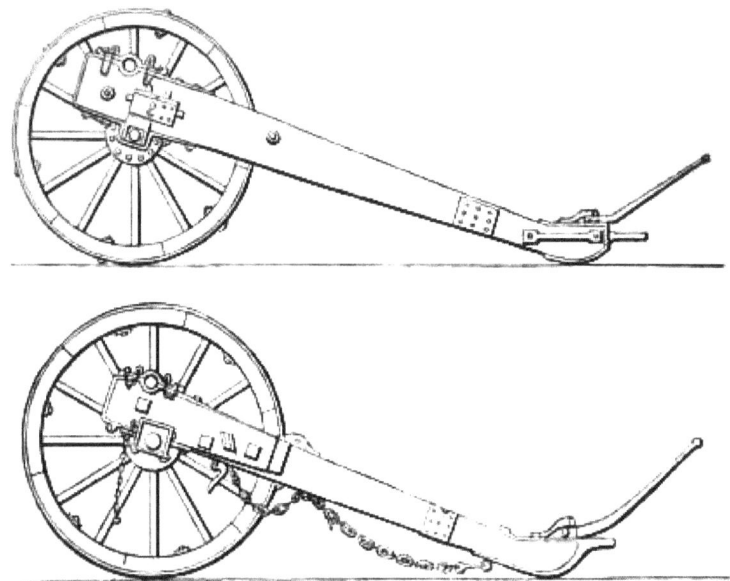

The armament of troops and field-batteries continued of these three calibres until the new arrangements, introducing the 9 and 6-pounder guns and 24 and 12-pounder howitzers, in 1828 and the following years.

The breaking out of hostilities with Nepal in 1814 called for a new species of carriages adapted to carry 3-pounders and $4^{2/5}$-inch howitzers in a hilly country. Lightness, strength, and a facility of being taken to pieces and put together were the points sought to be combined in the "mountain-train" carriages planned by Sir J. Horsford. They were not, however, much used during the war, for in general it was found that elephants could convey 6-pounders in the hills easier than men could the smaller pieces; and the former, being so much more effective, were, nearly in all cases, used.

The mountain-train carriages were found too slight, and quite unequal to bear the rough usage artillery meets with even from the hands of its friends; they required a degree of petting which appears not always to have been shewn them.

During a retreat in the Nepal country, several which had, for convenience and from the loss of their bearers, been limbered up to other carriages drawn by cattle, went to pieces in crossing the terrain at the foot of the hills. The fault was laid on the officers in charge, and not on the weakness of the carriages, by Sir John Horsford; but there will always be great difficulty in preventing these carriages experiencing the same treatment, if put together before entering the hills.

No. 14 is a sketch of the mountain-train pattern, which has remained unaltered up to the present day, excepting some changes introduced by Major Backhouse in the mountain-train of the late Shah Sujah, but which have not been made generally known.

Some changes are now probable, as a mountain-train 12-pounder howitzer has been substituted for the old $4^{2/5}$-inch howitzer. This new piece weighs 3 cwt., and its lines are drawn on the principles of the 12-pounder howitzer; the charge is 12 oz. of powder (an increase of 4 oz.), which, with the increased length, makes it a much more effective piece.

Sketch No. 14

The siege-carriages underwent little change during this time. From their solid nature they have been always less liable to injury than field-carriages; and, consequently, attention has been less forced to them by the repairs of daily accidents; less temptation has therefore offered to introduce improvements and alterations, and the pattern established in 1801 remained in use till 1823; indeed, at the present time there are many carriages of that kind in magazines.

In 1823 a new pattern siege-carriage (No. 15) was introduced; not, however, differing essentially from the old one; uniformity in axles, beds, limbers, &c., and improvements in *minutiæ*, were the chief alterations.

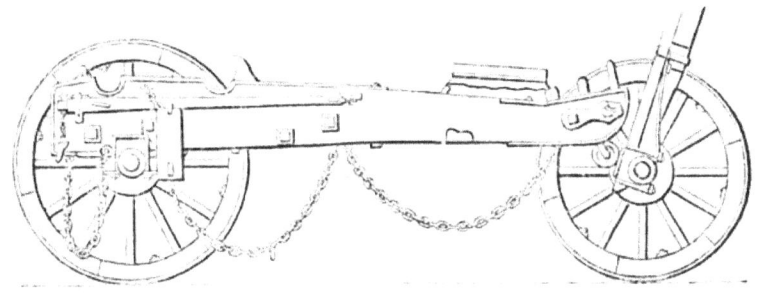

Sketch No. 15

A new kind of carriage was also introduced at this time for the iron howitzers, which superseded the brass 8-inch as a siege-piece; the trail was much shorter than that of siege-carriages, and furnished with small truck-wheels, to ease the recoil. (Sketch No. 16.)

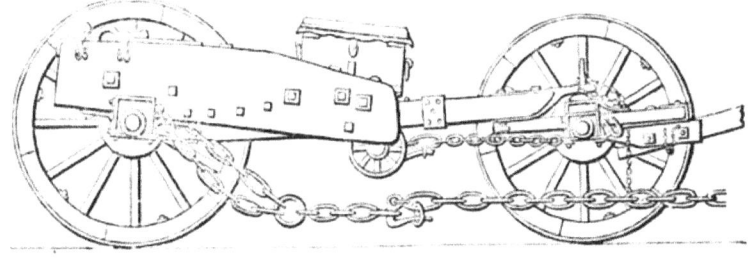

Sketch No. 16

Iron mortars and mortar-beds also superseded the brass mortars of 8-inch and upwards, and their wooden beds. No alteration has been made in any of these articles. In 1823, a general reform in the ordnance equipment in Bengal took place, and, with the changes above noted, the block trail pattern was introduced for the light field-carriages.

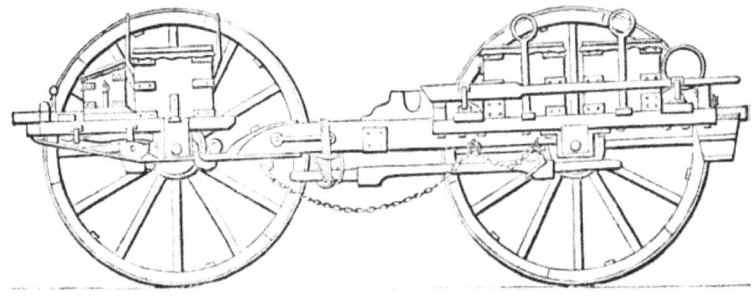

Ammunition Carriage (1823)

The ammunition-carriage was made with a limber exactly similar to that of the gun, and the ammunition was divided into six boxes, two on the limber, and four on the body of the carriage, easily removable; the wheels, axles, and beds were made similar, and pains were taken to render all parts as uniform as possible, so that one set might answer for the repairs of all. On their first introduction into Bengal, in the attempts to lighten the carriages as much as possible, some were made too weak, especially those for the 24-pounder howitzers, and slight alterations were made from time to time to obviate this defect.

At this time, the elevating-screws of the guns were fixed to the cascabel neck, while those of the howitzers were capstan-headed. In 1834, Captain Timbrell suggested the adoption of the fixed screw with all, and several howitzer-carriages were altered accordingly; in doing this, however, it became necessary to pierce the beams to receive the screw further to the rear than before, filling up the former hole with a plug: this double piercing weakened the beam so much, that with the increased action from the fixed screw, many broke down, and the change was discontinued at that time; the subject, however, was agitated for many years, and many trials made, and the result has been the retention of the original method.

The advantages of the fixed screw consist in its uniting the gun and carriage, and thereby preventing its jumping, in travelling or firing; greater facility of mending it, and an increased power in limbering up; it is also more economical, as a less depth of beam is required, the fixed screw adjusting itself by means of trunnions, while the capstan-headed requires a horizontal hump on the beam to receive it. On the other hand, the capstan-headed screw is supposed to strain the carriage less; to us, however, the advantages seem to be on the side of the fixed screw, and from the result of the experiments tried, there appears no doubt but that when applied to a new, *not an altered*, beam, the howitzer-carriages are strong enough to bear it.

In these ordnance arrangements, the European horse and all the foot artillery batteries were armed with 9-pounder guns and 24-pounder howitzers, while the native horse had 6-pounders; and this continued until 1834, when, under instructions from the Court of Directors, the whole of the horse artillery were armed with 6-pounder guns and 12-pounder howitzers.

In 1836, at the recommendation of Sir Henry Fane, then commander-in-chief, a special board of artillery officers from the three presidencies was convened at Calcutta, for the purpose of assimilating the ordnance equipment and arrangements throughout India. They sat for about two years, and during that time musters of the carriages they recommended for general adoption were built. This carriage, the "Indian pattern," was much like those in use with the Madras Artillery, and may be shortly described as having contracted cheek, narrow axles, and metal naves: the carriage was heavier than the Bengal pattern.

The proceedings of the board were transmitted to England and returned in 1841, with the orders of the Court of Directors (among other points), that if the pattern carriage had given satisfaction, it should be adopted throughout all India. In the interim, however, the Afghan war had taken place, and the carriages of the Bengal and Bombay presidencies been severely tried. The former stood the test of the service in that most difficult country, while the latter, constructed on a plan nearly similar to the Madras one, proved utterly worthless.

These circumstances, and the failure of some 6-pounder carriages of the "Indian pattern," with the Bombay horse artillery, during the short affair at Hykulzie, rendered the strength of the pattern doubtful, and after calling for reports from all who had been engaged in these campaigns, the Supreme Government in 1842 finally decided on adopting the Bengal block trail as the pattern for Indian light field-carriages.

This appears an appropriate place in which to detail the different means of draught adopted from time to time, and the arrangement will have the advantage of presenting the subject in one view, and saving the reader the trouble of searching for it through different periods.

To the end of the last century, bullocks were the only draught cattle in use for artillery purposes; they were attached to the carriage by yokes, most probably similar to those which may now be seen in every native hackery, and traces made of raw hide: these latter, during Lord Cornwallis's campaigns, were superseded by draught-chains, the whole chain in one long piece, very cumbrous and inconvenient. This pattern was early modified, we believe, by making the lengths for siege ordnance for three or four pairs of bullocks; but it was not until about 1825 that a separate chain was allotted to each pair, facilitating the lengthening, or reducing the line of draught greatly.

The yoke was attached by a swivel playing loosely on the pole, with a neck which passed through the upper part of the yoke, and was fastened with a nut. The yoke, at this period we think, consisted of two bars, and has remained up to the present day with little alteration. An attempt was made to supersede it by a single bar yoke with short stanchions, and chains to confine the bullocks in their places, by

General Hardwicke, about 1781. This was supposed to be an improvement on the native yoke, and more economical than the pattern in use; but an important point having been overlooked, viz. the native yoke-bar being fixed immovably to the pole, while the H. P. yoke was moveable on its swivel, the result was not satisfactory, as the bullocks were continually in danger of suffocation, from the bar twisting and tightening the chain round their necks. The double band yoke was therefore retained, and it was fitted on the pole with a clip-band, which, by embracing the upper bar, saved the necessity of piercing it for the reception of the swivel, and added much to its strength.

About 1801, horses were first used for the draught of guns in India. Experimental horse artillery was formed, and two galloper-guns were attached to each cavalry regiment. The original plan has been followed with little variation up to the present time; each horse of the team was ridden, and the guns were worked by the men who rode the horses. The chief advantages of this system are economy, greater exertion to be got out of the horses in a difficulty, and a smaller number of men and horses exposed to an enemy's fire; its disadvantages are, the horses being over-weighted, and a liability, from the paucity of numbers, of a gun being crippled in action by a few casualties. It may, however, after many years' experience, be pronounced a system combining with economy a very considerable degree of efficiency.

The bullocks, much improved by the arrangements of 1809, which transferred them to the care of the artillery, continued the sole draught animal of the foot artillery until 1818, when an experimental 12-pounder battery was horsed with a limited number of an inferior description of cattle: yet, under these disadvantages, so superior did this battery prove, that others were soon afterwards similarly equipped, and their numbers gradually increased until 1827, when it was decided that all the light field-batteries should be horsed; so convinced had the local government and the Court of Directors become of the utility of the measure. But scarcely were the orders issued, when one of those extraordinary changes, so often to be met with in Indian arrangements, consequent on the change in the head of the government, took place, and in 1828 the horses were ordered to be sold, and their place to be supplied with bullocks.

Against this arrangement, destructive of the efficiency of the regiment, the representations of the commandant of artillery were of no avail; and the remonstrances of a general officer, unwilling to be left with an inefficient field-artillery, were met by the reply that the change had been resolved on "not only from motives of economy, but from a conviction that the number and efficiency of the horse artillery rendered the maintenance of horse field-batteries unnecessary;" as if the duties and use of the two branches of the arm were not quite distinct and incompatible with one another!

The horse-batteries being thus extinguished, for many years there was not a foot field-battery that could be considered efficient for service; fortunately it was a period of profound peace, or the twelve troops of horse artillery would have proved but a "broken reed" to rest upon as the whole effective field-artillery of an army mustering, perhaps, 80,000 men, and scattered over a country twelve hundred miles in length, with hostile powers bordering on it in all directions.

In 1835, attempts were made to turn the enduring powers of the camel to gun-draught. Arguing on the fact that the animal had in former times been employed in draught, and that in the present day he is used in the plough in the Hurrianah and other sandy districts, Major Pew made many experiments, and at length succeeded so far, that government authorised a battery to be fitted for this draught at Dehli, and it was placed under the command of Captain W. Anderson. Its first performances, when with the camp of the commander-in-chief, appeared to promise well—so well, indeed, that on the formation of the Army of the Indus, it was attached to it under the command of Captain A. Abbott.

In the field, however, it did not keep up its character; while the ground was smooth and sandy, the camels worked well, but in moist or slippery soil they were continually liable to accidents, and in ground intersected by trenches they were peculiarly awkward; at all times they were found deficient in muscular exertion, weight constituting their sole power of traction; and when the work became hard, and food scarce, they knocked up completely and suddenly, without any warning; and on the army moving from Candahar towards Ghuznee, the camels were replaced by the horse and *yaboo* of the country.

A second battery, which proceeded to Scinde in 1843, fared no better. A third, stationed at Nusseerabad, seems to answer for cantonment duties, but we believe has not been tried in any other way. The result of the experiments appears to be, that though the camel will answer as gun-draught in particular localities, he will not do for a battery which is liable to move in all directions.

The war in Afghanistan forced on the government the necessity of improving their field-artillery, and as a commencement, a battery on the frontier was supplied with cast horses from the horse artillery and cavalry; but on the apparent termination of the war in 1840, with a view to economy, these horses were withdrawn and replaced, with much delay, with bullocks, leaving the frontier, on which our dubious friends the Sikhs could in a week have mustered 100,000 men and 200 pieces of artillery, with no other artillery than one or two 6–pounder troops of horse artillery, and this battery ill equipped with bullocks and drivers from the commissariat; and such was its state when the Afghan reverses broke upon India like a clap of thunder.

In 1841, the orders of the Court of Directors were received, to supersede bullocks entirely by horses, camels, and elephants, which were supposed likely to form cheap and efficient field-batteries, horses were given to a few, and one was furnished with elephants. We believe no one expected that this latter would answer. The awkward line of traction, the great power of the animal, and the fear of his becoming unmanageable under fire, were the obvious objections; to which might be added the disadvantage of the whole power of draught being concentrated in one animal, in case of this one being wounded, and which his great bulk rendered extremely probable.

After two years' experience, the elephant was rejected from field-artillery; but it was proposed to use his strength more advantageously in the movement of siege-guns, where several of the objections would not apply, particularly that of being exposed to an enemy's fire.

During the recent (as at 1852) campaign on the Sutlej, elephants were used in siege-guns, and also in a battery of iron 12-pounders; but although this battery was provided with spare limbers, with bullocks for carrying it into action, yet, by some mismanagement, the elephants were used at Sobraon, and, as had been anticipated, took fright at the first shot which passed over them, and ran off to the rear with the limbers, proving clearly the soundness of the opinion originally pronounced against their use for field-artillery.

We believe, too, that they are to be given up for siege-artillery, but not, we think, on such sound grounds; their adoption was an experiment; the harness intended for field-guns was transferred to siege, without alteration, and, as might have been expected, proved too weak: whether a stronger pattern, which was recommended, was used in the hurried march, by which the heavy guns were brought up from Dehli to the Sutlej, and how that answered; whether the animals proved themselves unequal to the work, or whether, as a means of instituting a fair comparison, a gun drawn by bullocks accompanied the elephants, and moved with greater ease or difficulty, we know not; but we think it is a pity that the animal has not been fairly tried, or if so, that the experiments have not been recorded and published for general information.

CHAPTER 5
Introduction of Horse Artillery

The supersession which the officers of the Indian Army suffered by those of H.M.'s service; the slowness of promotion; the absence of any furlough regulations enabling them from time to time to visit their native country without giving up their profession; the want of a provision on which to retire, together with other disabilities, had engendered much discontent in the army, and rendered it absolutely necessary that the defects in its constitution should be remedied, lest the whole machine should be rendered unfit for the duties required from it.

✶✶✶✶✶✶

So great had been the alarm at one time, excited by the desperate projects (of some officers), that Sir John Murray, the commandant of Fort William, without communicating his precautionary proceedings to the governor-general, placed the fortress in a state of defence, relying on the unshaken steadiness of the artillery; (*Life of Lord Teignmouth*, vol. i.) . . . and but for the firmness of the artillery at Calcutta, and the manly resistance of several officers at Cawnpore, the army would have dictated to the government their own terms.—*Idem, L. M. to Lord C.*)

✶✶✶✶✶✶

With this view, Lord Cornwallis prepared a plan on his voyage to England, and submitted it to the Home Government; previously, however, many representations had been made by the armies of the three presidencies, and they selected from their own officers in England agents to superintend their interests, and urge on H. M.'s ministers and the Court of Directors their claims to be placed on a liberal footing.

Captain Burnett on this occasion represented the Bengal Artillery, and in the committee combated the views of Lord Cornwallis and Mr. Dundas, of uniting the artillery of the three presidencies into one corps, and then incorporating it with the Royal Artillery.

In the remarks on Lord Cornwallis's propositions by Sir Henry Crosby (president of the Home Committee), we find that the Bengal Artillery officers declared that:

An union of the army of the three presidencies promises no advantage to the service in general, nor any fair one to the respective officers of each presidency in particular: it would but render the officers less acquainted with the language, manners, religion, and customs of the natives of their respective corps (*lascars*), who, in Bengal and on the coasts of Coromandel and Malabar, are scarce less different from each other than all are from Europeans, and in the adjustment of individual rank would create, perhaps, insurmountable difficulties.

Every officer now in the Company's service commenced his career at a particular presidency, and took, as was reasonable and inevitable, his chance of quick or slow promotion, according to the casualties of his own establishment. These casualties of natural death, of actual service, and of increased or diminished establishments, have made such an alteration in the general proportion of promotion, that he who went with General Goddard an old lieutenant to Bombay, would, in the event of an union of the three presidencies, find himself superseded by one whom he left a cadet on that establishment: the Bengal officers therefore could never agree, nor would the liberality of the officers of the other presidencies wish that all should be melted into one mass mutually interchangeable, without first equalizing the rank of the officers of each establishment by a reference to their original appointments as cadets; and the difficulties of such a reference, with its consequent effects, need not be pointed out.

They have likewise declared that an incorporation with the king's artillery will be a sacrifice of their dearest interests.

But that:

> In the event of a general transfer of the Bengal Army to the king's service, the three battalions of artillery on that establishment should be completed, agreeably to seniority, to a full complement of officers of all ranks above that of lieutenant-fireworker, and established to the same number of battalions of artillery, supposing each battalion in the two services to contain the same number of companies, if not in proportion to the number of companies in the king's service in the time of war; and, being thus completed, that they may be then transferred, and always remain independent; that the officers in the battalions do afterwards rise by regular gradation, as vacancies occur in either battalion, agreeably to the present practice, without

being, in either case, subject to removal to other corps, or to exchange with, or supersession from, officers in any other corps whatsoever; and that these three battalions, so transferred, be not relieved from Europe or any other quarter, at this present, or any future time, or in any manner whatsoever, but be stationed in Bengal as heretofore.

It was also urged that an incorporation of the artillery would tend to augment the mutual discontents, which had so long subsisted between the king's and Company's troops in India, in this branch, in proportion as the evil was removed from the other branches of the service; for as the incorporation would certainly be directly contrary to the wishes of all the Company's artillery officers, so it was believed that those of H.M.'s service would not be less averse to it, seeing that they were to admit strangers to a participation of their rights in return for a very distant and precarious advantage. Each would therefore consider the other as an intruder, jealousies and animosities would be the inevitable consequence of such a contest of opposite interests and inclinations, while the public service could not fail of being deeply injured by the constant operation of such destructive passions.

The contemplated transfer of the artillery (and European infantry) to the king's army was looked upon as highly prejudicial, not only to the interests of that branch, but to the Company's army at large, as tending to lower the respectability of the portion left, and on this account was strongly opposed by the whole of the agents from the armies of the three presidencies, and eventually their exertions were successful; the whole army was left with the directors (perhaps more from the ministry not being strong enough to carry the point, or sufficiently at leisure to organise the details immediately necessary), its organisation was however considerably altered, and the service of the East-India Company materially improved; furlough and retiring rules were introduced, a larger proportion of field-officers given, and a general code of regulations made.

It is only necessary here to notice these as they affected the artillery. The organisation detailed at the conclusion of the last chapter took place, and many officers (see list below) obtained brevet rank to equalise their ranks with the rest of the army, and a very fair proportion of officers was given to each company; *viz.* a captain, captain-lieutenant, two lieutenants, and a lieutenant-fireworker.

★★★★★★

Major-Gen. Duff,		Lt.-Col. Montague,		Major Holland,	
Col.-Gen. Deare,		Major Scott,		,,	Barton,
Lieut.-Col. Bruce,		,,	Rattray,	,,	Carnegie,
,,	,, C. Green,	,,	Mackintyre,	,,	Gordon,
,,	,, Woodburn,	,,	Burnett,	,,	Horsford.

★★★★★★

Seventy-four non-commissioned officers and gunners are not sufficient when they are liable to be much detached, and when vacancies cannot be filled by ready-trained men.

The artillery being found numerically insufficient for the duties required from it, in October, 1798, it was increased by an addition of two non-com. officers, two gunners, and (ten had been added in December, 1797), four *matrosses* per company, and a detail of *golundaz* of one *jemadar*, three *havildars*, three *naiks*, and forty privates to each of the eleven companies in Bengal (the other four companies were at Ceylon and Madras, and they were added to these early next year); thus adding upwards of nine hundred men.

These were raised by selecting the best-qualified men from age, size, and good conduct, from the *lascars*, and enlisting in general Mahommedans, "under an express stipulation, on oath, previous to their being enrolled," of "their engaging to embark on board of ship whenever the service shall require their proceeding by sea;" their age was limited from twenty to twenty-eight years, and their height from five feet seven inches to five feet ten inches. The required number was soon raised, and were so well drilled and disciplined by the following February, that the commander-in-chief on inspecting them "expressed his pleasure and surprise at the creditable state into which they had been so rapidly brought."

This admixture of natives with Europeans was injudicious, for although at first sight it might be supposed that the effect would have been the same on the native artilleryman as on the *lascar*, and that he would have acquired, from constant contact with Europeans, a portion of their hardness of character, and lost his own prejudices, yet it must be remembered that the *lascar* was looked upon as an inferior grade, and never took an equal part in the duties of the gun as was intended with the native artillerymen, and therefore the European never felt his own credit or safety entrusted to the former, while with the latter both were intimately connected; distrust and jealousy were the result, and the admixture was found to work so ill, that it was soon discarded; it being found that, valuable as native artillerymen are alone, they became worse than useless when mixed with Europeans. As the opinion of so practical and experienced a man as the late Sir John Horsford on this point will bear considerable weight, we quote it.

The European saw a native made a constituent part of that detail of the posts of the gun, of which he was one; he viewed this native with jealousy, and diffident of his ability (perhaps without reason) to serve the vent, or manage the portfire, he positively refused to stand between the wheels, as either spongeman or loader, urging, in spite of reasoning on the matter, that 'it was hard to be blown away by a black fellow.' The native, on the other hand, perceiving the European hostile to him, and suspicious of mischief, refused in his turn to take the spongestaff or be server; declaring that he might be 'blown away by the design or carelessness of the European.' Discord, recrimination, and hatred were the consequences.

But this was not all, the 'component part' looked around and saw itself a miserable handful of men isolated, and put down in a company composed of men of different language and country, and dissimilar habits and religion, unsupported by number and marked as an inferior body, by having no rank amongst them higher than that of a *jemadar*. They saw themselves considered as so many shreds and patches on the coat of a European company, and pointed at by the *sipahis* as a laughing-stock: lastly, that in the eyes of their own officers they were viewed as unprofitable interlopers, who brought no promotion in return for the trouble of disciplining them.

The regiment at this time (1799) therefore was constituted as below:—

Colonels	Lieut. Colonels	Majors	Captains	Capt. Lieutenants	Lieutenants	Lieut.-Fireworkers	Serjeants	Corporals	Drummers	Gunners	Mattrosses	Golundaz Jemadars	Golundaz Havildars	Golundaz Naicks	Golundaz Golundaz	Lascars Serangs	Lascars 1st Tindals	Lascars 2nd Tindals	Lascars Lascars	
-	-	1	1	2	1	5	5	2	10	70		1	3	3	40	1	2	2	70	per Company.
1	1	1	5	5	10	5	25	25	10	50	350	5	15	15	200	10	20	20	700	per Battalion.
3	3	3	15	15	30	15	75	75	30	150	1050	15	45	45	600	30	60	60	2100	Total.
3	3	3	15	15	29	13	73	73	30	146	751	10	28	27	358	30	60	60	2055	Returns Feb. 1799.

1,380 Europeans, 705 *golundaz*, and 2,250 *lascars*, or a total of 4,335. (The *lascars* can scarcely be called artillerymen; it is true that they fill certain *numbers* at the gun, but the greater portion were employed on the drag-ropes.) The infantry of the army at this period amounted to 40,000, (see list below), so that the artillery was in the proportion of one to every nine infantry soldiers, a proportion less than that usually considered sufficient in European armies, but considerably greater than has been preserved in the successive changes which have taken place in this regiment, and which we shall remark on as these changes come to be detailed.

★★★★★★

3 King's Regiment	3,000
2 Companies European Regiment	2,500
17 Native Regiments	35,360
	40,860

★★★★★★

In January, 1797, Major-General Duff being expected from England, whose arrival would supersede Colonel Deare in command of the artillery, it was declared this latter officer's tour for command in the field as colonel of the artillery, and in March (29) General Duff assumed the command of the regiment.

General Duff joined the regiment in September, 1762, and was present at the battle of Buxar, where his conduct elicited the laudatory mention of his name in the government reply to Major Munro. He does not appear to have been again employed on active service for some years; as a major he was selected to command the battalion of artillery raised for the *Nawab* of Oude in 1776, and on its reduction, he commanded the artillery at Futteygurh.

In 1780 he attained his lieutenant-colonelcy, and commanded the regiment during Colonel Pearse's absence on service in the Carnatic. In 1788, he went to England, and returning in 1791-2, was appointed to command the Bengal Artillery of the army under Lord Cornwallis, in which capacity he was present during the last campaign, and prepared the battering-train against Seringapatam.

At the conclusion of the war, he again returned to England, in consequence of the Court of Directors (to whom a reference had been made) refusing to allow him to command a battalion and the brigade of artillery.

The refusal may have originated in his rank of colonel, as the promotion, in the place of Lieutenant-Colonel C. R. Deare (killed at Sattimungulum), was delayed until the reply came from home; or from his junior officer Colonel G. Deare having been intermediately appointed. Whatever the cause was, it had ceased to operate in 1797, as he was then appointed to the command. He did not, however, hold it long, for the following month he was appointed to command at the Presidency, and Colonel Hussey succeeded to the regiment.

Major-General Duff was a man of a powerful frame of body; anecdotes of his strength are told to the present day; on one occasion, a leopard sprung suddenly upon him, but seizing the animal by the throat, they rolled over and over, the general never relinquishing his grasp until the animal was fairly powerless, when he was easily put an end to.

On another occasion, finding a sentry asleep over the park, he took a 6-pounder off its carriage and carried it under his arm (*doorbien ke mooafik*, as an old native officer, at that time his orderly, described it) "like a telescope." (The 6-pounder of that day was probably four hundred weight and a half.)

Major-General Duff returned to Europe in December, 1797—Major-General G. Deare succeeding him in the command at the Presidency, and as the vice-president of the Military Board, in the absence of the commander-in-chief; Colonel Hussey, the commandant of artillery, acting in the latter capacity till his arrival.

Colonel Hussey had but a short tenure of the command, for his promotion to major-general being known in India in September, 1798, it was declared in orders, that:

> Colonel Hussey having attained the rank of major-general, came under the influence of the Minutes of Council, 5 June, 1797, (and) Lieutenant-Colonel C. Green, the senior officer of artillery, under the rank of a general officer, was ordered to conduct the regimental duties and details, until further orders.

The unsettled state of the great Mahratta powers, and the threatening aspect of Zeman Shah, with whom the deposed *Nawab* of Oude, Vizier Ali, had been corresponding, rendered the assembly of an army of observation necessary to the defence of British India; a considerable force was assembled under Sir James Craig at Anopsheher, with which were five companies of artillery under Lieutenant-Colonel Woodburn; but this force appears to have been very ill equipped with ammunition, a circumstance noticed by Sir J. Craig to Lord Mornington:—

> Our proportion of musket ammunition is 120 rounds per man, and that for the small-arms of the cavalry is 40; with this, I certainly would not venture to stir a step from the Ganges, and how we are to gut up more, in the time in which I think it is probable that it may be requisite for us to do so, I know not: I have written in strong terms to the commander-in-chief on the subject. For our artillery, we have 300 rounds; but that is, if possible, still less equal to what we ought to have, at least, in a depot to which we could have a much more ready access than we have to Chunar or Allahabad. The latter should be our grand depot, in which should be lodged a quantity of stores of every species, equal to every possible emergency; while a field-depot, fed continually from it, should move successively from post to post as we advance, and be always at hand to renew our deficiencies.

The unprovided state in which the army in advance had been left, is an instance how ill the machinery of the Military Board had worked. A divided responsibility produced its never-failing result. No one member feeling it his particular duty to provide for the contingencies which might occur, the whole was left to chance, and the nearest magazine, on which the brigades at Cawnpoor and Futteygurh were dependent, was Chunar. Had there been one head to the Ordnance department, this would not have happened. In this instance, from Zeman Shah retiring, no harm occurred, but far from taking warning and being better provided for the future, we shall find that when, in 1805, Lord Lake sat down before Bhurtpoor, there was the same want of equipment, and that time it resulted in our lamentable failure.

While one portion of the regiment was in the field on the northern frontier, another was called on to form part of the army against Tippoo Sultan, whose proceedings had latterly been of so hostile a nature, that self-defence forced the British Government to curb his ambitious and dangerous designs.

The army was collected from all the presidencies. Bengal furnished three battalions of native volunteers and four companies of European artillery, with their *lascars* (eight companies) attached.

★★★★★★

Lieut.-Colonel Montague, Commandant; Lieutenant Drummond, Adjutant; Lieutenant R. Browne, Quarter-Master.

Lascar Companies.	Company.	Battalion.	Captains.	Captain-Lieutenants.	Lieutenants	Lieutenant-Fireworkers.	Non-Com. Officers and Gunners.
6, 20	3	1	{ Grace Dunn }	Caldwell	{ Pennington Green }	{ Bayle Richards }	56
11, 27	5	2	Clarke	Collier	{ Hetzler Douglas }	Graham	63
18, 25	1	3	Tomkyns	Toppin	... ...	Hay	69
10, 17	2	3	Glass	Balfour	A. Dunn	{ Ahmuty Brooke }	72

★★★★★★

One of these companies (5th company 2nd battalion) was taken from Ceylon; another (3rd company 1st battalion) had been despatched with Lieutenant-Colonel Errskine's force to Ganjam the preceding year, and thence to Hyderabad; and the two remaining ones, the 1st and 2nd of the 3rd battalion, sailed under command of Lieutenant-Colonel Montague towards the end of the year, and reached Madras in January, 1799.

The army under Lieutenant-General Harris was put in motion on the 3rd February, and entered Mysore on the 5th March. The artillery of the right wing, with which was the battering-train, consisting of four 24-pounders, thirty 18-pounders, eight 12-pounders, two brass 8-inch and eight 5½ mortars, was under Lieutenant-Colonel Montague's command.

On the 6th March the right brigade, under Colonel Montresor, was attacked at Seedaseer, but Tippoo's troops were driven off. On the 27th the grand army was attacked at Malavelly, but the loss was trifling, and on the 5th April the army encamped before Seringapatam, on which night and the following day the outposts of the army were engaged, in which action Lieutenant Brooke, of the artillery, was wounded.

Tippoo made no further attempts, but retired within the fort, against which approaches and batteries were commenced and carried on, the S.W. angle being the point selected for attack. Batteries were thrown up on both sides the river; and on the 4th May, the breach being practicable, the place was stormed.

But little personal record is to be found of the part the artillery took in this exploit; that their fire was well directed and kept up, the general orders of the day testify.

The merit of the artillery corps is so strongly expressed by the effects of their fire, that the commander-in-chief can only desire Colonel Smith (Royal Artillery) to assure the officers and men of the excellent corps under his command, that he feels most fully their claim to approbation.

These are the words; but in the routine of a siege on a large scale, their unremitting duty in the batteries leaves less to record than on many other occasions far less harassing and dangerous. Although their casualties were few, one took place which was deeply regretted:

> Lieutenant-Colonel Montague's arm was shattered near the shoulder on the 2nd May while in the battery, and required immediate amputation; for some days he appeared to be going on in a fair way; a contusion, however, on his chest, occasioned by the same shot, produced mortification, which caused his death on the 10th May. In him the regiment lost an officer of whom they may be deservedly proud. His talents, improved by a regular military education, and his long experience in active service, rendered him invaluable.
>
> In the early part of his career, his skill in his profession, his zeal and indefatigable activity, having been displayed on various occasions, he was afterwards selected for every important service. With General Goddard, with Sir Eyre Coote, and at the siege of Cuddalore, he was particularly distinguished, and in the campaigns of Lord Cornwallis he not only confirmed but increased his established reputation. He was called forth on the projected expedition against the Isle of France and Manilla, and finally was chosen to command the Bengal Artillery destined for the glorious enterprise against Seringapatam." (Beatson's *Seringapatam*.)

Lieutenant-Colonel Edward Montague was the fourth son of Admiral J. Montague, and brother of the late Captain James Montague, who commanded the ship *Montague* on the glorious 1st June, in which action he was killed by a cannon-shot while closely engaged with two of the enemy's ships, the *Impétueux* of 74, and *Le Républicain* of 110 guns.

Being originally designed for the army, he was placed in the academy at Woolwich, from whence he was sent out as a cadet to Bengal in the year 1770. On his arrival in Calcutta, there being a superabundance of officers, he was placed in a separate corps formed for the cadets of that year, and called the Select Picquet. In this situation he attended chiefly to his improvement in military knowledge and discipline, and from the gracefulness of his person, as well as an uncommon activity, he was soon distinguished by a superior skill and address in the performance of all military duties.

After serving twelve months in this corps, he attached himself to the artillery. While he was a lieutenant-fireworker, by the strict attention he paid to his duty, the interest he took in his profession, and the ardour with which he pursued every branch of it, he greatly improved himself in the knowledge of tactics, and his practice was proportionably advanced by being on several occasions employed on actual service.

About the year 1781 he was promoted to the command of a company. He was sent to join General Goddard, who was employed to demolish various forts in the Rohilla country, several of which were defended with the most obstinate bravery. In attacking one of them he was wounded by an arrow while attempting to force the gates, which, entering just below the eye, penetrated obliquely through part of the jaw, and almost reached the opposite cheek. Without a moment's hesitation, he broke the arrow off close to the iron barb, and continued at the head of his corps till the object of the attack was accomplished. The barb remained in his face several days, and was at length extracted with great skill by Dr. Brinch Harwood, now professor of anatomy in the University of Cambridge. (His brother was one of the council of revenue at Dinagepoor in 1766.) In these active scenes Captain Montague completely established his military character, gained the confidence and recorded approbation of his commanding officer, and greatly advanced the good opinion and regard which General Goddard had already entertained for him.

★★★★★★

N.B. There is some unaccountable error in the above. Goddard left Culpee in May, 1778, with Leslie's force. He was employed in 1781 at the Bhoreghat against the Mahrattas, who may have been mistaken for Rohillas. The detachment with Sir Eyre Coote sailed from Calcutta in October, 1780. Montague appears on the returns of one of these companies, but from the circumstantial account of his wound, we must suppose he went round and joined Goddard, and returned in the end of 1781. The regimental returns are blank from July 1780 to April 1781, and the companies absent on service are not included till their return. We had thought that Lieutenant Montague was quartermaster to the artillery in 1781.—E. B.

******

In the year 1782, Captain Montague was called forth to join Sir Eyre Coote on the coast of Coromandel. Captain Montague was in every engagement, and in services where so much real military merit was displayed, it is no common praise to say he was always peculiarly distinguished. He obtained the rank of major, and at Cuddalore, in 1784, he was appointed to command the artillery of one of the wings of the army, and there manifested his superior judgment by taking post on an eminence which produced the greatest advantages, and it was honourably acknowledged by a French officer of rank who was stationed to oppose him. On his return to Bengal, he was employed in Oude until the memorable expedition of the Marquis Cornwallis to Seringapatam. On this important service Major Montague was selected to attack the stupendous fortresses of Nunder-droog and Ramali-droog.

The chief engineer having reported Nunder-droog to be a fortress of uncommon strength, his lordship ordered Major Montague to proceed with his best train of artillery from Bangalore to join the army encamped about half-way to the place of attack. The expedition with which he performed that duty excited the astonishment, as it called forth the applause, of Lord Cornwallis; and though he was the youngest artillery officer with the army, he was entrusted with the conduct of the artillery employed in the reduction of that important fortress.

His skill, courage, and talents were crowned with complete success, and the thanks of the commander-in-chief expressed in the strongest terms the sense he entertained of his eminent services. The manner, also, in which he was entrusted with the command of the artillery employed against Severn-droog, manifested the great confidence which the Marquis Cornwallis possessed in his military enthusiasm and professional abilities.

******

N.B. The following conversation took place between the deputy adjutant-general and Major Montague as the latter passed headquarters on his march: "Lord C. has it in contemplation to give Colonel Smith the command of the artillery to be employed against Severn-droog, and he wishes to know if that circumstance will be any impediment to your exertions." The major replied, "that he did not expect to take the command; that his only wish was to be employed, and that his lordship might rely on his utmost exertions for the public service under Smith." The deputy adjutant-general did not think that answer sufficiently explicit; and said, "Lord C. wished to know whether Major M. could act with more effect when independent of Colonel Smith, than when under his command?"

The major answered, "that he could certainly carry a plan of his own into execution in the same time that it would require to suggest and explain it to another." The deputy adjutant-general therefore concluded that Major M.'s real opinion was that he should prefer to conduct the business by himself, and informed him that his lordship was disposed to give Colonel Smith an opportunity of knocking down the walls of the place where he had been so long confined in a former war; but as it might be attended with some risk to the service, he was at length determined to appoint Major M. to command and conduct the artillery against that important place, as the capture of it was absolutely necessary to the further progress of the campaign.

★★★★★★

In the year 1794, Major Montague was advanced to the rank of lieutenant-colonel, and was third on the list of the artillery officers when he was chosen to direct the artillery attached to the Bengal army, and which was destined to join General Harris, commander-in-chief, in the late glorious enterprise against Seringapatam, where this gallant and most distinguished officer found his most honourable grave.

If it is true, as has been asserted, that the commander of the artillery, Colonel Smith, a brave and deserving officer, had, from a long succession of illness, become too infirm to be continually in the trenches, the executive duty must have necessarily devolved upon Lieut.-Colonel Montague, who was next in command. But be that as it may, it is certain that three days previous to the capture of Seringapatam, a cannon-ball shattered his arm, while he was in the trenches, in such a manner as to require immediate amputation, and it was taken off within an inch of the shoulder. In this state, however, such was his zealous, active, and unconquerable spirit, he insisted on being carried into the trenches, where he continued to the last to encourage by his presence the troops, who adored him. During three or four days, it was hoped and believed that he was in a fair way of recovery; but having by the same shot received a contusion in his chest, it turned to a mortification, and carried him off on the eighth day after he had received his wound.

Thus fell Lieut.-Colonel Edward Montague, in the forty-fifth year of his age, lamented as he was beloved by the whole army; leaving a widow and three orphans, the youngest of whom was born a fortnight before his glorious but lamentable death. (He married a Miss Fleetwood at Masulipatam in 1792, when on his return to Bengal from the first campaign against Tippoo.) He served the Honourable East-India Company with zeal, fidelity, and superior military talents, during an honourable course of twenty-nine years; had been in more engagements than usually happens even to an active soldier, and had been noticed with the most flattering distinction by every commanding officer under whom he had served.

On this last occasion his being only mentioned in the general list of killed and wounded, without a single word of regret or eulogium, causes the mingled emotions of grief and astonishment in the minds of his afflicted family and friends. (The note in a former page may serve to explain this neglect, as the commanding officer of artillery was the same Colonel Smith to whom he had been preferred at Severn-droog.)

In private life he was not less distinguished than in his public services. He was benevolent and generous, possessing at the same time the most frank and candid disposition. He was an affectionate husband, a tender father, and a dutiful son. He loved his country with a patriotic ardour, and he died in the contest to extend its dominion and its glory.

He will live long in the remembrance of all who knew him; and it remains for the nation whom he served so well, and for whom he died too soon, to transmit his name to the times that are to come. (*Asiatic Annual Register*, 1800.)

After the fall of Seringapatam, one of the Bengal companies (5th company 2nd battalion) returned to Ceylon, and one (3rd company 1st battalion) to Cawnpoor with the 10th regiment native infantry, and the remaining two companies (1st and 2nd company 3rd battalion) continued with the brigades in Mysore, and were present at the occupation of Bednore and Hurryhur and pursuit of Doondia Khan, under Major-General Wellesley: they returned to Bengal in September, 1801.

******

Minute by governor-general, January 19, 1800.—"The conduct of the artillery and *lascars* attached to the regiment during the time of its absence from these provinces is equally entitled to commendation."

******

Medals of the annexed pattern were granted to all the native troops engaged in the expedition.

The following regimental order was issued by Colonel Green, R. O., September 19, 1801:—

> Colonel Green feels a particular pleasure in congratulating Captain Tomkyns, the officers and soldiers of his detachment, upon their safe return from a long and arduous service, to join the regiment he has the honour to command, and he deems it his duty, in justice to the meritorious zeal and professional exertions shewn by the Bengal artillery during the late various campaigns in Mysore and in the pursuit of Doondia Khan, to thank him and them thus publicly and in the name of the corps to whose general reputation the good conduct of the detachment has so highly contributed: at the same time that Colonel Green has to lament their diminution in point of numbers since they quitted Bengal, it must reflect additional credit on them that, however thus weakened by casualties incidental to

long warfare, they have ever manifested a cheerful, patient, and steady adherence to the active performance of those services they have been called upon for, under many trying and fatiguing exigencies; they are in consequence most justly entitled to the character of good and veteran soldiers, and as such, will ever merit his warmest support and good offices.

The 5th company 2nd battalion returned to Ceylon, and when the Kandian insurrection broke out, in 1802, marched with General M'Douall's army from Columbo, and assisted in the capture of Kandy; it remained as part of the garrison when the general returned in April to Columbo.

The following month the general came back, and trusting in the professions of the king, and thinking all was settled, again retired, taking with him the whole force except 200 men, H.M.'s 19th regiment, 500 Malays, and a detachment of artillery, Major Davies commanding the whole, and Lieutenant Humphreys the artillery.

Their position was attacked 23-24th of June, 1803, and the following day Major Davies capitulated, under the conditions that he was to march off, with arms and ammunition. The garrison retired to the river at Allemgonath, and halted, intending to pass the next day, but the Kandians set upon them, and, worn out with fatigue and hunger, they laid down their arms, and delivered themselves up as prisoners. The Europeans were immediately murdered, except nine of the officers; about 500 Malays and *lascars* were made prisoners; six 6-pounders, three howitzers, and a 5½ inch howitzer were lost.

★★★★★★

Captain Humphreys at the time of the massacre was seized by a junior assistant surgeon who rolled with him down the steep where the dead were flung; they remained concealed three or four days, but being discovered were taken before the king and separately confined.

★★★★★★

Lieutenant Humphreys was kept a prisoner for a time, but in September, on some solemn festival, was brought out and executed by order of the king. The native prisoners were mutilated by cutting off their noses and ears.

Reinforcements arrived, and the war was successfully prosecuted; most of the ordnance and many of the *lascars* were recaptured, and in October, 1804, the company, and the 5th company 1st battalion, returned to Bengal. On its departure the following order was issued:—

> The governor cannot allow Captain Edward Clarke, of the Bengal artillery, to leave this island, with the detachment under his command, without expressing his thanks to that officer for the useful and active services which he has rendered to the government of Ceylon during a period of more than eight years.
>
> He requests Captain Clarke to communicate to the non-commissioned officers and privates of the artillery, and to the detachment of *lascars*, his approbation of their conduct, and his wishes for their future prosperity.

In following out the services of these companies, we have anticipated a little, and it is now therefore requisite to go back a few years. Napoleon's expedition to Egypt, coupled, as it had been, with intrigues with Tippoo Sultan, alarmed government as to his views on India, and rendered it necessary to take some steps in self-defence, to check his career of conquest.

Lord Nelson had destroyed the French fleet in the Bay of Aboukir; an army from England, under Sir Ralph Abercrombie, had effected a landing in Egypt, and to co-operate with the latter, Lord Wellesley prepared detachments from the three presidencies, which, landing at Cossier or Suez, were to hem in the French Army, deprived of all communication with France between the two armies. Towards this detachment, Bengal contributed a detachment of horse and foot artillery. H.M.'s 10th regiment of Foot, and 1,200 *sipahi* volunteers.

Horse artillery, which had for some time been used in European warfare, was now about being introduced into India. It appears to have been first used by the Russians in the campaigns of 1757-8-9 against the Prussians, whose light cavalry often found themselves, at the time they felt sure of success, opposed by batteries of cannon, although no infantry were present. Frederick the Great introduced it into his army in 1759, and took great pains to exercise and instruct them himself in his camp near Landstruth, and soon found the arm of essential use.

The Austrians followed the example about 1780, and since that period it has been introduced into all European armies, though with considerable variation in the weight and calibre of the guns, and in the manner of mounting the gunners.

Some experimental horse artillery was raised, and part of it accompanied the expedition to Egypt; it was however embarked almost as soon as raised, so that no time was allowed for its acquiring any experience. From the returns, a portion of the governor-general's bodyguard was attached to it, and altogether but 36 horses.

European.							Body-Guard.								Gohundaz.			Lascars.				
Brevet Captain.	Act. Conductor.	Sergeants.	Corporals.	Farriers.	Gunners.	Matrosses.	Jemadar.	Havildars.	Naiks.	Troopers.	2nd Thidals.	Lascars.	Syces.	Grass-cutters.	Havildars.	Naiks.	Privates.	Serang.	1st Thidals.	2nd Thidals.	Syces.	Grass-cutters.
1	1	3	3	1	6	14	1	2	2	22	1	11	27	27	2	2	20	1	2	40	9	9

With a quartermaster's and train-artificer's establishment: Brevet-Captain Clement Brown commanded it.

The foot artillery, under Captain-Lieutenant Flemyng, consisted of—

European.						Gohundaz.				Lascars.			
Captain-Lieut.	Lieutenants.	Sergeants.	Corporals.	Gunners.	Matrosses.	Jemadar.	Havildars.	Naiks.	Privates.	Serang.	1st Thidals.	2nd Thidals.	Lascars.
1	2	4	4	6	24	1	3	3	40	1	3	6	93

Lieutenants Drummond and Starke were with this detachment.

A bounty of one month's pay and full *batta* was given to each native officer and soldier who embarked, and all possible attention was paid to the laying in the stock of provisions and water under their own inspection.

The foot artillery embarked on 27th November, reached Trincomalee on the 13th November, and Bombay on the 27th March, 1801; the horse artillery embarked in February.

The first division of transports reached Cossier on the 17th May; the disembarkation immediately took place, and on the 21st June the army commenced its march across the desert in successive small detachments, following each other at intervals, on account of the scarcity of water; *mussuls* were sent forward with each detachment, and returned for the use of the succeeding one; much suffering was experienced in this march; the extreme heat and want of water killed many men and horses; but it was observed in this, as in subsequent cases, that Europeans bore the exposure and drought better than natives.

The guns of the foot artillery were drawn by bullocks brought from Bombay; and the horse artillery joined the army which was collected at Ghennah about the middle of July, and the whole embarked in *jermes*, or country boats, on the 31st, and sailed down the Nile. The stream was rapid, and they floated successively past towns and ruins, pyramids and other monuments of mystic Egypt; and on the 7th August reached Gizah, and on the 8th and following days disembarked and encamped on the Isle of Roda, where they remained till the 28th, awaiting orders from General Hutchinson; on their reception they once more embarked, and arrived at Rosetta on the 31st August,—too late to participate in any of the service.

★★★★★★

On the march from Rosetta to Alexandria the axletree of one of the limbers broke, and for want of a forge-cart the detachment was detained eighteen hours on the desert without water or provisions; had a forge-cart been there, two hours would have sufficed.—Captain Brown to Colonel Green, 2nd April, 1803.

★★★★★★

The detachment remained in Egypt till May, 1802, when it marched from Gizeh (near Cairo) to Suez, detachments following each other successively, and completed it in five marches, losing only three Europeans by the way. On the 5th June the headquarters embarked on H.M.S. *Victor*, and reached Calcutta towards the end of July.

The foot artillery, under command of Lieutenant Starke (Lieutenant Drummond having returned to Calcutta on sick leave in September, 1801, and Captain-Lieutenant Flemyng most probably having sailed direct for England from the same cause, for he does not appear to have returned to India, nor to have been in Egypt in October, 1801, and he subsequently retired in England in December, 1802), returned in the *Commerce*, and the men composing the detachment rejoined their companies in Fort William on the 1st August, 1802. (Lieutenant Drummond returned to India on sick certificate September, 1801—Letter from Military Board to Military Secretary, 26th September, 1801.) The horse artillery disembarked on the 4th August, and rejoined the remainder of the experimental horse artillery.

The services of these detachments were acknowledged by the governor-general on their landing, in orders, from which the following is an extract:—

Under a grateful impression of the important aid derived to

the common cause of our country by the able and successful conduct of the expedition from India to Egypt, his Excellency is pleased to order, that honorary medals be conferred on all the native officers, non-commissioned officers, troopers, *sipahis*, *golundaz*, and gun-*lascars* who have been employed on the service in Egypt.

The insufficiency of the artillery in India had early attracted Lord Mornington's attention; in June, 1799, we find him writing to Mr. Dundas—

> Our artillery throughout India is very deficient. . . . . I cannot too strongly press the necessity of attention to the artillery in India: if you do not send out ample supplies of proper men and officers for this useful corps, it will soon fall to ruin; it is already on the decay,—a larger annual supply of cadets, and a reduction of the export of writers would tend to recruit it."

The Court of Directors had previously (July 5th, 1797) "advised the government of their intention to send out properly-qualified cadets for the artillery, and prohibited the transfer of any infantry officers" to that branch, and "with a view to promote emulation in the cadets for the artillery or engineer corps who are educated at Woolwich," the court "resolved (5th March, 1800) to make it a standing regulation, that those who by their progress in the different studies are first reported qualified to proceed to India, shall have precedence in rank in the general list of cadets appointed for the respective presidencies;" and this order was highly approved by the Governor-General in his minute on establishing the College of Fort William.

In July, 1800, Lord Wellesley writes again to Mr. Dundas—

> Every augmentation of native troops in India should be accompanied by a due augmentation of the European force, artillery

as well as infantry.

The Company's European artillery are everywhere extremely weak. The fixed establishment of this corps is defective at all the presidencies, and the numbers wanting to complete even that defective establishment are now so considerable that I intend without delay to reduce one of the Company's European regiments in Bengal for the purpose of augmenting the artillery of this presidency..... But the best remedy I may be able to apply will be insufficient, on account of the great deficiency of officers of artillery: some companies have now no more than one commanding officer doing duty with them. This deficiency proceeds, in a great measure, from the original deficiency of the establishment in point of commanding officers, and partly from the neglect of a regular supply of cadets.

It is probable that men were allowed to volunteer from the European regiments for the artillery at once, for the returns of the regiment shew that 277 men joined "from other corps" in the months of July, August, and September, 1801, but the 2nd European regiment was not reduced until the February following. At the same time, two companies were added to each battalion of artillery, and the strength raised to 1 captain, 1 captain-lieutenant, 2 lieutenants, 2 lieutenant-fireworkers, 5 sergeants, 5 corporals, 2 drummers, 10 gunners, and 80 *matrosses*; the companies, however, remained incomplete, for upwards of 800 men were deficient.

This increase was reluctantly sanctioned by the Home authority, for we find Mr. Dundas writing to the Court of Directors, 30th June, 1801, on the subject of the liquidation of their debts:—

> Mr. Wright observes, that if the addition to the artillery could be postponed, it would save £54,000; but I consider the addition to your artillery establishment to be of such deep importance to the security of your extended Indian empire, that I do not think the saving suggested should be adopted.

The authority was therefore given, and Lord Wellesley, in writing to General Lake, says:

> In issuing the order for the reduction of the 2nd European regiment, I request your Excellency to annex to it the order for the augmentation of the artillery, as directed by the Honourable Court. The improvement of our artillery is a point of such

importance, that I am resolved not to postpone it under any circumstances whatever.

The augmentation was accordingly carried into effect; the companies were levelled, so as to divide the old gunners and *matrosses* equally among the companies, and they were filled up as well as they could be from the volunteers who joined; and the regiment consisted, at the beginning of 1802, of three battalions, of seven companies each, with thirty companies of *lascars*: neither *lascars* nor *golundaz* details being added with the six additional companies; and the *golundaz* details, all except nine, were reduced in the following November.

The men composing the corps of horse artillery were borne on the rolls of the companies.

The remonstrances of Lord Mornington having thus obtained a numerical increase to the corps, and the Court's step of obtaining educated cadets from Woolwich having prepared men to fill the vacancies in the commissioned grades (the first of whom had arrived the preceding year), a new era may be considered as opening in the history of the regiment, and it may not be uninteresting to consider the state of the corps at this time.

Of the officers in its early years we have seen sketches in some of Pearse's letters already quoted, and from the specimens who lived on into this century, and of whom many anecdotes are current among the present seniors of the regiment, they appear to have been deficient not only in the scientific knowledge necessary for their profession, but many were without even the ordinary education of gentlemen of that period; boatswains and gunners in their original calling, they never rose to the manners and acquirements which are expected in commissioned officers; they therefore shewed to great disadvantage when contrasted with the lately-arrived cadets, who to the usual liberal education of gentlemen had superadded a course of study at Woolwich fitting them for the attainment of the higher degrees of their professional knowledge.

At the time, too, when they were studying, Indian affairs had awakened great attention; the wars with Hyder and Tippoo had just been brought to a conclusion, and all England rang with applause at the gallant and successful storming of Seringapatam and the expedition to Egypt; their minds were filled with these subjects, and themselves, on their arrival, either partaking in or watching the meteor-like career of Lake, how could they fail receiving a high tone, and infusing it into

		per Company.	per Battalion.	Total.	On the returns 1st April, 1802.
LASCARS.	Lascars.	70	700	2100	2113
	2nd Tindals.	2	20	60	60
	1st Tindals.	2	20	60	60
	Serangs.	1	10	30	30
GOLUNDAZ.	Privates.	40	200	600	575
	Naiks.	3	15	45	45
	Havildars.	3	15	45	45
	Jemadars.	1	5	15	15
EUROPEANS.	Drummers.	2	14	42	46
	Matrosses.	80	560	1680	891
	Gunners.	10	70	210	187
	Corporals.	5	35	105	106
	Sergeants.	5	35	105	96
	Lieut.-Fireworkers.	2	14	42	—
	Lieutenants.	2	14	42	28
	Captain-Lieutenants.	1	7	21	21
	Captains.	1	7	21	21
	Majors.	—	1	3	3
	Lieutenant-Colonels Commandant.	—	1	3	3
	Colonels.	—	1	3	3

those who immediately followed, and thus laying the foundation of a permanent improvement in the commissioned grades.

But while we must consider many of the old hands deficient in some qualities requisite to the formation of good officers, let us not forget the habits of the times in which they lived, nor that these men proved themselves good and brave soldiers in the many hard services in which they were employed; "*per mare, per terras*" might have been their motto. In the wars of Bengal and the Carnatic they filled their part with credit, and many are the names from among them which have been handed down to our respect and esteem both as good soldiers and men of high talent and conduct.

Pearse, Montague, Hutchinson, Duff, of the old hands, and others, such as Horsford, Clement Brown, Pennington, who living long into this century may fairly claim no small share in giving a tone to the present corps, are all names which we should not willingly allow to be forgotten; and although we may laugh at the anecdotes of the Hindes, Paschauds, and Greenes, and be tempted to rate the moderns highly when we look to the bright halo with which the Mahrattas, Nepal, Ava, and Affghanistan campaigns have encircled the heads of those whom we delight to honour, let us not forget those who shared in the wars with Hyder and Tippoo, and in the earlier campaigns in which the foundation of our Indian empire was laid. "*Vixerunt fortes ante Agamemnona, multi.*" (Many brave men lived before Agamemnon.)

The ranks were filled with men of an indifferent class; the great demand caused by European wars rendered it difficult to recruit for the Company's service, and, as a natural consequence, the worst men were enlisted. The Regimental Orders, as might be expected, record many courts-martial and the infliction of punishments to preserve order; still, however, when any portion was sent on service, they never forgot what was expected from them, and always supported the national character by their conduct in the field. (The uniform at this time consisted of the bearskin cap, long coat, with scarlet facings and embroidered button-holes, and grey trowsers with a red cord down the seam.)

A very mistaken notion as to the composition of the regiment has long prevailed, and is still repeated by those ignorant of the facts of the case; it is often affirmed that a large majority of the regiment is Irish, but from a reference to the long rolls at the period of which we are writing, we find the respective numbers—English 516, Irish 484, Scotch 74, Welsh 19, Foreigners 211, no description 32, and at a period six years anterior to it (1795), the proportion of Irish was still less, the English being 437 and the Irish 284.

At the present time (1852) the English and Irish are nearly equal. We purpose noticing the constitution of the regiment in this point from time to time at different epochs, and also adding the casualties wherever we are able to ascertain them, and this we trust will form a valuable addition to our knowledge of the statistics of Indian mortality.

Having detailed the formation of 1802, we must revert to the preceding year to bring up the record of the services of portions of the regiment.

In November, 1801, two complete companies were ordered for foreign service, to embark on the *Dover Castle* and *Asia* Indiamen.

Lascar Companies.	Company.	Battalion.	Captains.	Captain Lieutenants.	Lieutenants.	Lieutenant-Fireworkers.
4, 1	9	18	A. Fraser	A. Hinde	Fuller	C. H. Palmer
5, 3	5	12	C. Wittit	P. Paschaud	A. Dunn	S. S. Hay

The former company proceeded to Macao, and returned the following November, but does not appear to have been engaged in any active service during the expedition. The latter had a much longer absence; for, reaching Goa in January, 1802, it was sent on to Bombay, and thence to Guzerat in May, Surat in June, and back to Bombay in October; in December it was stationed at Tannah, having been detained by the Bombay Government. (Letter of John Duncan, 10th November, 1802, to Supreme Government.)

In August, 1803, it participated in the successful attack on Baroach, and then continued with the Bombay Army, under Major-General Jones, and joined the army before Bhurtpore in 1805, towards the conclusion of the siege; returned to Bombay in 1806, and reached Fort William in the *Sir William Pulteney* in July, 1806, after an absence of nearly five years, reduced to 33 men.

Captain C. Wittit, Captain-Lieutenant Paschaud, and Lieutenant-Fireworker S. Hay returned to the presidency in March, 1803. Lieutenant Drummond joined the company in December, 1802, and left in September following. Captain Watkins and Lieutenant T. D. Smith joined it at a later period. Lieutenant Dunn appears to have remained with it throughout.

Other portions of the regiment were called into the field, at the end of 1802, against a powerful *zemindar*, Bulwunt Sing, who was in possession of three forts, Sarsnee, Bidgegurh, and Cutchowrah, in the neighbourhood of Hattrass; these forts were situated in the districts ceded in 1801 by the *Vizier* of Oude and *Nawab* of Furruckabad, to maintain the stipulated British force. Mustering 20,000 followers, he trusted he could successfully resist the demand for his *jumma*, he therefore tendered a lower sum; this, of course, was refused, and as he appeared determined not to yield the point, a force was collected against him, which gradually increased to 4 battalions of infantry, 4 troops of cavalry, and detachments from 3 companies of artillery, with four 18-pounders, two $4^{2/5}$-inch howitzers, and ten 6-pounders.

Major Gordon, Commandant.

Company.	Battalion.	Lascar Companies.	Captains.	Captain-Lieutenants.	Lieutenants.
1	2	4, 23, 28	E. Constable		
3	2	7, 21, 22	W. Shipton	R. Best	
4	2	14, 16	J. Robinson	...	A. Mathews
			T. Green ...	...	T. D. Boyle

The trenches were opened against Sarsnee on the 27th December, and a battery erected on the 4th January, 1803, but at such a distance that the *rownee* was not breached; a storm was nevertheless made on the 15th, which proved unsuccessful.

Lieutenant Boyle was dangerously wounded by a cannon-ball on the 8th, and died on the 24th of January.

Reinforcements under the commander-in-chief arrived, and the siege was renewed; the approaches being advanced 200 yards, the town was taken on the 8th February, and on the 11th the garrison abandoned Sarsnee and fled to Bidgegurh; thither the army moved on the 13th; batteries were ready on the 21st February, and by the 27th a practicable breach was effected; during the night, however, the enemy were discovered evacuating the fort, and next morning it was taken possession of by the British.

Whilst proceeding round the fort in the morning, most probably with a view to ascertain the ordnance and stores, Major (Lieutenant-Colonel) Gordon was killed, along with several *sipahis* and *lascars*, by the accidental explosion of a powder-magazine. In reporting his death, the commander-in-chief says that he felt "particularly indebted for his exertions, directed by uncommon zeal and ability."

The governor-general, in the order published to the army, "deeply regrets the severe loss which the public service had sustained by the death of Lieutenant-Colonel Gordon;" he also notified:

> His high approbation of the gallantry and steadiness displayed by the troops, and of the readiness with which they submitted to extreme labour under circumstances of peculiar hardship from the unusual severity of the weather.

The force next moved to Cutchowrah, which, after some attempts at treachery and delay, was given up. Major T. Green had command of the artillery, and the troops then broke up and returned to their cantonments, small garrisons being left in Sarsnee and Bidgegurh.

In the contemporary accounts of these sieges we meet with no intimation of excessive rain having fallen, which, no doubt, adds exceedingly to the fatigues and hardships incidental to troops in trenches, and we are therefore rather at a loss to understand what the excessive hardships caused by the season, adverted to in the general orders, were; the heat in the month of March, in the provinces, is not overpowering, and we cannot help smiling when we recollect that within a few months these very troops were to form part of that army which Lake, contemning the seasons, led, in the hottest parts of successive years, through the Dooab and Rajasthan.

CHAPTER 6
Augmentation by Adding Golundaz

The conduct of the Mahrattas having rendered hostilities unavoidable, the governor-general determined to carry them on upon such a scale as would completely destroy their power, and, at the same time, eradicate the French party from the Dooab, where Mr. Perron, nominally a commander of Scindia's disciplined brigades, had in reality established a small independent principality of his own.

To carry out his intentions, the governor-general assembled forces in the Dukhun, Guzerat, Cuttack, Mirzapoor, Allahabad, and in the Dooab; with all of which, except the first, were portions of the Bengal Artillery.

The main army (in Bengal) was under the personal command of the Commander-in-Chief, General Lake; the corps composing it were put in motion early in August, 1803, and collected, on the 13th, at Arowl, on the Kali Muddee. They reached Coel on the 28th of the same month.

The following artillery were attached to it:—

Lieutenant-Colonel Horsford, Commandant. Lieutenant Brown, Brigade Major. Lieutenant Butler, Brigade Quarter-Master.

Company.	Battalion.	Lascars.	Captains.	Captain-Lieutenants.	Lieutenants.
1	1	19, 24, 26	T. Greene		
2	...	2, 15	Raban	Winbolt	
3	...	6, 8	Nelly		
1	2	4, 23, 28	Constable		
2	...	3, 13	Hutchinson		
3	2	7, 21, 22	W. Shipton	Best	Morris
4	...	14, 16	J. Robinson	... ...	A. Mathews

On the 29th August, General Lake attacked Perron's army, drawn up behind a *jheel*, with their right resting on Aligurh. The attack was made by the cavalry and gallopers, and the enemy drew off towards Agra. Mr. Perron was left in charge of the fort, with instructions to defend it to the last extremity.

General Lake determining to storm the fort on the 4th September, during the night preceding two batteries of four 18-pounders each, under Captains Greene and Robinson, were erected by Colonel Horsford at a village in the vicinity and at Perron's country house, to cover the advance to the party.

Before daylight the storming party, under Colonel Monson, moved out to within 400 yards of the fort, and there awaited the morning gun, the signal for the advance; on its being fired, they moved on, covered by a heavy fire from the supporting batteries. The fort had been alarmed, and the gates were closed. The ladders proved too short. A 6-pounder was sent for to burst the gate open, but proving insufficient, a 12-pounder was substituted, which succeeded after four or five rounds. During this delay, the party was exposed to a heavy fire, by which many were wounded; among others, Captain Shipton, who commanded the guns; notwithstanding this, he continued to advance with the party. The second and third gates were stormed, but at the fourth, his gun was again required, this gate resisted its fire, but the wicket being forced, the party entered, and obtained possession of the fortress, capturing 281 pieces of ordnance of all kinds.

The artillery lost but 2 Europeans and 4 *lascars* killed, 7 Europeans and 1 *lascar* wounded, in addition to Captain Shipton. The services of the artillery were acknowledged by the commander-in-chief in his report to the governor-general:—

> To Captain Shipton, of the artillery, who had charge of the guns which forced the gate, and who, though wounded, still remained at his post, I feel myself much indebted. To Colonel Horsford, who commanded the artillery, as well as Captains Greene and Robinson, who commanded the covering batteries, I feel myself under infinite obligations, and indeed the whole corps merit my warmest praise for the gallantry displayed on this occasion as well as in every other in which they have been engaged.

The governor-general in general orders, 15th September, 1803:

> Desires that his particular approbation may be signified to Captain Shipton, of the artillery, and also to Lieutenant-Colonel Horsford, Captains Robinson and Greene. . . . . . it is with the greatest satisfaction that the governor-general expresses his approbation of the bravery, discipline, and steadiness of the corps of artillery who were employed on this occasion.

A small detachment of half a corps, with one gun, under Lieutenant Winbolt, at this time in the cantonment of Shekoabad or Etawah, were attacked by a large body of horse, under a Mr. Fleury. The first attack, on the 2nd September, was beaten off, but being renewed on the 4th September, after several hours' resistance, the party capitulated, and were allowed to march off to Cawnpoor with their guns and arms. Lieutenant Winbolt was wounded in this affair.

The army reached the Jumna, near Delhi, on the 11th, and found the Mahrattas posted behind intrenchments, with their park of artillery in front, the whole covered by long grass. The commander-in-chief moved on to reconnoitre with the cavalry, and directed the artillery and infantry to follow; the front alone was accessible, and the cavalry were exposed to a heavy cannonade. They moved to the rear to avoid this, and to cover the advance of the line, but the enemy mistaking it for a retreat, moved out from their intrenchments.

The cavalry opened to allow the infantry to pass through, who attacked in line, the cavalry forming as a support in their rear. The advance was made under a tremendous fire of round and grape, without returning a shot until close, when, firing a volley, they charged, broke into open column, and allowed the cavalry and gallopers to pass through and complete the victory.

Colonel Horsford was employed covering the left with four guns and a battalion from a threatened attack by a body of Seik (Sikh) cavalry.

The loss of the artillery consisted of 3 Europeans and 1 *lascar* killed, 1 subaltern, 13 Europeans, and 16 *lascars* wounded. Lieutenant Mathews lost his leg by a cannon-shot; 67 brass and iron guns, 37 tumbrils of ammunition (besides 24 blown up), and 2 tumbrils of treasure, were captured on this occasion. The iron guns were of European manufacture, the brass nearly all cast in India on French models; the carriages were all fitted with elevating screws, strong and neat, and of the French pattern; the tumbrils stout, but clumsy; some with modern draught-chains, others with a trace of raw hide.

✶✶✶✶✶✶

Lieutenant Mathews was appointed fort adjutant at Agra the following year, and afterwards deputy commissary of ordnance at Futteygurh, and on his promotion to a captaincy was retained.

"At the particular recommendation of the commander-in-chief, in consideration of the peculiar services of Lieutenant Mathews, who lost his leg and thigh in the battle of Delhi, the governor-general is pleased to determine that Captain Mathews shall be exempted from the operation of the General Orders of 14th November, declaring the situation of deputy commissary of ordnance to be incompatible with the rank of regimental captain."

"This exemption is admitted as a mark of attention and indulgence to a deserving officer, who has suffered severely in the execution of his duty on active service against the enemy."— General Orders of May 15, 1806.

✶✶✶✶✶✶

General Lake wrote to the governor-general:—

To Colonel Horsford and every officer of the corps of artillery I feel myself infinitely indebted for their meritorious exertions on this occasion.

And in the general orders of the governor-general of 1st February we find:—

To Colonel Horsford and the artillery the governor-general in council repeats the public testimony of approbation which that meritorious corps has uniformly deserved in every exigency of the service

The officers present were the same as at Aligurh, with the exception of Captain-Lieutenant Best, who was left in charge of the ordnance in that fortress.

The governor-general in council deemed:

> It to be the duty of the government to anticipate the sanction of His Majesty and the Honourable the Court of Directors for the distribution of the treasure captured, as a testimony of the applause and gratitude with which the British Government viewed the exemplary valour, discipline, zeal, and firmness displayed by the army.

And directed that:

> The general principles of this order should constitute the proceedings of the governor-general in council with respect to all prize-money captured during the progress of the war.

The heavy artillery and stores intended for the siege of Agra were embarked on the Jumna in boats, the army marching down along the western banks. On the 7th October they reached Agra, and cut off all communication with the country, and on the 10th the enemy's battalions outside the fort were driven from the ravines and glacis, with a loss of 600 men and 26 guns. In this affair Lieutenants Beagham and J. Hay (who together with Lieutenant W. Parker joined the army a little previously) are mentioned as having distinguished themselves.

> The intrepidity and courage evinced by Lieutenant Beagham, of the artillery, employed in the assault, calls for his Excellency's warmest approbation and thanks.

> Lieutenant Hay, of the artillery, who went with a detachment of that corps to bring off the enemy's guns, merits my approbation for his successful exertions in this service.

The siege commenced, and by the 17th a breaching battery of eight 18-pounders and four howitzers, with an enfilading battery of four 12-pounders on its left and another of two 12-pounders on its right, were ready and commenced firing, and on the 20th the fort capitulated.

Seventy-six brass and 86 iron guns, 20 tumbrils, with two *lacs* of *rupees* and ammunition, &c. were captured; among them was the celebrated great gun of Agra, which lay on the banks of the Jumna until some twenty years afterwards it was broken up and sold, an attempt to carry it down the Jumna having failed, as also a fine brass 72-pounder, now in the barrack square at Dum-Dum.

General Lake wrote:—

> I attribute the early surrender of Agra to the great impression our breaching battery made on the walls, which opened yesterday within 350 yards, and which would have caused a practicable breach in a few hours more battering.
>
> To Colonel Horsford, of the artillery, as well as to every officer of the corps, I feel myself under great obligations for their unremitted exertions on this occasion, and to which I principally attribute my early success against this place.

Twenty-four *lacs* of *rupees* of prize-money were on this occasion divided among the troops, in accordance with the principle of the General Order 1st November, 1803, above quoted.

On the 27th October the army marched from Agra, and on the 31st (having previously left their baggage and heavy guns under a guard at Futtypoor Sicoree) had nearly come up with the Mahrattas. In the evening, General Lake moved on again with the cavalry, directing the infantry to follow at three o'clock next morning, and after a march of twenty-five miles overtook the Mahrattas at sunrise, near Laswaree, amounting to about 9,000 infantry and 5,000 cavalry, with 72 guns. As they appeared to be in some confusion, he was tempted to make an attack at once, without waiting for the artillery and infantry.

The enemy retarded this movement by cutting a *bund* and flooding the road, and availed themselves of the time gained to form their line, the right resting on Laswaree and the left on Mohalpoor, the front covered by the guns, and, as at Delhi, the country around covered with long grass. The cavalry charged boldly through the guns several times, the gunners falling down as they passed and reopening on their return, while the infantry plied them with musketry from behind an intrenchment formed of the baggage-*hackeries*: the guns could not be secured from want of infantry.

The loss having been great, and the men and horses much fatigued, the cavalry were withdrawn to wait the arrival of the infantry, the enemy having been effectually stopped and crippled. By noon the infantry reached the banks of the *nullah*, but some slight rest was necessary after a march of twenty-five miles; and as the enemy offered to surrender their guns on certain terms, a favourable answer was returned, though preparations were made for renewing the attack when the stipulated time should expire.

The enemy threw back their right, so as almost to encircle Mohalpoor, their whole front bristling with guns. The British infantry prepared to attack in two columns, the right, under Major-General Ware, against Mohalpoor, the left, under Major-General St. John, against the enemy's right, covered by the cavalry. All the guns which had come up were formed with the gallopers into four distinct batteries to support these attacks. The whole advanced under a heavy fire from the enemy's artillery, which were well and quickly served, and by four p.m. had entirely routed the enemy, capturing elephants, camels, 1,600 bullocks, 72 guns, 5,000 stand of arms, 44 colours, 64 tumbrils of ammunition and 3 of treasure, and 57 carts with stores.

In this brilliant action the artillery suffered but little—4 Europeans and 3 *lascars* killed, and 6 Europeans and 5 *lascars* wounded: the brunt fell upon the other branches.

From Laswaree the army returned towards Agra, sending in the wounded and captured stores, and remained in the neighbourhood till the end of the month, when Colonel White, with a proportion of artillery, was detached to aid the Bundelcund force in the siege of Gwalior. The main army soon after moved to a position near the Biana Pass, where the horse artillery troop (formed from the experimental horse artillery), under Captain Clement Brown, with Lieutenants Starke and Young, joined; but we must make a slight retrospect to bring up the proceedings of the other forces to this point.

The detachment of artillery, with Lieutenant-Colonel Fawcett's force, destined for Bundelcund, consisted of—

Major C. Wittit, Commandant.

Company	Battalion	Captains.	Captain Lieutenants.	Lieutenants.
1	3	Tomkyns	Feade	Richards.
2			Dowell	M. Brown. W. Hopper.

The force reached the banks of the Caine, near Tiroha, on the 23rd September, and on the 10th October crossed, and, after a long march over a rough country, came in sight of Shumsheer Bahadur's troops. A distant cannonade was all that occurred, the enemy made off as fast as he could, and the force proceeded against Culpee, which surrendered on the 4th December, as soon as a battery opened against it.

Its next move was to Gwalior, where the whole or a portion joined Colonel White, with whose detachment were Captain Green, Lieutenants Hay, Morris, Swiney, and Pollock. Batteries were opened, and on the 5th February, 1804, Gwalior had once again fallen into our possession.

The following general order was issued on its capture:

> The commander-in-chief is particularly happy to notice the valuable services of the artillery employed at Gwalior; and the great effect produced by the fire of the batteries under circumstances peculiarly unfavourable reflects the highest credit on the abilities of Captain Green, and on the officers and men under his command.

The detachments under Major-General Deare, of the artillery, and Lieutenant-Colonel Broughton, at Mirzapoor and Sumbulpoor, were equally successful, though not so brilliantly employed; their exertions frustrated the Mahrattas' hopes of plundering Mirzapoor and Benares.

The Balasore force met with complete success; they had chiefly, however, to contend against the difficulty of moving guns through a swampy, heavy country; the different towns surrendered with but little opposition. The fort of Barabutty alone required batteries to be erected against it; they were ready on the 13th October, and the defences being taken off, and the enemy's guns silenced, the storming party advanced, accompanied by some artillerymen, under Lieutenant G. Faithfull, with a 6-pounder, for the purpose of blowing open the gate. In passing the bridge, the party was exposed for 40 minutes to a heavy fire of musketry ere the gate could be forced, it was so blocked up with masses of stone: these removed, the attack was soon successful. Lieutenant Faithfull was wounded, though not dangerously, and his conduct, as well as that of Captain-Lieutenant Hetzler, was praised in general orders by the governor-general:—

> He trusts that Lieutenant Faithfull, of the artillery, will be speedily restored to the public service, in which his courage and resolution has already been distinguished.
>
> The governor-general expresses his sense of the conduct of Captain Hetzler, of the Bengal artillery.

To bring up the events of the campaign in all quarters, we must here turn briefly to the force in Guzerat, with which was the 5th company 3rd battalion. This force marched on the 21st August; at Bargood they met with but a feeble resistance on the 24th, and on the 26th a battery of two 18-pounders was completed against the fort of Baroach, and opened. By the 29th a breach was made, but the storm was delayed till 3 p.m., in hopes of profiting by the assistance of the *Fury* gun-vessel (on board which was a detail of Bengal artillery), and an armed boat, which were hourly expected, but which were prevented by the shallowness of the water; the storming party therefore advanced at the given signal (two 6-pounders fired in quick succession), and overcoming a vigorous resistance, gained possession of the fort.

With this company Captain-Lieutenant Dunn and Lieutenant Drummond appear to have been.

The main army, with the commander-in-chief, remained encamped near Biana until the 9th February, when they moved in the direction of Jeypoor, to which town a detachment under Colonel Monson was sent from Dowsah on the 18th April; on the 10th May, a second detachment, under Colonel Don, was sent against Tonk Rampoorah from Nurwalee; and on the 18th May, the main army broke up, and retraced its steps towards Agra, suffering much from the extreme heat of the weather ere it reached its destination in June.

Lieutenant-Colonel Don's force arrived before Rampoor on the 14th May, and to avoid exciting the enemy's suspicions and inducing him to block up the gateways really intended to be attacked, took up its position on the opposite side of the fort. At two a.m. on the next morning, the storming party advanced, headed by a 12-pounder, to blow the gates open, and followed by another, to keep in check a body of the enemy's cavalry; while Captain Raban, with one 12-pounder and four 6-pounders, took up a position from which he was enabled to fire upon any point of the works which the enemy might man to meet the attack; a picquet of the enemy was driven in, the first gate was blown in by the gun, the second was found open, and the third and fourth were also blown in; the storming party entered, and the town was taken possession of.

Thanks were given to Captain Raban and every officer and soldier of the detachment; the 2nd company 1st battalion, or a portion of it, was employed on this duty.

Hitherto the operations of the army had been perfectly successful, but we have now to recount two failures, in both of which, but particularly in that in Bundelcund, the artillery suffered heavily.

The Bundelcund force, under Lieutenant-Colonel Fawcett, had

been protecting that province from Holkar's incursions, and was encamped in May, 1804, near Kooch. A detachment of seven companies of native infantry, under Captain N. Smith, and fifty European artillery, from the 1st and 2nd companies 3rd battalion, under Captain-Lieutenant Feade and Lieutenant Morris, were sent against a small fort, named Baillah, in the neighbourhood.

The guns having opened on the 21st May, the *killidar* offered to surrender on the following morning if the firing was directed to cease; his offer was accepted, but availing himself of the respite, he immediately despatched intelligence to Ameer Khan, who was in the vicinity, and requested him to fall on the detachment, which he did the next morning with 8,000 cavalry, and cut up two companies of the infantry, and the whole of the artillery, with their officers, and took possession of the guns, (2 12-pounders, 1 6-pounder, 2 howitzers, and tumbrils), except one, which, with the remaining five companies, made good their retreat to Lieutenant-Colonel Fawcett's headquarters.

★★★★★★

In moving for the production of papers in the House of Commons on this occurrence, Sir Philip Francis said it had cost "two complete companies of *sipahis*, some cannon, and fifty European artillerymen, every man of whom were cut to pieces: the loss of the *sipahis* is to be lamented, that of the artillerymen is invaluable." A most infelicitous expression for the author of Junius.

★★★★★★

Lieutenant-Colonel Fawcett, alarmed at the reports he received, and unequal to the emergency in which he was placed, immediately retreated to Betwah; which movement caused much annoyance to the commander-in-chief, as it opened Bundelcund to Holkar, and left him undistracted to turn his whole force against Colonel Monson's detachment in Rajasthan. Lord Lake would have ordered the command of this force to have been previously made over to "Lieutenant-Colonel Wittit, of the artillery, a most excellent officer; but for his ill-health;" this was very indifferent; so much so, indeed, that he died on the 27th May. In him the regiment lost a most valuable officer; as a subaltern he had served with his company in Lord Cornwallis's campaigns on the coast, and was considered by Sir John Horsford one of the most superior officers in the regiment.

Colonel Martindell, after some changes, was appointed to the command of the force, and in June succeeded in capturing Mahobar, and defeating the Ram Rajah and Nagahs, and with this the campaign closed.

We must now follow Colonel Monson's force, with which was the 2nd company 2nd battalion of artillery, commanded by Captain Hutchinson and Lieutenant Winbolt, in its unfortunate retreat. Advancing, after the capture of Hinglaizgurh to the Mokundra Pass, with the object of co-operating with Colonel Murray's force from Guzerat, on the 7th July Colonel Monson received intelligence of Holkar's having crossed the Chumbul, and moved to meet him; but almost immediately learning that Colonel Murray had fallen back on the Myhie, he retired to the pass on the 8th, beating off the attacks of the enemy. Fearful, however, of the enemy getting behind him, he commenced his retreat on Kotah.

On the 12th he was again attacked, and again beat Holkar off; he pushed on for the Janee Nuddee, but the rain falling heavily, he did not reach the *ghat* till the morning of the 13th, and then finding the rivulet not fordable, he was obliged to halt till the 15th; the state of the roads was such that the guns sunk deep in the mud, several were abandoned, and most of the ammunition destroyed. On the 17th the Chumbul was reached; the Europeans were passed over on elephants, and sent on to Rampoorah, while the main body crossed over in detachments wherever fords could be found.

On the 24th there was another severe contest with the enemy, and it was not until the 27th that the last battalion, with Colonel Monson, reached Rampoorah; but here this unhappy detachment found no rest,—want of provisions forced them to push on, and after leaving a garrison under Captain Hutchinson, of the artillery, they again moved (they were however reinforced by two battalions, four guns, and some irregular cavalry, under Major Frith) to the Bunass.

On the 22nd August they reached its banks, and found it so swollen that the largest elephants could scarcely pass; three boats only could be found, and in them the treasure was sent across. On the 23rd the enemy appeared in force, and on the 24th, the river having run off a little, the baggage was got over, Monson covering the retreat by an attack on the enemy, which was at first successful, but the enemy rallying, forced him back, with the loss of his last gun; the baggage was abandoned, and, harassed by the enemy's cavalry, the broken army reached Koosialgurh during the night; from hence they moved in a square to the Biana Pass, where they hoped for some respite; but Holkar, bringing his guns to bear, forced them to continue their flight, and parties of broken and disordered fugitives were all of Monson's army that arrived at Agra.

In crossing the Bunass on the 24th Lieutenant Winbolt, of the artillery, was drowned. He was an officer of high promise, and one who stood high in the opinion of Sir J. Horsford, in whose company he had served on the coast in the campaigns of 1790-1-2.

To check Holkar, the army was called out again; the horse artillery and other troops from Cawnpoor marched on Agra on the 3rd September, and towards the end of the month the camp was formed between Agra and Secundra. Holkar was too wary to be led into a general action, and moving northwards with his main body, he was followed by Lord Lake, who reached Delhi and relieved the siege on the 15th October. Holkar moved towards Parriput, and crossed the Jumna into the Upper Dooab; Lake (with the horse artillery, cavalry, and reserve brigade, under Colonel Don) crossed near Delhi on the 31st, and leaving all private wheel-carriages and all baggage that could possibly be spared, pushed on, determined to give Holkar no rest.

This rapid movement relieved Colonel Burn, who, with some *nujeebs*, was shut up in the ruined fort of Shamlee by Holkar. Following closely, Lord Lake came in sight of him near Meerut, but he fled with all speed, by the route of Hassur to Futteygurh. On the 16th, Lake was within sixty miles of Futteygurh, and starting again at night, he made great exertions to come up with him. Just as he mounted his horse, news came of the decisive victory gained by Major-General Fraser over the Mahrattas at Deig, an inspiriting omen to his own troops. At dawn on the 17th, they reached the skirts of the enemy's camp; the horses were at their picquets, the men sleeping beside them, when their sleep was either broken or rendered final by discharges of grape poured in upon them from the horse-artillery guns; the dragoons charged, and the enemy took to flight,—Holkar among the first.

The blowing up of a tumbril had first alarmed him, but he was persuaded it was the morning gun being fired at Futteygurh; but the firing continuing, the cry of "Lord Lake's army" arose, and a general flight followed; some took refuge in trees, and might have escaped, but from their indiscretion in firing on our troops, who, thus taught in what direction to look, soon brought them down with their pistols. The pursuit continued for upwards of 10 miles, which, added to the previous march of 58, made a total of 68 miles in 24 hours, and when it is recollected that this had been preceded by 350 miles in a fortnight, it may be considered one of the most surprising feats on record, and speaking more powerfully to the state of efficiency of the regiments so employed, than words can do.

The services of the horse artillery were acknowledged by Lord Lake; in writing to the governor-general, he says:

> I have great satisfaction in reporting to your lordship the very meritorious conduct of Captain Brown and the corps of horse artillery under his command, who, by the rapidity of their movements, were able to do great execution. Captain Brown's great attention in the management of his corps, and his zeal and activity when called into action, have on every occasion merited my best acknowledgments.

And in the General Order, November 18th, he returned his thanks:

> To Captain Brown, and officers and men of the horse artillery, for their highly meritorious and intrepid behaviour in the engagement of yesterday.

The officers with the horse artillery were Captain C. Brown, Lieutenants H. Starke and J. Young. The wounded were 1 European, 1 Indian, and 4 horses; the killed 1 *lascar* and 7 horses.

The main body of the army, which had been left at Delhi on the 1st November, moved in the direction of Govindhur, and on the 13th attacked the Mahratta Army under the walls of Deig, gained a complete victory, and captured 87 guns, all mounted on field-carriages, and fitted with elevating screws and every apparatus; among them were six of the 18-pounders presented to the Mahrattas in 1791, and (which must have been a pleasing circumstance to Colonel Monson, who fell into the command on the death of Major-General Fraser) fourteen of the guns, nine tumbrils, and four casts of those which had been lost in his disastrous campaign.

In this action the artillery lost 4 Europeans and 5 natives killed; 6 Europeans and 19 natives wounded: Captain Butler had a horse killed under him.

Lord Lake followed Holkar from Futtehgurh on the 20th; crossed the Jumna near Muttra, on the 28th; sent on the captured guns to Agra, and ordered out a battering-train, which joining him on the 10th, he moved towards Deig, and on the 13th took up a position. Trenches were opened during the night, and a breach being ready by the 23rd, the place was carried by storm. Captain Raban accompanied the storming party with a detail of artillery to spike the guns, and distinguished himself by the way in which he performed this duty.

Lieutenant Groves, of the artillery, was killed on the 20th December, and Lieutenant T. D. Smith wounded; 100 guns were taken, together with many tumbrils.

The details of this siege, as well as those of Bhurtpoor, Gunnourie, Komona, and Adjegurh, are so fully recorded in that valuable publication the *East-India Military Repository*, that it would only unnecessarily swell this work, were more than the briefest allusion made, compatible with our object.

For this siege six or eight 18-pounders, four 8-inch and four 5½-inch mortars were all the siege ordnance available.

The insufficient provision of ordnance and stores for siege purposes will henceforth often strike the reader; and the question why—possessed, as Bengal is, of an inland navigation from one extremity of the presidency to the other, offering every facility for a speedy and cheap conveyance of stores—ample materials had not been pushed forward to meet our wants, must continually recur. The suddenness of the campaign cannot be admitted as a valid reason; the war had been deliberately entered on eighteen months before, and it was known that the enemy possessed many strongholds which required battering-trains for their reduction.

The first campaign had given us Agra, a place admirably situated for a depot, with reference to the scene of war, to which an adequate equipment should have been forwarded; but it was not done, and the want was severely felt in the course of this campaign. If ample supplies are not available against a fortified place, and it is absolutely necessary to reduce it, men's lives must be substituted for shot and shells; in some cases, no doubt, *time* is most precious, and it may be a matter of calculation whether time or men can best be spared; but when near our own frontier, there can be no excuse for the improvidence which has failed to provide the requisite stores, and by that means to take from the commander the choice between expenditure of his troops or of the munitions of war.

In most we must attribute the blame to the cumbrous and inefficient machinery of the Military Board, in whose province lies the supervision of the magazines; but the board, composed of many members, becomes a screen for individual responsibility, and this must always be the case until each member is vested with the sole control of the details of his own department, subject only to a discussion in the board of the general question, that each may have the benefit of his colleagues' opinions, and be made aware of what is going on in other departments, that all may work in concert.

The opinion above given of the inefficient state of our siege-trains is fully borne out by that recorded by the Marquis of Hastings in his *Summary*, when, speaking of Hattrass, he says, "One of my earliest military cares on arriving in India had been to satisfy myself why we had made so comparatively unfavourable a display in sieges." The details at once unfolded the cause: it is well known that nothing can be more insignificant than shells thrown with long intervals; and we never brought forward more than four or five mortars where we undertook the capture of a fortified place. Hence the bombardment was futile, so that at last the issue was to be staked on mounting a breach and fighting hand to hand with a soldiery skilful as well as gallant, in defending the prepared intrenchments.

This was not the oversight of the Bengal Artillery officers, for no men can be better instructed in the theory, or more careful in the practice of their profession than they are; it was imputable to a false economy on the part of government. The outlay for providing for the transport of mortars, shells, and platforms in due quantity would certainly have been considerable, and it was on that account forborne; the miserable carriages of the country, hired for the purpose, where a military exertion was contemplated, were utterly unequal to the service, and constantly failed under the unusual weight in the deep roads through which they had to pass. Therefore, we never sat down before a place of real strength furnished with the means which a proper calculation would have allotted for its reduction.

These remarks have been particularly brought out by studying the details of the attack on Bhurtpoor, which next employed Lord Lake's army, but which we shall not enter into, referring the reader to the same authority as mentioned when speaking of the siege of Deig, and contenting ourselves with a very concise account of the operations.

The army marched from Deig to Bhurtpoor; trenches were opened on the 4th of January, 1805; batteries were erected, a breach effected, and an unsuccessful storm attempted, on the 9th; other batteries were raised and a fresh breach made, but the enemy were so active in stockading it every night, that a second attack could not be made until the 21st: this, also, was unsuccessful. During the storm, the British cavalry were forced to turn out to keep off Holkar.

On the 23rd, a convoy, slenderly escorted, was plundered; a second and a larger one was successfully brought in on the 28th, containing, among other stores, 8,000 18-pounder shot. On the 6th February the army changed ground; Meer Khan crossed the Jumna on the 7th, and was pursued by Major-General Smith, with all the cavalry and horse artillery, who came up with and defeated him at Afzulgurh, near Moradabad, on the 2nd of March; the scattered remains of this army recrossed the Ganges, and Major-General Smith returned to camp on the 23rd, after a march of 700 miles.

The siege had been still carried on; the Bombay Army joined on the 10th February, but the troops, although nearly exhausted, petitioned to be allowed to finish the operation; the artillery were particularly eager, for, though few in number, and fatigued beyond conception by working the guns without a relief since the commencement of the siege, the thoughts of being deprived of their post distressed them exceedingly, and they entreated permission to be allowed to discharge the duties of their station alone.

Regular approaches were made, and the batteries pushed on to within 400 yards of the walls, but the means of arming them were very insufficient; six 18-pounders, four heavy mortars, four light mortars, and two 12-pounders to take off the defences, appear to have been the extent of ordnance preparations brought against a place six or eight miles in circumference! On the morning of the 21st, a sally made by the enemy was driven back, and in the afternoon a storm was attempted, covered by the artillery guns drawn out on the plain, but without success. A fourth attack was made the following day, but it equally failed. The siege was still continued, but the enemy offering to give up the fortress on certain terms, it was accepted, and the army finally broke up from its melancholy camp at Bhurtpoor on the 21st April, and after remaining a short time on the banks of the Chumbul, watching Scindiah, retired to Agra the following month.

During the siege, the artillery lost Lieutenant Percival, killed on 9th January; Lieutenant Gowing, killed on 22nd February; Captain Nelly, wounded on 21st February; Captain Pennington, wounded on 22nd February; and Lieutenant Swiney, wounded on 21st February.

From this melancholy detail it is cheering to turn to the successful proceedings of Captain Hutchinson, of the artillery, who, it will be recollected, was left during Monson's retreat in command of Rampoorah, and whose judicious application of a small force led to the most brilliant results.

On the 17th January, 1805, he marched with his company, 2nd company 2nd battalion (or a portion of it), 320 *sipahis*, a few irregulars, and two 6-pounders, against Gemeena; reaching it as the moon rose on the 18th, he instantly commenced the attack. The road to the gate was blocked up by loaded *hackeries*, their wheels removed, and thus the approach of the guns was prevented; the *hackeries* were set fire to, steps were cut in the side of the ramparts, and the *sipahis* mounted; their only officer, Lieutenant Purvis, being wounded. Captain Hutchinson supplied his place, and aided by Corporals Cross and Hislop, mounted the ramparts; a hole was made through the parapet, and the assailants increasing in number, the enemy were driven back on the gate; but the wicket being forced open by the butt ends of the muskets, the place was captured with but little loss.

Lord Lake, reporting the above to Lord Wellesley, says:

> The enterprise and gallantry this meritorious officer has on every occasion manifested during his command at Rampoorah has never been more conspicuous than on the present occasion, where he appears to have accomplished a most arduous and dangerous undertaking, with a spirit and perseverance which reflects on him the highest credit.

On the 22nd February, he went against Bommongaon, a mud fort, with high ramparts and a ditch; the gates built up and remarkably well defended by a garrison of 300 men. His party consisted of his own company and 160 *sipahis*, with two 6-pounders and two howitzers; these light guns made no impression, but on the 24th two 12-pounders arrived, and by the evening a practicable breach was effected, but the assault being delayed till morning, the garrison made off in the night.

On the 25th February he moved to Karawul, a large walled town, with a number of bastions, four small guns, and 1,100 men as a garrison; he placed his two 12-pounders and one 6-pounder in battery within 300 yards of the walls; his battery was formed with empty tumbrils and ammunition-boxes filled with earth, finished up with bags of grain; his two howitzers and remaining 6-pounder were placed in a similar manner in another direction. By the afternoon of the 26th a breach was made, which he immediately stormed.

Captain Hutchinson was not unmindful of the deserts of his subordinates; he says:

> I should be proud if his Excellency General Lake would notice Corporals Cross and Hislop; they are soldiers who have distinguished themselves more than once, and there are not two better or braver men in the 2nd company 2nd battalion of artillery.

★★★★★★

Cross was appointed to the Ordnance Commissariat Department, and at the present moment (1852) is living at Penang, having, after a long, laborious, and honourable career, been allowed to retire on a pension with the rank of captain.

★★★★★★

His next exploit was against Darrara, a fort with a broad and deep ditch and high ramparts, the gate defended by a ditch and covered with an outwork. Captain Hutchinson placed his garrison in two batteries, one at 35 yards from the counterscarp, one still nearer, and by noon on the 21st March, a breach was effected; the storming party, headed by six artillerymen, whom it would be injustice not to name,—Corporals Cross and Hislop, Gunners Campbell and Johnstone, Matrosses Muller and Hudson,—moved to the attack, and after overcoming a severe opposition, succeeded in gaining possession of the fort; of the enemy between 60 and 70 were killed, and the remainder taken prisoners.

Of the artillerymen, Johnstone was killed, and Hudson shot through the body and arm, after which he charged and killed three of the enemy.

But we must once more return to Lord Lake's army, whom we left at Agra. The rainy season limited their repose. Holkar's restless spirit urged him to collect his scattered followers, at the head of whom, equipped with 60 guns, he approached Muttra in October; Lord Lake followed, and Holkar moved to the north. It soon became a perfect chase. Holkar fled into the Punjab; Lake crossed the Sutlej on the 7th December, and was on the point of engaging him on the banks of the Beas on the 25th, but was prevented by positive instructions from the Governor-General, who probably wished to avoid embroiling himself with the Seikhs. A treaty was therefore reluctantly entered into, and the army returned slowly to Dehli.

Captain Pennington was commissary of ordnance with this force; Captain C. Brown, Lieutenant-Fireworkers Frith and Boileau, were with the horse artillery, and Captain T. Greene, Lieutenants Hay and Rodber, with the 1st company 1st battalion.

In closing the account of these glorious campaigns, it will not be out of place here to record the names of the officers sharing in them, and we fortunately have a memorandum, in Sir John Horsford's writing, of those entitled to share in the prize-money, which gives the necessary information.

1st Campaign.

Lieut.-Col. Horsford,	Capt. Best,
Capt. Butler,	„ J. Robinson,
„ T. Greene,	„ Mathews,
„ Raban,	Lieut. M. Browne,
„ Nelly,	„ Morris,
„ Constable,	„ S. Hay, ⎫ Agra and
„ Hutchinson,	„ Beagham, ⎬ Laswaree
„ W. Shipton,	„ W. Parker, ⎭ only.

2nd Campaign.

Lieut.-Col. Horsford,	Lieut. Young,
Capt. C. Brown,	„ Grove,
„ Raban,	„ Gowing,
„ Nelly,	„ Pollock,
„ Hutchinson,	„ Parker,
„ Best,	„ Hay,
„ Butler,	„ Percival,
„ Paschaud,	„ T. D. Smith,
„ Mathews,	Capt. Hinde, ⎫ Bhurtpoor
Lieut. M. Browne,	„ Dunn, ⎬ from
„ H. Starke,	„ Pennington, ⎨ January
„ Swiney,	Lieut. W. H. Frith, ⎭ to April,

The paucity of British troops in the ceded provinces induced several of the *zemindars* to resist the revenue authorities, and, among others, Doondia Khan, who possessed two strong mud forts in the vicinity of Aligurh. The failure of the attacks on Bhurtpoor added to their contumacy, but the want of power to punish, rendered it necessary to pass it over for the time, and be content with some show of submission, which Doondia Khan made to Major-General Smith on his return from Afzulgurh to Bhurtpoor.

Causes of complaint continued to arise, and towards the end of 1806, the collector reported he had strengthened Komona with a new outwork and attacked a neighbouring *zemindar*. All efforts at accommodation proving useless, a force was collected in August, 1807, under Major-General Dickens, and proceeded against Komona on the 12th of October. With this force were—

Company.	Battalion.	Captain-Lieutenant.	Lieutenants.
3	1	Lindsay	M'Quake, Harris, Pryce, Forrester, and Parlby.
2	2		

Lieutenant-Colonel Horsford was also present, commanding a brigade, but also specially directing the artillery.

An assault was made on the 18th November, but proved unsuccessful, owing to the determined opposition the enemy made, and the way in which he defended the breach, with mines, powder-bags, burning *choppahs*, &c. The assailants were beat back with heavy loss, but the enemy deserted the place during the night.

Lieutenants Harris and McQuake, acting as engineers, were wounded; 5 Europeans and 9 natives killed; 10 Europeans and 10 *lascars*, of the artillery, were wounded.

From Komona the force proceeded to Gunnouree on the 22nd November, and carried on the attack of that fort until the 11th December, when the enemy evacuated it.

For the detail of these operations we would refer the reader to the fourth volume of the *East-India Military Repository*.

The strength of the artillery, as fixed in 1802, having proved itself quite insufficient for the duties of the Presidency, in August, 1805, five companies of *golundaz* were raised; they were formed from the "component parts" which remained on the alteration in 1802. These companies were added without any officers, but in the following year (19th June, 1806) a lieutenant-colonel and major were added to each battalion.

The regiment, therefore, at this period consisted of—

Colonels	Lieut.-Colonels	Majors	Captains	Capt.-Lieutenants	Lieutenants	Lieutenant-Fireworkers	Sergeants	Corporals	Gunners	Horse. Trumpeters	Horse. Matrosses
3	6	6	21	21	42	42	4	4	10		40

Foot.					Golundaz.				Lascars.				
Serjeants	Corporals	Gunners	Drummers	Matrosses	Native Officers	Havildars	Naiks	Drummers	Privates	Serangs	1st Tindals	2nd Tindals	Lascars
105	105	210	42	1680	10	40	40		500	40	81	81	2750

The staff are omitted in this abstract, as they would only tend to swell the headings, and their number is trifling.

In July three additional companies of *golundaz* were added of similar strength.

In Bundelcund disturbances still continued, and during several years a force continued to find employment in that district. In February, 1806, Gohud was taken, and in January, 1807, Chumar, near Kooch. The general orders on the capture of the latter, notice:

> The professional ability and zealous emulation displayed by Captain Hopper, of the artillery employed on that service in preparing the way for which all are entitled to his lordship's particular praise and thanks.

Captain Turton and Lieutenant G. Faithfull also appear to have been in this campaign.

The following year, towards the conclusion, the force again took the field to reduce Adjeegurh, which Luchmun Dowlah refused to yield, agreeably to stipulation.

A portion marched against Heerapoor, with which were Major Brooke, Lieutenants Granishaw and C. H. Campbell, of the artillery; after ascending the pass on the 19th December, with much difficulty, the fort was reconnoitred, and batteries formed of fascines and sandbags on the 20th, and by 3 p.m. a breach was made; a fire was kept up at intervals during the night, the enemy made a feeble attack on an outpost, and evacuated the fort during the night.

The report of the governor-general's agent to the secretary to government said:

> The exertions of the pioneers and their officers, and those of Captain Brooke, Lieutenants Granishaw and Campbell, the Europeans and *lascars* of the artillery, in preparing the batteries and serving and laying the guns, could not be surpassed.

Captain Brooke's services were also acknowledged in orders by Major-General Martindell.

On the 22nd January the force was brought into contact with the enemy, who, surrounded in the strong position of Rugowley, made a desperate resistance, and, although driven to a corner, rendered it necessary to withdraw the troops from the attack.

Major Brooke, Captain-Lieutenant Ferris, Lieutenants D. Macleod, Granishaw, Campbell, and Marshall, were present in this action.

On the 27th January the army took up their position before Adjeegurh; a battery was erected on the plain, but the distance was found to have been miscalculated, probably from the overhanging appearance which forts built on hills assume, and it was found necessary to occupy the spur up which the road ran to the gate. Much labour was required to convey the heavy guns to their positions, and it was not until the morning of the 11th February that they opened their fire; it continued during the 12th and the morning of the 13th, when the whole of a wall came down; the *killidar* then came out, and the fort was given up.

> To the artillery the heavy duties of the siege more particularly fell; their exertions were great, and vied with the natural objects they had to encounter. Their fire was inimitably well directed, and the commanding officer must ever feel himself indebted to the officers and men who conducted it.
>
> The judgment, zeal, and energy of Captain Brooke, commanding the artillery, his personal and unremitting exertions, were so conspicuous during the siege, that to do ample justice to the merits of that valuable officer, the commanding officer cannot convey in terms too strong his high sense of approbation and approval.

A small force was also employed this year in reducing Bhowanee, a fort in the Hurrianah country. The inhabitants had been in the habit of plundering all travellers, and at length ventured on the baggage of a British detachment. The chief met a representation by a peremptory denial of reparation in terms of insolence. The force in Rewaree, under Lieutenant-Colonel Ball, moved out towards the end of August, and arriving on the 27th, allowed the enemy twenty-four hours to consider. The terms were absolutely rejected, and on the 28th batteries were quickly erected; their fire opened the following morning, and by noon a breach was made, and the place carried by assault after a vigorous resistance.

> To Captain Mason, in the general command of the artillery, the very able arrangement of that officer's department throughout, but particularly in conducting the duties of the breaching-batteries, with the very heavy and well-directed fire that was so rapidly kept up, in covering the advance and approach of the storming party to the points of attack, entitles Captain Mason to every commendation, and reflects great credit on the officers and men under his command.

This detachment order was republished in the government General Order, detailing the service.

We have been unable to ascertain what portion of the regiment, and what officers, were on this occasion employed.

We must now advert to two important additions which were made to the regiment in the course of this year. In August the governor-general, adverting to the original establishment of the experimental horse artillery, the success of which on various occasions in the field has fully confirmed the judgment which was formed of the superior efficiency of a corps of that description for service in India, determined to make a considerable augmentation to the corps, and place it on a permanent establishment. It was accordingly directed to be increased to three troops; the officers and men to be drawn from the foot artillery.

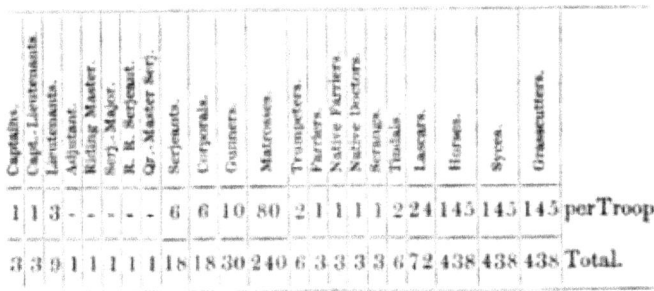

The senior captain exercised the command over the whole, in addition to the command of his own troop, subject to the orders of the commandant of artillery.

In December orders were issued for the formation of a corps of ordnance-drivers. Hitherto the drivers for the ordnance carriages had been hired as required, and discharged when the service was over; this system had worked so ill, and its faults had been so strongly brought to light in the late campaigns, that it was now resolved to introduce a better plan. An organised corps was raised, sufficient to provide a driver to every two bullocks, and divided into companies, which were attached to companies of artillery, in the same manner as the *lascars*, with whom they were assimilated as much as possible. They were clothed in uniform, and were not to be discharged except by the authority of the commandant of artillery or officers commanding the principal stations of the army.

Raised from the middle *castes*—the Gwalas and Aheeas chiefly,—

and attached to the service by the regular pay, the pension when worn out, and the treatment they received, this proved a valuable addition to the regiment.

In November two companies of independent *golundaz* were raised, to take the duties of Prince of Wales' Island.

We have omitted to state that in May, 1808, Colonel Carnegie resigned the command of the regiment and sailed for England. He was succeeded by Colonel Horsford, who had, with so much credit to himself, been commanding the artillery in the field. Colonel Horsford originally entered the corps as a private; he was born of a good family, and well educated, but his friends wishing him to enter the church, he evaded it by enlisting in the Honourable Company's service, and coming to Bengal as a private in the artillery, under the assumed name of Rover, and in 1778 he was a sergeant in Captain Thelwall's, or the 1st, company.

Inquiries having been made for him, it is said he was suspected by Colonel Pearse, who had employed him in copying some papers, from his pointing out an error in a Greek quotation; his appearance answering to the description may also have furnished a clue. Colonel Pearse tried him by calling out his name suddenly as he was leaving the room; the test was successful; his confusion betrayed his identity, and he was promoted to a cadetship in the regiment, and continued to rise by seniority. He was employed in the campaigns against Tippoo in 1791-2 and 1799, establishing for himself a high name, both as a practical and scientific artillery officer; his advent to the command of the regiment was hailed with universal pleasure and satisfaction, for much benefit was expected to the corps by the manner in which he would exercise his authority, increased as it was by the great personal influence which his character had established.

In 1810 the regiment was again called on to take part in an expedition, beyond seas. In the preceding year a force, chiefly of Madras troops, was sent against the Isle of France, and occupied Rodriguez; it was reinforced by Bengal troops, and directed against the remaining islands in 1810.

The 6th company 1st battalion of artillery sailed on the expedition, but had little opportunity of gaining distinction. Bourbon was occupied in July, and the force sailing for the Isle of France, landed at an unexpected point, and moved forward with rapidity and decision. Fort Malartic was carried by assault, and the town surrendered in December.

The officers, Capt.-Lieutenant A. Graham; Lieutenant T. Pereira; Lieut.-Fireworker Ewart, I. Rawlins, H. C. Baker and T. D. Fordyce, accompanied the artillery; and the native troops were decorated with a medal, not so much for the service, probably, as for the purpose of stimulating the native army to embark with alacrity for service beyond seas.

In this year the regiment furnished a portion for a far more serious conflict, in which native troops were once again brought into personal contest with Europeans, an event which had not occurred since the destruction of the French power in the Carnatic; we refer to the expedition to Java.

The artillery detachment was as follows:—

Major Caldwell, Commandant.   Lieut. J. Scott, Adjutant.

Company.	Battalions.	Lascar Companies.	Captains.	Captain Lieutenants.	Lieutenants.	Lieutenant-Fireworkers.
7	1	15, 16	W. Richards	J. D. Smith	Harris	Archer
1	2	19, 24	J. Dundas H. Faithful	J. Farrington Cameron	... ...	Farmabie W. Bell

3rd Independent Golundaz.

The detachment embarked on the 11th March, and reached Malacca in April, where the Madras division joined; the expedition remained inactive till the 11th June, almost the only event being the burning of one of the Bengal store-ships laden with powder; and this occurred fortunately without doing any damage to the fleet. Lieutenant Archer died on the voyage.

On the 4th August the fleet anchored near Chillingching; the troops were landed, and took possession of Batavia without opposition on the 8th; an attempt by the enemy to drive them out the following night failed; and on the 10th the British advanced and drove the enemy from their intrenched camp at Weltervreeden. Captain Noble, with the Madras Horse Artillery, performed the chief artillery duties on this occasion.

The enemy having concentrated their force in the strong lines around Fort Cornelis, a battering-train was landed, and trenches were opened at about 800 yards from the position. These the enemy flooded by cutting dams on the 19th; on the 20th batteries for twelve and eight 18-pounders and nine howitzers and mortars were commenced; on the 21st the enemy opened a heavy fire on the unfinished batteries; but nevertheless the guns were mounted by the 22nd, when the enemy made a vigorous sally, and overcoming the unarmed working parties, who were not even protected by a guard, succeeded for a moment in capturing the batteries; but they were quickly driven back.

On the 23rd and 24th a heavy fire was kept up by the enemy from twenty-four 32-pounders on the batteries and trenches; but although, on the 24th the fire of the nearest redoubt was repeatedly silenced, and towards evening several of the enemy's guns were dismounted by the fire from the batteries, yet it became evident that without regular approaches the place could not be carried (unless by a *coup de main*), and this would require time, labour, and exposure in a baneful climate, which was to be avoided by all means.

Lieutenant Farnabie was killed by a stray shot while standing in the trench, and Captain Richards was wounded by some cartridges taking fire in the battery during these two days.

It was determined to storm the lines on the 26th. To occupy the enemy, a party, covered with nine guns, took post behind a rising ground on the right, and opened their fire, while the main column, under Major-General Gillespie, attacked the left, and after sustaining a severe loss, finally succeeded in carrying the lines,—capturing 6,000 prisoners and 280 pieces of fine brass ordnance.

In the orders issued to the army after this exploit, no mention is made of the artillery; and this omission has been attributed to a dislike said to have been taken to the Bengal Artillery. That some such feeling was supposed to exist, we may conclude from the following passage, which appears in a letter from an engineer officer on the island to Colonel Horsford, written in October:—"

> You will see that the artillery were left out in the thanks to the army on the 26th August; but allow me to say, and that *decidedly*, that had it not been from the fire of our 18–pounders on the

23rd, 24th, and 25th, I believe not a man would have returned from the storm of the 26th without some remembrance, as the day before the storm 130 men and 4 officers were killed and wounded by our batteries; the consequence was, that their artillerymen positively refused to work at the batteries, and hardly a gun was fired by the enemy during the storm, although they had plenty of time; in short, I declare to you that I scarcely ever saw a more destructive fire kept up than by our batteries; indeed the killed and wounded in a hospital four miles to the south of Cornelis showed it, as well as the number of guns that were dismounted.

I was constantly in the batteries. The effect of our artillery, when they did fire, was so conspicuous, that at a *practice* I never saw better firing, *especially* of three guns on the right of the twelve-gun battery, commanded by Lieutenant Cameron. I declare to you I never witnessed anything like it, for every shot he fired went into the enemy's embrasures; the consequence was, that in an hour and a half the redoubt which was opposed to it was silenced.

In Sir Samuel Achmuty's report to Lord Minto, the following mention is made of the ordnance branches:—

I have the satisfaction to assure you that both the artillery and engineers were actuated by the same zeal in performing their respective duties which has been so conspicuous in all ranks and departments, though, from deficiency of the means at their disposal, their operations were unavoidably embarrassed with uncommon difficulties.

From Cornelis, General Jansens fled to Bintenzorg, and thence to Samarang, near which town he took up a position, Jattoo, on high and rugged hills, defended by thirty pieces of artillery, and the road cut off by *cheveux de frise*; he was attacked on the 16th of September by a detachment of 1,200 men, under Colonel Gibbs, with whom were 110 artillerymen and six guns; with the artillery were Major Caldwell, Lieutenants Scott, Farrington, Cameron, and Ralfe. Two of the guns were sent to the right with a force to seize on a hill which overlooked the enemy's left, while the remainder were placed in a position in front to throw their shot across the valley into the enemy's position. As soon as the two detached guns opened their fire, the advance rushed on; the enemy were surprised and fled, doing little execution with their artillery, which was all taken.

This was the last effort of General Jansens; he fled to Salatiga and capitulated; Fort Ludovick was surrendered, and the war, as far as the Dutch were concerned, may be said to have ended; but to avoid returning to Java again, we will here notice such other affairs as occurred during the time the British held possession of the island. But before continuing the narrative, we will here insert a sketch of the medal granted to the native troops employed in the expedition; and we may also state that medals were for this service granted to officers in H.M.'s service, but to none under the rank of commanding officer of a corps, or holding an important staff office.

The next service on which this force was employed was the expedition under Gillespie to the Palmsbury River, in April, 1822, in which were Captain S. Shaw, Lieutenants Hill and Delafosse.

In June, they again started for Samarang. Major Butler, who had previously come round, commanded the artillery; Lieutenants Farrington, Cameron, and Hill accompanied. They reached Djocjocarta on the 17th of June, and prepared for the attack of the "*kraken*," or fortified residence of the *Sultan* of Mataram, three miles in circumference, armed with many guns, and defended by a broad wet ditch with drawbridges, by 17,000 regular troops, and an armed population of 100,000. The enemy were kept on the alert by a heavy fire till three in the morning of the 20th, they were then allowed a respite, and two hours before daylight the troops moved to the assault and carried the works. Major Butler, one drummer, and eleven rank and file of the artillery, were wounded.

In the orders, we find:

> The commander of the forces performs a pleasing task in recognising the valuable services of Major Butler, commanding the artillery, who has uniformly displayed his wonted zeal and

indefatigable exertion; the commander of the forces is therefore happy in the opportunity of bearing public testimony to the professional superiority and valuable acquirements of this excellent officer.

And Lieutenant Cameron's conduct is also spoken of.

Other expeditions took place during the time we held possession of the island, in which, Captain-Lieutenant Shaw, Lieutenant Farrington, Lieutenants Cameron, Harris, and Delafosse, took part; in those against the town of Boni, in 1814, and against Macassar, in 1816, Lieutenant Farrington is mentioned in orders, and attention drawn to his exertions.

******

In the 'other expeditions' mentioned during that time, the Java Light Cavalry, with H. A. attached, was formed; Capt.-Lieutenant Boileau, Lieutenant Gowan, and Lieutenant Parlby accompanied it; but we believe this corps was never engaged.

******

Bundlecund still continued the seat of war; Gopal Sing, availing himself of the natural fastnesses of the country, evaded our troops continually. He was overtaken near Perereea in February (and Lieutenant Timbrell is mentioned on this occasion), but escaping, he fled to the hills, from whence he came out the following month, and before assistance could be sent, burned the cantonment of Tiroha, maintaining a harassing and desultory warfare, which, without producing any marked events, kept the troops constantly on the move during that and the following year; and it was only brought to a close by the siege of Callingur, in February, 1812; after which, Gopal Sing returned to his allegiance.

Callingur is a fort situated on one of those detached rocky eminences abounding in Bundlecund, and which require little aid from art, as they are almost natural fortifications. The rock at the summit forms a natural scarp, of from ten to twenty feet high, and the whole side of the hill is very difficult of access. The only entrance is in the centre of the northern wall, and the approach to it is by a steep pathway winding up the face of the hill; this gained, a succession of gates bar the entrance to the fort.

The force under Colonel Martindell assembled on the 19th January; on the 21st occupied a small hill, within 800 yards, which promised to be the most favourable point for attack. The 22nd, 23rd, and 24th were employed in clearing the jungle and making a road for the guns, and, on the 25th, two 18-pounders were, with great labour, got up. In the night, two more guns and two mortars followed, and were placed in battery: two other batteries were erected at the foot of the hill, against the main gateway, and the whole being ready by the 28th, opened with great effect. The enemy's guns were immediately dismounted, and the bastion opposed to the guns on the hill demolished.

The town was taken this day; and the batteries continuing to play till the 2nd of February, the breach was supposed practicable, and a party advanced to storm it, but finding a perpendicular ascent of twenty feet, their ladders crushed and broken by the showers of large stones the enemy rolled down, the party were forced to retire with heavy loss: the *killadar*, however, was glad to come to terms, and capitulated on the 8th February.

Major Fuller commanded the artillery in this siege, and their exertions were acknowledged in general orders:—

> The governor-general deems it his duty to express his concurrence in the honourable testimony borne to the distinguished services of the artillery and engineer departments by Colonel Martindell.

The neighbouring districts of Boglecund and Rewah were, during the next year, the scenes of petty warfare, similar to what had taken place in Bundlecund; marked by no features of great importance, yet involving much exertion on the part of the troops, particularly the artillery employed, from the mountainous and rugged features of the country and the number of *nullahs* and rivers intersecting it. We have but few records of this campaign, and are therefore unable to give the details, interesting as they would be to those who are acquainted with the country, and can, from the present state of the Heerapoor, Bisramgunge, and Bundry Ghats, easily imagine the difficulties they presented at the time of which we are now writing.

About this period an alteration took place in the *matériel* of the regiment, by the introduction of the Gribeauval pattern of gun-carriage and the long caisson for ammunition, a description of which will be found in the fourth chapter. The *matériel* and the means of draught occupied much attention at this period, and there is every reason to believe that the recently organised driver corps and the gun bullocks about this period, under the particular care and attention of Lieutenant-Colonel Grace, commanding the artillery in the field, were in a most efficient state. The bullocks were carefully selected and trained, fairly worked and well looked after, and the consequence was, that we find the gun bullocks condemned as past their work, selling, from the high condition they were in, for the purpose of slaughter, at a higher rate than the good young cattle bought to replace them were costing.

As the next war in which the army was engaged proved how insufficient the strength of the regiment was, and caused a considerable addition to the native portion of it, we propose here to notice the additions to the end of 1815, although the war commenced the preceding year: by so doing, we shall avoid breaking the thread of the narrative of the Goorkha war.

The last additions we have noticed were two companies of independent *golundaz*, added in 1809; a third company was raised in February, 1812, and a fourth in August, 1814; in 1815 four additional companies of *golundaz* were raised to meet the wants of the service; so that the regiment now consisted of 1 horse brigade of three troops, 3 European battalions of 7 companies each, and 1 Native battalion of 16 companies, together with *lascars* (42 companies) and ordnance-drivers (26 companies); but these additions to the numerical strength of the regiment had been made without any corresponding increase to the ranks of the commissioned officers.

This was peculiarly galling; for while struggling with the difficulties of their position, the officers had the mortification of seeing the numbers of the infantry increased by whole regiments at a time, bringing fair promotion with the augmentations, while, in their own branch, from 1802 to 1815, the troops and companies had increased from 21 to 40, yet, with the exception of the field officers added in 1806, not an officer had been given: the infantry had during that time risen from 25 to 31 regiments.

An important change in the location of the regiment took place in 1813. The headquarters had hitherto been in Fort William, and moved out to Dum-Dum during the cold months for practice and exercise; this year, barracks having been completed, Dum-Dum was permanently occupied as the headquarters of the artillery,—a change, no doubt, adding much to the comfort of all ranks, for there can be no comparison as to the comfort and health of men cooped up within the narrow limits of a fortress, and those occupying an airy roomy cantonment,—even if a cantonment surrounded with swamps, as Dum-Dum is; and in spite of which it is now one of the most salubrious of stations for European troops.

As it had been used as a practice-ground for upwards of thirty years, many bungalows of different degrees of stability had sprung up,—chiefly, we believe, of mat and thatch; and as the officers doubtless were not idle while the barracks were building, we may believe that they found plenty of accommodation ready for them; and houses, of a more durable nature, soon began to spring up, some on new sites, others replacing the temporary habitations. A mess-house, we believe, had been previously built by Government; occupying the site of the centre room of the present building, which, by gradual additions and alterations, has reached its present handsome proportions. These were chiefly made in 1824-5, in 1836, and in 1841-2, when the verandah was raised and the portico added. The last improvement was made in 1845, when the roof, put on twenty years before, requiring to be renewed, the centre rooms were raised several feet.

The other houses in the cantonment have hardly undergone less change: brick walls first replaced the mats, and then *puckah* roofs superseded the thatch; the usual additions of rooms and verandahs taking place. The very last of the old bungalows was recently transformed into a *puckah* house, and, save the old avenue, which all declare to have been exactly in its present state when they landed half a century ago, there is little in the present cantonment which can be recognized by those who first occupied it permanently. The barracks had an upper story placed on them about 1830; the church was built in 1819; and a year or two ago a racket-court, for the men of the regiment, was built: the officers erected one for themselves in 1834.

For many years Dum-Dum was a very favourite station; its mess, its amateur theatre, its band, and, at one time, its pack of fox-hounds, rendered it a place of resort to many from Calcutta and the neighbouring stations; but the gradual change in the location of the artillery has necessarily reduced the numbers there, and the heavy tax upon the means of living, caused by the station being placed on half-*batta* in 1829, causes all who can to avoid it; and consequently hardly any are to be found there save the staff of the regiment of the station and the battalions quartered there, with the young men just arrived from England and awaiting their dispatch to the provinces.

CHAPTER 7
Rocket Troop Raised

The overbearing conduct of the Nepaulese having forced the British into war, Lord Hastings prepared to carry it on with vigour, and bring it to as speedy a termination as possible; and with this view no preparations were spared which the most consummate foresight and consideration could suggest.

A nearly simultaneous attack on four different points, necessitating the Goorkhas to spread their forces and resources along their whole extensive frontier, was the plan originally adopted, and carried out with some alterations, suggested by an increased knowledge, or forced upon us by those obstacles and failures which must ever attend upon extended combinations.

Major-General Sir D. Ochterlony, with about 6,000 native infantry and a small train of artillery, was to attack the western or extreme right of the Goorkha territories—the districts in the neighbourhood of the present hill station, Simlah.

Major-General Sir R. R. Gillespie, with about 1,000 Europeans and 2,500 native troops, with artillery, was to penetrate the valley of Deyrah, and, after dislodging the Goorkhas from their positions in it, to attack Gurhwal; this done, another force was to attack Kumaon from Rohilcund.

Major-General J. S. Wood, further to the eastward, was to penetrate by Bootwul to Palpa: about 1,000 Europeans and 3,000 native troops, with a small artillery, composed this force.

Major-General Marley was to operate on the east, or left, against their capital at Katmandro, by the passes between the Gunduck and Bagmuttee Rivers: a moderate train of artillery, 1,000 Europeans, and 7,000 native troops, formed this division.

With all these forces were portions of the regiment, which we shall enumerate as we notice the actions of each division.

The first which came in contact with the enemy was Gillespie's. This force marched from Meerut, and entered the Dhoon by the Kheeree pass, and seized Deyrah on the 22nd October, 1814: the horse artillery under Major Pennington accompanied this division, (see list below.)

1st Troop,—Major Pennington; Lieutenants Gowan, Kennedy, Campbell, Moreland.

2nd Troop,—Capt. Starke; Capt.-Lieutenants Whish, Boileau; Lieutenants Playfair, Curtis, Lumsden, Sconce.

3rd Troop,—Captain Brooke; Capt.-Lieutenant Rodber; Lieutenants Parlby, Hyde, Luxford.

Captain-Lieutenant McQuake was quartermaster to the reserve.

Colonel Mawbey having been sent forward to seize Nalapanee

(Kalunga), found it so much stronger than was expected, that he fell back, and the whole force advanced; one end of the ridge was seized on the 30th, and under cover of this party a hasty battery was raised during the night to receive ten field guns, about 600 yards from the fort; at daylight they opened their fire, and four columns were to have advanced to the assault, but by some misunderstanding only two advanced; the enemy, throwing open a wicket, pushed out a gun, took them in flank, and forced them to retire.

A fresh attack by three companies of H.M.'s 53rd was equally fruitless, and, rendered impatient by the repulse, Gillespie rushed on at the head of a small party of dismounted dragoons from his own regiment, the 8th Royal Irish: in this attack he fell. The force now retired to Deyrah, and awaited till the 24th November the arrival of siege guns (4 18-pounders, 2,400 shot; 2 8-inch mortars, 400 shells), from Delhi. On the 25th operations were recommenced; a battery for the 18-pounders was raised at about 300 yards, and by the 27th the wall was brought down.

The enemy made a spirited sally on the battery, but were driven back by discharges of case shot. The assault was attempted, and failed, and a gun was run up by Lieutenant Luxford, who volunteered, and was shot in the attempt to clear the breach. The troops would not advance.

Open force having thus failed, a successful attempt to cut off the supply of water was made, while shells were continually poured into the fort. Cooped up in so small a space, without shelter, their execution was great, and on the 30th the brave garrison evacuated the place, leaving to their victors a scene which none could look on without shuddering.

With the siege guns, parts of the 5th and 6th companies 3rd battalion arrived, with the officers, Capt.-Lieutenant Battine; Lieutenants Tennant, Lyons, C. Smith, C. G. Dixon; and Chesney, adjutant. The horse artillery also remained:

> As the professional advice and opinion of so able an officer as Major Pennington on the subject of artillery as affected by local circumstances, could not fail of being of the greatest use to Captain-Lieutenant Battine.

The artillery losses were not severe: Lieutenant Luxford was the only officer killed; and in reporting it Colonel Mawbey said:

> Lieutenant Luxford, of the horse artillery, is so severely wound-

ed that I have no hopes of his recovery. This excellent officer had gone to the foot of the breach in command of an howitzer and 12-pounder gun, which I sent in hopes, with the assistance of shrapnel shells, of lessening the astonishing exertions made by the Goorkhas.

A detachment being left near the Jumna, the main body marched for Nahun by the plains on the 5th December, and on the 20th Major-General Martindell assumed the command. His first efforts were not successful. A combined attack on the enemy's positions on the heights by columns under Majors Ludlow and Richards, was beaten back, the former with much loss, and the division took up its position before Nahun.

Major-General Ochterlony's division was accompanied by the 4th company 3rd battalion artillery, and early in November attacked Nalagurh. The place was breached, and the garrison capitulated on the 5th November, on which occasion the major-general considered it his "particular duty to express his obligations to Major McLeod and officers and men who manned the batteries." These were, Major McLeod, commandant; Lieutenant Cruikshanks, adjutant; Captains Webbe, G. Brooke, Mason, Fordyce, Cartwright, C. Graham, Timbrell, and Hall and E. P. Gowan, who joined at Nahun.

The next object was the attack of Ramgurh, and some manoeuvring was necessary. The news of the failures at Kalunga arriving, gave fresh confidence to the Goorkhas, and made the British cautious. Sir David waited for reinforcements till near the end of the year. Light guns arriving, the force moved, and manoeuvred to place itself in rear of the Goorkha position, who, to meet it, changed their front, and occupied the heights of Maloun, exposing Ramgurh, which was the immediate object of the movement.

With incredible labour and perseverance, two 18-pounders were carried up the hills and placed in battery about 700 yards from the fort by the 12th November. Their fire was ably directed by Captain Webbe, and the walls having crumbled away under it, the garrison were glad to capitulate on the 17th, and were suffered to join their comrades in Maloun.

Before following this division to its victorious conclusion, we shall find it more convenient to glance at the proceedings of the other forces, which were acting against the Goorkha line of frontier.

Major-General J. S. Wood's division left Gorukpoor late in December: the 5th company 2nd battalion artillery was attached to it. (Captain McDowall; Lieutenants De Brett, Crawford, Twemlow.) In January it entered the Teraie, and, coming suddenly on a stockade at Jeilgurh, carried it at once, in which operation Captain McDowall was wounded. Fearing that he could not retain the stockade if attacked, Major-General Wood retired to Nichloul, and, though reinforced by more troops, remained inactive till the end of the season, when he made an attempt with his guns on Bootwul, and retired to Gorukpoor.

To the eastward, Major Bradshaw, with the advance of Major-General Marley's army, on the 25th November attacked and carried the post of Burhurwa, on the Baghmuttee, on which the Goorkhas evacuated the Teraie, and Major Bradshaw occupied posts at Boragurhee, Sumunpoor, and Pursa.

Major-General Marley, with the main army, arrived on the 12th December: the 6th company 2nd battalion, and detachment, were with this force, and the artillery officers listed; Major Mason, commandant; Lieutenant Walcott, adjutant; Capt. Lindsay; Lieutenants Roberts, Kempt, Blake, Mathison, Counsell, Vanrenen, Fulton, Pereira, Scott, Croxton; and a small train of heavy guns, some field and mountain train guns, and wall pieces. The force moved in four columns; the main one towards the Bicheea-koh and Hetounda passes; the second towards Hurheehurpoor; the third by the Sookturdurree pass and Joorgooree; while the fourth was kept in Jusspoot. The end of the month of December found the main body at Puchroutee Tuppah, with the posts of Pursa and Sumunpoor twenty miles on the left and right flanks of the army, the posts in the same state they had been three weeks previously, and no steps taken to strengthen them. They were garrisoned by about 500 men each, and Pursa had, in addition, a single 6-pounder, commanded by Lieutenant Mathison.

On the night of the 17th January, 1815, both posts were attacked by the Goorkhas; the party at Sumunpoor was taken by surprise and cut to pieces; that at Pursa was a little better prepared, and, aided by Mathison's gun, defended themselves for some time; but the enemy, availing themselves of the shelter the trees afforded, picked off nearly every artilleryman. Mathison then proposed to charge the enemy, but the sepoys refused, and a retreat was attempted, Lieutenant Mathison serving the gun by himself, when all his men were killed or wounded, by which the enemy were kept back; the gun being lost, the retreat became a flight, and had the enemy followed, all must have perished.

Lieutenant Mathison, in his report, says:

I cannot refrain from particularly mentioning the persevering bravery displayed by Matross William Levey, who, though wounded by a musket-ball through one leg and one arm, yet gallantly continued to keep his station until the priming-pouch was blown away from his side, and his wounds becoming too painful to endure, obliged him to sit down. 'Sillaree,' gun-*lascar* of the 42nd company, is also deserving of particular mention; who, although wounded in both hand and foot, continued alone to assist me to the last, and was the person who seized and carried away with him the silver spear planted by the enemy close to the gun at the commencement of the action, and now in the possession of Major-General Marley.

In the orders of the day, the major-general:

Expressed his best thanks to Lieutenant Mathison for his gallant conduct in defending his gun till every man, European and native, fell around it, and all the ammunition was expended.

The artillery in this unhappy affair lost 4 Europeans and 6 natives killed, and 6 Europeans and 11 natives wounded; and it is probable that many of the wounded died afterwards. Want of foresight in not strengthening the position, and want of proper information of the enemy's movements, seem to have been the chief causes of this catastrophe: we may add another—the detaching a single gun. Two guns mutually support each other, and in case of a misfire occurring, the second gun is ready to pour in its fire, should it be attempted to carry the first by a rush; and we have heard it said that Lieutenant Mathison declared on this occasion, that had he had another gun he could have beaten off the enemy. A general order has since prohibited the practice by declaring that never less than two are to be detached.

After this, Major-General Marley gave up all idea of penetrating the hills; he strengthened the post of Baragurhee, and never again entered the forest. On the 10th February he left his division, and Major-General G. Wood arrived on the 20th, but the season passed away in inactivity.

In February detachments of irregulars under Lieutenant-Colonel Gardiner and Major Hearsey advanced on Almorah from Kasheepore and Pilheebheet, and were followed by a small division of regulars under Colonel Nicolls, with which was a detachment of European artillerymen under Lieutenants C. H. Bell and R. B. Wilson, with ten pieces of artillery. On the 5th April the force entered the hills, and heard of the defeat of the irregulars before Almorah; on the 23rd, a detachment from it overtook Hastee-Dull with his troops, near Gunnanath; an action followed, in which the Goorkhas were beaten and their leader slain.

On the 25th the whole force attacked the breastworks on the Seetolee heights, and, following up their success, drove the enemy into Fort Almorah, and formed a lodgement on the ridge.

> With considerable exertion on the parts of the officers of artillery, Lieutenants Bell and Wilson, the small mortars were laid in the battery, and opened at six in the evening, and the larger ones (8-inch) at midnight.

Several shells were thrown into the fort, which compelled the garrison to remain concealed; many Goorkhas and Cassiahs having quitted the fort, it was supposed that the garrison had fled, but during the night a sharp attack on the outposts proved that they had determined to make a last effort; this failing, on the 27th they evacuated the fort.

In Colonel Nicolls's report he says:

> I feel much indebted to Lieutenants Bell and Wilson for their activity in laying and bringing these mortars into use so soon.

And in the general orders the governor-general records that these officers "are mentioned in terms of strong commendation."

This well-executed expedition materially affected the aspect of the war; in the language of the Goorkha chief, it "broke the camel's back," it separated the extremities of the frontier, and prevented reinforcements being sent from Katmandoo to Maloun, and it stood out in brilliant contrast with the other events of the campaign; but we must now return to the divisions employed against Nahun and Maloun.

Major-General Martindell's force, which we left in front of Nahun, remained inactive till February; its subsequent operations were marked by vacillation; with great labour, 18-pounders were carried up the hills, and, after the time and labour thus expended, no further result was obtained than levelling a stockade, which was found to be of no use to the general plan of the campaign. Operations were commenced against Jythuck, and a position taken up on the ridge on the 1st April, although opposed by the enemy; this advantage was followed up, and Punchul Point seized; other positions were taken up, which straitened the enemy's post, and would have eventually forced him to evacuate the fort, had not the operations at Maloun caused the Goorkhas to leave the province. To these operations we must now turn.

We left Major-General Ochterlony in possession of Ramgurh, with his forces interposed between the enemy on the Maloun ridge and Belaspore. Great exertions were made by the artillery in moving the ordnance up the heights; but on the 10th March a battery was raised against Taragurh; on the 11th a breach was practicable, and the enemy fled; Chumba was attacked and breached by the 16th, and the garrison capitulated; other forts were reduced, and the detachments joined the main body which was in front of the Goorkha lines. These extended from the forts of Maloun to Soorujgurh, all the peaks crowned with stockades, except those of Ryla and Deothul, the former, convenient for future operations against Soorujgurh, the latter, in the heart of the Goorkha line, within 1,000 yards of Maloun. The main attack was against Deothul, while a second was made on Kyla, while other columns moved, as if against Maloun, to distract the enemy.

Five columns were prepared, and on the night of the 14th April, Kyla was occupied, and on a signal made, two other detachments moved to that point; this done, two other columns moved on at night and occupied positions till daylight, when they attacked Deothul from opposite sides: with these columns were two field-guns, to assist in holding the height when gained, as considerable efforts were expected from the enemy.

The position was carried after a severe contest, and much desultory fighting continued till evening; but on the morning of the 16th the Goorkhas, 2,000 in number, made a furious attack on the hill; the artillerymen were nearly all killed at their guns, and at one time, Lieutenant Cartwright, with one artilleryman only, was left; but, aided by Lieutenant Hutchinson of the Engineers, and Lieutenant Armstrong of the Native Infantry, they kept up a fire which tended materially to check the Goorkha onset; and reinforcements and ammunition arriving opportunely from Ryla, their efforts slackened, and they were driven back by a charge headed by Major Lawrie.

A road was made for heavy artillery to Deothul, and with incredible labour the 18-pounders were placed in battery against Maloun early in May; but news of the fall of Almorah having arrived, the Goorkhas urged their chief, Ummer Sing, to yield, and on his refusing, they left him, and he was forced to capitulate on the 5th May.

The exertions of the artillery in this campaign were acknowledged in the following general orders:

The unwearied alacrity, the labour, the conspicuous gallantry, and the skill, displayed by the whole of the artillery, engineers, and pioneer departments throughout the course of the service, have been pointed out to the special notice of the Governor-General, and His Excellency accordingly expresses his earnest sense of the meritorious conduct exhibited by Major McLeod, commanding the artillery, and by Captain Webbe, of the same corps.

Early in the following year it became evident that the court of Nepal intended evading the treaty they had agreed to, and the force was assembled again in the neighbourhood of Dinapore, and placed under Sir D. Ochterlony's command, with the object of occupying the capital.

In addition to the former artillery, the 7th company 2nd battalion, and 3rd company 3rd battalion, with the following officers, Captains Pollock and Biggs; Lieutenants Marshall, Denniss, Geddes, Buck, and O. Baker, joined the force. On the 10th February the main body entered the Sal forest, and took up a position at Bicheea-koh; four days were spent in reconnoitring and inquiry, when it was discovered that the regular road, which was fortified, might be turned by some very difficult passes in the Chooriaghati range; on the 14th, at night, a battalion (3rd) marched, and entering a ravine, called Baleekola, followed its course five or six miles, then striking up a water-course, came to a steep acclivity of 300 feet in height; the advance clambered up, and were followed by the brigade, and the heights were gained.

The other brigade (4th) marched by the direct road on the 15th, and the Goorkhas, hearing that the *ghat* was turned, retreated on Muckwanpore with but little resistance. Lieutenant Walcote of the artillery was wounded severely in reconnoitring the stockaded position. On the 27th the two brigades united at Muckwanpore; a reconnoitring party came in contact with the enemy, and Lieutenant Pickersgill with difficulty regained the camp; but reinforcements proceeding from each side brought on a general action, which was eagerly contested; the artillery came into full play, and the effect of the guns upon the enemy's masses moving on the opposite ridge considerably aided in the victory gained.

The only other action was that in which Colonel Kelly's brigade was engaged in the attack on Hurryhurpore Hill. The infantry were engaged from six to eleven, when "two 6-pounders and two 5½-inch howitzers being brought up on elephants, in a few minutes decided the affair, and left us in possession of an almost natural redoubt."

Amongst the wounded you will see Captain Lindsay; although his wounds are not severe, I fear I shall lose his active service for a time, which I lament exceedingly, having found Captain Lindsay a most zealous, able officer, both as an artillerist and engineer. (The words of Colonel Kelly in reporting the affair.)

With this campaign the war ended; the pride of the Nepalese was effectually humbled for the time, on finding a British force in full march on their capital, and they were compelled to execute the treaty; but since that period they never ceased to look forward to the arrival of the time when an opportunity of revenge might offer.

The services of the native troops were rewarded by a medal to all native officers who had served within the hills, and to such of the native infantry officers and privates as had distinguished themselves by their gallantry or energy. This medal we have never seen, though by the records we observe several were given to the native branches of the regiment. The sketch here given is copied from one which appeared in the *East-India United Service Journal*, in 1837.

In the early part of the present century the attention of the Ordnance department in England was turned towards a weapon which had long been in use with the native armies in India—the rocket; and, under Sir William Congreve's superintendence, rockets of a large size and great power of flight had been manufactured and used with much success in the bombardment of Boulogne and Copenhagen. (*The Details of the Rocket System* by Sir William Congreve is also published by Leonaur.) Experience suggested improvement in details, and the results seemed so satisfactory, that a troop equipped with cars for firing volleys and tripods for single rockets was added to the corps of Royal Artillery, and employed with considerable effect at the battles of Leipsic and Waterloo.

Acting upon this example, and considering that it would be advantageous to beat our Indian enemies at their own weapons, the government decided this year on adding a rocket troop to the Bengal Artillery. It was ordered in September, and consisted of European artillerymen mounted on camels, and volley-cars drawn by horses. Its strength is as detailed, 1 captain, 2 lieutenants, 1 lieutenant-fireworker, 10 non-commissioned officers, 80 troopers, 5 *sirdars*, 60 *surwans*, 70 camels, 20 horses, 4 cars, 20 *bouches à jeu*, and 960 rockets.

Captain Whish, Lieutenants G. N. Campbell and G. Brooke, and Lieutenant-Fireworker Cartwright were posted to this troop, and it was soon in a state of efficiency. It was attached to the horse brigade, which was at this time commanded by Major Pennington, who was retained in the command, although:

> His promotion to the rank of major rendered him in excess to the establishment of officers attached to it, at the recommendation of His Excellency the commander-in-chief, in consideration of his general merits as an officer and his particular qualifications for the command of the corps of horse-artillery, which had attained such an eminent degree of discipline under his superintendence.

The dress of the regiment in January underwent some change; the dress-jacket had embroidered button-holes on its scarlet facings; the breastplate was gilt, with the Company's arms embossed in silver; the pantaloon continued to be worn as dress with the Hessian boots; but trousers or overalls were worn on all duties; the shako was introduced, displacing the bearskin cap. There are pictures in existence which give a good idea of the dress at particular periods, and in them all the changes may be traced.

A large portion of the regiment was this year called into the field against Diaram, the *zemindar* of Hattrass, whose fort and territory had been ceded by Scindia to the British in 1803, at which time no terms were made exempting Diaram from the general laws in force in the Company's territories; but, in the expectation that, finding no necessity for armed followers, his force would gradually have dissolved and his fort gone to ruin, the government took no steps to break it up at once.

Mistaking this forbearance, in spite of several warnings, he persisted in a course of aggrandisement and opposition to the civil officers, which drew down on him the powerful hand of government, who determined that no ill-timed economy should interfere with the rapid and complete reduction of his power. Lord Hastings directed the preparations to be made on such a scale to convince all that our failures heretofore were caused not from a want of skill or resources, but from our failing to bring them forward, and being more lavish of the blood of our troops than the *matériel* of our magazines.

For this siege two troops of horse artillery and the rocket-troop, seven companies of European, and four of native artillery, and eighteen companies of *lascars*, moved from different points and collected before Hattrass, together with a battering train of six 24-pounders, fourteen 18-pounders, four 8-inch howitzers, six 10-inch mortars, fourteen 8-inch mortars, and twenty-two 5½-inch mortars; total, 20 guns, 8 howitzers, and 42 mortars. The general command of the artillery was held by

Major-General Sir J. Horsford; Captain C. H. Campbell, M. B.; Major Pennington, commanding horse artillery; Lieutenant Lumsden, adjutant and quarter-master; Majors Mason, McLeod, and Butler, fort adjutants.

Troop.	Captains.	Captain-Lieutenant.	Lieutenants.	Lieutenant-Fireworkers.
1	Boileau	...	G. Gowan	Morland, Pennington
3	J. Brooke	Rodber	Hyde, MacAlister, Sconce	
Rocket	Whish	...	G. Brooke	Cartwright

Company	Battalion.	Captain-Lieutenants.	Lieutenants.	Lieutenant Fireworkers.
2	2	Fraser	Croxton	G. R. Scott, R. B. Wilson
3	2	Curphy	Pereira	Hele, Vanrenen
4	2	Pryce	Carne	Sanders, Crommelin
6	2	Lindsay	Roberts	Coulthard
4	3	...	L. Lawrence	Smith, Whinfield
6	3	Battine	Fordyce	R. Dickson, Delafosse
7	3	Tollemache	Timbrell	Wood, E. P. Gowan

1st, 2nd, 3rd, and 4th companies of golundaz battalion; 1st, 5th, 6th, 8th, 12th, 18th, 20th, 27th, 30th, 31st, 32nd, 37th, 38th, 40th, 41st, 43rd, 44th, and 45th companies of gun lascars.

The force assembled on the 11th February, and from that time till the 21st was employed in collecting and preparing *matériel* for the siege and waiting for the train; on its arrival, three batteries were erected against the *kuttra*, which opened on the 22nd, and continued firing during the 23rd: a breach was effected, and during the night the enemy left the *kuttra*.

On the 25th, batteries were commenced against the fort, three armed with guns, and two with mortars from the *kuttra*, and on the right, two guns, and three mortar batteries, one of the latter of sixteen 5½-inch mortars; the trenches were pushed up to within 50 yards of the ditch, a rocket-battery was erected between the *kuttra* and fort; much delay occurred from want of fuses or from those sent turning out bad, so that fresh had to be driven and materials sent for from Agra; the time was employed in completing the batteries and approaches; a slight fire was kept up till the 2nd March, when preparations being all made, the bombardment commenced, at a signal from the rocket-battery, by a general salvo. An eye-witness writes:

> The effect and sight was beautiful, and was only excelled by a spectacle which took place about 5 in the afternoon. While in the battery watching the flight of a shell, it scarcely touched the ground before an explosion took place, the most awful and grand I ever beheld—a powder-magazine had been exploded. It is hardly possible to give an accurate description of it; it was more like an immense column of red smoke, forming itself like an enormous *chattah* in rolls, continually changing form as it ascended to an incredible height: several fragments fell in the trenches and hurt some people.

Another writes:

> The effect of our shells and the ruins they have occasioned, are indescribable; the house and *zenana* of Diaram is a complete riddle—shot and shell holes in every direction; the mortality is great, men and horses lying in the gateway and works.

For the details of this operation, the first in India in which artillery was used on a large scale, we would refer our readers to a journal of the siege, which appeared in the *East-India United Service Journal*, in 1837, and content ourselves with adding the orders issued on the occasion.

Major-General Marshall's order says:

The science and skill displayed by the engineers and artillery department were eminently conspicuous, and the bombardment and explosion of the enemy's principal magazine, which, without derogating from the merits of others, must be allowed to have given us almost immediate possession of the place, will long be regarded as the most memorable among the brilliant events of the last fortnight, and as demonstrative of the extent and soundness of that judgment and penetration which, in the avowed anticipation of the very consequences, enabled the army, by the provision of adequate means, to insure them.

The practice of the artillery has answered the expectations of that high authority to which the major-general has ventured to allude in the forgoing observations. Another motive for them is to bring forward and illustrate the fact more closely, that where the means are equal to the science and practical knowledge known to pervade every branch of this army, the results must invariably be rapid and successful, even against such strong and formidable forts as Hattrass proved to be.

We cannot refrain from quoting the order issued to the artillery by Major-General Sir John Horsford; the more so, as it proved the last he was permitted to pen to the corps, his valuable life having terminated suddenly, soon after returning to Cawnpoor from this service:—

Major-General Sir John Horsford, commanding the artillery brigaded before Hattrass, performs with pleasure the last exercise of his command in conveying to the horse and foot artillery and rocket-troop his congratulations on the brilliant services which their united exertions have effected for the state, Government having through their means principally been placed in possession of Hattrass, the rapid reduction of which has caused the surrender of the important fortress of Morsaum and eleven other forts.

The acknowledgments of Major-General Marshall, commanding the army, and the favourable sentiments entertained by the army at large, must be much more satisfactory to the artillery than any tribute of praise which Sir John Horsford could bestow in confirmation of their meritorious services.

But the major-general considers public acknowledgments due to Major Mason, commanding the foot artillery, who, with Majors MacLeod and Butler, superintended in turn the several batteries. He begs to offer his best thanks to Major Mason and the experienced field-officers above mentioned, for their several important services.

The major-general duly appreciates the labour and exertions of every officer and man employed in the batteries before the *kuttra* and fort, and more particularly the heavy duty all had to perform on the 2nd instant during the general bombardment. To the officers commanding batteries, and to their juniors doing duty under them, the major-general's notice is particularly due. The state of the fort after its capture evinced to all that the means employed for its reduction had been directed by hands well acquainted with their use. Where every officer was equally zealous, the major-general hopes he will be excused for not naming all who deserve his praise and thanks.

The mature judgment of Major Pennington was displayed on every occasion which offered itself.

The spirit and conduct of the officers and men of the horse artillery throughout the service deserve the major-general's warmest approbation.

The zeal evinced by Captain Whish, the officers and men of the rocket-troop, require the major-general's notice in public orders.

The major-general's personal feelings are much gratified by the important consequences which have resulted from the unanimity which prevailed amongst every branch of the artillery to forward the objects of the service. The preparations which were made caused much to be expected from their exertions, and the major-general is satisfied that the expectations of the most sanguine have been realised. It is a source of great pleasure for the major-general to reflect that the last period of his service with a corps in which he has long served, should be distinguished by events which call forth the admiration of all who witnessed them, and by services which conspicuously increase the credit and the established high character of the regiment of Bengal Artillery.

From Hattrass Sir John Horsford returned to Cawnpoor, and on the 20th April closed his honourable career. His death was sudden, and it is believed was occasioned by a disease of the heart. To his public character the governor-general bore testimony in the following order:—

> The governor-general cannot direct the succession in the regiment of artillery without expressing his deep concern at the loss the Honourable Company's service has suffered by the death of Major-General Sir John Horsford, K.C.B. The ardent spirit, the science, and the generous zeal of that admirable officer, were in no less degree an advantage to the public interest than an honour to himself. It is consolatory to think that when sinking under the malady which so early deprived his country of an energy incessantly devoted to her glory, he had the consciousness of having just displayed with signal triumph the skill and superiority of the corps which he had so materially contributed to fashion and perfect.

The part Sir John Horsford had borne in some of the severest service the regiment had been engaged in, his thorough knowledge of the profession, his high talents and commanding character, gave him great influence in the regiment, and secured for his opinions great weight with the authorities; and, had he been spared to exercise the command for a few years more, the regiment would undoubtedly have been placed on a far more efficient footing than it hitherto had been. From the time of Pearse's death to Horsford's succession to the command, no man of talent or influence had been at its head; and the consequence was, that while the other branches of the army were increased on a scale more adequate to their wants, the artillery was added to by driblets, kept in the lowest state, and its organisation made a subject of continual experiment.

Just before his death, Sir John Horsford submitted to the Marquis of Hastings a memoir, pointing out the faults which had thus been committed, and detailing the principles upon which the corps of artillery ought to be formed; going on from these principles through all the details, he presented a complete scheme of a regiment of artillery adapted to the wants of Bengal. His character insured attention to the subject, and the result was, that in the following year the corps was reorganised, not indeed upon the scale Sir John Horsford proposed, but upon the most efficient it had yet been.

Major-General Hardwicke was appointed commandant in succession to Major-General Sir John Horsford.

We must pause at this point for a time to consider a circumstance which was of great importance to the regiment—the question of general officers of the ordnance branch being eligible to the general staff of the army. In the arrangements for remodelling the army in 1796, no doubt existed on the point. In the Minutes of Council, 5th June, 1797, it was directed that the artillery regimental command was to be held by the senior officer present, "not being a general officer," and several artillery general officers had been employed on the general staff; such was the state of the case up to 1814, when the Court of Directors thought proper to annul the existing orders, for reasons which may be briefly thus stated:—

1st. That the services of the artillery and engineer generals are required by the state in their own departments.

2nd. That the practice, though not the theory (so to speak), of His Majesty's service excludes ordnance generals from any employment on the staff.

******

The subject is fully gone into in *Considerations on behalf of the Officers of the Indian Artillery and Engineer Corps,* by Lieutenant-Colonel James Young, of the artillery. Published in 1816.

******

To the first, it might be replied, that even supposing one artillery and one engineer general are wanted at the heads of the corps, it is no reason why the others should not be employed on the general staff during the period they are not required with their own. That till now a general officer was never allowed to serve in this position; and if while debarred from the general staff and holding the regimental command on the regimental allowances, his position would be a very unfavourable one, as contrasted with that of a general officer of cavalry or infantry.

To the second we would say, that if true, some compensation would be found to the Royal Ordnance general officers in the numerous regimental superiorities they enjoy in Europe over regiments of the line; such as rising regimentally to colonelcies, the greater proportion of field officers, higher pay, the use of a horse, superior regimental rank, ordnance staff offices, and many other points which it would require more space than we can afford to go fully into; but, in reality, Royal Ordnance officers were not excluded, and at the time of publication of the order there were twelve or fifteen of them employed on the home and foreign staff of the army.

Feeling that their prospects were much blighted by being thus debarred from those honourable and lucrative commands to which every officer hopes (though few live) to succeed, the officers of the ordnance corps in Bengal (and also in Madras and Bombay) memorialised the Court of Directors, praying for a revision of the orders in question, and their reply was published in August, 1817. The Court did not enter into the question; they refused the point at issue, but directed that general officers of artillery and engineers in command of their regiments should be placed on a similar footing as to allowances with other general officers serving on the army staff. But although at this time the representations of the ordnance officers had no effect, there is little doubt that they were subsequently reconsidered and their justice admitted, for in the general remodelling of the military system in 1824:

> An additional general officer on the Honourable Company's establishment was authorised for the staff of each presidency, and the generals of artillery and engineers were rendered eligible to the staff, the command of those corps devolving on the senior colonels or field-officers.

The comparative efficiency of guns collected into batteries kept in order and directed by officers of the artillery, and of the same scattered as battalions and galloper-guns, had been proved so strongly in favour of the former, that the government now resolved on following up the practice of European powers. The gallopers from six native regiments were directed to be embodied into two troops of native horse artillery at Meerut and Cawnpoor, and placed under the command of Captains G. Gowan and Biggs in July, and those of the two remaining regiments were some months later withdrawn and formed into a third troop at Nagpoor under Lieutenant George Blake, and subsequently Captain Rodber. The horses and troopers accompanied the guns; and as the best horses had generally been given to the galloper-guns, these troops were exceedingly well provided with draught cattle. For officers the foot-artillery was again indented on, but this time not without an augmentation, for:

> Adverting to the number of officers withdrawn from the foot to the horse artillery, and to the total inadequacy of the number of officers which would remain with the battalions of foot artillery, and for the numerous and important duties required of them, the governor-general was pleased to determine that the officers actually attached to the horse artillery should be struck off the strength of the foot artillery, and the vacancies supplied by promotion.

And accordingly, one major and six captains were now (25th October) added to the corps.

Before adverting to the campaigns which the Marquis of Hastings's grand combinations against the Pindarees caused, we will notice the additions made to the regiment previous to its reorganisation in October, 1818, and detail its strength when that change had taken place, and then succinctly refer to those well-planned operations which with very little bloodshed rooted out the Pindarees, and humbled the Mahratta power.

In continuation of the system of collecting guns in batteries, an experimental horse field-battery was formed in November, and placed under Captain Battine with the 6th company 3rd battalion. The battery consisted of eight guns and eight waggons (two 12-pounders, two 5½-inch howitzers, and four 6-pounders), and ninety-six horses were allowed to drag it; these horses were led by "*Syce* drivers," a class of *syces* placed on the same footing as *lascars* with respect to pay, clothing, and pension.

The rocket-troop was modified as to the numbers of its men and cattle, but camels were still continued with it, nor was it till 1822 that they were superseded by horses, and two additional companies of independent *golundaz* were raised for the Islands and Bengal. Colonel Sherwood was appointed acting commandant during Major-General Hardwicke's absence on sick leave.

The regiment now was composed of the horse artillery, consisting of seven troops, including the rocket-troop; three European battalions of seven companies each, twelve regular and six irregular companies of *golundaz*, forty-five *lascar* and twenty-six driver companies. The new organisation directed it to consist of seven troops of horse artillery, three European battalions, of eight companies each, one native battalion of fifteen companies, with a company of *lascars* attached to each company, European or native (39), and seventeen bullock and two horse field-batteries, each of eight pieces, with a driver company to each.

The officers were allotted to the different portions of the regiment in the following proportion:—

Horse Artillery.	3 European Battalions.	Native Battalion.	Total.
1 Colonel	3	...	4
2 Lieutenant-Colonels ...	6	...	8
2 Majors	6	1	9
7 Captains	24	13	44
28 1st Lieutenants	48	4	80
— 2nd Lieutenants	48	4	52

The rank of 2nd captain was abolished, and that of 2nd lieutenant substituted for lieutenant-fireworker; *serangs* of gun-*lascars* were made *jemadars*; *serang*-major, *soobahdar*; 1st and 2nd *tindals, havildars* and *naiks*; gunners were styled bombardiers, and *matrosses*, gunners.

European Troop or Company.										Native Troop or Company.													
Serjeants	Corporals	Bombardiers	Trumpeters	Farriers	Rough riders	Gunners	Jemadars Havildars	Naiks	Lascars	Soobahdars	Jemadars	Havildars	Naiks	Trumpeters	Rough riders	Farriers	Troopers	Staff-Serjeants	Jemadars Havildars	Naiks	Lascars	Sirdars	Drivers
7	6	10	2	2	2	80	1	2	24	1	1	6	6	-	-	90	-	1	2	24	4	85	
6	5	10	2	-	-	80	12	2	70	1	2	8	8	2	-	-	100	-	12	2	70	-	-

See the following page for a list of the whole regiment.

Forming a total of 8,094, including *lascars*, and excluding drivers.

The infantry of the army at this period amounted to about 64,000 men, or nearly in the proportion of eight infantry to one artilleryman, bringing the relative numbers of the two branches pretty much to what they were in 1796, at which time the infantry were 7½ to one artilleryman.

In a preceding page we have alluded to the operations of the governor-general for the purpose of rooting out the Pindaree hordes by whom Central India was overrun, and the Company's provinces yearly threatened, and in some instances plundered. Their numbers may have reached some 20,000 horse, undisciplined, and prepared to run rather than fight, and were scattered about in small *durras* or bands, so that no large bodies of troops would have been necessary to overcome them had it not been for the tacit protection afforded these freebooters by the Mahratta powers, and whose attitude was such, that preparations were forced to be made on a scale sufficient to meet their armies, and this called a far larger portion of the armies of India into the field than would otherwise have been required.

The Bengal divisions took the field about November, 1817. The masterly position taken up by Lord Hastings, with the centre division of the grand army threatening Scindeah's capital, his park and magazines, in case he ventured to move from Gwalior to join the Mahratta confederacy, completely paralyzed him; but the Peshwah and Nagpoor *rajah* being unawed by any sufficient body of troops at hand, attacked the residents at their courts, and it was only by the heroic

				Returns Dec. 1818
FOOT ARTILLERY	DRIVERS	Drivers	1615	2640
		Birdars	761	1292
	LASCARS	Privates	1562730	1903261
		Non-commissioned Officers		
	NATIVE	Native Officers		
		Buglers		
		Privates	150030 39	1632 32 49
		Non-commissioned Officers	240	245
		Non-commissioned Staff	—	—
	EUROPEAN	Native Officers	43	39
		Buglers		
		Bombardiers and Gunners	2160	1469
		Non-commissioned Officers	364 249	233
		Non-commissioned Staff	—	—
HORSE ARTILLERY	NATIVE	Lascars	168	—
		Non-commissioned Officers	21	—
		Farriers, Rough-riders, Trumpeters	18	12
		Troopers	270	246
		Non-commissioned Officers	36	56
	EUROPEAN	Native Officers	6	6
		Farriers, Rough-riders, Trumpeters	24	13
		Bombardiers and Gunners	320	321
		Non-commissioned Officers	52	46
		Non-commissioned Staff	—	7
		2nd Lieutenants	80 52	75 43
		1st Lieutenants	44	44
		Captains		
		Majors	9	9
		Lieutenant-Colonels	8	8
		Colonels	4	4

exertions of the small escorts, and which have immortalised the names of Poonah and Seetabuldee, that the posts were made good till reinforcements could arrive.

Many portions of the regiment were employed with the five divisions of Bengal troops, and in operations extending over so great a space, must necessarily have undergone much severe marching; but as the actual service was partial, and we do not pretend to enter into a detailed account of the whole campaigns, we shall only refer to the occasions on which they came in contact with the enemy.

We have already mentioned that the galloper-guns of the cavalry regiments were incorporated into troops of horse artillery; the gallopers of two regiments employed on the Nerbudda were formed into a troop under Lieutenant G. Blake, and, with a squadron of native cavalry, detached by Colonel Adams to Nagpoor on the first news of the expected attack on the residency, to share in the noble defence of Seetabuldee; they arrived too late, but they joined Brigadier Doveton's force on the 16th December, and were employed in the action fought against the Arabs, who formed the chief strength of the Nagpoor Army.

In the Battle of Mahidpoor, fought by Sir T. Hyslop's army on the 21st December against Holkar and the Peshwah's forces, one Bengal Artillery officer was present—Lieutenant Sotheby, commanding the *golundaz* company of the Russell brigade.

Major-General Brown was detached with a column from the grand army against Jawud, and on the 20th January, 1818, attacked the troops of Holkar, drawn up under the walls, and drove them into the fort by a charge of cavalry, supported by a fire of shrapnel from two guns of the 2nd troop horse artillery under Lieutenant Mathison, silencing the enemy's guns.

✶✶✶✶✶✶

During the most severe part of this affair, a circumstance occurred truly creditable to the character of this officer, and fully substantiated by the testimony of an eye-witness. An European horse artilleryman fell deadly wounded, and on his comrades attempting to carry him to the rear, he entreated them to desist, adding, "I know I must die, and I only wish to shake Lieutenant Mathison by the hand before I die." His wish was immediately gratified, and he expired uttering "God bless you."

✶✶✶✶✶✶

This success was followed up by an immediate attack; the guns of Captain Biggs's native troop were drawn up on the right and left to destroy the defences of the entrance, while a 12-pounder, under Mathison, was dragged up by the European artillery and pioneers to blow open the gate, and which was not effected until the third round, during which time the party were exposed to a heavy and galling fire.

In the field orders issued on this occasion:

> The major-general desired to express his particular satisfaction at the manner in which the artillery under Captain Biggs and Lieutenant Mathison was served, and at the soldier-like manner in which Lieutenant Mathison took up his 12-pounder to force open the gate.

Lieutenant-Colonel Pennington, in writing to Lieutenant Mathison on this occasion, said:

> Accept my best thanks for the great credit you brought the horse artillery by the ability and gallantry you displayed in the attack on Jeswunt Rao Bhao and his town, and my cordial congratulations on your personal safety.

The next action we have occasion to notice was that of Lieutenant-Colonel Adams at Seonee on the 16-17th April, in which Captain Rodber's troop (who had been appointed to the troop lately engaged at Nagpoor under Lieutenant Blake) did good service.

The Peshwah's army flying from Brigadier Doveton's division, was intercepted by Lieutenant-Colonel Adams, who immediately attacked with the cavalry and horse artillery, driving the enemy from position to position.

✶✶✶✶✶✶

The artillery were in front, and the first gun that opened was a Madras horse-artillery gun under Lieutenant Hunter, which killed the enemy's *beenee-wala*, or quartermaster-general, upon which they took to flight. One of Captain Hunter's two guns sticking on the stump of a tree, Lieutenant Crawford moved on with the other, accompanying Captain Rodber's guns.

✶✶✶✶✶✶

Colonel Blacker says:

> Great praise, has been given to the horse artillery on this occasion, and, from a comparison of several accounts of this affair, whatever loss was sustained by the enemy is chiefly attributable to their fire. The ground was unfavourable for cavalry, yet

the guns, by admirable exertion, were advanced and the cavalry may be said to have only covered them.

✶✶✶✶✶✶

Lieutenant Crawford says, "After a five-mile gallop we pulled up, having no troops near but about 80 of the 5th cavalry, and so dead beat were we all with the long march and gallop, that the Peshwah and those with him, being fresh, got off easily."

✶✶✶✶✶✶

It must be borne in mind, too, that these exertions were preceded by a march of unparalleled length. Captain Rodber was sent from Nagpoor to join Colonel Adams's force, and in a letter written many years afterwards, he says:

> I could not have gone less than ninety miles. At 1 a.m., on the 16th April, I commenced my march (after going the previous day eighteen miles over an execrable road, large loose stones and hills) to join Colonel Adams at Hingun Ghat; on the road I received a letter, informing me that Colonel Adams had marched and encamped at Alundaboo; this information obliged me to retrace my road for some distance; I reached the colonel's camp between 2 and 3 p.m. (I am quite positive to the time exactly); I could not have gone less than fifty-six miles, as I pushed on. At 8 p.m., same day, I mounted again, and moved with the detachment in pursuit of the Peshwah, and was not dismissed till between 12 and 1 next day. About six of the last miles were over a succession of wooded heights covered with large loose stones, and hollows deep and wide enough to hide both gun and horses in. From what we see of roads in any part of India I have visited, no notion can be formed of the ways here; in a march sometimes, you have to cross seven or eight *nullahs* with swampy bottoms and difficult approaches.

In the same letter Captain Rodber, speaking of this service, says:

> I dined with Jenkins (at Nagpoor) the night before I marched, and late some of his *hurkarus* came in and reported that the Peshwah's army had got round Colonel Adams, and was in full march on Nagpoor, said to have eighty guns, and 10,000 Arabs, and a number of horse. It was not for me to say a word about my little party marching into the very jaws of this host, but I thought it very inconsiderate allowing me to move. I remember one morning, when quite dark, a trooper from the advance

guard coming into the line, and declaring he heard the noise of horses' feet, and when I had satisfied myself of the fact, I put all in the most defensible position, firmly believing it was the van of the Peshwah's army; it proved, however, a large body of the *Nizam's* horse, sent to me by the colonel; I do not know that I ever felt greater relief.

Major-General Marshall's division occupied Sagur in March, 1818, and a portion of the force moved out against Dhamoney, a small fortress about thirty miles distant, at the head of a ravine or valley leading to the Dussan River, the neighbouring country being very rugged and broken. The detachment took possession of the town on the 20th March, and by the 24th had raised batteries against the fort, in which two 24-pounders, four 18-pounders, one 12-pounder, and two 5½-inch howitzers, were placed; a mortar-battery also was completed to the rear. These opened on the 24th March, and after six hours' firing the *killidar* surrendered. The 4th company 2nd battalion artillery was employed in this service—Captain Hetzler, Captain Lindsay, Captain-Lieutenant Coulthard, Lieutenants Carne, W. Bell, Lieutenant-Fireworkers Saunders, Crommelin, and Patch.

This force then marched, *viâ* Dumoh, to Jubbulpoor, and proceeded against "Mundlah," on the Nerbudda, and by the 25th, batteries had been formed for thirty-two pieces of artillery; they were immediately armed, and by the next day a breach was open, which was successfully stormed.

The artillery operations were directed by Captain Hetzler. The following officers were present:—Captain Lindsay, Lieutenants Dickson, Carne, Saunders, Patch, D'Oyley, Kirby, and Crommelin.

Lieutenant-Colonel Adams's division was employed against the fortress of Chandah in May, 1818. Both Bengal and Madras artillery were with him; of the former, the three native troops of horse artillery, under Captain Rodber, Lieutenant Twemlow, the 5th company 2nd battalion, Captain MacDowell, Lieutenant Crawford, acting field engineer, Lieutenant Walcott, commissary of ordnance.

On the 9th May the force arrived, and on reconnoitring, it was found to be nearly six miles in circumference, and mounting eighty guns; the ordnance available for the attack consisted of three 18-pounders, four brass 12-pounders, six howitzers, and twelve 6-pounders. On the night of the 13th, a battery was raised on an eminence to the south of the fort, from which four pieces of ordnance, to divert the enemy's attention, played on the town with shells and hot shot, while materials were being collected, and a thorough reconnaissance made. The south-east angle was finally determined on for the breach.

On the 17th, the four 12-pounders were placed in battery to destroy the flanking defences, as well as the howitzers and three 6-pounders. During the night of the 18th, the three 18-pounders were placed in a breaching battery within 250 yards of the place, and opened their fire on the 19th. By 4 p.m., the breach was practicable; the assault was, however, delayed till the following morning, but a fire was kept up at intervals during the night to prevent the enemy retrenching the breach, which they attempted. In the morning the assault took place; the storming party was accompanied by a detail of artillerymen with spikes and sponges for spiking or turning the enemy's guns. The storming party were completely successful, and obtained possession of the town and fort after overcoming a very serious resistance.

In noticing this action, the general order says:

> The rapid demolition of the enemy's defences, and the speed with which a breach was effected, would sufficiently testify the service of Lieutenant Crawford, Bengal Artillery, acting as engineer, in indicating the positions for the batteries, even had not Lieutenant-Colonel Adams professed his obligations to those officers so warmly.
>
> Captain Rodber, Captain MacDowell, and Lieutenant Walcott, seem to have highly deserved the praise their commander bestows upon them. Indeed, the efforts of all the officers and men of the artillery appear to have been highly laudable.

The Sagur troops under Brigadier-General Watson, in October, 1818, again took the field against Urjun Sing, Rajah of Gunakota, who refused to give up his fort, agreeably to treaty. It was situated about thirty miles from Sagur, on the banks of the Sonar, at a point where a small *nullah* ran into it, so that the river and *nullah* formed ditches on two sides, while the third, in which was the gateway, had a well-formed artificial ditch; but it was not a place of any strength. On the 23rd October, a battery of fourteen mortars and four howitzers was formed on the opposite bank of the Sonar, near the city of Hardynugger, and opened its fire on the fort.

An accident occurred next day in the battery, which caused several casualties. The shells for expenditure had been placed in the rear of the mortars covered by *paulins*, and by some mischance a spark got among and ignited them, upwards of one hundred blowing up. (The explosion of a shell we believe.) On the 26th, a breaching battery was ready, and opened from two 24-pounders, four 18-pounders, and two 12-pounders, to which two more 24-pounders were added on the 29th. The battery was 900 yards from the wall, but a breach was soon accomplished, and the enemy capitulated without standing an assault.

The 4th and 6th companies 2nd battalion artillery were present, with Captain Hetzler, Captain-Lieutenant Coulthard, Lieutenants Pew, Saunders, D'Oyley, Patch, Kirby, and Crommelin.

In June a detachment from the 4th company 2nd battalion, with Lieutenants Carne and Saunders, were sent with a column against the fort of Satunwaree; a breach was effected by the 18-pounders on the 8th June, and assaulted, but unsuccessfully; the place, however, was evacuated during the night.

The unsuccessful assault led to a report that the breach had not been sufficiently cleared, and charges were preferred against Lieutenant Carne for bad practice of the artillery, for serving out an excess of liquor to the men on duty, leading to their intoxication, and for being intoxicated himself.

Of the first and third he was acquitted by a general court-martial, and partially of the second; the fact probably was, that the men, being much exposed and overworked under the burning sun of June, a small quantity of liquor, which in other circumstances would have been taken with perfect impunity, flew to their heads.

The Nagpoor subsidiary force, under Major-General Doveton, marched against Assurghur to receive charge of it from Scindia's *killidar*, but the *killidar*, according to the native custom, pretended to have received no orders, and it therefore became necessary to proceed against it; all the available trains were sent for, including those from Sagur and Hoshunabad, and when collected, amounted to the number detailed in the list following; but the siege commenced with those with the force.

2 ... 24-pounder guns	4 ... 10-inch mortars
22 ... 18 do. do.	8 ... 8 do. do.
4 ... 12 do. do.	9 ... 5½ do. do.
3 ... 12 do. do. brass	6 ... 8 do. howitzers
16 ... 6 do. do.	7 ... 5½ do. do.
14 ... — do. do. gallopers	4 ... 4⅜ do. do.

Many difficulties were experienced in carrying on the approaches up the steep sides of the hills; an accident, though fortunately attended with but little loss, occurred, by the magazine in rear of the breaching battery, containing 130 barrels of powder, exploding on the 21st March. Towards the end of the month, half of the 5th company 2nd battalion under Lieutenant Debrett arrived with the Hoshunabad train, and on the 31st, the Sagur force, with the 4th and 6th companies 2nd battalion and 22 heavy guns; from this time the siege was pressed with vigour, and on the 9th April the garrison surrendered, having made a very stout resistance. Lieutenant-Colonel Crossdill, of the Madras Artillery, commanded the artillery. Captains Coulthard and Pew, Lieutenants Debrett and Counsell, appear to have been present at this siege; the latter officer was slightly wounded.

Having thus brought our history to the close of the Pindaree war and its consequent service, we may notice such internal changes as were going on in the regiment and ordnance department generally, following their chronological occurrence until held service shall again call for our attention.

Originally the gun-carriages were constructed by a contractor in Fort William, under the inspection of the commissary of stores; in 1800, the system was altered, and an agency for this purpose was formed with a superintendent on a staff salary of *Rs.* 1,200 *per mensem* and his military pay and allowances. The agency was established at Cossipoor, and connected with it was another for the supply of seasoned timber.

In 1814, a second agency was found necessary to meet the wants of the department, now scattered over a very extended space, and established at Allahabad, under Major Clement Brown. In 1817, it was transferred to Futteygurh; this agency was dependent on a half-wrought *matériel* yard at Cawnpoor. The Honourable Company's timber-yards at Cossipoor and Cawnpoor were annexed to the gun-carriage agencies in 1823 and 1825 respectively, and in the year 1829, the Cossipoor agency was incorporated with that at Futteygurh.

In May, 1818, the ordnance commissariat officers were organised into a department upon the principles which had governed the previous formation of an army commissariat department; it was made one generally of seniority, and a provision was made for a certain number of warrant officers in the grade of deputy commissary, as well for two other ranks above that of conductor.

To carry out the reorganisation of the regiment, adverted to in a former page, in November, the 8th company to each European battalion was added; a draught of 100 men from the European regiment was taken for this purpose. Two companies of *golundaz* (11th and 12th) and five companies (41st to 45th) of gun *lascars* were reduced. (The 6th independent company of *golundaz*, and 40th company of gun *lascars* were reduced on their return from Ceylon in March, 1819.) The driver companies were reduced to nineteen, two for the horse, and seventeen for the bullock batteries; nine were reduced (2nd, 3rd, 4th, 5th, 6th, 7th, 9th, 10th, and 12th), and transferred to the commissariat; each company was fixed at four *sirdars* and eighty-six drivers, and the batteries consisted of eight pieces.

The *lascar* companies were strengthened by the addition of one *havildar* and fourteen privates to each company, with European battalions, and by one *havildar* with the companies attached to the 4th battalion.

The field-train establishments, which in 1809 were placed entirely under the control and care of commanding officers of artillery at Agra and Cawnpoor, were now transferred to the magazines, and kept in order by the commissaries under the general control of the commanding officer of artillery.

The horse field-batteries were increased to three, and considered part of the permanent establishment, making the number, fourteen bullock and three horse-batteries. Another bullock-battery was shortly added, on Mhow becoming a Bengal station.

The governor-general, adverting to the important, responsible, and laborious duty which the recent signal alterations in the constitution of the artillery have imposed on the commandant, and considering the staff salary at present allowed to him, when not a general officer, to bear no proportion to the extent and variety of his command, was pleased to sanction a personal allowance, in addition, of *Rs.* 500 *per mensem*; and also, on the same principle, the commanding officer of artillery in the field was allowed to draw 600, and all field commanding divisions, 300. The major of brigade was raised to an assistant adjutant-general of the regiment, and a brigade-major permanently sanctioned in the field.

A model department was formed at Dum-Dum under Captain Parlby, and the establishment for bouching guns and preparing tangent-scales was attached to it. In this department a very valuable collection of models was made up, and which, on the breaking up of the establishment in 1829, were transferred to the expense magazine, and thence to the regimental mess in 1839, the regiment having added a room for their reception.

A permanent select committee was formed, consisting of certain regimental and staff officers of artillery, at Dum-Dum and in the neighbourhood, to whom every question involving change in the *matériel* equipment of the department was to be submitted in the first instance, and their opinion was to be forwarded to assist government in coming to a decision, and they were soon fully occupied with the important questions of windage, brass ordnance, and patterns of light field-carriages.

In August the *lascars* of the regiment were very much reduced; the use of drag-ropes as a means of moving guns, except for trifling distances, or out of a difficulty, was given up, and with that, the necessity of such strong bodies of *lascars* with artillery companies ceased. They were reduced to a detail of one *havildar*, two *naiks*, and twenty-four privates, to each troop and European company, and taken away entirely from the native battalions; the men thus struck off from the regiment were formed into sixteen companies of store *lascars*, each consisting of one *subahdar*, one *jemadar*, four *havildars*, four *naiks*, and eighty privates, and were posted to the different magazines. But this arrangement was not found to answer, and the *lascar* companies were, on the war breaking out in 1824, increased to forty privates, partly, perhaps, from the insufficiency of Europeans to keep the companies up to their proper strength.

An interpreter was allowed to the regiment at headquarters, and attached to the *golundaz* companies at Dum-Dum.

Lieutenant-Colonel A. MacLeod was appointed commandant on Major-General Hardwicke's sailing for Europe in December, and with Colonel MacLeod the command of the artillery in the field ceased; the brigade-majorship was also abolished, and Captain Tennant, who held it, was appointed assistant secretary to the Military Board.

In February five companies were added to the *golundaz* battalion, raising its number to twenty companies, to meet the exigency of the war with Ava.

In June, to meet the deficiency of Europeans, three additional companies of *lascars* of eighty-four men each were raised; four privates were added to each *golundaz* company, and the *lascar* companies increased, as above mentioned, to forty men each, those who had been transferred to the store *lascars* being taken back again.

In May, a fundamental change took place in the Indian Army; the battalions were formed into regiments, and the officers of all branches of the service were placed on the same footing as to the chances of promotion, by the regiments being of equal strength in this particular. This new organisation caused a considerable degree of promotion throughout the army, and in this the artillery shared.

The officers of the regiment continued, as previously, to rise in one general gradation list, and the regiment was to be composed of

3 brigades of horse artillery, each consisting of	3 European and 1 Native troop.	
5 battalions of European foot artillery	,, ,,	4 companies.
1 battalion of Native foot artillery	,, ,,	20 companies.

The rocket-troop was to form one of the troops of a brigade.

Lascar details were attached to the troops, and a company to each European company, and a driver company to each field-battery.

These changes, however, were not even nominally carried into effect until the middle of the next year, owing to the scattered state of the regiment, the occupation the Burmese war gave, and the difficulty in obtaining a sufficient supply of European recruits to meet the demand.

In reality, some of the troops of horse artillery were not formed until the end of 1826; we therefore shall not in this place give a tabular statement of the strength of the regiment, but reserve it until we arrive at the year 1826, when a reorganisation of the native battalion made another change, and the state of the regiment, before and after its alteration, will then be seen at one glance.

The aggression of the Burmese on our frontiers, and the contempt with which they treated all remonstrances, forced the Indian Government reluctantly to declare war in 1824.

Unfortunately, little was known of the country, and a most injudicious plan of operations was drawn out, which, by seizing Rangoon and the numerous native craft the maritime capital was expected to furnish, embarking the troops in them, and sailing up the Irawaddy in the rainy season, and threatening Amerapoora, was to terminate the war in one campaign.

With this intention the expedition sailed in April, and was joined by the Madras portion early in May at Port Cornwallis in the Andaman Islands.

Two companies of the Bengal Artillery with their *lascars* accompanied the expedition.

Major Pollock, Commandant; Lieutenant Laurenson, Adjutant; Lieutenant B. Brown, Deputy Quarter-master General.

Company.	Battalion.		Company.	Battalion.	Captains.	Lieutenants.
7	3	afterwards	3	5	Timbrell	G. R. Scott, Rawlinson, G.R. McGregor.
8	3		4	5	Biddulph*	Counsell, E. Blake, O'Hanlon, McDonald.

★ Joined in December, 1824.

On the 10th May the fleet reached Rangoon, and, overcoming a very faint resistance by a few broadsides from the *Liffey*, the troops landed and took possession. They found it deserted by its inhabitants, and incapable of affording either subsistence or the means of advancing. No choice was left; nothing could be done till the cold weather, except shelter themselves against the approaching rainy season, to which the Bengal monsoon is but as summer showers in comparison. During this season, the troops suffered much from exposure, from bad and insufficient supplies, harassment by the enemy, and continual petty attacks on stockades, so that when the season for operations arrived, it found an army of invalids, instead of one fit to take the field.

The Burmese recalled their army under Bundoola from Arracan, and it arrived in the vicinity of Rangoon in November. Rangoon was invested, but, awaiting reinforcements and supplies, Sir Archibald Campbell offered little opposition, contenting himself with strengthening his own position and placing all his artillery in battery, to bear on the enemy's trenches. Things remained thus till the 5th December, when the guns all opening, the columns moved out under cover of their fire, attacked and overcame the enemy's left; Bundoola, however, rallied again, and pushed on his attack on the Shevé-da-gon *pagoda*.

On the morning of the 7th the attack was renewed; every gun that would bear on the enemy was opened, and continued firing till noon, when the infantry moving out, completely routed the enemy. He rallied in a strong position at Kokaing, from which, on the 13th, he was with difficulty dislodged, and in which action the regiment lost a fine young officer, Lieutenant O'Hanlon, who, volunteering with the bodyguard, was shot in a gallant charge, made to cover a column hard pressed by the enemy.

This action cleared the vicinity of Rangoon of the enemy, and reinforcements, stores, and supplies arriving, health was restored to the army, and preparations for an advance were strenuously made. Among the reinforcements, were a troop of horse artillery and half the rocket-troop, "corps which excited great hopes, and never disappointed them."

Troop.	Brigade.	Captains.	Lieutenants.	Sub-Lieutenant.
1	1	Lumsden	Thompson, Timmings, C. Grant.	
2	2	Graham	Paton, G. Campbell	Allen.

But, leaving the force at this point, let us trace the steps of the other divisions, and then return to the Rangoon column, on which the chief exertions of the war fell.

The small advanced party at Ramoo, unsupported by the force at Chittygong, fell an easy prey to Bundoola's force, which gradually closed on and cut it up; a detail of artillery, with two 6-pounders under Lieutenant J. W. Scott, formed part. Lieutenant Scott, severely wounded, was placed on an elephant and carried into Chittygong, whither the few who escaped fled.

After this reverse, the force at Chittygong was strengthened and formed into a division, under Major-General Morrison, for the purpose of driving the Burmese out of Arracan, crossing the Yemidong mountains and joining the Rangoon force about Prome. With it were two companies of artillery.

Lieutenant-Colonel Lindsay, Commandant;
Lieutenant Kirby, Adjutant.

Company.	Battalion.	Captains.	Lieutenants.
3	2	Rawlings	Lawrence, Fenning, Lewin, Greene, Dyke.
4	2	Hall	Cardew, Fordyce, Gaitskell, Hotham.

Lieutenant J. W. Scott was attached to the pioneers.

This column marched in the cold weather slowly, for it experienced much difficulty both from the wild and swampy country it traversed, and from the breadth of the rivers it had to cross, which, from its route being as near the coast as possible, were complete estuaries. Transporting the guns and stores over these deep and rapid streams required no small exertions from the artillery, as also in traversing the swampy delta of the Koladine River, leading to the capital. No opposition was offered until the army reached the Padhna pass, on the 25th March, 1825; there the advanced guard was fired upon, and it became necessary to drive the enemy from the heights. On the 28th, the army debouched into an open plain, under a line of hills, covering the town of Arracan.

The foot of these hills was a swampy thicket, the upper part cleared from jungle and strengthened by a breastwork. Without much reconnaissance, the guns were pushed on into battery under the hills, and a general assault took place. It was unsuccessful; such as effected their way through the tangled thicket at the foot were driven back by the musketry and volleys of stones of the defenders. The guns were abandoned for the time, and withdrawn under cover of the night.

During the night of the 31st, some troops with two 9-pounders on elephants ascended the ridge to the right of the enemy's position, moved along the crest at daylight, and bringing the guns into play, the enemy fled, leaving the city at our mercy. And here the operations of this army may be said to terminate; disease, engendered by the pestilential locality, soon raged most fearfully, and converted the town into a large cemetery. Small detachments were sent against Ramree; Lieutenant Hotham, with two guns, engaged in the attack, which was at first unsuccessful; it was, however, finally occupied, as was Aeng, a station on the pass leading through the hills.

In the following cold season reinforcements were sent, among them the 4th company 4th battalion, Lieutenants Rutherfurd and Buckle, and it was intended that the force should attempt the passage of the hills, and for that purpose it was partially collected at Amherst Island; but the difficulties and want of transport were too great, and the idea was abandoned. Arracan was evacuated, and the troops located at Ackyab, an island at the mouth of the Koladine and Myoo Rivers, Cheduba, Ramree, and Sandoway, and finally withdrawn in 1826.

That the passage of the hills was possible, there is no doubt; two regiments from Prome succeeded in the attempt by the Aeng pass, while Lieutenant B. Browne; Lieutenant Brady, of artillery; and Captain Trant, deputy quartermaster general, reached Arracan by another, early in 1826.

In 1823, a squadron of gun-boats was sent to cruise on the Burrampooter, probably with the intention of protecting that frontier from threatened incursions of the Burmese. Captain Timbrell, Lieutenants Bedingfield and Burton, were with this flotilla.

On the Sylhet frontier detachments of the 6th battalion were with the army, Captain J. Scott, Captain C. Smith, Lieutenants Brind and Lane, Lieutenant Turton, adjutant; but this force never came in contact with the enemy. The country proved impassable.

Lieutenant Huthwaite was with a detail of native artillery employed against Munneypoor, and engaged in the successful attack on the enemy's blockaded position at Daoudputlee.

Let us now return to the Rangoon Army. Such preparations as circumstances admitted of being made, the army advanced on the 11th February, 1825, in two columns, one by land and one by water: the main portion of the artillery was with the former; with the latter, Lieutenant Paton and some of the rocket-troop were placed in the *Diana* steamer.

The inadequacy of the supplies of the land column may be easily imagined when it is stated that it was with the utmost difficulty Captain Lumsden obtained four bullocks for his forge-cart!—its value, however, was repeatedly acknowledged, and its aid gladly sought, almost daily, to repair public carriages of every department.

To the water column was intrusted the operations of dislodging Bundoola from his strong position at Donabeu, while the land column pushed on as rapidly as possible for the capital. The enemy were driven from their stockade below Donabeu, but on approaching that position, it was found far more formidable than represented. The attack on it proved unsuccessful, and Sir Archibald was forced to retrograde to assist in its capture. On the 1st April, the attack was renewed by land and by water; from the latter, a brisk cannonade and effectual flights of rockets were poured in, and the batteries on the land side were equally effectual; the rockets, however, then failed; the heat and shaking they had been exposed to in the march rendered them nearly or worse than useless.

One, however, is claimed as having decided the day, by killing Bundoola. His energy alone kept the enemy together, and after his death they fled from the stockades during the night. The march was resumed, and Prome occupied by the army for the rainy season. Here

Lieutenant Thompson died on the 11th May.

During the rains, Lieutenant Timmings came round to Dum-Dum for his own health, and returned in October, carrying back with him reinforcements in men and horses for the artillery; Lieutenants G. Graham, Daniell, Begbie, and Brady also accompanied him.

The enemy rallied, and towards the middle of October had nearly surrounded Prome with stockades.

On the 2nd December, Sir Archibald Campbell attacked and defeated them, following up his success the next day. The horse artillery were pushed on in advance through *nullahs* and over rocks, to obtain a position bearing well on the enemy at Nassadee, and during the cannonade an howitzer missing fire twice, Captain Lumsden directed the shell to be withdrawn; this was done, but the fuse having ignited, the shell burst, just as it reached the muzzle, killing a *lascar*, wounding a gunner and Captain Lumsden; but he immediately rallied, and continued, in spite of his wound, directing the operations of his battery. Six guns, manned by the 3rd company 5th battalion, with Lieutenant-Colonel Pollock, Captain Biddulph, and Lieutenant Laurenson, were also engaged in this successful attack.

The enemy retired on Melloon, a stockaded position on the opposite bank of the river, there about 500 yards wide. Negotiations commenced on their part, and an armistice was concluded, to last till the 18th January, 1826. The ratified treaty not having been received, at midnight preparations for the attack commenced; batteries for the guns were got ready; boats in waiting for the troops, and at 11 a.m., when the fog cleared up, the whole of the guns, mortars, rockets, heavy and light, opened with a salvo.

The range was hit at once, and shot, shells, and rockets flew into all parts of the stockades, the interior of which, from their being planted on the side of a rising ground, was distinctly visible. The "hurtling of this iron shower" continued for about an hour and a half, when the storming columns crossed in the boats of the flotilla, and were soon masters of the place.

The rocket practice was particularly efficient, scarce a rocket failed; a strong contrast to the rockets carried by land, which had proved worthless on several occasions: those used at Melloon were brought up with the flotilla, and perhaps never has there been an occasion since the invention of the weapon where they were more successful, or their effects could be so distinctly seen, as when blazing and roaring, their long trails of smoke marking their course, they plunged into the stockades of Melloon and raked them from side to side in their eccentric courses after grazing.

The army pressed on, allowing no respite. "Officers' chargers were put in requisition to drag the guns of the invaluable horse brigade;" horses of the rocket-troop were similarly employed, and their place supplied by Burmah ponies. The horse artillery, bodyguard, and H.M.'s 13th Light Infantry now formed the advance guard, and on the 9th February came up with the enemy at Pagahen-Meen; the guns immediately opened, and the enemy were soon broken, but, in pursuing them too rashly, the 13th regiment got entangled in the difficult ground, and the main body coming up, in endeavouring to debouch from a defile, got wedged together, artillery, rockets, guns, and carriages.

Of this confusion and delay the enemy took advantage and rallied, and had they not been held in check by the gallant conduct of the horse artillery, bodyguard, and the 13th, much mischief might have been done. The confusion was soon remedied, and a complete victory rewarded the troops.

This was the last action. The enemy, thoroughly humbled, now opened negotiations in earnest, which were soon concluded. A deputation proceeded to the "Golden Fort," at Amerapoora, and returned with the ratified treaty of peace. Among those selected for this distinguished duty was Captain Lumsden, than whom and his gallant troop, none had borne a more honourable and useful part during these laborious campaigns.

A silver medal, of the annexed pattern, was awarded to all the native troops engaged in the war, either in Rangoon, Arracan, or Sylhet.

Among the general orders we find:

> The governor-general entertains the highest sense of the efficient services and honourable exertions of Captains Timbrell of the artillery; and the services of the Bengal foot artillery, under

Lieutenant-Colonel Pollock, and of the Bengal rocket-troop and horse artillery, under Captains Graham and Lumsden, demand also the special acknowledgments of government.

Early in 1825, British interference in the state of Bhurtpoor became necessary, (Maharajah Bulwunt Sing succeeded his father in 1824, and was dethroned by his cousin, Durjun Sal in March, 1825), and Major-General Sir D. Ochterlony, the agent to the governor-general at Delhi, exercising the authority vested in him, ordered the assembly of a force for the purpose It was disapproved by the governor-general, and many portions of the regiment had in consequence the *désagrémens* of a useless march in the months of April, May, and June.

In the cold weather, however, affairs in Bhurtpoor continuing the same, and those in Ava more satisfactory, the project was resumed, and a force ordered to collect at Agra and Muttra, in November, under the command of Lord Combermere, who had just been appointed to the chief command in India.

For this army the whole of the available artillery was drawn together and the provinces were denuded. The field batteries were thrown into the magazines, and their bullocks appropriated to the siege-trains, and yet when collected, the whole were barely sufficient to work the guns in battery, without one single relief. In like manner the magazines from Cawnpore to Kurnal poured forth all their munitions of war, but this afforded only 114 siege-pieces, with about 1,000 rounds of shot per gun, and 500 shells per mortar and howitzer, with a proportion of shrapnel and case.

16	......	24-pounders,		2	......	13-inch mortars,	
20	......	18	„	12	......	10	„	„
4	......	12	„	46	......	8	„	„
12	......	8-inch howitzers.					

A reserve was formed at Allahabad to be pushed on as opportunity offered.

The *personnel* consisted of five and a-half troops of European, and two of native horse artillery, nine companies of European, and five of native foot artillery, (see list below), forming a total of about 1,200 Europeans, and 700 native artillerymen, with 500 *lascars*, but of these only 1,100 were foot artillery, barely sufficient to man the guns, even when augmented by a body of horse artillery recruits, who, just drafted into that branch on the augmentation, were not qualified for the duties of mounted artillerymen.

2nd company, 1st brigade		1st company			
1st "	⎫	2nd "	⎫		
2nd "	⎬ 2nd "	3rd "	⎬ 3rd battalion		
3rd "	⎭	4th "	⎭		
4th "		2nd "	⎱ 4th "		
1st "	⎫	3rd "	⎰		
2nd "	⎬ 3rd "	3rd "	⎫		
4th "	⎭	4th "	⎬ 6th "		
2nd "	⎫	5th "			
3rd "	⎬ 1st battalion	13th "	⎭		
4th "	⎭	17th "			

The following officers were present:—

Brigadier M'Leod, C.B., Commanding ; Captain Tennant, Assistant Adjutant-General ; Lieutenant Dashwood, Aide-de-Camp.

Brigadier C. Brown, Commanding Horse Artillery ; Lieutenant Winfield, Major of Brigade.

Brigadier R. Hetzler, Commanding Foot Artillery and Park ; Lieutenant Johnson, Major of Brigade.

Horse Artillery.

Lieutenant-Colonel Stark, Commanding 2nd Brigade.
Major Whish, Commanding 1st Brigade.
Captain J. Scott, Commanding 3rd Brigade.

Capt. Hyde,	Lieut. Maidman,
" N. Campbell,	" MacLean,
" Farrington,	" Ewart,
" Blake,	" M'Morine,
" R. Roberts,	" Garbett, Adj. 2nd Brig.
" W. Bell,	" Wakefield,
" Wood,	" Alexander,
Lieut. Moreland,	" W. Anderson,
" Nicholl,	" Wiggins,
" Pennington, Adjutant 3rd Brigade	" Backhouse,
	2nd Lieut. Pillans,
" Bingley,	" Grote,
" Mackay, Adj. 1st Brig.	" Boileau.
" Cullen,	

Foot Artillery.

Lieutenant-Colonel Parker, Commanding 6th Battalion.
„ „ Biggs, Commanding 3rd Battalion.

Major Battine,	Capt. Woodroofe,
Capt. Pereira, Commissary,	„ Brooke, Commissary,
„ Curphey,	„ Oliphant,
„ Pew,	Lieut. R. C. Dixon,
Lieut. Huthwaite,	Lieut. Clerk, Adj. 6th Bat.
„ Sanders, Adj. 3rd Bat.	„ Mowatt,
„ Hughes,	„ McGregor,
„ Rotton,	„ Edwards, Adj. 1st Bat.
„ A. Abbott,	„ Ellis,
„ Torckler,	2nd Lieut. J. Abbott,
„ Cautley,	„ Bazely,
„ Garrett,	„ Duncan,
„ Horsford, Adj. 4th Bat.	„ Todd,
„ Wade,	„ Sage.

The trains and stores were collected at Agra and Muttra, and started, in two divisions, on the 9th December. On the 17th they were united before Bhurtpoor, and the grand park formed. The cavalry and horse artillery had preceded the army and secured the *bund* of the lake, just as the enemy were about to cut it, to flood the ditch of the fortress.

The laboratory tents were pitched on the 16th, and the preparation of the platforms and stores commenced upon. On the 23rd, the first battery was armed, and it opened its fire on the 24th; daily the approaches, parallels, and batteries were extended, under a fire from the enemy always hot, and generally well directed. In addition to breaching-batteries, a mine was driven under the N.E. bastion, and sprung, but without effect, on the 7th January, the charge being too small. The gun breach was by this time practicable, and Lieutenant-Colonel Stark and his adjutant ascended it; the firing was directed to be continued, to improve it, but the shot buried themselves, pounding the earth into fine dust.

On the 9th a depot of ammunition, formed to supply the batteries, was blown up by a shot from the enemy passing through a tumbril; the whole was consumed with a fearful explosion; but although the enemy kept up a heavy fire all night, from every gun which would bear upon the spot, clearly indicated by the burning stores, the casualties were few. A mine was sprung in the counterscarp opposite the gun breach, making the descent into the ditch easy. On the 12th, a mine was commenced under the long-necked bastion; it was ready and loaded by the 18th January, and the firing it was to be the signal for the assault. A heavy fire was kept up from all the batteries on the morning of the 18th; the mine was sprung, and scarcely had the heavy mass of dust and smoke cleared away, when the columns moved out to the assault and were shortly in possession of the place.

The artillery casualties in this siege were remarkably few; the labours undergone by both officers and men in the batteries for twenty-six days were extreme, but borne with the utmost cheerfulness and good temper. The ammunition expended was,

24-pounder round shot 18,331	18-pounder case	391
,, ,, shrapnell 345	Shells, 13-inch	236
,, ,, case 639	,, 10 ,,	4,506
18-pounder round shot 22,533	,, 8 ,,	13,720
,, ,, shrapnell 524	,, ,, ,, shrapnell	119
	Grand Total	61,446

The average rate of firing was forty-eight rounds per gun, and twelve per mortar *per diem*; the greatest, 142 and 20. Nine 24-pounders, sixteen 18-pounders, one 10-inch and seven 8-inch mortars, were rendered unserviceable, and the carriages of six 8-inch (brass) howitzers broke down during the siege. (The daily expenditure of ammunition and artillery details of this siege will be found in the *East-India United Service Journal* for 1837.)

General orders of the commander-in-chief:—

To Brigadier MacLeod, C.B., in the general command of the artillery, and Brigadiers Hetzler and Brown, commanding the siege and field artillery respectively, the Commander-in-Chief feels greatly indebted for their highly creditable exertions, as, also, to the whole of the officers and men of the artillery, for the excellent display of scientific correctness in the batteries, as well as for their commendable endurance of fatigue which the nature of the service necessarily exposed them to.

The commandant issued the following regimental order:—

The commandant begs to offer to officers and men of that part of the regiment engaged in the field under his more immediate command his best thanks for their conduct and exertions during the siege, which have, in general orders today published, obtained the approbation of the Right Honourable the Commander-in-Chief; and to Brigadiers Hetzler, C.B., and C. Brown, he has more especially to tender his acknowledgments for the assistance he has derived from them in their respective commands.

To Captain Tennant, the assistant adjutant-general of the arm, he feels much indebted for his able assistance on this and many other occasions, for which he is entitled to his warmest acknowledgments and thanks. To Lieutenant Dashwood, his *aide-de-camp*, he also tenders his best thanks for his conspicuously useful exertions.

In a former page we stated our intention of reserving a tabular statement of the organisation of 1824, until we reached the year 1827, when a fresh arrangement of the native artillery took place; we have now reached that period, (see table following page) for the year 1826 has little to be recorded, except that in November four companies of *golundaz* and three of *lascars* (those raised in 1824) were reduced.

In September, 1827, an additional battalion of officers was added to the regiment, and the native artillery divided into two battalions, of eight companies each, denominated the 6th and 7th battalions.

CHAPTER 8
Establishment of Retiring Fund

At the conclusion of the Burmese war, the horses from the Sylhet local corps were transferred to Dum-Dum, for the purpose of being attached to a battery, and in the early part of 1827, the undersized stud horses, which had hitherto been sold to the public, were directed to be admitted into the service for the light field-batteries, as government had decided on horsing them all, the uselessness of bullocks for the purpose having been thoroughly proved. The number of batteries was, in July, 1827, fixed at twelve.

The arrangement was immediately commenced on, and, by the end of the year, six batteries were in an effective state, and the remainder would soon have been ready. It will, however, scarcely be credited that in April, 1828, these orders were countermanded, and bullocks directed to be retained and the horses of the batteries so equipped sold off.

							HORSE ARTILLERY.											FOOT ARTILLERY.											
							EUROPEAN.				NATIVE.					LASCARS.		EUROPEAN.				NATIVE.					LASCARS.		
—	Colonels.	Lieutenant-Colonels.	Majors.	Captains.	1st Lieutenants.	2nd Lieutenants.	Brigade Staff.	Non-commissioned Officers.	Trumpeters, Farriers, Rough-riders.	Gunners.	Native Officers.	Brigade Staff.	Non-commissioned Officers.	Trumpeters, Farriers, Rough-riders.	Troopers.	Non-commissioned Officers.	Lascars.	Battalion Staff.	Non-commissioned Officers.	Buglers.	Gunners.	Native Officers.	Battalion Staff.	Non-commissioned Officers.	Buglers.	Privates.	Native Officers.	Non-commissioned Officers.	Lascars.
1824	9	9	9	45	90	45	27	207	54	720	6	6	36	28	270	36	288	43	424	40	1620	60	3	320	40	2080	20	80	800
1827	10	10	10	50	100	50	27	207	54	720	6	6	36	28	270	36	288	46	424	40	1600	48	6	256	32	1664	20	80	800
On Returns, 1st Dec. 1827	10	10	10	50	100	50	27	218	57	732	7	6	36	28	270	36	288	46	436	40	1600	50	6	293	32	1700	21	82	921

It is difficult to penetrate the veil of mystery which shrouds the acts of the Council Chamber, so as to ascertain the real author of such vacillating policy; the reasons which induced the equipment of 1827, and which were the accumulated experience of years, were equally cogent in 1828, and that they were sound, everyone who has had experience of Indian warfare will vouch. That there is no reason to suppose the change was made consequent on orders from home, we may conclude, for in 1834, we find the Court of Directors "satisfied of the superiority of horses over bullocks for light field-artillery," directing "their gradual substitution," an order to which no attention was paid by the then governor-general.

Under these circumstances, rumour, with her hundred tongues, is perhaps not wrong in attributing it to a "malignant influence," which for a quarter of a century opposed every suggestion for the improvement of the prospects or efficiency of the ordnance branch. A late military member of the Council of India, long secretary to government in the military department, who, repeating the one argument, equally applicable against every advance, "We won India with bullocks, and why should we not keep it with bullocks?" supported the late Lord W. Bentinck in putting aside the Court's orders of 1834, and Lord Auckland in paying a slow and partial obedience to them when repeated in 1841.

Cotemporary with this retrograde movement, was the reduction of the field-batteries from eight to six pieces each, a good arrangement, had it been accompanied by a proportionate increase in their numbers; but this was not done, and it therefore reduced, by one fourth, the field-artillery, already far too low, in reference to the other branches of the army. The gun contract was at this time transferred from the senior artillery officer at the station to the officer commanding the battery, a very judicious change, as it placed the power in the hands of the person most properly responsible for the efficiency of the battery, and left to the superior officer his proper duty of supervision unfettered by personal considerations.

The rocket-troop was converted into a gun-troop; but, that the use of the weapon might not be forgotten, a proportion of rockets was directed to be attached to each field-battery. For this purpose, the commandant submitted a proposition to add a car, capable of carrying 120 6-pounder rockets, to each field-battery, and capable of manoeuvring in line with it; but after the pattern car had been prepared, the subject was, somehow or other, allowed to fall into oblivion, probably, we believe, from the supplies of rockets having been countermanded; and thus for many years neither officers nor men had any opportunities of accustoming themselves to their use. From 1828 till 1840, when at the headquarters of the regiment their use was resumed previous to despatching a supply to China, and at Kurnal and Ferozepore, where, in 1842, some which were sent for service in the passes of Affghanistan were used, not a rocket was fired.

Another reduction followed, causing great excitement in the army at large, but which pressed more heavily on the artillery than any other branch. We refer to the orders of December, 1828, placing certain stations on half-*batta*; of these, Allahabad, Benares, Dinapore, and Dum-Dum, were artillery stations, and the latter, that of the headquarters of the regiment, the artillery being a European regiment, and therefore considered not liable to be called on for sudden movements: the officers were placed on half-tentage likewise.

That the reduction in allowances was such as to bear heavily on individuals, especially in the lower grades, the statement following will show, and this, moreover, was subject to another tax of 4½ *per cent.*, the exchange between *sonat* and *sicca rupees*, the former being the coin in which the military accounts are kept, while the latter was that current in Calcutta, and in which the troops were actually paid.

	R.	A.	P.		R.	A.	P.	
Lieut.-Colonel	1,032	4	0	...	752	14	0	per mensem.
Major	789	3	0	...	580	14	6	,,
Captain	433	10	0	...	354	13	0	,,
1st Lieutenant	265	12	0	...	209	14	0	,,
2nd Lieutenant	213	5	0	...	167	10	6	,,

The headquarters of the regiment being at Dum-Dum, the mess, band, library, and other regimental institutions, were there, and officers were naturally fond of being stationed there, for various reasons; such as its gaiety and amusements, and the opportunities it offered for studying their profession or improving their prospects in the service.

From these circumstances, the regimental head-quarters generally had in a time of peace a large number of officers of the higher ranks present, and this contributed to render it a desirable station. But all this was reversed by the half-*batta* order; instead of thronging to the head-quarters, the station was avoided by all ranks, and the discipline of the regiment suffered much in after years from the difficulty of keeping sufficient officers of standing for the common routine duties of the place and instruction of the young officers joining the regiment. The want of a sufficient body of officers at Dum-Dum of known talents and experience is also felt when vacancies suddenly occur in any of the important artillery situations dependent on it for the temporary arrangement in cases of exigency. We refer to the arsenal, foundry, powder-works, expense magazine, acting assistant quartermaster, and ordnance secretary in the Military Board; in several of these situations much difficulty has at times been experienced, and has only been met by doubling-up the duties of two appointments on several occasions in one person.

The regiment (and the army) memorialised strongly on the occasion, but without effect, though some years afterwards the hardship was partially ameliorated by the grant of full tentage to the artillery, it having been clearly shown that the officers of no branch of the army are subject to such sudden and repeated movements, and these as individuals, and not with the aids and conveniences which the officers of a wing or detachment of infantry find by combining their means. In the table following is noted the receipts of officers at half-*batta* stations, as sanctioned in 1835, and since continued.

	R.	A.	P.
Lieutenant-Colonel .... per mensem	827	14	0
Major	580	14	6
Captain	392	5	0
1st Lieutenant	234	14	0
2nd Lieutenant	192	10	6

Recently, (as at 1852), a further modification of the order, limiting its effects to stations within two hundred miles of each presidency, has taken place, and as the saving caused by it is now reduced to so very a trifle, and its weight laid so unequally on the different branches of the army, a strong feeling of hope exists that the order will finally be totally repealed.

Further reductions followed; two troops and companies were struck off from each regiment of cavalry and infantry, and with them two lieutenants and one ensign. Although the reduction of the companies neither was nor could be made applicable to the artillery, yet the three subalterns per battalion, or thirty in all, were reduced, the twenty first lieutenants remaining supernumerary till absorbed, and thus stopping the promotion of the second lieutenants about four years. The results of this were not felt for some time, because the actual number of officers present with the regiment continued much the same, and the number of cadets sent out to replace casualties was not altered, the supernumerary list continued long, and it was even attempted to retain the cadets unpromoted until vacancies occurred; but we believe that the government law officers decided that it would not be legal, and they were accordingly all promoted to commissions.

With the reduction above noticed, was coupled what was thought a boon, at the time, but which in fact has proved the cause of much supersession by the royal service—the promotion of all lieutenant-colonels commandant to the rank of colonel. Every lieutenant-colonel in H.M.'s service in India who happened to be senior in that rank to any one of the lieutenant-colonels commandant now promoted, was also breveted with the rank of colonel, and as in each presidency there are no less than four distinct gradation-lists leading to this rank, viz., artillery, engineers, cavalry, and infantry, each of which has had its fortunate period, the confusion and supersession which followed may easily be imagined.

It was brought to a crisis by Lieutenant-Colonel MacLeod, a lieutenant-colonel of 1827 (a cadet of 1794), obtaining his regimental colonelcy in four years, and, of course, all lieutenant-colonels of H. M.'s service senior to him were also promoted, and the anomalies became so stupendous, that an alteration was made in the plan, and the Bengal native infantry, as the largest body, was made the guide; but this destroys the only chance the other branches had of ever retrieving in the higher grade the slow promotion they may have had in the lower, and gives the royal service, with its promotion by purchase and regimentally to the rank of lieutenant-colonel, a fearful advantage (see note following), over the Company's service, which has been increased by the power exercised by the commander-in-chief in India to grant brevets of major-general to such colonels in India as H.M.'s brevet to Company's officers may supersede.

> The effect is clearly shown in the brigading the late army of the Sutlej, where the army, consisting of fifteen cavalry and thirty-seven infantry regiments, formed into six divisions and sixteen brigades, was thus commanded:—
>
> | | | | | |
> |---|---|---|---|---|
> | Cavalry regiments | .... | 3 Queen's, | 12 | Company's |
> | Infantry　　　„ | .... | 8　　„ | 29 | „ |
> | Division Commanders | ...... | 4　　„ | 2 | „ |
> | Brigade　　　„ | .... | 7　　„ | 9 | „ |
>
> Of the cavalry, although four-fifths were Company's regiments, the division and three of the brigade commands fell to H.M.'s service.

The rank thus given is of a double nature, and may be made use of or laid aside at pleasure, allowing them to be lieutenant-colonels or major-generals, as most convenient, and thus enabling them to reap the benefits of high rank without its drawback—removal from lucrative commands in India.

In 1828, the uniform of the officers of the horse artillery was changed; the jack-boots and leather breeches were superseded by the overalls, and the equipments and horse furniture of a similar pattern to those worn by light cavalry were adopted; but the uniform of the non-commissioned officers and gunners remained unchanged. For actual hard work on horseback, such as is riding in the guns, few will deny that the boots and breeches are the most serviceable dress, but they are inconvenient when dismounted, and ill-adapted for exposure to wet, and at no time can they be endued in a hurry.

The foot artillery about the same time discarded their short jacket faced with scarlet and embroidered with gold, for the present plain but handsome uniform: the second epaulette to the subaltern ranks was ordered in 1833. The undress remained a blue jacket with scarlet cuffs and collar, unrelieved by a button or atom of lace until 1841, when a row of studs down the front, and gilt shoulder-scales, were added; the latter adding as much to its appearance as they detracted from its comfort.

Several years now passed away void of internal change or external employment. Such universal quiet reigned, that it appeared as if swords and spears might be most usefully turned into ploughshares and reaping-hooks, and the army looked round in vain for employment. Central India was at rest, Nepal not likely to disturb the quiet, and the Punjab, under the strong rule of Runjeet Sing, seemed removed from the chance of inimical contact with the Indian Government.

Suddenly rumours sprung up of disturbances in Rajasthan, which, by degrees, assumed a more determined aspect, and Maun Sing, of Joudpoor, was mentioned as the delinquent, and an army was about to assemble against him, but, humbling himself, he averted his ruin, and a portion of the force was sent against the robber tribes of Shekawut.

With the force were three troops of horse artillery, eight companies of foot, and a siege-train of twenty-six pieces.

Brigadier Parker commanded the artillery; Captain Sanders, commissary of ordnance; but the force met with no opposition, and after destroying many of the robbers' strongholds, returned to cantonments.

The reductions which took place in 1828 by this time began to tell, as the supernumeraries were absorbed; and to provide even a small number of officers for the foot artillery, the subalterns of the horse artillery were reduced to two per troop; a very inadequate number when the Indian contingencies are borne in mind.

For many years the officers of the Bengal Army had been accustomed to procure the retirement of their seniors by the donation of a sum of money, varying in amount according to the value of the step and the abilities of the donors. The custom, it is true, was contrary to the orders of the Court of Directors, but they were aware of and permitted it. In the artillery the same custom prevailed; and this year it was systematized by the establishment of a fund by monthly contributions from all captains and subalterns to provide for two retirements annually. Its advantages have been most apparent in its working, and the principle of a mutual insurance tontine, on which it was formed, has rendered it more effective even than was expected.

The other branches of the army were not successful in establishing funds of the sort; but the question being much agitated, led to a memorial, from Lieutenant-Colonel Powel, of the Bombay Army, to the Court of Directors, praying that the system might be put a stop to, on the plea of its interfering with the seniority system of the Company's army. It was met by several counter-memorials, and, on replying to the whole together, the court gave the proceedings their sanction, by declaring that, although they would not cancel the orders forbidding purchase, they would hold them in abeyance, unless there appeared such a probability of the pension-list being overloaded, that their interference would be necessary, and that of this, due warning should be given.

These years passed off without any portion of the army being called on to take the field, if we except a slight *émeute* among the Bheels in the neighbourhood of Mhow, in 1837, to check which, a small body of troops with two horse artillery guns, from the 2nd troop 3rd brigade, under Lieutenant Kinleside, were detached; but towards the end of the next, a storm appeared to be gathering in the north-west. The Persians besieged Heerat, and were only foiled in their attempt by the steady persevering gallantry and resources of Lieutenant Eldred Pottinger, of the Bombay Artillery, who, throwing himself into the fortress, inspired its defenders with a portion of his own dauntless spirit.

Persia was supposed to be egged on by Russian intrigue, and India to be its ultimate object. Self-defence called upon the Indian Government to check these designs, and having vainly endeavoured by negotiation to render Affghanistan under Dost Mahomed a barrier, the government resolved to espouse the cause of its exiled sovereign, Shah Soojah-ool-Moolk, with the hopes that, when replaced on the throne of his forefathers, he would prove a stanch friend.

To carry this plan out, an army was assembled after the rains, at Ferozepore; but information arriving of the Persians, baffled by Pottinger's cool resolution, having decamped from before Heerat, the plan of the campaign was altered. In fact, our end was gained; and had it not been for the very unnecessary connection with Shah Soojah as a reason for our interference, and which would have stood better on the simple plea of self-preservation, not a soldier need have moved from Ferozepore. But before entering on the eventful campaigns which followed this step, let us glance at events in other parts of India which necessitated the assembly of a force in Bundlecund, though the campaign was a bloodless one.

The Jhansee *raj* having lapsed through the failure of direct heirs, the widow of a former *raja* endeavoured to place, as the adopted son of the previous ruler, a boy on the throne. A disturbance arose, which ended in the murder of the minister supported by the British authority. This act of the *Bhaiee* was called in question by the governor-general's agent; his authority was treated with disrespect, and he found it necessary to call in the aid of a regiment and a couple of guns.

At these, the insurgents, who had seized the fort, laughed, and on his attempting a parley with them, attacked and wounded his elephant and *chuprassees*, and forced him precipitately to retreat. Reinforcements and a battering train were sent for from Sagur; but the country had been so denuded of troops to form the army of the Indus, that, had it not been for the Mhow troops just being relieved from Bombay, a very insufficient force could have been collected.

A train of four 18-pounders and four 8-inch mortars, with as much ammunition as carriage could be obtained for, was got ready, and, in the absence of available artillery officers, the commissary of ordnance at Sagur, Lieutenant Buckle, who had offered his services, started in charge of it early in December, and after a march of twelve days, rendered difficult and fatiguing by the badness of the roads, the steep banks and rocky beds of the rivers and *nullahs* which abounded, and the broken rocky *ghats* leading from table-land into Bundlecund, reached Jhansee on the 18th December.

The troops collected by degrees, and the artillery, when reinforced from Cawnpoor, amounted to that detailed in the list following.

1st company, 3rd battalion, and field-battery.	Major Bell.
Detail of golundaz, and 2 6-pounders.	Captain Lane.
	Lieut. Buckle, commissary of ordnance.
Gwalior contingent battery.	„ Richardson.
	„ Kinleside.
6 18-pounders.	„ Abercrombie.
2 8-inch howitzers.	„ Salmon, adjutant.
4 „ mortars.	„ J. H. Smyth, Gwalior contingent.

The engineer park was placed in the charge of the commissary of ordnance, the field engineer, Major Smith, having joined *dak*, and the preparation of *matériel* instantly commenced.

Continual communications passed between the *Bhaiee* and the agent, which were warlike to the last, and, as she had collected bands of Nagas, resistance was expected; but on the preparations being completed, the force moving down to invest the fort, carrying their train and the stock of gabions and fascines which had been prepared, she fled during the night, and the fort was taken possession of without firing a shot.

The labour of conveying the heavy ordnance over a broken country was the chief difficulty, but this was not much felt, owing to the season of the year.

The army of the Indus assembled at Ferozepore, and a meeting took place between the governor-general and Runjeet Sing. The news of the Persians breaking up from before Heerat determined government on sending only one division of the army, accompanied by the troops which were being raised for Shah Soojah, under British officers, into Affghanistan. The artillery for the *Shah's* service consisted originally of two troops of horse artillery, to which were afterwards added a mountain train and some body-guard guns.

Captain W. Anderson was intrusted with the formation of the horse artillery, and though but little time was allowed him, and many difficulties arose from the demand for men and horses for the other branches, his exertions succeeded in overcoming them, and he marched in good time from Dehli, with his two troops fully equipped, but, of course, untrained. His endeavours were well seconded by his two subalterns, Lieutenants Cooper and Turner. The *Shah's* guns were in Lieutenant Warburton's charge, and the mountain train was organised by Captain Backhouse, but not until 1840.

The regular artillery, with this division from Bengal, consisted of

Major Pew, commanding ; Captain Day, commissary of ordnance ; Lieutenant Backhouse, M.B.

Company.	Brigade.	Battalion.	Captains.	Lieutenants.
2	2	–	Grant	Duncan, J. Anderson.
4	3	–	Timmings	Mackenzie, Hawkins, E. Kaye
2	–	6*	A. Abbott	Dawes, R. Shakespear, Warburton.
4	–	2	Garbett	J. Abbott, Walrek, Green.

* (No. 6 battery.)

Captain Todd, of the artillery, who had been employed in Persia, was attached to the political department.

The army commenced its march on the 10th December, and met with no difficulties until the 16th March, 1839, when they entered the Bolan pass, a pass as terrible to the Indian, as that of Avernus to the classical, imagination. Here the toils of the campaign began, and, as usual in such cases, a double share fell to the artillery. The horses, overweighted and ill-fed, with difficulty dragged the carriages through its stony lengths; the camels and bullocks, over-driven to keep pace with the column, and escape the new danger arising from the matchlocks of the Murrees and Brahoos perched on the rocks, stumbled and fell, many never to rise again: store-carts and baggage were lost by these accidents.

The difficulties of procuring provisions were increased after clearing the pass by the arrival of the Bombay column, though the country became easier until reaching the Kojuck pass; narrow, steep, and in places blocked up by large rocks, it was with the greatest difficulty, and by incredible perseverance, that the heavy and light artillery were got through this obstacle. Great loss of baggage occurred here from the deaths of camels. At this point, the camel battery, which had hitherto got on very well, showed symptoms of knocking up; the animal's conformation, from want of power of muscular exertion, being quite unfitted for draught in situations of difficulty.

All at length reached Candahar towards the end of April, but the horses of the horse artillery and cavalry so worn, that a long rest was necessary to fit them for work; the troops, too, required rest and food, and the halt continued till the end of June, though not entirely without employment, for the camel battery took part in the expedition against Girisk, and two guns of the 4th troop 3rd brigade, under Lieutenant E. Kaye, were detached with the *Shah's* troops against refractory chiefs in Tezeen.

From Candahar a mission was sent to Heerat; Captain Todd was placed at the head of it, and Lieutenants J. Abbott and R. Shakespear were his assistants. Of the results of this mission, or of his assistants, to Khiva; of the difficulties and dangers endured and overcome by Abbott as the pioneer, and the success which crowned Shakespear, in following his path, nothing need be said in this place. Their own accounts have already been published.

On the army moving forward, the 2nd troop 2nd brigade, 2nd company 6th battalion, with No. 6 light field battery, alone accompanied it. The *Shah's* artillery, the 4th troop 3rd brigade, the 4th company 2nd battalion, and the heavy guns, remained at Candahar. On the 21st July the fortress of Ghuznee was reached, reconnoitred the next day, and the artillery placed in position, by 3 a.m. of the 23rd, to cover the assault which was ordered at dawn. On the gate being blown in by two bags of powder, every gun opened to cover the advance of the storming party, which was perfectly successful, and, by 5 o'clock, the place was in our possession.

The exertions of the troops were rewarded by a medal from Shah Soojah, and which is remarkable for one thing—being the first given in India to all engaged. Hitherto, these decorations had been granted to the native troops alone; but on this occasion the medal was given to all, without any distinction whatever. It was suspended from a crimson and green ribbon.

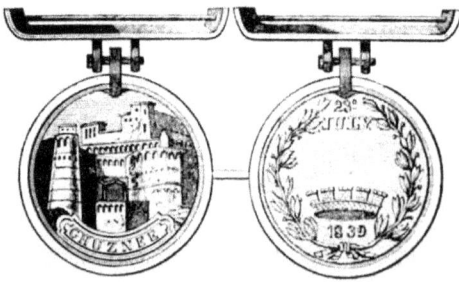

The army continued its march to Cabul without opposition. Deserted by his followers, Dost Mahomed fled, leaving his guns at Maidan a spoil to the invaders; and himself narrowly escaping from a band of officers, among whom was Lieutenant Backhouse, of the artillery, who, under Major Outram, followed him closely, but were misled by the arch traitor Haji Khan Kokur.

But while the main army was thus employed, a small column, chiefly of irregulars, with Colonel Wade, escorted the Shah-Zada by the Khyber Pass to his father's capital. With this column were two howitzers, manned by a detachment of the 4th company 2nd brigade, and commanded by Lieutenant Barr: Lieutenant Maule, of the artillery, was attached to the prince's suite. This column met with no opposition, except on first entering the Khyber Pass, where they were engaged with the Afreedis at Koulsir, and again at Alee Musjid. The names of Lieutenants Barr and Maule are both mentioned in Lieutenant-Colonel Wade's despatches on the occasion.

The main army reached Cabul on the 6th August, and Colonel Wade's column on the 3rd September. The Bombay column returned in October, and, picking up four of the *Shah's* horse artillery guns, under Lieutenant Cooper, proceeded against Khelat. Reaching it on the 13th November, the troops advanced to the assault under cover of the fire from the guns, which drove the enemy from the neighbouring heights; the guns were now directed against the gates, and, these being forced, the place was soon won. In his despatch, General Wiltshire says:

> To Lieutenants Forster and Cooper, I feel greatly indebted for the scientific and steady manner in which the service of dislodging the enemy from the heights and afterwards effecting an entrance into the fort was performed.

The main army left Cabul for Hindustan in October, 1839; the 2nd company 6th battalion with No. 6 battery alone remained. The camel draught had proved so useless for such a country, that horses were now directed to be substituted, and so promptly was this order carried out by Captain Abbott, that within fifteen days after receiving it, half the battery was equipped, and marched against the Ghilzies, under Lieutenant Dawes, moving upwards of 400 miles ere it returned. The other half of the battery was employed in the following January in the Koh-i-daman under Captain Abbott. Pushoot held out, and the 9-pounders being placed in battery at daylight, a breach was formed on both sides of the outer gate, but an inner one existing, against which the guns could not be brought to bear, bags of powder were tried without avail, and the troops were forced to withdraw; but the enemy fled during the night. Colonel Orchard wrote:

> To Captain Abbott, the highest praise is due, for the manner in which he has conducted the arduous duties devolving on him, as well as the great service rendered by him yesterday.

We have now to notice perhaps the most extraordinary march ever performed by artillery—that of a native troop of horse artillery across the Hindoo Kosh to Bamian; extraordinary both from obstacles overcome, and the circumstance of the men of this troop being natives of Hindostan. The 4th troop 3rd brigade was ordered for this trip in September, 1839, and, Captain Timmings having just died, it was under the command of a subaltern, Lieutenant M. Mackenzie, with whom was Lieutenant E. Kaye.

The valley of Bamian lies about N.W. from Cabul, distant only 112 miles; but it is separated from the valley in which the capital is situate by a broad belt of stupendous mountains, the highest range of which exceeds in altitude 12,000 feet. The troop entered upon its mountain road near the village of Urghundee, and while toiling up the first laborious ascent (steep in itself, but rendered still more difficult by huge stones and fragments of rock), it was met by Major Thomson, of the engineers, and some other officers, (Major, later Lieutenant-Colonel, Salter of the cavalry, and Lieutenant Sturt of the engineers, since killed in action), who were just returning from an excursion to Bamian.

Major Thomson immediately declared the road to Bamian to be impracticable for guns—that the passes in advance were still more difficult in their nature than that of Urghundee, and said that he would, immediately on arrival at Cabul, report to the envoy that it would be useless to attempt to reach Bamian. The troop, however, continued its march, and, the passage of the Urghundee Ghât accomplished, descended into the beautiful valley of the Cabul River, along the banks of which the route continued for three marches, passing Julraiz and Sir-i-Chushmeh. The road was at times difficult, being frequently in the rocky bed of the stream, and always ascending, gradually becoming steeper and more toilsome.

The summit of the Oonai pass is said to be 11,400 feet in elevation; at this great elevation, even in September, the cold was intense. The passage of the range was a work of great toil, as the ascents and descents were numerous. The summit of the range is in general a table-land, gradually sloping towards the north-west; not one continuous table-land, but intersected by numerous deep glens, running parallel to each other, with steep precipitous sides, difficult to ascend or descend. On the 21st, a small mud fort, named Youatt, was reached, and on the 23rd the troop, after crossing several spurs from the range just surmounted, descended to the banks of the Helmund, beyond which towered the snow-capped peaks of Koh-i-Baba.

In consequence of the report received from Major Thomson of the impracticable nature of the road to Bamian, the envoy had sent instructions for three guns and all the ammunition-waggons to return to Cabul, the other three guns to halt until elephants sent from Cabul should arrive; it was then intended that the three guns should be dismounted and carried over the remaining passes on elephants. These instructions were received at Youatt, but the neighbourhood being entirely destitute of forage, it was considered advisable to move the troop on to Gurden Dewaal, on the River Helmund.

Having arrived there, the troop halted, and Lieutenant Mackenzie went forward and examined the pass over the Hindoo-Koosh range. This officer having considered the passage practicable, forwarded a report to that effect to headquarters, and requested permission to proceed with the whole of the troop. Permission was at length received, and on the 30th the march was resumed.

The foot of the Irak pass was attained in three difficult marches, the ascent being constant and fatiguing. The passage was commenced immediately, nearly all the guns and carriages being pulled up by hand (the horses being taken out); at this work, the artillery and infantry soldiers and some 200 Hazarehs were employed during the whole day, and it was not until dark that the entire battery had reached the foot of the western face of the mountain, which was found to be considerably steeper than that up which the ascent led.

On the following day the march was resumed through a deep and dreary defile, abounding in rocks, and the precipices enclosing it so steep and lofty, that the sun's rays scarcely ever penetrated to its lowest depths. Through this tortuous glen the troop wound its way, until, after many an interruption from rocky ledges of dangerous descent, the small valley of Meeanee Irak was reached on the 4th of October, and vegetation and human habitations were once more seen.

The whole of the 5th was occupied in passing the Kuski Ghât, over a range of no great elevation (a spur only of the Hindoo-Koosh) but of great difficulty. The ascent was occasionally so steep (at an angle of 45°) that the men working at the drag-ropes could not keep their footing; horses, of course, were out of the question. The ascent was, however, accomplished in the afternoon, and the descent by the edge of a precipice, where a false step would have insured instant destruction, commenced. This, too, was effected, but night found the troop in a defile so narrow, and enclosed by such steep walls, that it seemed to be but a fissure in the mountain, caused by some convulsion of nature. Nothing further could be done till daylight; early on the morning of the 6th of October, the troop crossed the last intervening ridge and entered the valley of Bamian at Zohauk. Next day the troop reached Bamian, and encamped close to some mud forts, which were destined now, for the first time, to become the dwelling-places of British officers and soldiers.

This march to Bamian has been dwelt upon somewhat longer than is altogether suitable to the pages of a work of this nature; but, within a smaller space it would have been scarcely practicable to give an idea of the service performed. It was certainly one of the most arduous undertakings ever accomplished by horse-artillery. (The highest point surmounted, the Irak pass, was 12,400 feet above the sea.)

Nor less singular the position of the troop after its arrival; in the midst of a belt of mountains more than 200 miles in width, separated from Cabul by the highest range, impassable by troops during some months in the year, and in a valley scarcely ever exceeding 500 yards in breadth (generally much less), and only a few miles long. As might have been expected, the horses had suffered, though not in a very great degree, from the severity of the march, the cold, and the great scarcity of forage. The two latter evils continued to press upon the troop for many months, until the returning summer brought the green crops and more genial weather. The carriages of the troop had, however stood the hard work over rocky roads admirably, and a most favourable report was made on them by Lieutenant Mackenzie.

On the 15th of October, the troop went into winter quarters in a large mud fort.

With the exception of a movement to Syghan, at the beginning of November, in which sixty horse-artillery troopers, acting as cavalry, took part, and an attack on Mahomed Ali Beg's fort in December, when two small mortars and a 3-pounder mountain-gun, mounted on ponies, were sent with the troopers, the long dreary winter season passed over quietly—the soldiers of the artillery and infantry being employed for some time in throwing up entrenchments, connecting the various forts in possession of the British.

This was done at the suggestion of Dr. Lord, the political agent, there having been some probability of a coalition among the Usbeg powers to support the ex-*ameer*. Had such an event occurred during the winter, the Bamian detachment would have been thrown entirely on its own resources, as no help could come from Cabul, while, on the other hand, the roads from Toorkhistan were open. The cold was intense during the winter, the thermometer at sunrise being often as low as 12° below zero. All the rivers were frozen over.

On the 1st of March, 1840, Captain H. Garbett (who had been posted to the troop on the decease of Captain Timmings) joined, and took command of all the troops at Bamian; he had been obliged to walk 100 miles through the snow, as the mountains were now only passable by men.

On the 14th of March, two guns of the troop were present in a small affair with the Hazarehs at Fouladee, about six miles from Bamian. A mud fort had to be captured, and the surrounding hills to be cleared of a considerable body of Hazarehs; the gateway was knocked down by a few round shot, and the fort was then carried by the infantry, while a few rounds of shrapnels cleared the neighbouring hills of the Hazarehs. The whole affair did not last much above half an hour. The artillery lost one European laboratory-man, one *syce*, and one horse killed, and one trooper wounded. Dr. Lord admitted the chiefs of the refractory tribe to terms, and affairs resumed their wonted peaceful aspect.

In July, however, there seemed to be every prospect of hostilities being renewed; Dost Mahomed, who had for months been a prisoner at Bokhara, had effected his escape to Kooloom, and the Usbegs began to arm in his cause. The British infantry had been pushed forward to Bajgah, twenty-five miles northward of Syghan, and had come into contact with the unfriendly tribes. At the beginning of August, a small affair occurred near Kamurd, in which two companies of infantry suffered a very severe loss.

On the 4th of August, two guns of horse-artillery were sent to Syghan, (a good practicable road across the mountains had, ere this, been made), more as a demonstration than with any other object, as the roads to Kamurd and Bajgah, across the Dundan-Shikun and Nal-i-Ferish passes, were totally impracticable. The Dost was now advancing from Kooloom, accompanied by the Wallee of that place, at the head of about 10,000 men, and every prospect of his force increasing daily.

On the 13th of September, Brigadier Dennie arrived from Cabul with reinforcements, which had been despatched on hearing of the *ameer's* advance. The force at Bamian, besides the troop, consisted now of the 35th native infantry, the Goorkah regiment, a *resallah* of irregular cavalry, and 400 *janbaz*, or Afghan horse. The Afghan infantry had been disarmed and sent to Cabul.

On the 17th, in the evening, the Dost's piquets entered the Bamian valley at Soorukdhurrah, about four miles distant, and on the following morning the brigadier having received information which led him to believe that merely the advanced guard of the enemy had arrived, took out a small detachment of only eight companies, and engaged the whole Usbeg force, who were completely routed and driven from the field in great confusion. Two guns of the troop, under Lieutenant Mackenzie, were present in this affair.

The Usbegs fell back almost immediately when the guns opened on them, abandoning in succession three positions in which they attempted to make a stand, but from which they were instantly dislodged by the guns advancing. Thus, in the valley itself, where the main body of the enemy was, the contest was decided by the horse-artillery, but on the heights the infantry were engaged with some other parties of the enemy, mostly foot-men. The cavalry pursued the Usbegs for some miles up the defile of Soorukdhurrah. The enemy has been variously computed at from 5,000 to 10,000 men in the field.

Four guns of the troop accompanied Brigadier Dennie in his subsequent pursuit of the enemy, but the movements of the Usbegs had been too rapid to allow it to be effectual; but the results were most happy, as it induced the *ameer* to leave the Usbeg camp, and forced the Wallee to abandon his cause. The rest is well known: the *Dost* threw himself into the Kohistan of Cabul, and the theatre of war being thus changed, the British troops were recalled from Bamian, and on the 8th October (exactly a year and a day after its arrival), the troop marched in progress to Cabul with Colonel Dennie. At the commencement of the following year the troop returned to India with the escort in charge of the captive *ameer*.

In the expedition to the Kohistan, under Brigadier Sale, Captain A. Abbott and his battery, and Lieutenant Warburton with two of the *Shah's* bodyguard guns, were employed. The fort of Tootundurra was carried with little loss, a fact attributed:

> In a great measure to the dread inspired by the excellent practice of the artillery under the able direction of Captain Abbott, assisted by Lieutenants Maule and Warburton.

In breaching Julga in October, these same guns were again employed, and Captain A. Abbott and Lieutenant Warburton are reported as having distinguished themselves in the service of the artillery.

In November the detachment was engaged with the *Dost's* followers at Purwundurrah, and two guns of No. 6 battery, under Lieutenant Dawes, covered the successful attack on the heights after the shameful flight of the cavalry.

At this period, a brigade marched from the provinces under Colonel Shelton, to relieve part of the Cabul force; with it was Captain Nicholl's (1st company 1st brigade) troop of horse artillery— Lieutenants Waller and Stewart, subalterns—and the newly-formed mountain-train under Captain Backhouse and Lieutenant Green. The brigade advanced as far as Jellalabad, when rumours arising of the disaffection of the Sikhs in the rear, it returned by forced marches to Jumrood, but finding its presence not required, again marched without rest to Jellalabad.

By the difficulty and rapidity of this march the horses of the troop were much knocked up, and their distress was much increased by the officer commanding the brigade having insisted, in spite of Captain Nicholl's remonstrances, on the troop marching in rear of the infantry, checking the natural pace of the horse, and subjecting the troop to continual halts.

Two of its guns, under Captain Nicholl, were employed in February in reducing forts in the Nazian valley, as also was the mountain-train.

While the artillery with the Cabul force was thus employed, that at Candahar was not inactive. In April, 1840, Captain W. Anderson, with one of his troops of horse-artillery and a body of the *Shah's* troops, marching in the direction of Ghuznee, fell in with a large body of insurgent Ghilzies, and defeated them near Tazee, on the Tornuck River. The enemy made a firm stand, twice charged our line, and were driven back by the steadiness of the troops and the well-sustained fire of the guns under Lieutenant Cooper.

Colonel Wymer's detachment was attacked at Ealmee on the 19th May, on its route to Khelat-i-Ghilzie, by a large body of Ghilzies. Two of the *Shah's* horse-artillery guns under Lieutenant Hawkins were present:

> And opened upon the enemy's dense masses of attack at about 900 yards, with beautiful precision and effect, causing them to

break into three columns, which still continued the attack

But were driven back by the steady fire of the line, though they continued their efforts from five till nearly ten at night.

Too much cannot be said of the scientific and destructive manner in which the artillery practice was conducted by Lieutenant Hawkins, which created awful havoc in the ranks of the enemy, to the admiration of the troops present.

In July, Lieutenant Cooper, with two guns, accompanied Captain Woodburn against Uctar Khan, in the neighbourhood of Girisk. The enemy attacked the left:

With great boldness, but were repulsed by the well-directed fire of the guns, and three companies on the left; failing in this, they attacked the right, but were again met by a most destructive fire from the guns and five companies which were on the right.

The rear was then attacked, but a gun being reversed, and the rear rank of the infantry facing about, the enemy were driven off, after standing three rounds of case shot.

Lieutenant Cooper deserves my best acknowledgments for the rapidity and admirable manner in which he brought his guns to play upon the enemy; and I had frequent opportunities of noticing the precision of his practice. His guns are never in difficulty.

These are Captain Woodburn's words in his official report, in which also he speaks in another place of the "admirable conduct of the artillery."

In August, this same officer, with four guns, when attached to Captain Griffin's force, was again in action with the enemy near Khawind, and again rendered effectual assistance, and earned the praises of his superiors for himself and his details.

On the arrival of Shah Soojah at Cabul, a grand *durbar* was held, and a new order of chivalry was instituted—that of the "*Dur-i-Dooranee*," or Pearl of the Dooranee Empire, consisting of three ranks, similar to those of the Bath.

The annexed is a representation of the star of the order. It was conferred on several artillery officers at various times previous to Shah Soojah's death.

Hitherto we have had the gratifying task of recounting the exploits of a victorious army; a darker page must now follow; but though success no longer brightens the narrative, we have still the consolation of knowing that those parts of the regiment employed, heroically performed their duty in scenes of no common trial, and that their exertions, in a cause which from the first was evidently hopeless, only ceased when the cold hand of death laid them low in the dark defiles of the Koord Kabool and Jugdulluck.

In October, the Eastern Ghilzies occupied the passes between Bhootkhak and Jellalabad. Brigadier Sale, with a brigade, was sent to clear them; No. 6 battery and the mountain-train accompanied. Lieutenant Dawes with the two 9–pounders was with the advance-guard, on whom, in forcing the Kabool pass, the chief brunt fell. In the Tezeen valley, all the guns were brought into action, in a succession of skirmishes which lasted till dusk, with much effect.

The march was now a daily struggle; two guns, sometimes commanded by Lieutenant Dawes, sometimes by Captain Backhouse (part of whose train, under Lieutenant Green, had returned with the 37th regiment of Native Infantry to Cabul), on the rear-guard, were engaged daily; at Jugdulluck a severe struggle ensued, and its favourable conclusion was insured by the guns seizing an unoccupied position, which took the enemy's line in reverse; the rear-guard was, however, suddenly attacked and the baggage seized:

> Soon, however, by the praiseworthy exertions, and cool and soldier-like orders and example of Captain Backhouse, confidence was restored and the rear-guard extricated from the defile.

The report continues:

> I have been much pleased with the address and able arrange-

ments of Captain Abbott, who has twice commanded the advance-guard.

The insurrection burst out on all sides; myriads of Ghilzies, &c., re-occupied the passes in the rear, and cut off all communication with Cabul, forcing Sir Robert Sale to seek the safety of his brigade by occupying Jellalabad. The Kohistanees rose in Charekar, and murdered Lieutenant Maule, of the artillery. Candahar was surrounded. Ghuznee fell. The Khyberees sealed the mouth of their pass. Colonel Wild's attempt to force it failed, and the last act of the tragedy was completed in the annihilation of the Cabul garrison on its fatal and ill-judged retreat.

★★★★★★

The 4th company 6th battalion, with Lieutenants A. Christie and Robertson, formed part of this force. Captain Lawrence, as political agent, accompanied it, and procured four guns from the Seiks, which, however, were of little use, as their carriages broke down.

★★★★★★

The details of these sad events have been so graphically described, that we need here do no more than record the losses of the regiment, and extract from the accounts of eye-witnesses their testimony to the admirable conduct of that noble troop, the 1st troop 1st brigade horse-artillery, both during the siege and the retreat.

After detailing the disastrous action of the 23rd November, Captain Melville says:

> Here, amidst so much that was condemnable, let me again bear just and heartfelt testimony to the behaviour of that brave, though small, body of men, whose conduct on this, and every other occasion during the war, was that of a band of heroes, and who, preferring death to dishonour, met their fate, nobly fighting to the last for the gun they had so ably served.
>
> I allude to the horse-artillery; when Sergeant Mulhall and six gunners, whose names I feel deep sorrow I cannot here record, sword in hand awaited the advance of the foe, and it was not until they saw themselves alone in the midst of thousands of the enemy, that they dashed at full gallop, cutting their way through them, down the hill; and though surrounded by cavalry and infantry, yet they managed to bring their gun safely to the plain, where, however, only three of them being alive, and they des-

perately wounded, they were obliged to leave it, and contrived to reach cantonments.

Again, during the retreat, he says:

> On reaching the extremity of the (Khoord Cabool) pass, the horse-artillery, that noble branch of the service, whose courage, even in extremity, never failed, and who supported all their misfortunes cheerfully, halted, and, turning a gun on the pass, awaited the debouchment of our troops and the arrival of the enemy's. This soon happened, and we received them with some well-directed rounds of grape.

After their guns and horses were lost:

> The artillerymen, those few that remained, formed in the ranks of the 44th, and gallantly supported on foot that deathless reputation they had gained when urging their steeds into the heart of the battle.

Lieutenant Eyre, speaking of the siege, says:

> The gunners, from first to last, never once partook of a full meal or obtained their natural rest; of the hardships and privations undergone, it would be difficult to convey an adequate idea.
>
> On the retreat from Cabul, owing to the starved condition of the horses, which disabled them from pulling the guns through the deep snow and rugged mountain-passes, the guns were, one by one, spiked and abandoned. In the Khoord Cabool pass, a whole gun's crew perished rather than desert their charge; on nearing Jugdulluck, some horse-artillerymen, headed by Captain Nicholl, acting as dragoons, charged and routed a party of the enemy's cavalry.
>
> Throughout the last struggle, up to Gundamuck, all eye-witnesses concur in testifying to their stubborn valour.

Of his troop, Captain Nicholl, Lieutenant Green (who joined it on the loss of the mountain-train early in the retreat), and Lieutenant Stewart, were killed; Lieutenants Eyre and Waller, both of whom were wounded during the siege, were given over, with their families, by the orders of Major-General Elphinstone, to Akbar Khan; 8 non-commissioned officers and gunners were killed in Cabul, 30 in the Khoord Cabool pass, 26 between that and Jugdulluck, 32 in reaching

Gundamuck, 3 were taken prisoners at the close, 3 left wounded at Cabul, and 3 doing duty with No. 6 battery and the mountain-train at Jellalabad. Sergeant Mulhall was killed at Gundamuck on the 13th January, 1842.

The regiment raised a monumental column to the memory of this gallant troop, on the base of which, on one marble slab, the circumstances under which they fell are narrated, and on another, the names of every non-commissioned officer and gunner are inscribed.

Previous to the insurrection breaking out, the 3rd company (Captain Sotheby, Lieutenants Cornish and Brougham), 2nd battalion moved from Ferozepore to relieve the 4th company at Candahar; it dropped down the Indus to Sukkur, and marched to Quettah, where it arrived on the 27th November, 1841, and remained, on account of the communications with Candahar being closed. Here it was employed in throwing up defences and field-works, for the protection of the cantonment, whenever the frost and snow intermitted.

The only building available for their barracks becoming unsafe, during the winter they were forced to occupy their tents, and the severity of the weather in which they were exposed to this insufficient shelter, may be judged of by the fact of 180 camels of the company having perished from it. In the second advance of Major-General England, and the successful attack on the heights of Hykulzye, this company shared; a party under Lieutenant Cornish assisting in working the guns of Captain Leslie's troop of Bombay Horse Artillery, and with that force it joined the headquarters of the Candahar Army on 10th May.

Before this junction occurred, the Candahar force had been on more than one occasion moved out to clear the neighbourhood of the insurgents. In January, they came up with them on the Urghandab, and after driving them from their position, the horse-artillery and cavalry pursued them some distance. In the report of this action, Captain W. Anderson's name was brought to the favourable notice of government.

In March, the army again took the field, and on the 9th the horse-artillery under Captain Anderson got within range, and opened on the enemy with good effect; they broke and fled too rapidly for the infantry to come up with them. While the main body was absent, an attack was made on the city, but without success: part of the 4th company 2nd battalion was present with the garrison.

On the 25th March, the insurgents were attacked near Baba Wala by Colonel Wymer. The well-directed fire of two guns under Lieutenant Turner soon drove in on the pass a large body of the enemy, and they were finally put to flight by the arrival of the main body under Major-General Nott. In his report, Colonel Wymer writes:

> I trust that I may be permitted to bring to the Major-General's notice the admirable practice of the artillery under Lieutenant Turner's guidance, every shot from which told with beautiful effect on the dense masses of the enemy.

A small garrison, with which was one-half the 3rd company 2nd battalion artillery, under Lieutenant Walker, had been left in Khelat-i-Ghilzie in November, 1841; the insurrection isolated them from the Candahar force, and for several months they underwent very great hardships; an insufficient supply of firewood exposed them to cold, barracks without doors, and piercing cold winds, bread and water for rations for days together, and an enemy at the gates; under these privations the artillerymen never grumbled nor lost their good temper, but continued to work as if they had been highly fed. The enemy gradually closed in round the fort, and on the night of the 21st May commenced a simultaneous attack on two points; at one point, there were two 6-pounders, under Lieutenant Walker, at the other only one.

The enemy came on in a determined manner, crossing the ditch by means of scaling-ladders, and some even reached the parapets; so closely were the artillery assailed, that at one time they were forced to turn to their small-arms to assist in driving them off; towards morning the attack ceased, and the little garrison was left in quiet possession of their fort, and in the course of a few days Colonel Wymer arrived from Candahar with a force to relieve them.

This service was rewarded by a medal to all engaged, the handsomest of any by which the campaigns in Afghanistan are marked.

Brigadier Sale's force, on reaching Jellalabad, immediately occupied themselves in rendering its defences tenable, collecting provisions, preparing ammunition, and mounting their guns on the most advantageous positions. In availing himself of the resources of the country, and keeping up our communications, Captain MacGregor's services were most conspicuous and successful, and perhaps to his exertions it may mainly be attributed that the "illustrious garrison" were enabled to hold out, and earn for themselves the undying honour they have gained.

The exertions also of Captain Abbott, Captain Backhouse, and Lieutenant Dawes, are honourably recorded in the records of that siege, records which have been so fully published that little is left to us beyond extracting a few passages; and we shall first refer to the report of the construction of the works.

> With the exception of a few of the larger bastions, all the batteries were prepared by the artillerymen themselves, both Captain Abbott's company and Captain Backhouse's mountain-train, under the superintendence of their own officers; besides this, a party of Captain Abbott's artillerymen was always ready to assist in the works generally, and they were most ably superintended by Lieutenant Dawes, to whom I am indebted for aid as constant as it was valuable, and willingly given.
>
> Captain Backhouse, with his own men and detachment of the 6th infantry Shah Soojah's force, not only prepared the parapets and embrasures for his own guns, and repaired the damages done to them by the earthquake, but he undertook and completed several of the most useful and laborious operations executed.

Brigadier Sale writes:

> Captain MacGregor, political agent, gave me the aid of his local experience, and through his influence and measures our *dâk* communication with India was restored, and a great quantity of grain collected. Captain Abbott made the artillery dispositions in the ablest manner, and used every exertion to add to and economise our resources, in the way of gun and musket ammunition.
>
> The artillery practice of No. 6 light field battery has ever been excellent, and has been equalled by that of the mountain-train. Captains Abbott and Backhouse and Lieutenant Dawes have proved themselves excellent ordnance officers.
>
> The siege, or rather blockade, continued from November to April.

The greatest want at times prevailed of everything but grain; but the men preserved their cheerfulness under all privations, the native artillerymen of the 2nd company 6th battalion vying with the Europeans of H. M.'s light infantry in setting an example of good discipline and patient and cheerful endurance of hardship and danger. In April, Akbar Khan collected a large body of troops in the neighbourhood, both to overwhelm the garrison and meet the army advancing to its succour through the Khyber.

This body the garrison attacked on the morning of the 6th April, and completely overthrew, capturing standards and baggage, and four of the guns lost by the Cabul force.

In the action, No. 6 battery, with which, in addition to Captain Abbott and Lieutenant Dawes, were Captains Backhouse and MacGregor, as volunteers, was most effective; moving rapidly to the front, it covered the advance of the infantry, and held in check a large body of cavalry which threatened the flank.

This success was most complete, and the garrison achieved its safety by its own prowess. Its gallantry was rewarded by a medal to all engaged; the corps were permitted to wear a "mural crown," with the word "Jellalabad" on their appointments, and a donation of six months' *batta* was granted as a compensation for the various losses suffered, and at the close of the campaign the rank of major, with the companionship of the Bath, was bestowed on Captains Abbott, Backhouse, and MacGregor.

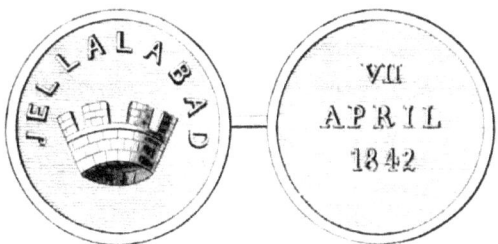

On the news of the insurrection reaching India, steps were taken for despatching a force to aid the troops in Affghanistan. Major-General Pollock, C.B., of the artillery, was selected for its command, and joined it at Peshawur in February.

The artillery with it was very insufficient. A troop of horse-artillery and half a light field battery, a second troop (Captain Delafosse's), and the remainder of the field battery, did not join until after the entrance to the Khyber was won.

Troop.	Brigade.	Company.	Battalion.	Captains.	Lieutenants.
3	1	–	–	Delafosse	Richardson, Money, Abercrombie.
3	2	–	–	Alexander	A. Fitzgerald, Larkins.
–	–	2	2	—	L. Smith, Douglas.
–	–	4	6	—	A. Christie, Robertson.

Captain Lane, commissary of ordnance, Lieutenant Pollock, *aide-de-camp*, Lieutenant Sir R. Shakespear, military secretary, Captain H. M. Lawrence, political agent.

On the 5th April, the attack was made on the pass; the guns were directed on the barriers raised to defend the entrance; two columns attacked the heights on either side, and the main body carried the pass when the way had been opened by the fire of the guns. The arrangements of General Pollock were admirable. The attack was completely successful; and the enemy evacuated Ali-Musjid at our approach. Captains Alexander and Lawrence, Lieutenants Shakespear and Pollock, are mentioned in the despatches.

Jellalabad was reached, but the enemy had disappeared, and here the force halted, pending the receipt of orders for an advance on Cabul, and till arrangements for carriage could be made to enable them to carry out the order. This halt was not altogether inactive; in July, No. 6 battery, with Captains Abbott and Dawes, was engaged with Brigadier Monteith's force in the Shinwaree valley with much credit. Captain MacGregor accompanied the brigade, and "when opportunity offered itself, served with the guns."

While the force remained halted, a supply of rockets reached the artillery, which had been forwarded by *dâk banghy* from Allahabad, under the impression that the weapon was particularly calculated to be serviceable in the passes at points where artillery could not be used at all, or without the greatest difficulty. The expectation was not realised—the rockets being too delicate to bear the shaking they underwent; this, together with the expansion of the iron case and the contraction of the composition from the heat to which they were exposed, rendered them nearly useless on reaching their destination.

Towards the end of August, the arrangements were completed, and the force moved on; the artillery strengthened by No. 6 battery and the mountain-train, which had formed part of the "illustrious garrison." On the 24th, the enemy were driven by General Pollock from

Mammoo Khel, in which action the services of Captains Abbott and MacGregor, and Lieutenant Pollock are mentioned. On the 8th September, some fighting occurred near Jugdulluck, and on the 10th, the enemy assaulted the rear-guard on all sides, but "were checked by the very effective fire of the guns, ably directed by Captain Lawrence (political agent), who volunteered his services, and by Lieutenant Abercrombie." The brigades were collected in the Tezeen valley, for which purpose Major-General Pollock halted on the 12th, and on the 13th were attacked by the whole of Akbar Khan's troops, who were defeated with much loss.

Two of the guns, a 24 and 12-pounder howitzer, lost on the retreat, were here recaptured. The rear-guard was hard pressed in defending the entrance to the pass as the troops moved on, and the effective services of Captains Alexander and Lawrence, and Lieutenant Douglas, in the use of the guns at this period, are acknowledged. In the despatches of Major-General Pollock, the names of Major Delafosse, Captains Abbott, Backhouse, Alexander, MacGregor, Lieutenants Fitzgerald, Shakespear, and Pollock, are mentioned with applause.

On the 15th, the force reached Cabul, and on the 16th possession was taken of the Bala Hissar, under a salute from Major Delafosse's troop.

Major-General Nott, after being joined by Major-General England's force, as related in a previous page, continued to hold Candahar, pending final instructions. Towards the end of May, the enemy, collecting in numbers, endeavoured to carry the town, when Major-General Nott moved out against them. Both Captain Anderson's troops were engaged in this affair with credit. Early in August, Candahar was evacuated: one column with the baggage retired by the Kojuck pass; with this was Lieutenant Cooper's troop of horse-artillery and the 3rd company 2nd battalion artillery under Lieutenant Walker. In its route to Sukkur this force met with little or no opposition.

The main force marched on the 8th August. The artillery consisted of Major Sotheby, commandant; Lieutenant Brougham, adjutant, S. S. Horse Artillery, Captain W. Anderson, Lieutenants Turner and Hawkins; 3rd company, 2nd battalion, Lieutenant Cornish, four 18–pounder guns attached.

On the 31st August, within forty miles of Ghuznee, the governor, with about 12,000 men, moved out to meet the British, but he was defeated with the loss of guns, tents, &c. Major Sotheby was mentioned in the despatch, which concluded by saying:

I cannot close this despatch without expressing my admiration of the dashing and gallant conduct, rapid movements, and correct practice, of Captain Anderson's troop of horse-artillery; nothing could exceed it, and I beg to bring this officer and Lieutenant Turner, attached to the same troop, to the particular notice of his lordship, as officers who have on many occasions rendered me most essential service.

Ghuznee yielded without opposition; its walls and bastions were destroyed—the gates of Somnath and the Zubber Jung rewarded the conquerors and graced their triumphant march to Cabul, which they reached on the 17th, after defeating the enemy at Beni Badam and Mydam on the 14th and 15th, in which actions "the artillery" are reported as having "distinguished themselves," and the names of Captain Anderson and Lieutenant Turner are particularly mentioned.

A body of Kuzzilbash horse, despatched under Sir R. Shakespear towards Bamean, to aid the prisoners, met them on their return, they having effected their escape; of the artillery, Lieutenants Eyre, Waller, and Warburton; Sergeants MacNee and Cleland; gunners A'Hearne, Kean, and Walton, were the sole survivors.

A force was sent against Istaliff on the 30th September, in which the mountain-train under Captain Backhouse, and two 18-pounders under Lieutenant Cornish, were employed. Lieutenants Richardson and Pollock accompanied the force, and the former was slightly wounded.

The combined armies now turned homewards, meeting with many difficulties from the exhausted state of the cattle and the obstacles in the passes; so much so, that the four 18-pounders which had originally marched with the Army of the Indus were burst in the passes and their carriages burnt.

Daily skirmishes took place, and in passing a ravine near Alee Musjid just at dusk, a rush was made by the Afredis on a small detachment of artillery with a gun of the mountain-train under Lieutenant A. Christie. He was killed, and the gun carried off, but afterwards recovered.

Of the trophies, the Zubber Jung was burst at Cabul; the Kazee travelled with difficulty as far as Lundi-khana, in the Khyber, where, upsetting into a ravine, it was burst and abandoned; the Somnath gates alone reached Hindustan, travelling on a spare 18-pounder carriage; but they were fated, even after 800 years of absence, not to pass their kindred threshold; they got no further than Agra in the attempt, and were there deposited in the armoury of the magazine.

The troops were received on their return by the Army of Reserve at Ferozepore, assembled in case its aid should have been wanted, and medals bestowed for the different services, bearing the inscriptions of Candahar—Candahar, Ghuznee, Cabul, 1842—Ghuznee, Cabul, 1842—and Cabul, 1842; the obverse of all was similar, and this, and all the medals since that for Ghuznee, were worn on a particoloured ribbon of light tints, called "the ribbon of India," ill fitted for a military decoration.

For these distinguished services General Pollock was rewarded with the first class of the order of the Bath, and received the thanks of both Houses of Parliament. He was subsequently appointed a member of the Supreme Council of India, and on being compelled to quit the country on account of ill-health in 1846-7, a pension of £1,000 *per annum* was bestowed upon him by the East-India Company, with the unanimous approbation of the Court of Proprietors. The freedom of the city was also voted him by the corporation of London.

Of the artillery officers who served under Generals Pollock and Nott, the following received honorary distinctions:—Captains Anderson, Alexander, Lane, and Lawrence, were gazetted brevet-majors; and Majors Delafosse, Sotheby, and Anderson, companions of the Bath.

Before closing this account of the war in Afghanistan, it should be mentioned, that in the political department several artillery officers were greatly distinguished.

The names of Captains Todd and MacGregor are associated with important historical events at Herat and Jellalabad; whilst Captain Abbott and Lieutenant Richmond Shakespear (who was subsequently knighted for these services) will be remembered for their enterprising and perilous journeys to Khiva and the Caspian for the purpose of liberating the Russian slaves confined in the former place.

CHAPTER 9
Reorganisation of the Regiment

In the following year (1843) the attention of the Supreme Government was directed towards a new quarter. The death of the Maharajah Junkojee Rao Scindiah was followed by alarming disturbances at Gwalior. The army became dominant in the State. The regent, who had been nominated to preside over the *Durbar*, during the minority of the adopted son of the deceased ruler, was incompetent to control the rebellious soldiery; the widow of the late king took part against the minister, and the hostilities, which commenced with a bed-chamber intrigue, ended in a civil war. Such, indeed, became the anarchy and confusion at Gwalior, that the British Resident quitted Scindiah's court, and the governor-general, though not contemplating immediate interference, began to watch with some anxiety the progress of events at the Mahratta capital.

As the year advanced, the *ranee's* party, at the head of which was the Dadur Khasgeewallah, a man whose temper and designs were notoriously hostile to the British, became stronger and stronger. Such of the officers, in the service of the *maharajah*, as were known to be friendly to the paramount state, were ill-treated and dismissed. Covert hostility began to rise into open defiance; and it now became apparent, that from the other side of the Sutlej, the Sikhs were watching, with undisguised satisfaction, the excitement at Gwalior, and waiting to take advantage of any disaster that might befall us, to declare themselves on the side of the Mahrattas.

As the cold weather approached, the aspect of affairs became more and more threatening. To bring about a satisfactory settlement by mere diplomacy, appeared difficult, if not impossible; and Lord Ellenborough determined on assembling an army on the banks of the Jumna. The force assembled at Agra, in the month of November, under the personal command of Sir Hugh Gough, the commander-in-chief, and was called the "Army of Exercise." At the same time a left wing was formed, under the command of General Gray, to operate upon Gwalior from the Bundlekhund country, whilst the main army advanced from Agra.

On the 16th of December, Sir Hugh Gough commenced his march. Affairs were growing worse, and armed intervention was inevitable. When at length, the Khasgeewallah was given up, with the hope of arresting the progress of the British, the Army of Exercise was in full march upon Gwalior, and was not to be stayed.

The artillery division of the Army of Exercise was commanded by Brigadier G. E. Gowan, Captain J. H. Macdonald being his assistant adjutant-general. Colonel J. Tennant was appointed, with the rank of brigadier, to the command of the foot-artillery; Lieutenant and Brevet-Captain A. Huish, acting as major of brigade; and Captain E. F. Day, as commissary of ordnance. The components of the horse-artillery force were the 2nd troop 2nd brigade, commanded by Captain C. Grant, with Lieutenants Clifford and P. Christie, as subalterns; the 3rd troop 2nd brigade, commanded by Brevet-Major Alexander, with Brevet-Captain A. Fitzgerald (adjutant of the brigade, who had volunteered to do subaltern's duty with the troop), and Lieutenant Wintle; and the 2nd troop 3rd brigade, with which were Brevet-Major Lane (commanding), Brevet-Captain C. Mills, and Lieutenant Moir.

The foot-artillery consisted of the 1st company 1st battalion (with No. 10 light field-battery) under Brevet-Major Saunders; Lieutenants Bruce, Milligan, and Sladen, subalterns; and the 1st company 4th battalion, commanded by Captain B. Brown, with Lieutenants Holland and Remington. In addition to these were the heavy batteries, consisting of six 18-pounders and four 8-inch howitzers, manned by the reserve companies of the 4th battalion (European) and the 6th *golundauze*; the former under Lieutenant-Colonel Farrington, with Lieutenant Whiteford, adjutant; and the latter under Lieutenant-Colonel Denniss, with Lieutenant Warner, adjutant.

The artillery with the left wing was commanded by Lieutenant-Colonel Biddulph (Captain Austin, major of brigade), and was composed of the 1st troop 3rd brigade, commanded by Captain F. Brind, Lieutenants Coxe and Bourchier, subalterns; the 3rd troop 3rd brigade, under Captain George Campbell, with whom was Lieutenant Humfrays; and the 6th company 6th battalion, with No. 16 light field-battery, under Lieutenant W. Olpherts.

On the arrival of the advanced columns at Dholpore, they were met by the Khasgeewallah, whose surrender, now become a matter of fact, was regarded as a prelude to a general compliance with the terms dictated by the Governor-general. The bulk of the siege-train was therefore halted, and eventually ordered back to Agra.

On the 27th of December information was obtained that the enemy had advanced to Choundah, a village within eight miles of the position occupied by the "Army of Exercise" at Hurgonah, and arrangements were made next day to attack them on the 29th. On the morning of that day, the army advanced upon the village of Maharajpore. It was believed that the enemy were some miles distant; but, as the British troops ascended the rising ground, the Mahratta batteries opened suddenly upon our advancing columns; and as our own heavy artillery was in the rear, it was no easy matter to silence the destructive fire kept up by the enemy, with a spirit and a precision which could scarcely be excelled by the best gunners in the service of any European state.

Our light field-batteries were overmatched by the heavy metal of the Mahratta ordnance; but their steadiness under fire was never exceeded, and the determined resolution with which they carried on the unequal contest, elicited the highest praise. Captain Grant's troop of horse-artillery came into action about half-past eight o'clock, when it engaged one of the enemy's batteries, drawn up on the left of the village of Maharajpore. Here it was joined by Major Alexander's troop, when, says Brigadier Gowan, from whose report to the commander-in-chief these details are taken:

> Both advanced to within 500 yards of the enemy, and soon drove him from his guns, which were taken possession of by the 3rd brigade of infantry. On following up the enemy, the two troops were suddenly exposed to a cross fire, from two of the enemy's batteries, which had hitherto been concealed; one in front, and the other on our left flank.
>
> Captain Grant was ordered to oppose the former, and Major Alexander the latter, which was soon after stormed and taken by the 3rd brigade of infantry; upon which Major Alexander followed up the retreating enemy with great effect, and Major Lane, with the 2nd troop 3rd brigade, joined them in the pursuit. In the meantime, Captain Grant had advanced to within 600 yards of the Choundah position, and was opposed singly to the fire of a heavy battery of 12 guns, for upwards of half an hour, and I regret to say, sustained a considerable loss in men and horses.
>
> So well chosen, was the enemy's position, that even on horseback, I could only discern the muzzles of their guns, which in weight of metal, as well as in number, were very superior to the troop's. More than once, however, the enemy were driven by our fire from their guns, but being unsupported at the time, except by a weak troop of cavalry, no advantage of this could be

taken, and he returned to his guns.

In another letter, addressed to the assistant adjutant-general of artillery, Brigadier Gowan, with reference to the other details of field artillery, says:

> Major Lane's troop (2nd troop 3rd brigade) advanced with the 4th brigade of cavalry, under Brigadier Scott, forming the left column, and Nos. 17 and 10 light field-batteries, with the 4th and 5th brigades of infantry, respectively forming the centre column of attack. These came into action on the opposite side of the village of Maharajpore from that on which we were first engaged. The conduct of officers and men was highly satisfactory, and everything I could desire.

Nothing could have exceeded the resolute courage with which the Mahratta batteries were defended, alike by infantry and artillerymen, or the precision with which the guns were served by the latter. The commander-in-chief wrote:

> I never witnessed guns better served, nor a body of infantry apparently more devoted to the protection of their regimental guns, held by the Mahratta corps as objects of worship.

Brigadier Gowan wrote:

> The fire of the enemy was remarkably accurate, and was maintained with a smartness which surprised me. At one time they got the range of Captain Grant's troop so exactly, that nearly every shot fell between the guns and waggons of the battery.

It was only by the steady gallantry of the British infantry, who charged the enemy's batteries in the face of destructive showers of grape and round shot, that their position at last was carried. Her Majesty's 39th and 40th regiments headed the columns. Nothing could have been more gallant than the attack, more obstinate than the resistance. The enemy's *golundaz* stood to be bayoneted in their batteries, and only yielded up their guns with their lives.

It is probable that, if in this engagement better use had been made of the artillery, the loss that fell upon the British Army would have been much less severe. Brigadier Tennant, who commanded the foot-artillery, had brought up four 8-inch howitzers in line with H. M.'s 39th, but he was not permitted to advance. Had he been allowed, as was his expressed desire, to move up within 800 yards' distance, where he could see the enemy's position more distinctly, and therefore operate with greater precision, he might, it was the opinion of those present, have knocked the Mahratta batteries to pieces, and enabled the infantry columns to advance in comparative safety to the attack.

On the same morning of the 29th of December, General Gray, who, with the left wing of the army, had been advancing upon Gwalior from the Sindh River, came up with the enemy at Punniah, a village a few miles to the south of the capital. Here the Mahratta batteries were strongly posted, as at Maharajpore, on commanding ground, and in gorges flanking one another. The 3rd Buffs, who led the column sent forward to attack the enemy's position, were supported by Captain Brind's troop of horse-artillery, 1st troop 3rd brigade, which:

> Opened upon the guns to the left of Mangore, whilst Major Geddes, with Captain Campbell's troop, 3rd battalion 3rd brigade, and two guns of Captain Brind's, opened upon the battery of seven guns in rear of Mangore; and their practice was beautiful, silencing all but one of the enemy's guns, which was served with the greatest accuracy to the last moment. Lieutenant Olpherts, with four guns of No. 16 light field-battery, took up a position south of Mangore, and opened on the enemy as they retreated up the hills, with good effect. Lieutenant Tombs, with two guns of light field-battery attached to the rear-guard, fired with great precision several shots upon the enemy's left. (From the report of Brevet-Captain Reid, assistant quartermaster-general. The latter portion of the extract is adopted word for word by General Gray in his despatch.)

The Mahrattas made a gallant defence, but were driven from their guns with considerable loss; and night closed upon their total dispersion.

In these engagements on the 29th of December, the artillery lost at Maharajpore, 1 2nd lieutenant, 1 sergeant, 1 gunner, killed; and 1 sergeant, and 21 gunners, wounded; besides *syces*, ordnance-drivers, and a considerable number of horses. At Punniah, the loss was much smaller, only one man and one horse having been killed. The officer who fell at Maharajpore, was Lieutenant Leathes. He was posted with the rear-guard, and had ridden forward, it would seem, to watch the progress of the action, when coming too close to the Mahratta batteries, a round shot carried off his head.

For services rendered during this campaign, Colonel Gowan received the companionship of the Bath; Majors Geddes, Sanders, Alexander, and Lane, were promoted to the rank of lieutenant-colonel by brevet, and Captains Brown, Grant, Brind, Campbell, and Macdonald, were gazetted as brevet-majors.

In the political transactions with which these military operations were connected, Lieutenant Sir Richmond Shakespear, of the artillery, took a conspicuous part. He acted as an *aide-de-camp* to the commander-in-chief, during the battle of Maharajpore, and was thanked in his Excellency's despatch. Captain Macdonald also received the thanks of the commander-in-chief. On the subsequent settlement of the affairs of Gwalior, four batteries were raised for service with the new Gwalior contingent; and placed under the command of Lieutenants Eyre, Warburton, T. H. Smyth, and Hawkins; Brevet-Captain Frank Turner being appointed brigade major.

In honour of these victories, a bronze star, with "Maharajpore" or "Punniah" in the centre, was struck, and distributed to the troops engaged.

Early in the year 1844, the 4th troop 1st brigade of horse-artillery, and the 4th company 6th battalion of foot, which formed part of the relief ordered to Scinde, had their fidelity severely tried by the conduct of two native infantry regiments who refused to cross the Sutlej, on the plea that their just allowances had been withdrawn. The artillery, consisting of a native troop and a native company, who must have come under the operation of the same order, do not appear to have taken a leading part in the mutinous movement.

In the autumn of this year (1844), a reorganisation of the ordnance commissariat department was ordered by the Supreme Government. Instead of a principal commissary of ordnance, resident, as heretofore, in Fort William, an inspector of magazines, with his head-quarters at Allahabad, was appointed; and the arsenal of Fort William was placed under the charge of the deputy principal commissary of ordnance.

In the beginning of the year 1845, Sir Henry Hardinge, then governor-general, directed his attention to the state of the artillery, and, in conjunction with Sir George Pollock, the military member of council, introduced several important improvements.

"The number of regular horse field-batteries had been gradually increased to five. (This, and the following paragraphs distinguished by inverted commas, are taken *verbatim* from a very valuable article on the "Bengal Artillery" in the *Calcutta Re-*

view, No. xviii.) These were at first equipped with 89 horses, which allowed six horses each for six guns and six waggons, one spare per team, and five for the staff; the gun-teams were subsequently allowed eight horses to each. In 1845, the number of batteries was increased to nine, and the complement of horses to each fixed at 120, which gave eight horses to each gun and waggon, and allowed a team for the forge-cart, with six saddle-horses, including one spare and one spare draught-horse per team. On the frontier or on service, ten additional horses were sanctioned.

******

Note:—The following extract from a minute by Sir Henry Hardinge, dated January 20, 1845, relates to this important subject. "In reference to the 4-horse field-batteries, it appears to me essential that 9-pounders should be drawn by eight horses instead of six; that a battery of six pieces should therefore have, when ordered on field service, a complement of 120 horses, instead of 98; and considering the immediate result of a few weeks' campaigning, the number ought to be 130 horses. When not under orders for field service, the number may remain at 98. On this matter, and every other relating to the artillery, the governor-general requests the Honourable Sir George Pollock to make the arrangements which his experienced judgment may decide, so as to secure the utmost efficiency; for in all these matters, efficiency will be found to be true economy." (The number of horses would seem to have been raised in the first instance from 89 to 98.)

******

"In July, 1845, a new organisation of the whole of the Indian artillery took place, by which the corps in Bengal received a nominal increase, but a practical decrease, except in the establishment of officers. The five European battalions of five companies each, were formed into six battalions of four companies each, and the two *golundaz* battalions of ten companies, into three battalions of six companies each, causing a total reduction of one European, and two native companies.

"One important advantage was, however, obtained by the increase of European officers, the want of which had been seriously felt on various previous occasions. The relief thus granted could not of course be felt immediately, but its beneficial effect is now becoming manifest.

"This gave an establishment of three brigades and nine battalions, each having a complement of officers similar to the infantry, with the exception that an additional captain was allowed to the latter, which has not been accorded to the artillery, although greatly wanted."

The important subject of elephant-draught at this time engaged the attention of the governor-general. These animals had been long in use with the light post-guns in Arracan and other places, and an experimental elephant-battery had been recently established at Dumdum. But Sir Henry Hardinge now turned his thoughts towards the application of this description of draught to heavy ordnance, convinced that, for the transport of siege-guns, artificers' carts, &c., elephants would be found more serviceable and more economical than bullocks. During the Sikh campaign, the services of the former were tested, especially on the march to and from Kote Kangra; and the result more than justified the expectations of the governor-general.

CHAPTER 10
Battles of Aliwal and Sobraon

As the year 1845 drew towards its close, the state of affairs in the Punjab demanded the most anxious attention of the governor-general. Eager to maintain peace, but at the same time determined to be prepared for war, Sir Henry Hardinge had noiselessly increased the strength of the frontier army, and had himself proceeded, in September, to the North-west, apparently on an ordinary tour of inspection. In July, 1844, there had been between Meerut and Ferozepore 24,000 men, and 66 field-pieces. This force he had, with as little ostentation as possible, increased to 45,500 men, and 98 field-guns. The most important position was Umballah.

As it was from this point that any attack from beyond the Sutlej must have been met, the governor-general, by December, 1845, had placed there, in the front line, 32,470 men, and 66 field-guns, where before, in July, 1844, there had only been 13,530 men, and 48 field-guns. But all these preparations were made in the manner least calculated to alarm or to irritate the Sikhs, and it was hoped that, in spite of the boastings of the turbulent soldiery, they would be restrained by their own intestine feuds from advancing to the attack of their neighbours. The middle of December, however, saw them preparing to cross the river; and the great event, which had for many years been talked of in every cantonment in India, was now on the eve of accomplishment; the war in the Punjab was about to commence.

We come now to speak more in detail of the disposition of the artillery at this time. At the commencement of the war, there were stationed at Ferozepore, the 5th troop 1st brigade, under Captain E. F. Day; the 3rd troop 3rd brigade, under Brevet-Major George Campbell; the 4th company 6th battalion, with No. 19 light field-battery, under Captain J. Fordyce; and the 2nd company 7th battalion, with No. 6 light field-battery, under 1st Lieutenant A. G. Austen (Captain Boileau, lately posted, not having joined), in all 12 horse-artillery guns and howitzers (6 and 12-pounders), and 12 foot-artillery guns and howitzers (9 and 24-pounders). Besides these troops and companies, there was a reserve company (the 2nd company 2nd battalion) for the service of heavy guns and rockets. The whole were under the command of Lieutenant-Colonel Huthwaite, of the 3rd brigade.

At Loodianah were posted the 1st troop 1st brigade, under Captain F. Dashwood; and the 4th troop 3rd brigade, under Captain H. Garbett (total 12 guns); the whole commanded by Lieutenant-Colonel Geddes.

But the largest force of artillery was posted at Umballah, under Lieutenant-Colonel George Brooke, of the 1st brigade horse-artillery. At that station were the 2nd troop 1st brigade, under Captain D'Arcy Todd; the 3rd troop 1st brigade, under Captain G. H. Swinley; the 1st troop 3rd brigade, under Major F. Brind; the 3rd company 4th battalion, under Captain Jasper Trower; and the 2nd company 6th battalion, under Captain R. Horsford; Nos. 7 and 9 light field-batteries being attached to these two companies. There were also at Umballah, the 2nd and 4th companies (reserve) 4th battalion, under Lieutenant-Colonel G. Denniss.

******

On the deaths of Captains Dashwood and Todd, Captain Mills (of the political department) commanded the 1st troop 1st brigade at Ferozeshuhur, and Lieutenant Mackinnon commanded the 2nd troop in the same action; Captain Waller commanded the latter at Sobraon.

******

Thus, the Sirhind division of artillery, commanded by Lieutenant-Colonel Brooke, numbered forty-two horse-artillery and twenty-four foot-artillery guns and howitzers. The four 9-pounder batteries were horsed; but No. 19, at Ferozepore, having only lately been changed from a bullock-battery, and being incomplete in harness, was obliged to take the field with bullock-draught. The governor-general was at this time at Umballah; and he had with him on escort duty, two horse-artillery guns, under 1st Lieutenant George Moir, of the 2nd troop 3rd brigade horse-artillery, commanded by Lieutenant-Colonel Lane, then at Muttra.

The Sikhs crossed the Sutlej on the 11th and 12th. On the latter day Sir Hugh Gough marched from Umballah to Rajpoora, with the headquarters of the Sirhind division, a distance of 18 miles; and on the 13th, Sir John Littler moved his troops into camp, to protect the cantonments of Ferozepore; one regiment being detached with three guns, from No. 6 battery, under Lieutenant Tulloch, to defend the city. On the same day, he brigaded his force; Lieutenant-Colonel Huthwaite, of the 3rd brigade, being temporarily appointed a brigadier of artillery; Lieutenant Abercrombie, adjutant of the 3rd brigade, being his brigade-major.

On the 13th, the governor-general and the commander-in-chief being then only a few miles distant from each other, and in constant communication, the Army of the Sutlej was formed into brigades and divisions. Lieutenant-Colonel Brooke was appointed brigadier to command the artillery; consisting of all the troops and companies before mentioned, as stationed at Ferozepore, Loodianah, and Umballah, as well as the two guns under Lieutenant Moir, from the escort of the governor-general. Brevet-Captain Murray Mackenzie, adjutant of the 1st brigade, was appointed major of brigade to the artillery, and Brevet-Captain Warner, adjutant of the 4th battalion, commissary of ordnance.

On the 13th, the troops at Loodianah received orders from Sir H. Hardinge to march to Busseean, a distance of twenty-eight miles; and at the same time, the two horse-artillery guns from Muttra, and the 5th cavalry, which formed part of the governor-general's escort, were sent thither to join them. The object of this movement was to cover Busseean, full as it was of supplies for the British Army, which, but for the interposition of the Loodianah force, would in all probability have been destroyed by the enemy. By this movement also, the force under the commander-in-chief, marching up from Umballah, was augmented by 4,000 men and 12 guns.

On the 15th the troops halted, and on the following day moved on to Wudnee, of which place a Sikh garrison was in possession. On their refusal to furnish supplies to the force, the two troops of artillery were brought into position before the town—a movement which had the desired effect. Here the Umballah force, with the main body of the artillery, under Brigadier Brooke, joined the troops from Loodianah.

On the 17th the army made a short march of ten miles to Chirruck, where the troops suffered much from scarcity of water.

On the 18th the whole force moved to Moodkee. During the march a message was received from Major Broadfoot, who was reconnoitring in front, to the effect that the Sikhs were in possession of the fort and village of Moodkee, and that a portion of their cavalry were in advance of that place. The horse-artillery and cavalry were immediately ordered to form line to the front; the enemy's pickets, however, had abandoned their advanced position, and Moodkee opened its gates at the sight of a few guns.

It was half-past two o'clock before the army was encamped. The horses had been picketed, and men and officers were about to seek some refreshment after the fatigues of the march, when Major Broadfoot brought intelligence that the enemy was within three miles of our lines. The governor-general himself rode down the front of the artillery camp, and the guns were quickly in motion.

The camp of the British Army was, at this time, formed on a tract of cultivated ground immediately to the west of Moodkee. In front, for about a mile, extended ploughed fields, beyond which there stretched a dense jungle of low brushwood and stunted trees. Through this the Sikh columns were now advancing. The horse-artillery, with cavalry on the flanks, moved rapidly across the ploughed fields.

The dust caused by the march of the Sikh columns rose densely against the blue sky above the brush-jungle; but when the enemy perceived that the British line was in motion, they halted in the jungle to make their arrangements for the battle. The horse-artillery proceeded in line across the fields, but halted before entering the jungle. The light field-batteries, which had been directed to follow, with the infantry columns, came up soon after the action commenced; and in a short time 30 horse-artillery and 12 field-battery guns were in full play.

Our fire soon told upon the enemy, who were hidden in a thick jungle, and their position only indicated by the smoke from their guns. Soon, apparently, some of the Sikh pieces were either silenced or withdrawn, for their fire gradually slackened. Brigadier Brooke, in his official despatch, reports, that "the line of artillery kept up a heavy fire on the enemy, nearly silencing their guns;" and the commander-in-chief corroborates this statement, saying, that the enemy "opened a very severe cannonade upon our advancing troops, which was vigorously replied to by the battery of horse-artillery under Brigadier Brooke, which was soon joined by the two light field-batteries. The rapid and well-directed fire of our artillery appeared soon to paralyze that of the enemy."

Rather more than half an hour after the commencement of the action, the commander-in-chief directed Colonel Geddes to take two troops of horse-artillery, and to proceed with the 4th light cavalry and 9th irregulars to the left, to oppose a demonstration of the Sikhs from their right flank. The 1st and 4th troops of the 3rd brigade (under Major Brind and Captain Garbett), being on the left of the line, were those which accompanied Colonel Geddes. The two troops with the cavalry moved rapidly into the jungle towards the left front, and came into action against some Sikh cavalry and infantry, who had apparently been creeping round with the intention of turning our left flank.

Colonel Geddes, who was the senior officer on the left, perceiving this body of the enemy retiring before the fire of our guns, directed the 9th irregular cavalry to charge. This was accordingly done. As the cavalry moved forward, the guns ceased firing, and again advanced through the jungle, which at every step grew denser and denser, and much impeded the movements of the horse-artillery.

At the same time that this occurred on the left, a similar movement was made from our right to turn the enemy's left flank, and to check their cavalry, who were endeavouring to circle round our right. The 1st (2 guns of the 2nd troop 3rd brigade accompanied this troop throughout the action), and 3rd troops 1st brigade, under Captains Dashwood and Swinley, and Captain Trower's battery, were pushed forward to support the 3rd dragoons and a brigade of native cavalry, who were now ordered to charge the enemy's left flank.

The 2nd troop 1st brigade, under Captain Todd, and Captain Horsford's battery, still remained in the centre, covering the advance of the infantry brigades. After the brilliant and successful charges of our cavalry on both flanks, the troops and batteries detached to the right and left were ordered to close in to the centre, in order to support the attack of the infantry.

It was nearly dusk. The early evening of a winter day had set in whilst the action still raged furiously. The jungle at every pace grew denser, and it was with difficulty that the guns could force their way through the brushwood. Captain Swinley's troop, in covering the advance of an European regiment, suffered much from a close discharge of grape and musketry, and one gun, having lost all its horses, was temporarily disabled. The 1st troop 1st brigade sustained great loss from the close fire of the enemy's artillery and infantry. Captain Dashwood, who commanded the troop, was, at this period of the action, with his staff-sergeant and several of his men, struck down by grape. Lieutenant Pollock, of the 3rd troop 1st brigade, also received a mortal wound; and Captain Trower was shot at the head of his battery by a Sikh soldier concealed in a bush.

At this time darkness was rapidly covering the field, and the artillery, being within a few paces of the enemy's line, were suffering much from their galling fire. But at length the Sikh line gave way before the advance of the British infantry, who, supported by a part of the artillery, pursued for a considerable distance the retreating enemy; but, as the commander-in-chief observed in his despatch, "night saved them from worse disaster."

The action commenced at half-past three in the afternoon, and, as the day was one of the shortest of the year, the rapid closing in of night prevented the British force from taking full advantage of its success. The Sikhs saved a portion of their ordnance, some of their guns being apparently withdrawn early in the action. It is supposed that they had in all from thirty to forty guns engaged, of which seventeen fell into our hands.

The artillery suffered more in this action from grape and musketry than from the round shot of the enemy, which did comparatively little mischief. Only one or two waggons were blown up, and in fact scarcely any loss was sustained until the troops and field-batteries were pushed up through the jungle close to the enemy's fire. It was then that Captains Dashwood and Trower, and Lieutenant R. H. Pollock (son of Major-General Sir George Pollock, G.C.B.), received their death-wounds. The first was struck down by grape, receiving two wounds, one on the arm and the other on the foot, the latter of which proved mortal. Lieutenant Pollock had his knee smashed by a musket-ball, and being for a long time exposed to the cold night air, lying in a waggon, though the limb was amputated immediately upon his arrival in camp, sunk on the 19th. Captain Trower, as we have said, was shot by a Sikh concealed in the jungle; the ball passed through his body, and he died during the night.

There were several Sikhs—Akalis and others—lying concealed behind the bushes, who waited until our troops came close upon them, to pick out our officers. The total loss of artillery was (*killed*) 2 European officers, 4 sergeants, 13 rank and file, 5 *syces* and grass-cutters, 3 drivers, and 45 horses;—and (*wounded*) 4 European officers, 1 native officer, 2 sergeants, 22 rank and file, 11 *lascars*, 2 drivers, 7 *syces*, and 25 horses. The officers killed and wounded were, Captain Jasper Trower, killed; Lieutenant R. Pollock, killed; Captain F. Dashwood, severely wounded; 1st Lieutenant C. V. Cox, slightly wounded; 1st Lieutenant C. A. Wheelwright, wounded; 1st Lieutenant C. Bowie, slightly wounded. Captain Dashwood died soon afterwards.

The morning of the 19th was devoted to the mournful duty of bringing in the wounded and burying the dead.

★★★★★★

During the night of the 18th and the morning of the 19th the ammunition-boxes of the horse-artillery and light field-batteries were replenished, as far as practicable, from the spare waggons attached to each troop and battery. The two guns of the 2nd troop 3rd brigade, which had originally marched from Muttra merely on escort duty, being unprovided with spare ammunition, borrowed a few rounds from other guns, but not sufficient to complete.

★★★★★★

The artillery sent out limbers and cattle to bring in the captured ordnance. Whilst thus employed, our working parties were disturbed and obliged to retire towards camp, by some bodies of the enemy's horse, who had returned to the field probably with the same intention. As large bodies of the enemy's horse were still hovering about, the commander-in-chief drew up his troops again, prepared, if necessary, to renew the action; but nothing, at this time, worthy of note in our memoir, occurred.

On the night of the 20th, two 18-pounder guns and two 8-inch howitzers arrived in camp from Umballah, under Brigadier Denniss and Captain Warner, commissary of ordnance. Short as the time was, ammunition was prepared for the howitzers, which were thus enabled to accompany the force on the following morning. The 18-pounders were, however, left behind in camp at Moodkee.

An hour before daybreak on the 21st, the army broke ground. The main body of the artillery moved in rear of the centre column under General Gilbert. Two troops of horse-artillery were, however, detached, one with the column under Brigadier Wallace, and the other was attached to Major-General Sir H. Smith's division. The distance from Moodkee to Ferozeshuhur, where, according to intelligence received in camp, the main body of the enemy were posted, is not above twelve miles; but the army moved slowly, led by the infantry columns, and a very considerable detour was made to the left, in order that a junction with the Ferozepore division, under Sir John Littler, might be made, at a sufficient distance from the intrenched position of the enemy. (Ferozeshuhur is a small village between Moodkee and Ferozepore, and about five miles south of the high-road from the latter place to Loodianah.)

Although the communication with Ferozepore had been lately interrupted, as the Sikhs had interposed between that station and the headquarters force, instructions had been sent to the major-general to move out of his camp at Ferozepore on the morning of the 21st, so as to form the desired junction. The Governor-General's despatches had been duly received; and Sir John Littler, with 5,900 men and 21 guns, marched early on the 21st to Misrèe-wallah, a village a short distance from the Sikh position. This movement was skilfully accomplished by the general, who left the whole of his camp standing, and threw out the usual mounted picquets in front, thus deceiving that portion of the Sikh force under Tej Singh which had been employed in watching him.

The *sirdar*, ignorant of Littler's march, remained in front of the empty camp during the whole of the day, and did not learn the general's movement until the next morning. The junction of the two forces was effected about half-past one p.m.; and "dispositions were made for an united attack upon the enemy's intrenched camp." About 4 o'clock the British troops moved forward under their veteran commanders; Sir Hugh Gough leading the right wing, and Sir Henry Hardinge, who, after the Battle of Moodkee, had chivalrously volunteered his services as second in command, placing himself at the head of the left.

The nature of the ground was somewhat similar to that at Moodkee, covered with thick jungle, and, as on that day, the sun was rapidly sinking when the action commenced. It was the shortest day of the year, and but a few hours of daylight remained. The line of attack was formed, Sir John Littler on the left, Brigadier Wallace in the centre, and General Gilbert on the right. Sir Harry Smith's division, the reserve, was in the second line. The cavalry was in reserve and on both flanks.

The artillery was thus posted—Lieutenant-Colonel Huthwaite, of the 3rd brigade, was with Sir John Littler. He had under his command the 5th troop 1st brigade, under Captain E. F. Day—3rd troop 3rd brigade, under Major G. Campbell—4th company 6th battalion (bullock-battery attached) and three guns of No. 6 horse field-battery—the other three guns having been left with a detachment to protect the city of Ferozepore. Captain D'Arcy Todd's troop—the 2nd of the 1st brigade, was on the left of Brigadier Wallace's division; and Captain G. H. Swinley's, the 3rd troop of the 1st brigade, was on the extreme right of the line, beyond her Majesty's 29th foot. The 4th troop 3rd brigade, under Captain Garbett, and the 1st troop 1st brigade, now under Captain C. E. Mills, with Lieutenant Moir's two guns, were on the left of Gilbert's division.

Major Brind's troop was with Sir Harry Smith's in the second line; but just as the action commenced was moved up to the first line, and took post to the right of Captain Garbett's troop. These three troops, the 1st and 4th of the 3rd brigade, and the 1st of the 1st, were under the command of Lieutenant-Colonel Geddes. To the left of these were two horse field-batteries under Captain Horsford and Lieutenant Atlay, and the heavy howitzers and rockets under Brigadier Denniss and Captain Warner.

The action commenced on the left, Colonel Huthwaite pushing forward with his two troops of horse-artillery and his light field-batteries, to the attack of the enemy's position. The heavy guns and rockets and 9-pounder batteries next came into action, and almost immediately afterwards the horse-artillery in the centre and on the right. The action now became general with the artillery on both sides. The roar of the ordnance was tremendous. The British had 65 pieces in action—but, with the exception of two heavy howitzers, all light guns. The enemy had upwards of 100 guns in battery, and most of them of large calibre; whilst even those of smaller dimensions, being of much heavier metal than our own field-pieces, were fired with increased charges and carried greater distances.

The ground in front of our line was, in the first positions taken up, covered with jungle as at Moodkee, but afterwards, as we neared the enemy, became clear and open. After a few rounds, the horse-artillery in the centre of the line were advanced to a closer distance, and the troops moved through the jungle at a rapid pace, the shot from the enemy's guns tearing up the ground on all sides, but as yet causing little loss.

As before mentioned, the detachment of artillery under Colonel Huthwaite on the left, commenced the action. Pushing the guns forward from one position to another, until within grape distance, he had for a time completely silenced the batteries opposed to him. Meanwhile the infantry on his left moved forward to the attack, but the movement was not successful. Subsequently, however, the 9th Foot and 26th Light Infantry (with a portion of the 14th N.I.), under Brigadier Wallace, carried the enemy's battery.

Meanwhile the other troops and batteries, from their different positions in line, had advanced through the jungle. The 2nd troop 1st brigade, under Captain Todd, being on the left of Brigadier Wallace, approached the artillery attached to Littler's division. Major Brind's troop, the 1st of the 3rd, after advancing to a great distance, was despatched to the right to join Captain Swinley's, which had accompanied the 29th foot. Two troops under Colonel Geddes, after several positions, emerged from the jungle and came into a clear open space in front of the southern face of the enemy's intrenchments, and within reach of their grape-shot; and now the artillery fire ceased, the infantry were moved forward and (forming line) advanced to the storm. The batteries in front were carried at the point of the bayonet, notwithstanding the most determined resistance, and the great loss sustained, just as the line reached the battery, by the explosion of a large under-ground magazine, which had all the effect of a mine.

The sun had now set, and darkness was rapidly falling on the field. The obscurity was much increased by the dust and the smoke from the batteries and the exploding magazines. From the frequency of these explosions, and the quantity of earth thrown up by them, it was at first supposed that the enemy's position had been mined; but they were nothing more than under-ground magazines, which, some by accident, some by design, were now exploded, adding to the confusion and din of the fight.

Several regiments having penetrated the batteries, reached the Sikh tents, many of which were now on fire. Here the troops became partially broken and entangled; nothing could be distinguished clearly amidst the smoke and obscurity. It was difficult to ascertain in which direction lay friend or foe. Shots were falling thick on all sides, and even now the troops of horse-artillery, halting unemployed before the Sikh position, suffered material loss. Two waggons of Captain Mills' troop exploded simultaneously—giving at first a momentary impression that the mines extended even so far from the enemy's batteries. The 3rd dragoons, who had charged from the right of the line on the batteries immediately opposed to them, carrying everything before them in their course, now at length emerged from the enemy's position in scattered parties.

It was now dark. All our infantry were engaged. The reserve, under Sir Harry Smith, had been called up and had penetrated beyond the batteries, most of which had been captured; and one brigade had even reached the village of Ferozeshuhur. Yet all opposition had not ceased, and the enemy still held a great portion of their intrenchments. Amidst, however, the darkness and intricacies of the camp, it was impossible then to push our success further. It was advisable, therefore, to withdraw our shattered regiments, which within the Sikh position were exposed to hidden dangers, without any compensating advantage.

Accordingly, a bivouac was formed within two or three hundred yards of the batteries. Here were collected, under Gilbert and Wallace, the 9th, 29th, 31st, and 80th regiments of Foot, and the 1st European Light Infantry. The 1st troop of 1st brigade, and 4th troop 3rd brigade, under Colonel Geddes, joined this division of infantry, near which the governor-general and commander-in-chief remained throughout the night. The 2nd troop 1st brigade, now under Lieutenant Mackinnon (Major Todd having fallen in the action), and some field-battery guns, under Captain Horsford, soon afterwards came up to the ground. The 5th troop 1st brigade, 3rd troop 3rd brigade, and 9-pounder batteries attached to the 4th company 6th battalion, and 2nd company 7th battalion, bivouacked a short distance to the left. The 3rd troop 1st brigade, 1st troop 3rd brigade, with some field-battery guns, bivouacked during the night near Misrèe-wallah, which was occupied by British troops of all arms.

The night passed wearily away in cold and watching; the enemy, occasionally firing, allowed our harassed troops little rest. One gun was particularly troublesome during the greater part of the night, until the governor-general ordered its capture by the 80th Foot and 1st Europeans. Other guns were playing during the night with little or no effect. The uproar in the Sikh position was tremendous; the shouting was incessant, and the beating of drums, the sounding of bugles, and the firing of matchlocks and musketry continued, with short intervals, until daybreak. Frequently their drums beat to arms, and it was supposed that the enemy were preparing to attack us. Accordingly, a few guns were got into position and held ready with grape; but nothing came of these indications.

About midnight the troops, having originally bivouacked as they came upon the ground, were formed up in order; the guns in front, and the infantry in two lines in their rear. At length day broke, and the Sikh position was now comparatively quiet. The uproar had gradually diminished, and it was generally supposed that the enemy had begun to abandon their intrenchments. At first a thick mist shrouded all surrounding objects; but the beams of the rising sun soon dispelled it, and the three troops of horse-artillery, under Captain Mills, Lieutenant Mackinnon, and Captain Garbett, pushed forward and again opened on the Sikh position.

But there was no longer the determined resistance which had marked the contest of the previous day. It is true that some batteries of heavy metal replied to our fire for a time, and did some little mischief, a few of our waggons being blown up; but the enemy's fire soon grew feeble. The infantry, who were close in rear of the guns, formed into line, and with a hearty cheer sprang forward. Soon the intrenchments, here most insignificant, were gained and passed; and the British line swept through the camp, meeting with but little opposition. The horse-artillery, after ceasing their fire, limbered up and accompanied the infantry line under command of Lieutenant-Colonel Geddes.

There was no check to the progress of our troops. No steady resistance was offered by the enemy. The village of Ferozeshuhur was carried as the line advanced. There was a smart skirmishing fire in front, but it was evident that many of the Sikh battalions had already fled, and that our advance expedited the retreat of the others. The line having passed the village of Ferozeshuhur, leaving it to the left, and having reached the extremity of the enemy's position, halted. Upwards of seventy of the Sikh guns, and the whole of their *matériel* and camp equipage, fell into our hands. And thus, apparently the battle terminated.

But such in reality was not the case. We now come to a period of the engagement sufficiently difficult to describe. Orders had been given to allow a certain number of men to fall out for the purpose of procuring water, and arrangements were also being made for securing the captured ordnance. It was generally believed that the contest had ceased, when suddenly to the left of the British line, and extending over a considerable arc of the horizon, a dense cloud of dust was seen rising from the jungle. The *sirdar*, Tej Singh, who had been uselessly watching Sir John Littler's empty camp, had now marched from his position before Ferozepore to join the main army under Lal Singh, whom he supposed to be still in possession of the intrenched position. But to his surprise he found himself in the presence of the victorious British Army.

Our ammunition was getting scarce.

✶✶✶✶✶✶

Sir Hugh Gough has stated in his despatch, that the ammunition of the artillery had been completely exhausted in this protracted engagement. And an able writer in the *Calcutta Review* (No. XI.) has made a similar assertion, which, however, is not quite correct as to the time indicated, as all the troops of horse-artillery present were engaged with Tej Singh. The author of the article on the "Sikh invasion of British India" adds, "We believe the complement of a horse-artillery gun on service is 300 rounds." This is not quite accurate. Each 6-pounder gun carries with it 128 rounds of all sorts; and each 12-pounder howitzer has 80 rounds. The troops of horse-artillery from Umballah and Loodianah had each two spare 6-pounder waggons, and one howitzer waggon, making up the complement to $166^{2/5}$ rounds per gun, and 140 per howitzer. The Ferozepore troops brought out with them no extra waggons, and the two guns of the 2nd troop 3rd brigade had no spare ammunition at all.

★★★★★★

The horse-artillery was at this time in three separate bodies. Two troops (and a part of a field-battery, under Lieutenant Austen) were with Colonel Huthwaite on the left of the field. The troops commanded by Major Brind and Captain Swinley were, early in the morning, with Sir Harry Smith's division; and Colonel Geddes commanded three troops with headquarters. Colonel Huthwaite moving through the jungle on the left of the village, came unexpectedly on the *Sirdar* Tej Singh. He immediately opened upon the Sikh force, and drew down a heavy fire. This was the commencement of the affair. Major Brind, in command of his own troop and that of Captain Swinley, soon after became engaged with the enemy on the left front of the village.

His fire was answered by about thirty pieces of all kinds from the Sikh batteries. The three troops under Colonel Geddes were also directed to move forward to the attack. The artillery under Colonel Huthwaite, being entirely unsupported, and his ammunition failing, was compelled to fall back, as the enemy was within a few hundred yards, and appeared to be moving round his flanks. At the same time the two troops of horse-artillery under Major Brind, being exposed to an enfilading fire from some heavy guns of the enemy, were obliged to retire upon the village where the supports were posted. About this period, Colonel Geddes, after sustaining a very heavy fire, finding his ammunition expended and that he was entirely unsupported, was compelled to fall back upon the hollow square which, in the meantime, had been formed by the infantry on the right front of the village.

The greater number of the guns were now placed on the prolongation of one of the sides of the square. Some were in the village, and three guns of the 4th troop 3rd brigade were posted in one of the angles of the square immediately fronting the direction of Tej Singh's advance. There was now a pause—the army quietly waiting the expected attack of the Sikh *sirdar*. Most of our guns were now without, or nearly without, ammunition, only a few rounds of grape remaining. Near the village to the left of the large square were several Sikh ammunition-carts, and the commander-in-chief directed the artillery to seize as much of the enemy's ammunition as time would admit of, to replenish the exhausted boxes.

But unfortunately, most of the guns, being on the right of the square, were too far removed to avail themselves of this opportunity. The three guns, however, which were in the angle, procured each some fifteen or sixteen rounds, which proved of material assistance. Meantime the Sikh line under Tej Singh continued to advance. At length, when he had arrived some six hundred yards from the British position, Major Brind's troop in the village, and the three guns of the 4th troop 3rd brigade in the angle of the square, opened upon the enemy, and drew down a furious cannonade from some forty field-guns. Those of our guns which were on the right of the square, besides being short of ammunition as before mentioned, were placed with their left flank towards the enemy, and therefore could not, even had they ammunition, take part in the conflict.

From their position they suffered much from the enfilading fire of the enemy, as did also the regiments on that side of the square. For some twenty minutes, the few guns which we had opposed to the enemy kept up this unequal contest. Whilst the Sikh artillery were playing upon our position, the *sirdar* appeared to be gradually crossing our front. It was about this time that the commander-in-chief changed the front of the line, bringing a portion of it within shelter of the village. The fire of the artillery on our side now entirely ceased.

Major Brind, who had been in the village with two troops, was directed to join the entire mass of the artillery which was on the extreme right, in column with the cavalry—as did also the three guns of the 4th troop of the 3rd brigade, which had expended all their ammunition, including that which they had captured from the Sikhs. But by this time the Sikh fire was gradually lessening, and the *sirdar* appeared to be withdrawing from the field.

It was after the change of front had been effected, and whilst the artillery and cavalry, in a mass of contiguous columns (the cavalry on the right, left in front), were moving round the right of the village, that orders were given to the latter to form line to the right preparatory to charging. The cavalry accordingly, whilst the artillery halted, moved forward in line, and made a demonstration against the enemy—which was the last offensive movement made on either side.

During this movement of the cavalry, the artillery halted, to be able, if necessary, to support the former. But on the cavalry re-forming and again forming column, the march was resumed, and orders were received (the order was given to the brigadier, without authority from the commander-in-chief), by the senior officer, Brigadier Harriott, to escort the whole of the field-artillery into Ferozepore for the purpose of refilling their ammunition-boxes. But the action was now entirely over, and the Sikh *sirdar* was making the best of his way towards the river.

In this action the artillery lost 31 killed, including officers; and 77 wounded (exclusive of *lascars*, &c.). Major D'Arcy Todd had his head carried away by a cannon-shot on the 21st; Captain J. F. Egerton, at the time attached to the quarter-master general's department, was cut down on the 22nd, near the village of Ferozepore, whilst carrying a message. He lingered more than a month under very severe sabre-cuts, and died on the 23rd of January, 1846. 1st Lieutenant P. C. Lambert, a very promising young officer of horse-artillery, was killed by a cannon-shot on the 22nd. The wounded officers were Captain W. K. Warner, commissary of ordnance (slightly), Captain M. Mackenzie, brigade major (slightly), 1st Lieutenant R. M. Paton (slightly), and 1st Lieutenant E. Atlay (slightly).

The artillery had several pieces disabled at different periods of the action, and some six or seven limbers or waggons were blown up.

The exhaustion of the ammunition with the field-artillery at Ferozeshuhur was a matter of too pregnant and suggestive a nature to be lost, in the way of warning, upon the sagacious practical mind of the governor-general, who, soon after the conclusion of the war, addressed himself to the remedy of the evil which had threatened such serious consequences during the campaign. It was obvious that the guns had gone into the field with a scanty supply of ammunition, and that the Indian system, which allowed a smaller number of rounds than is sanctioned by the regulations of the royal army, was unequal to the exigencies of such trying service.

★★★★★★

The royal waggons carry 146 rounds a gun, the Indian waggons, I believe, only contain 96 rounds. In the royal service, the (6-pounder) gun and waggon carry 194 rounds a gun. The extra waggons in the royal service have 29 rounds a gun, and in the Indian service only 19 rounds a gun. The waggon in the Indian service is, I have no doubt, best adapted to the country and the draught animals, but if a battery of five guns had ten waggons (and the howitzer one waggon), the number of rounds a gun would be about 220. The 9-pounder field batteries, I understand, take into action 139 rounds a gun. The royal 9-pounder takes 166.—*Minute of Lord Hardinge, Feb. 2, 1847.*

✶✶✶✶✶✶

To remedy this for the future, it was recommended by Lord Hardinge, that there should be allotted to each gun of every troop and battery, whether a 6-pounder or a 9-pounder, two ammunition-waggons, giving to each 6-pounder 224 rounds, and to each 9-pounder 168 rounds. One waggon, it was proposed should always be close at hand with each gun in action, and the other in reserve, the whole supply of ammunition being under the charge of the officer commanding the troop or battery. The Military Board, whilst concurring in the expediency of the proposed increase of ammunition, suggested that the six waggons with the troop or battery, should be under the charge of the officer commanding; and the six spare waggons in magazine, a proposal which was readily concurred in by the Governor-General.

On the 24th of December the army moved to Sultan-Khan-Wallah, and thence, in a few days, to Hurruff, with an advanced division at Mulloowal. On the 1st of January the army was again brigaded. Colonel Gowan, C.B., was appointed to the command of the artillery division; Captain Edward Christie was nominated deputy assistant adjutant-general; Captain Warner, commissary of ordnance; Lieutenant H. H. Maxwell, deputy assistant quartermaster-general (originally appointed at Wudnee). Lieutenant-Colonels Biddulph, Brooke, and Dennis, were appointed brigadiers; with Captains Austin, Mackenzie, and Lieutenant Kaye, as brigade majors.

Great exertions were now made, in anticipation of the renewal of the struggle, to strengthen our ordnance force, especially by the addition of a siege-train. To the artillery formerly specified were accordingly added three troops of horse-artillery from Meerut, and one from Muttra—the 1st troop 2nd brigade, under Captain Turton—the 2nd troop 2nd brigade, under Major Grant—the 3rd troop 2nd brigade, under Lieutenant-Colonel Alexander; and the 2nd troop 3rd brigade (two guns of which had been previously with the army), under Lieutenant-Colonel Lane;—also, the 1st company 4th battalion, under Captain Waller, with twelve 9-pounder iron guns, reamed out to 12-pounders, and drawn by elephants, with some reserve companies of the 3rd and 6th battalion, under Lieutenant-Colonel Wood. The horse-artillery from Meerut, and Captain Waller's guns, joined the army early in January, and the remainder at a later period.

On the 12th of January the headquarters of the army changed ground to Bootawallah, with its extreme flanks resting on Mukkoo and Attaree. On the 13th and 14th there was an interchange of a few distant rounds between the British and Sikh artillery, which led to no results. On the 18th, a force under Sir Harry Smith was detached towards Dhurrum Khote. The artillery which accompanied this division, consisted of the 1st and 3rd troops of the 2nd brigade, and No. 6 horse field-battery, under Colonel Lawrenson. The 1st troop 1st brigade, under 1st Lieutenant J. Mill, followed with Brigadier Wheeler, who was sent to the reinforcement of Sir Harry Smith, but did not take part in the affair of Buddowal. It was on the 21st that this incident occurred, in which the artillery assisted in covering the retirement of Sir Harry Smith to Loodianah. A few store-carts, which were in the rear with the baggage, fell into the hands of the enemy.

A week after this, the Battle of Aliwal was fought. Reinforced by a body of troops under Brigadier Wheeler, which joined the division on the 26th of January, Sir Harry Smith made his arrangements to attack the enemy's position at daybreak on the 28th. The general, in his well-known despatch, writes:

> My order of advance was the cavalry in front, in contiguous columns of squadrons of regiments; two troops of horse-artillery, in the intervals of brigades: the infantry in contiguous columns of brigades, at intervals of deploying distance; artillery in the intervals, followed by two 8-inch howitzers, on travelling carriages, brought into the field by the indefatigable exertions of Lieutenant-Colonel Lane, horse-artillery.

About 10 o'clock the enemy's batteries opened on our advancing columns, and the action soon became general. All arms distinguished themselves greatly on this memorable occasion:—

> Lieutenant-Colonel Lane's and Captain Turton's troops of horse-artillery, under Major Lawrenson, dashed almost among the flying infantry, committing great havoc, until about 800 or

1,000 men rallied under the high bank of a *nullah*, and opened a heavy but ineffectual fire from below the bank.

Sir Harry Smith adds:

> I immediately directed the 30th Native Infantry to charge them, which they were able to do upon their left flank, while in a line in rear of the village. This native corps nobly obeyed my orders, and rushed among the Avitabile troops, driving them from under the bank, and exposing them once more to the deadly fire of twelve guns within three hundred yards. The destruction was very great, as may be supposed, by guns served as these were. Her Majesty's 53rd moved forward in support of the 30th Native Infantry, by the right of the village. The battle was won; our troops advancing with the most perfect order to the common focus, the passage of the river. The enemy, completely hemmed in, were flying from our fire, and precipitating themselves in disordered masses into the ford and boats, in the utmost confusion and consternation.
>
> Our 8-inch howitzers soon began to play upon their boats, when the 'debris' of the Sikh army appeared upon the opposite and high bank of the river, flying in every direction, although a sort of line was attempted, to countenance their retreat, until all our guns commenced a furious cannonade, when they quickly receded. Nine guns were on the verge of the river by the ford. It appears as if they had been unlimbered to cover the ford. These, being loaded, were fired once upon our advance. Two others were sticking in the river; one of them we got out; two were seen to sink in the quicksands; two were dragged to the opposite bank, and abandoned. These and the one in the middle of the river were gallantly spiked by Lieutenant Holmes, of the 11th Irregular Cavalry, and Gunner Scott, of the 1st troop 2nd brigade horse-artillery, who rode into the stream, and crossed for the purpose, covered by our guns and light infantry.

The highest praise has been bestowed by Sir Harry Smith on the artillery, for its conduct throughout these operations—He continues, in his despatch to the commander-in-chief:

> The guns literally being constantly ahead of everything. I would beg to call His Excellency's marked attention to Major Lawrenson, commanding the artillery; in Lieutenant-Colonel Alexan-

der, Captain Turton, and Lieutenant-Colonel Lane, the service has officers of the very first order; and I am equally satisfied with Captain Boileau, in command of the 9-pounder battery, and with Lieutenant Mill, in charge of four light guns. The two 8-inch howitzers did right good service, organised, equipped, and brought into the field by the exertions and determination to overcome all difficulties of Lieutenant-Colonel Lane, equally well served and brought forward always with the infantry by Lieutenant Austen.

Lieutenant Tombs, who was present as acting *aide-de-camp* to the general, also received the thanks of Sir Harry Smith.

In this engagement the artillery lost 3 men and 30 horses, *killed*; 15 men and 9 horses, *wounded*; 5 men and 12 horses, *missing*.

We come now to the crowning action of Sobraon. It was on the night of the 7th of February that the long-expected siege-train arrived from Delhi, with four companies of foot-artillery, under the command of Lieutenant-Colonel Wood. The commander-in-chief, overjoyed by this accession to his strength, determined upon the immediate attack of the enemy's intrenched position. But short time was allowed to the artillery to prepare ammunition for the heavy ordnance. On the 8th, the artillery, which had been detached with Sir Harry Smith, rejoined headquarters: on the 9th, the plan of operations was sketched out for the following day. A little before midnight the heavy ordnance moved out of camp to the advanced position of Rodawallah, there to be joined by Brigadier Ashburnham's brigade of infantry, to which was added the 62nd foot, which, owing to some mistake, did not reach that post till near gun-fire. The following account of the Sikh intrenchments and of the plan of attack is taken from the *Calcutta Review*:—

> The Sikhs had taken up one of the falsest positions possible; *viz.* with their rear resting on the Sutlej; yet, by dint of much labour, some foreign science, and the ingenuity natural to a military people, they contrived to convert it into one of the strongest fortifications against which troops were ever led;—being nothing less than a series of vast semi-circular intrenchments, the outer one of which was two miles and a half from end to end, and three quarters of a mile in depth; the whole surrounded by a deep ditch and 'bristling' with sixty-seven pieces of artillery. A bridge of boats united this formidable camp to another on

the opposite bank of the Sutlej; where also were planted some heavy guns, whose range swept easily across the river.

Sir Hugh Gough's plan of attack was as follows:—The heavy guns were to commence operations by a cannonade upon the intrenchment, into which, crowded as it was with upwards of 30,000 men, their fire was expected to carry confusion and dismay. Sir Robert Dick's division, on the extreme left of the British line, was then to advance and storm the right, or western corner of the Sikh position; General Gilbert's division on the centre, and Sir H. Smith's division on the right, were simultaneously to make false attacks, with the view of diverting the enemy's attention from the real attack of Sir Robert Dick. Brigadier Cureton, with a brigade of cavalry and a troop of horse-artillery, was directed to threaten the ford of Huríkí Puttun, about a mile distant from the eastern corner of the intrenchment, on the opposite bank of which the enemy's cavalry were posted.

Agreeably to this plan, at about 7 o'clock a.m., the artillery opened; the fog rolled off as it were a curtain, and the surprised Khalsa at once heard and saw that the avenger had come upon them. In an instant the Sikh drums beat to arms; and many rounds had not been fired from the British guns before an answering thunder from the intrenchment told that the works were manned and the struggle had begun.

Owing to the delay above mentioned, it was not until a little after sunrise that the heavy guns were placed in position. Opposite the enemy's centre was a mortar-battery, under command of Lieutenant-Colonel Wood. On the prolongation of the right flank of the enemy's intrenchment, at a distance of 1,300 yards, were placed three batteries of heavy ordnance—six 18-pounders under command of Lieutenant-Colonel Lawrenson—six 10-inch howitzers under Brigadier Dennis—and eight 8-inch howitzers under Lieutenant-Colonel Huthwaite. Further to the left of these batteries, and slightly in advance, were the rockets, under Lieutenant-Colonel Geddes; Brigadiers Biddulph and Brooke superintended these batteries; the first on the right, the second on the left. The attack was commenced by Major Grant's howitzer-troop. The surprise was most complete.

The Sikh position, which up to this time had been wrapped in profound silence, now became a scene of uproar and commotion.

Their drums beat to arms; and they began to busy themselves in preparations for the engagement. The 12-pounder reamers, manned by the men of the 5th troop 1st brigade, under the command of Captain Day, were the next to open. These, after a short interval, were followed by the heavy batteries. Then, to use the words of the commander-in-chief's despatch:

> The whole of our artillery fire was developed. It was most spirited and well directed. I cannot speak in terms too high of the judicious disposition of the guns, their admirable practice, or the activity with which the cannonade was sustained; but notwithstanding the formidable calibre of our iron guns, mortars, and howitzers, and the admirable way in which they were served, and aided by a rocket battery, it would have been visionary to expect that they could, within any limited time, silence the fire of seventy pieces behind well-constructed batteries of earth, plank, and fascines, or dislodge troops covered either by redoubts or epaulements, or within a treble line of trenches.

As already mentioned, but a short time had been allowed for the preparation of ammunition for the heavy guns; to this and to the great distance at which they were posted from the enemy's works, is to be attributed their inability to silence the Sikh fire. But the practice both of guns and rockets was considered highly effective. It had been proposed by the commanding officers of artillery, to place the guns in battery nearer the enemy's entrenchments; and had this been done, some satisfactory results might have been obtained.

★★★★★★

In a memorandum on this subject left by Captain Buckle, the author says:—"At Sobraon, the heavy guns, which had been waited for nearly a month, were placed on the plain about 1,300 yards from the intrenchments, instead of in batteries prepared for them at half that distance, and the facilities for which were great in the abundance of men and material, and in the softness of the soil. They might easily have been erected during the night of the 9-10th of February, had previous arrangements been made; and had this been done, the enemy's intrenchments, instead of being nearly uninjured, would have been swept away by the storm of shot poured upon them. As it was, the effect of the fire was greater on the defenders of the works than upon the works themselves; and quite as much as was expected by those competent to form an opinion, considering the greatness of the distance, and the shortness of time during which they fired. And for the selection of the distance we are credibly informed that the artillery are not responsible."

******

But the commander-in-chief was unwilling to hazard the delay which the formation of the necessary parapets would have occasioned. Hence, at the time when Sir Robert Dick, who was on the extreme left, was ordered to advance to the attack, the ammunition of the heavy guns had been well-nigh expended.

The writer in the *Calcutta Review*, says:

> The attack was led by Brigadier Stacy with Her Majesty's 10th and 53rd regiments, and the 43rd and 59th Native Infantry, supported on the flanks by Captains Horsford's and Fordyce's batteries, and Lieutenant-Colonel Lane's troop of horse-artillery. Beyond all comparison this was the finest attack of the campaign. The artillery galloped up and delivered their fire within 300 yards of the enemy's batteries, and the infantry charged home with the bayonet, and carried the outworks without firing a single round.

The governor-general says:

> A forbearance, much to be commended, and most worthy of constant imitation.

As it was the finest attack, so also did it meet with the most determined hand-to-hand resistance which the Khalsa soldiers had yet opposed to the British. Like lightning, the real plan of the attack seemed to flash on the minds of all the desperate men in that intrenchment; and, disregarding the distant feints of Gilbert's and Smith's divisions on their left and centre, they rushed to the right to repel the real danger that was upon them.

In vain, Stacy's brigade tries to withstand the mass which every moment is growing denser; in vain, Wilkinson's brigade comes up to the support; in vain, Ashburnham's reserve swells the furious tide of the assault.

It was like the meeting of two mighty rivers, one swifter and one deeper than the other;—and as the swifter for a moment penetrates its duller neighbour's stream, then, yielding to the overpowering waters, is rolled back and swept away; so would the conquered trenches of the Sikhs have been wrested again from the brave division of the British, had not Sir Hugh, with the intuitive quickness of a general's eye, marked the crisis and the struggle, foreseen its issue, and ordered up Gilbert's and Smith's divisions to the rescue.

They advanced; the enemy beheld it, and, returning tumultuously to the posts they had abandoned, poured upon these new enemies, from every foot of the intrenchment, a destructive fire of grape, round shot, and musketry.

In spite, however, of a loss, unprecedented in so short a time,—Sir H. Smith's division losing 489, and General Gilbert's 685 men, in about half an hour, these two indomitable divisions persevered in storming what proved to be the strongest part of the enemy's position; and the intrenchment being thus carried by the British at three different points, the gunners, who drew their swords when they could no longer fire, were bayoneted beside the guns they had so murderously served,—while the cavalry and infantry, driven from three sides into a confused and disordered mass, but fighting to the last, were inch by inch forced to retreat where alone retreat was possible.

Preferring death to surrender, they recklessly plunged into the river. The bridge, of which they were so proud, and to which they had so confidently trusted, broke down under the first party of flying horsemen, and became impassable; while the Sutlej, having risen seven inches in the night, had flooded the ford. The graphic narrative of the commander-in-chief says:

> In their efforts to reach the right bank, through the deepened water, they suffered from our horse-artillery a terrible carnage. Hundreds fell under this cannonade; hundreds upon hundreds were drowned in attempting the perilous passage. Their awful slaughter, confusion, and dismay, were such as would have excited compassion in the hearts of their generous conquerors, if the Khalsa troops had not, in the earlier part of the action, sullied their gallantry by slaughtering and barbarously mangling every wounded soldier whom, in the vicissitudes of attack, the fortune of war left at their mercy.

******

N.B. For the severe punishment inflicted on the Sikhs during their retreat across the river, we are indebted to the singular forethought and cool calculating judgment of the Governor-General. Owing to the paucity of artillerymen, men had been taken from the horse-artillery to serve the heavy guns in the field; and the troops—three if not four—to which they belonged, were *left behind in camp.*

The services of these troops would have been lost to the army on the 10th February, had not Sir Henry Hardinge, while the battle was yet raging, ascertained that the ammunition of the heavy guns was nearly expended, and deduced, from this misfortune, the more than *fortunate* conclusion, that the horse-artillerymen would soon be again available for their proper duties. He accordingly sent back orders to the troops left in camp to move down without delay to *Rhodawallah*; and they *were* brought down *by their drivers alone*, to that post, where they found their own artillerymen waiting for them, and were galloped into action.

The anecdote is not generally known, but is worthy of record as highly characteristic of a mind peculiarly happy in the arrangement of *details, whose judicious combination alone produces military success."—Reviewer.* (Colonel Alexander's, Major Campbell's, and Captain Turton's troops were on the right; Colonel Lane, with Sir R. Dick's division. Major Grant, as before mentioned, had commenced the action with his 24-pounder howitzers. The officers and men of the 2nd troop 1st brigade, 3rd troop 1st brigade, 5th troop 1st brigade, and 1st troop 3rd brigade, were employed with the heavy batteries, rockets, and reamers. The 1st troop 1st brigade had remained with Wheeler near Loodhianah.)

★★★★★★

"Sixty-seven pieces of cannon, upwards of 200 camel swivels, numerous standards, and vast munitions of war," were left in possession of the victors.

The loss of artillery in this action was not very severe; Lieutenant Faithfull, of the 1st troop 2nd brigade, was killed by a cannon-shot. Major Grant was wounded in the arm. The total of killed and wounded in the different troops and batteries, was (*killed*), 1 European officer, 3 rank-and-file, 3 *syces*, and 17 horses; (*wounded*), 1 European officer, 1 sergeant, 33 rank-and-file, 5 *lascars*, 5 *syces*, and 23 horses.

The following officers were especially named by the commander-in-chief:—Brigadiers Gowan, Biddulph, Brooke, Denniss; Captain Christie, deputy assistant adjutant-general; Captains Pillans and Warner, commissaries of ordnance; Lieutenant Maxwell, deputy assistant quartermaster-general; Captains Austin, Mackenzie, and Lieutenant Kaye, brigade majors; Lieutenant-Colonels Wood, Huthwaite, Geddes, Alexander, and Lane; Majors Lawrenson, Grant, Brind, and Campbell; Captains Day, Turton, Swinley, Fordyce, Horsford, Waller, and Lieutenant Holland.

It should be mentioned in this place, that, on the death of Major Broadfoot, the political agent on the north-western frontier, Major H. M. Lawrence, of the artillery, then political agent at Catmandoo, was summoned from Nepaul to take charge of our relations with the Punjab, and to execute the congenial policy of the governor-general.

The summons was responded to with remarkable despatch, and, within a fortnight from its receipt, he had joined the camp of the governor-general. He was present at the Battle of Sobraon.

We subjoin here a complete list of the honours conferred on the artillery:—

To be A.D.C. to the Queen:—Lieut.-Col. Gowan, C.B.

To be Lieut.-Cols.:—Majors F. Brind, G. Campbell, H. M. Lawrence, C. Grant, and G. S. Lawrenson.

To be Majors:—Captains H. Garbett, R. Horsford, E. F. Day, G. H. Swinley, J. Fordyce, W. S. Pillans, F. Boileau, R. Waller, and E. Christie.

To be Companions of the Bath:—Lieut.-Cols. Biddulph, Brooke, Denniss, Huthwaite, Geddes, Alexander, Lane, Lawrence, and Lawrenson.

Immediately after this action, the British Army crossed the Sutlej, and marched upon Lahore. Indeed, the firing had scarcely ceased, when the governor-general despatched a staff officer to Khoondah ghaut, directing Sir John Littler to commence the passage of the river at that point. Captain Garbett's troop of horse-artillery and two native infantry regiments were ferried across the Sutlej, and thus, both banks being in possession of the British Army, an excellent bridge of boats was thrown across, and the passage of the river was effected without opposition.

Thus, closed the first Sikh war—one of the most memorable and glorious in the annals of our eastern empire. Upon the history of the subsequent treaties, this memoir need not enter. In April, 1846, the greater part of the army returned to India, leaving a strong body of troops to occupy Lahore.

CHAPTER 11
Chillianwallah and the Close of the Sikh War

In accordance with the treaties entered into with the Sikh government, the Jullundur Doab, and the hill country immediately bordering upon it, became a portion of the British territory. Within the latter stood the celebrated fortress of Kote Kangra, the *killedar* of which refused to deliver up possession of the place to the British authorities, declaring that, unless the Maharajah Runjeet Singh himself appeared before the gates, he would not surrender the keys.

> The fort of Kangra is one of those which is strong from its position: it is built near the conflux of the Bub Gunja with the Beeas; and is bounded, for the most part, by precipices nearly perpendicular; and where the declivities are less formidable, the aid of masonry has been had recourse to, so as to render the place, in the opinion of Vigne, impregnable under European engineers. The occupants of the fort were believed to amount to about 500, principally Akalis, and their guns were said to be ten in number. (MacGregor's *History of the Sikhs*.)

It now, of course, became necessary to reduce this fortress to subjection. Accordingly, a force, under Colonel Wheeler, was sent against it. It consisted of the 2nd, 11th, 41st, and 44th native infantry, with a wing of the 63rd, and a siege-train composed of three 18-pounder guns, two 8-inch howitzers, and six mortars, under Lieutenant-Colonel Wood, with Captain Swinley's troop (3rd troop 1st brigade), and Captain Fitzgerald's (2nd company 7th battalion), and Captain Christie's (4th company 6th battalion) batteries. The march was one of the most arduous character. It seemed impossible that heavy guns could be transported up the precipitous defiles which led to the fort. An officer of the force writes:

> With our heavy guns, we had to cross the River Gooj no less than fifty-six times between the Beeas and Kote Kangra; and the last day we crossed it, rain having fallen on the hills, it swelled to a roaring torrent. Frequently the guns got completely fixed between enormous boulders of rock, so as to defy all the ingenuity both of artillery officers and engineers; when the united strength of men, horses, and bullocks, aided by two elephants dragging had failed, one fine old *mukhna* (a male elephant, with tusks like a female) was always called for. Coming

forward with an air of pitying superiority—his look seeming to express clearly, 'What! can't you do it without me?' he would look carefully at the gun in every direction, and when he had found the point where his power could be best applied, he put his head to it, and gave it a push, as if to weigh the opposition; then followed another mightier push; and if that did not suffice, a third, given with tremendous force, almost invariably raised the gun out of its fixed position, and sent it on. He would then retire with the air of Coriolanus, when he said to Aufidius, 'Alone I did it!'—a more valuable ally than Coriolanus, because he said nothing, and was always willing.

Such, indeed, were the difficulties of the march, that the enemy, believing that our heavy ordnance could never be brought under the walls of the fort, determined to hold out. The same opinion of the impracticability of the road was entertained by many of our own officers. The writer above quoted—Colonel Jack, of the 30th Native Infantry—says:

> The brigadier was recommended to leave his 18-pounders on the other side of the River Beeas; he, however, determined to take them on as far as possible, and, by extraordinary management and exertion, he succeeded in taking them all the way. They turned out, as the Europeans quaintly remarked, to be the really influential *politicals*.

On the 25th of May this tremendous march—one of which it has been rightly said, that it "reflects everlasting credit on the artillery"—had been successfully accomplished. Preparations were commenced for the erection of batteries and the planting of the guns in position; but siege operations were rendered unnecessary by the unconditional surrender of the fortress. A portion of the artillery force, including the heavy guns, remained at Kote Kangra throughout the greater part of the year, being finally withdrawn in December. The return march of the heavy ordnance was little less difficult than the ascent; but on this, as on the former occasion, the elephant-draught was found to be admirably adapted to the required service. Lieutenant Clifford in an elaborate report says:

> From the experience of this march, I am satisfied, that from their intelligence, docility, and strength, elephants are admirably adapted for the draught of heavy ordnance through a mountain-

ous country; and I doubt whether the heavy guns could possibly have been taken up to Kangra and back without the assistance of these animals; for though bullocks answered sufficiently well for the draught of carts and lighter carriages, the number requisite to move a siege-gun could not have been used at many of the windings and declivities met with during this march, to say nothing of the difficulty of guiding bullocks over narrow, dangerous roads, in which the elephants appeared to show a sense of the necessity of caution. Throughout the march, ten elephants were immediately attached to the four guns; *viz.* two in draught with each piece, accompanied by two spare.

The year 1847 was one of almost uninterrupted tranquillity. During the first quarter of the following year little occurred to break the quiet that reigned in the Punjab; but in the month of April, affairs began to wear a more threatening aspect. The refusal of Moolraj, the Dewan of Mooltan, to give up that fortress to the British officers commissioned to transfer it to the hands of another chief, and the murder of those officers (Mr. Agnew and Lieutenant Anderson) by the people of the garrison, led, in the course of that year, to the celebrated siege of that stronghold. Before, however, we dwell upon this important event, it should be mentioned that, in the month of May, some disturbances having been created in the Manjha country by a Sikh Ghooroo (Bhaee Maharaj), two guns of the 4th troop 1st brigade (which had marched from Loodianah to Lahore early in the month), under Lieutenant A. Bunny, accompanied the detachment sent in pursuit of the rebels; and subsequently, the entire troop, under Captain Murray Mackenzie, proceeded on a similar service.

The operations of Lieutenant (now Major) Edwardes having brought him before the walls of Mooltan, it became matter of discussion between the commander-in-chief and the resident at Lahore, Sir F. Currie, (Colonel Lawrence had by this time proceeded to Europe for the recovery of his health), whether a regular force should be sent against the fortress at that time, or delayed to a later period. Eventually, the resident took upon himself the responsibility of ordering the advance of the force; and Major-General W. S. Whish, commandant of the Lahore division, an old and experienced artillery officer, proceeded in command of it.

The artillery with this force was commanded by Major Garbett. Lieutenant J. Mill was appointed major of brigade. The 4th troop of the 1st brigade, under Captain Murray Mackenzie, marched down with the Lahore column, along the left bank of the Ravee. The 4th troop 3rd brigade, under Captain John Anderson, marched with the Ferozepore column along the right bank of the Sutlej. The 2nd company 2nd battalion, the 3rd and 4th companies of the 3rd battalion, and the 6th company 7th battalion, under the command of Major E. F. Day, went by water down the Sutlej with the heavy ordnance. Lieutenant Peter Christie was appointed commissary.

These details set out towards the close of July. The land column reached Mooltan before the end of August. On the 4th of September the siege-train arrived. On the 5th, General Whish, in the name of the *maharajah* and the Queen of England, called upon the garrison to surrender. No answer being returned to the summons, the engineer officers were called upon to submit their plans for the attack of the place. It was finally determined to commence regular siege operations; and on the morning of the 7th, the first parallel was commenced. It had previously been in contemplation to attempt the seizure of the place by a *coup-de-main*; and on the 6th, our mortar batteries had commenced playing on the town. On the 7th, 8th, and 9th, there was some slight skirmishing.

At daybreak on the 10th, some of our guns were got into position, and a tolerably heavy fire was maintained throughout that day. On the following day orders were issued for an attack upon a position which the enemy maintained in advance of the city. The column named for this service was accompanied by 4th troop 1st brigade of horse-artillery, under Captain Mackenzie. The attack took place on the morning of the 12th, and was highly successful, though attended with considerable loss. Among the officers wounded, was Lieutenant Bunny, of the horse-artillery: General Whish had a horse shot under him.

This successful attack placed all the defensible points on this side the city in our hands, and by enabling the heavy guns to be advanced to within 600 yards of the city walls, would have considerably shortened the operations of the siege, but the defection of Shere Singh, which took place on the 14th, entirely altered the aspect of affairs. This circumstance, combined with other causes, the most prominent of which was the numerical inefficiency of the force employed to carry on the various duties of the siege, embracing the formation of trenches and batteries, the protection of the camp and lines of ammunition, as well as the thorough investment of the place, induced the general most unwillingly to suspend operations until the arrival of reinforcements should enable him to proceed with the siege.

In the meanwhile, the standard of revolt had been raised in the countries beyond the Indus, and on the banks of the Chenab. The Sikh troops at Bunnoo had mutinied and murdered their officers; and Chuttur Singh, a chief of considerable note, headed the insurrection in the Hazareh. Towards this point the eyes of Shere Singh were directed. He was the son of Chuttur Singh, and after his defection, did not long remain with Moolraj, but marched northward to join the rebels, taking with him 5,000 men, 12 guns and howitzers, and 80 *zumbooruks*. It was now no longer an isolated case of rebellion in remote provinces.

The whole Sikh nation appeared to be rising up in arms against us. The very troops which had been despatched by the Durbar to assist General Whish in his operations, had joined the insurgent force, and it was doubtful whether we had a single friend, Sikh or Mahomedan, in the country. It became necessary, therefore, to take the field on a more extended scale, and the commander-in-chief determined to place himself at the head of the army.

It was thus that in vain General Whish applied to Simla for reinforcements. All the available troops were required for the campaign, which appeared inevitable, on the Chenab. Accordingly, orders were sent to the Bombay Government to afford the necessary assistance. Here for a time we must quit that division of our army, and follow the movements of the commander-in-chief.

In October, 1848, orders were issued for the assembly of the Army of the Punjab, under the personal command of Lord Gough; Brigadier Tennant was nominated to the command of the artillery, with the rank of brigadier-general; Brevet-Captain Abercrombie, adjutant of the 3rd brigade horse-artillery, was appointed deputy assistant adjutant-general; Lieutenant H. Tombs, deputy assistant quartermaster-general; Captain Hogge, commissary of ordnance, and Lieutenant P. Christie (with General Whish at Mooltan), deputy commissary of ordnance; Lieutenant H. A. Olpherts was subsequently nominated *aide-de-camp* to the brigadier-general. Lieutenant-Colonel Brooke, C.B., 2nd brigade horse-artillery, and Lieutenant C.V. Cox, his adjutant, were respectively appointed brigadier and brigade-major of horse-artillery; and Lieutenant-Colonel Huthwaite, C.B., 1st brigade horse-artillery, and Lieutenant E. Kaye, his adjutant, were nominated to the same situations in the foot-artillery.

The artillery division was constituted as follows: Headquarters and

4th troop (at Mooltan) 1st brigade horse-artillery; headquarters and 1st, 2nd, 3rd, and 4th troops 2nd brigade horse-artillery; headquarters, 1st, 2nd, and 4th troops (at Mooltan) 3rd brigade horse-artillery; 1st company 1st battalion (No. 10 horse field-battery); 3rd company 1st battalion (No. 17 horse field-battery); 2nd company 2nd battalion (at Mooltan); 3rd and 4th companies 3rd battalion (at Mooltan); headquarters, 1st, 2nd, and 4th companies 4th battalion; 2nd company 7th battalion (No. 6 horse field-battery); 3rd company 7th battalion (No. 5 horse field-battery); and 6th company 7th battalion (at Mooltan).

The several components of the army crossed the River Sutlej near Ferozepore, at different times—the majority during the month of October, or early in November; but some of the corps and the artillery train, with No. 6 field-battery, and some reserve companies, did not move across the bridge till the middle of November. Brigadier Huthwaite was intrusted with the equipment and preparation of the train and park, and all arrangements regarding a plentiful supply of ammunition.

Some regiments of cavalry and troops of horse-artillery had been early pushed forward, under command of General Cureton; and Brigadier-General Campbell followed him across the Ravee with his division of infantry and some field-batteries. The commander-in-chief followed with General Gilbert's division.

At the time that our troops crossed the frontier, the Rajah Shere Singh was in force on both banks of the Chenab, with his advanced parties pushed forward to Eminabad and Goojranwallah, and occasionally even to the banks of the Ravee. These, however, fell back before the advancing columns under Brigadier-Generals Cureton and Campbell, and the Rajah abandoned the town of Ramnuggur, and placed the principal part of his force on the right bank of the river, but still holding the left with large masses of cavalry, and some smaller bodies of infantry. The town of Ramnuggur, on the left bank of the Chenab, is situated about two miles from the river, from which it is divided by a low tract of waste *cander* land, subject to occasional inundation, and intersected by a few easy *nullahs*. Nearly midway between the town and the river was a small but dense grove of trees, around which hovered the advanced bodies of the Sikh Army.

On the 20th November, Brigadier-Generals Cureton and Campbell were within an easy march of Ramnuggur, and during the night they were joined by the commander-in-chief. The following day the first collision took place between the Army of the Punjaub and the Sikh troops under Shere Singh. It was an unfortunate affair, which led to the loss of some valuable lives without any corresponding advantages to ourselves. Lord Gough was on the ground or in its neighbourhood, but Brigadier-General Campbell was that day in command. However, as the work was entirely confined to the cavalry and horse-artillery, Brigadier Cureton was the actual leader. It was his lordship's wish to drive Shere Singh completely across the river. The Sikh cavalry were, as before mentioned, hovering between the grove and the left bank. Our cavalry and two troops of horse-artillery (Lane's and Warner's) were pushed forward rapidly to dislodge them.

The 14th Dragoons, charging inconsiderately too far in advance, came unexpectedly upon a *nullah* filled with Sikh infantry, and were received with a heavy musketry fire, which caused them considerable loss. Colonel Havelock and many others fell in the skirmish, and also the brave old General Cureton. Nor was this all; one of our troops of horse-artillery (2nd troop 3rd brigade) advancing too close to the river's edge, got under a heavy fire from the enemy's batteries, and was compelled to retreat with the loss of a gun, which stuck against the bank of a *nullah* and could not be extricated. Such was the unpropitious commencement of the campaign. The Sikhs were certainly compelled to confine themselves to the right bank, but no doubt the same object might have been gained without so great an expenditure of life.

Meantime the heavy train, with No. 6 horse field-battery, and Penny's brigade of infantry, were moving up as rapidly as possible. After crossing the Ravee, the detachment diverged from the main road for the purpose of attacking a fort of some strength, called Jhubber, into which a rebel *sirdar*, Attar Singh, had thrown a small garrison, when he proceeded to join the camp of the *sirdar*. Two guns of No. 6 field-battery, with small detachments of infantry and irregular cavalry, proceeded in advance against the fort, while the main body followed. The garrison, however, refused to surrender to the nine-pounders, and the walls were too strong for field-pieces. It needed, however, but a sight of the elephant-guns to induce the garrison to throw open their gates, and yield themselves prisoners. Some small pieces of ordnance were captured in the fort, which, together with the neighbouring village, were destroyed by orders from headquarters.

On the 30th November, the heavy ordnance, anxiously awaited by Lord Gough, joined headquarters at Ramnuggur, and that very night several pieces were placed in battery near the grove, and also farther to the right and higher up the stream, while Sir J. Thackwell, with nearly all the cavalry, Campbell's division of infantry, and three troops of horse-artillery, and two field-batteries, marched up the stream to find a ford whereby to effect a passage, and so turn the enemy's position. (Thackwell marched without baggage or camp equipage.) This Lord Gough expected could be effected about nine miles above Ramnuggur; but Sir J. Thackwell found himself under the necessity of moving nearly as far as Wuzeerabad before he could effect the passage. This of course occasioned considerable delay.

On the 1st and 2nd there was some exchange of shots between our batteries and those of the enemy on the opposite bank; but the distance was too great to allow of any effect being produced. On the night of the second, our batteries were advanced to within 400 yards of the river's edge; but in the morning it was apparent that the enemy had drawn back a great part of his camp, though he had left some batteries near the river, between which and ours some desultory firing took place. In the afternoon heavy firing was heard some few miles up the river. This was Thackwell, who had been attacked while resting after several long marches.

There was nothing more than a cannonade from either side. Shere Singh tried to dislodge Thackwell, but could effect nothing by his fire, while, on the other hand, he himself was soon driven from the field by three troops of horse-artillery, 1st and 3rd troop 2nd brigade, and 1st troop 3rd brigade, under Huish, Christie, and Warner, and two field-batteries (No. 5 under Captain Kinleside, and four guns of No. 10 under Captain Austin). Thackwell made no pursuit; being ignorant of the strength of the enemy both in men and guns, and his own troops being somewhat weary, he was unwilling to become more closely engaged. The enemy suffered considerably, but our loss was trifling, and principally in the artillery; Captain E. G. Austin, of No. 10 heavy field-battery, was severely, and Lieutenant J. E. Watson, of 1st troop 2nd brigade horse-artillery, slightly wounded.

As day broke on the morning of the 4th, it was discovered by the indefatigable General Gilbert, as he rode from our batteries to the river's edge, that the enemy had entirely deserted his position. A ford was immediately sought for, and soon discovered; Thackwell, reinforced from headquarters, pursued the retreating Sikhs until they entered a thick belt of jungle, into which he did not consider it prudent to follow them. (A brigade had been sent across previously by pontoons a few miles up the river, but too late to take part in the action of Sadoolapore.) He accordingly encamped at Hailah, his camp equipage and baggage having been sent to join him from Ramnuggur.

About the 8th or 9th he was again reinforced. The remainder of the horse-artillery, under Brigadier Brooke, C.B., crossed the river, also No. 17 heavy field-battery under Captain Dawes, and the 1st company 4th brigade with four 18–pounders and two 8–inch howitzers, under Captain Sir R. C. Shakespear. Thackwell had with him now nearly all the force; two brigades of infantry, Hearsay's brigade of irregular cavalry, Miles's battery (No. 6), and the park, being all now left at headquarters.

His camp was formed at Hailah, in an extensive and for the most part uncultivated plain. In his front was the broad belt of jungle before mentioned, which extends from the sandy ridge on the banks of the Jhelum, some twelve or fifteen miles into the Dooab. At the further edge of this belt lay Shere Singh, his left resting on Russool, at the western extremity of the sand-ridge, his right flank being at Futtehshah-ke-chuck, and his back towards the river. After the 5th December, each force remained inactive for a considerable period, save that the Sikhs occasionally sent small parties of horse through the jungle, who annoyed Thackwell by carrying off baggage, camels, &c.

On the 18th, a pontoon bridge having been constructed across the river, headquarters, Mountain's brigade of infantry, Hearsay's of irregular cavalry (with the exception of the 11th under Holmes, left at Ramnuggur), and Brigadier Huthwaite and his staff, crossed the Chenab, and were then joined by No. 10 light field-battery under Lieutenant Robertson. On the 1st January, the headquarters force moved to Janu-ke (about 1½ miles in rear of Hailah), when the artillery train and park joined from Ramnuggur, at which place a bridgehead had been constructed, armed with two 24–pounders and the guns of No. 6 heavy field-battery.

On the 9th, headquarters force and that under Madwell changed ground, and effected a junction at Lussooria and Loah Tibbee, on the main road from Lahore to Attock, and about 12 miles in advance of the Chenab. Here it was supposed that the force would remain for a considerable time, and no doubt such was the original intention; but Attock, long defended by the gallant Herbert, fell, and Chutter Singh was known to be in full march to join his son, the *rajah*, on the Jhelum; and Mackeson, the governor-general's agent, impressed upon the commander-in-chief the advisability of overthrowing the latter before reinforced by his father. His lordship, willing always to follow warlike counsels, readily consented: he reviewed his army, ordered up two corps of native infantry from Ramnuggur, on the 12th moved through the jungle, to Dhingee, and on the 13th fought the Battle of Chillianwallah.

The strongest part of the enemy's position was supposed to be his left, at Russool, on the extremity of the sand ridge, where it abuts on the River Jhelum. The immediate neighbourhood of Dhingee was pretty free from jungle, but along the base of the sand ridge, and in front of the whole of the Sikh position, it was exceedingly dense—rendering all military operations (especially movements of cavalry or artillery) most difficult and hazardous; and concealing effectually the enemy's line. It was Lord Gough's original intention to attack Russool with his right (Gilbert's division), while General Campbell should operate upon Lallianwallah and Futteh-shah-ke-chuck; but there was so much counter advice offered to him on the night of the 12th, that he was induced to forego his intention of attacking the enemy on the following morning.

The force, however, marched from camp on the 13th, and the line of contiguous columns at first bore steadily down towards the enemy, the right directed on Russool. After a time, the right was brought more forward, so that the direction of our march became parallel to the enemy's line, and Lord Gough gave orders to his quartermaster's department to find a suitable spot for encampment, without going too near the enemy, and, at the same time, without the necessity of retracing our steps towards Dhingee. This was somewhat difficult, as the army had just passed some villages—Burra and Chota Oomrao, between which and Chillianwallah there was no water. At Chillianwallah, on a mound, or small hillock, was the enemy's most advanced post; of this, however, we were not aware, till a small party of our cavalry came upon it unexpectedly, and was fired upon; and thus, Lord Gough was *forced* to fight the action on that day.

Our cavalry (with exception of 3rd and 9th irregulars, under Hearsay, our rear-guard) was divided between the two extreme flanks. Gilbert's division formed the right wing, Campbell's the left, and Penny's brigade was in reserve.

The 1st troop 2nd brigade, 3rd troop 2nd brigade, and 2nd troop 3rd brigade, under Lieutenant-Colonel C. Grant, were with the cavalry on the right; Captain Dawes's, H.F.B. (No. 17), was with Gilbert; No. 5, H.F.B., and three guns of No. 10 (the other three guns being on rear-guard), were, under Major Mowatt, with Campbell. The 2nd troop 2nd brigade, 4th troop 2nd brigade, and 1st troop 3rd brigade, were under Lieutenant-Colonel Brind. The heavy guns (consisting of six 18-pounders and four 8-inch howitzers), under Major Horsford (the respective batteries commanded by Majors Ludlow and Sir R. C. Shakespear), were in the centre of the line. These were all drawn by elephants, which were, however, exchanged for bullocks before the action commenced.

Brigadiers Brooke and Huthwaite were, with their respective brigades, on the march, but during the action with the commander-in-chief's staff. The army moved in line of contiguous columns of brigades, at first directed towards the enemy's position, but subsequently changing front to the left, parallel to the Sikh line, our right towards it. As soon as the Sikh post on the mound at Chillianwallah had been discovered, line was formed from the columns. The outpost was of course soon driven in; after which, Lord Gough again changed front—to his right this time, so as to bring our front again opposite the Sikh line. The army halted, arms were piled, and the quartermasters proceeded to mark out ground for encampment. But the Sikhs, determined to bring matters to an issue under cover of the jungle, brought up some light pieces, and fired upon us.

As it was evidently impossible to encamp within reach of their guns, which the denseness of the jungle enabled them to move up unobserved by us, and as we could not encamp elsewhere from want of water, without retracing our steps, which would have borne too much the appearance of retreating, Lord Gough was *compelled* to fight, and that, too, under peculiar disadvantages, as he knew little or nothing of the ground in his front, nor did the thick jungle admit of his reconnoitring. He was forced, too, to abandon his original plan of attacking Russool, as we had now got opposite their centre; the enemy, too, had frustrated all, by moving out of their position into the jungle in front of it.

The enemy's position was a very extensive one, and Lord Gough was forced to lengthen his own line. The consequence was, that our left and right wings were at a considerable distance apart. The cavalry on the right was divided into two parties; the one under Brigadier Pope comprised the 14th Dragoons, a wing of the 9th Lancers, the 1st Light Cavalry, and a wing of the 6th; with these were Huish's troop (1st troop 2nd brigade) and half of Christie's (3rd troop 2nd brigade), under Colonel Grant. Further to the right, and somewhat to the rear, so as to cover the right flank of our army, were a wing of 9th Lancers and a wing of 6th Light Cavalry, with Lane's troop (2nd troop 3rd brigade), and half of 3rd troop 2nd brigade, under a subaltern.

To the left of Brigadier Pope was Gilbert's division, with Dawes's battery; and left of these again the heavy guns. Campbell's division and the remaining cavalry, with which were three troops of horse-artillery, under Lieutenant-Colonel Brind, were far removed to the left, and could not be seen from the centre of the line. The action commenced with the heavy guns. It would have been well had they had the battle to themselves a little longer. They produced soon a very considerable effect on the enemy's fire. In the words of the commander-in-chief:

> After about an hour's fire, that of the enemy appeared to be, if not silenced, sufficiently disabled to justify an advance. I then ordered my left division to advance.
>
> Campbell soon became closely engaged. Lord Gough then deemed it necessary to push forward his right wing, and the heavy guns were ordered to cease firing. The commander-in-chief soon received intelligence of a great misfortune having happened to Pennycuick's brigade (one of Campbell's division)—the 24th regiment of Foot especially suffered severe loss.

✶✶✶✶✶✶

> With regard to Pennycuick's brigade, the commander-in-chief says in his official despatch: "In justice to this brigade, I must be allowed to state that they behaved heroically, and but for their too hasty and, consequently, disorderly advance, would have emulated the conduct of the left brigade, which, left unsupported for a time, had to charge to their front and right wherever an enemy appeared. The brigade of horse-artillery on their left, under Lieutenant-Colonel Brind, judiciously and gallantly aiding, maintained an effective fire."

✶✶✶✶✶✶

The other brigade, consisting of 61st Foot and two native corps, had, however, made a more successful advance. The reserve under Penny was now ordered forward to support Gilbert's division; but this consisted of but two native regiments (one having been left on rearguard). Sir W. Gilbert's division, well supported by Dawes's brigade, met with but little loss, with the exception of the 30th and 56th Native Infantry, which corps suffered severely. But further on the right, Pope's brigade of cavalry, and the horse-artillery under Colonel Grant, were driven back with much loss. The cavalry, it seems, had formed line on the right of the guns, and were then ordered to advance through the jungle. From some unexplained causes, they had only just come within sight of the enemy, when the brigade—notwithstanding the efforts of the officers to stop the movement—retreated, not, however, without loss, for the Sikh cavalry hung closely on their heels.

Unfortunately, the men did not retreat directly to the position from whence they had advanced, but, obliquing, came in front of the guns (some of which were unlimbered) and galloped through them, the Sikhs mixed up with them, or close behind; so that our men could not fire without slaying our own cavalry. The consequence was, many of the gunners were cut down at their guns, and six of the pieces fell into the enemy's hands (two were afterwards recovered by Lieutenant C. Cookworthy, of 3rd troop 2nd brigade, who, after the action, took limbers and horses, and sought for his division). Major Christie received several severe sword and spear wounds, of which he died on the 15th. The other three guns and the cavalry retreated through the jungle, until they reached an open space, near which stood the chief and his staff. Here the guns drew up, and the cavalry rallied, with the exception of a small party, which continued its flight as far as the field hospital, established on the mound near Chillianwallah.

The Sikh cavalry, who had followed in pursuit, halted at the edge of the jungle, and a few rounds from our remaining pieces soon forced them to retire. Colonel Lane, who commanded on the extreme right, had also been attacked by cavalry, but he had repulsed them with a grape fire from his guns. Meantime our cavalry and artillery on the left had made a successful advance, and Campbell, at the head of the 61st foot and some native infantry, had swept all before him, taking several batteries. Gilbert too, in his advance, had overthrown everything, capturing a great quantity of ordnance. The enemy was everywhere driven from his ground and forced back upon his positions, and our troops, somewhat shattered, remained in possession of the field.

But night had now come on, and, seeing the great loss that we had met with, the difficulty of the ground, and that our men were weary and exhausted, the commander-in-chief, after consultation with Campbell, considered it expedient to bivouac on the edge of the jungle, at the foot of the mound at Chillianwallah. Unfortunately, this caused the loss of nearly all the guns which we had taken from the enemy—most of them were recovered by them in the night—four of our own too, were carried off, and we secured only thirteen of the enemy's. Whether the Sikhs claimed the victory, or whether it was in exultation at the trophies gained—some colours besides the guns—or whether it was merely to inform their friends that they still held Russool, they fired a salute that night from the summit of the ridge.

Our loss in this action was severe. Of the artillery, Major Christie, as before mentioned, died of his wounds, as also did Lieutenant Manson, of the 4th troop 2nd brigade; Captain Dawes and 1st Lieutenant Dundas were wounded. The total loss of *killed* was 2 sergeants, 14 rank-and-file, 1 *lascar* and 1 *syce*; *wounded*, 1 sergeant, 1 trumpeter, 28 rank and file, 8 *lascars*, and 1 *syce*; *missing*, 2 rank and file, and 6 *syces*.

The morning of the 14th set in wet and gloomy, and the chief then issued orders to pitch camp upon ground marked out immediately in rear of the mound, fronting the enemy's position. Whatever intentions Lord Gough may have half-formed of resuming the attack on the 14th, the heavy fall of rain which commenced that evening and continued during several following days, induced him to abandon them. He immediately set about strengthening his position, and the sad task of collecting and burying his dead. And so, the British and Sikh Armies sat down in sight of each other, with scarcely four miles of ground between their respective camps.

Such was the Battle of Chillianwallah; a victory, certainly, insomuch as we remained in possession of the field of battle; but a failure, inasmuch as Lord Gough did not accomplish his object—to drive Shere Singh across the Jhelum, and to completely overthrow him before Chuttur Singh could form a junction with his son.

A month of inactivity succeeded. Our position was a bad one; it covered no road, did not protect the country in our rear, nor guard our communications; neither did it in any way confine the enemy. Our communication with Dhingee was exceedingly precarious; supplies and forage, as well as water, were scarce. We should have felt the want of the latter severely, had it not been for several heavy falls of rain, which filled some dry hollows. As considerable reinforcements were in progress to join Shere Singh, it seemed not at all improbable that he might venture to attack us in our camp. The commander-in-chief therefore strengthened our position as much as possible.

A good deal of jungle which might conceal the enemy's designs was cut down; several trenches were dug in front of the line, to afford temporary protection to picquets; the heavy ordnance was placed in battery at the mound to sweep all the ground in front,—and subsequently, a square redoubt was erected to strengthen our right flank, which approached the sand-ridge, and was more liable to attack than any other part. This redoubt was at first armed with some spare field-pieces, drawn by bullocks, but afterwards by the 3rd company 2nd brigade horse-artillery, to which Captain Kinleside, of No. 5 heavy field-battery, had been appointed—Major Ludlow succeeding him in command of the battery. (This troop had been on the detachment system experimentally, but, after Chillianwallah, when new guns were given, it reverted to the old system.) The right flank of our camp was thrown back nearly at right angles. In it were two troops of horse-artillery under Colonel Grant. Fordyce's troop (2nd company 2nd brigade) of 9-pounders was at the angle, and afterwards placed in a small battery a short distance to the front.

Dawes was in the front face with Gilbert, sending out two guns on picquet; the heavy ordnance at the mound; No. 5, with Campbell's division near the village; No. 10, in rear with Penny. Beyond the village were three troops of horse-artillery under Colonel Brooke (when the 3rd troop 2nd brigade was removed to the redoubts, the number with him was reduced to two). Our left, beyond the village, was slightly retired in an oblique direction. The park was in rear of the mound. As the enemy became stronger and more threatening, several changes took place. The whole of the left was thrown back so as to unite the village of Mojawalla in rear of camp—with the front face, and our right flank was also connected with the village by a rear face—thus our camp formed an irregular quadrilateral figure, or rhomboid, and four pieces of heavy ordnance were placed near Mojawalla. But it was some time before our camp had assumed this form.

The enemy almost daily received accessions of strength. Chuttur Singh joined the Sikh force, and salutes were common in their camp. Reports were frequent of their intention to attack, but little credit was given to them. The chief, however, considered it prudent to be prepared; half the men, and latterly all, were ordered to sleep in their clothes, and a signal (three guns from the mound) was agreed upon, at which all the troops should turn out. The enemy occasionally made some demonstration. Sometimes his whole line turned out, but more frequently he brought small parties into the jungle, below Russool, and then attacked our right wing, which was frequently on the alert.

But the Sikhs gave us the greatest annoyance by capturing our baggage-cattle. This they did frequently, and we were obliged to send out very strong parties of cavalry to protect them. Our horse-artillery, too, had very fatiguing work, guns being frequently out with detachments sent to protect convoys of grain, &c. These had to make long, harassing marches, and latterly it became necessary to send out parties of cavalry and horse-artillery to reconnoitre the country in our right rear.

Thus, wearily passed the time, news from Mooltan being most anxiously looked for. At length we had the pleasure to fire a royal salute for its capture and to discuss the circumstances of the successful siege. What those circumstances were, should be here briefly recorded:— On the 26th of December the Bombay troops joined General Whish under the walls of Mooltan. The force now amounted to 17,000 men, with sixty-four pieces of artillery. The time for renewed action had arrived, and Whish was ready to commence operations. Indeed, on the morning of the 26th, before the Bombay division had come up, he had issued an order, expressing his hope that within twenty-four hours after their arrival, "all the enemy's posts that are a requisite preliminary to the commencement of a regular attack on the citadel," would be carried; and in the course of the following day they were in our possession.

In these operations, four guns of the 4th troop 3rd brigade of horse-artillery, under Captain Anderson, and four guns of the 4th troop 1st brigade, under Captain Mackenzie, were engaged; the former with the centre column, and the latter with the right column. On the following day Whish, reporting these operations to the adjutant-general, wrote:

> I hope tomorrow morning to have an 8-inch mortar-battery of six pieces playing on the citadel, at five or six hundred yards' distance.

On the 30th the general reported that our batteries were in full play, and that already a shell from a mortar, laid by Lieutenant Newall, had exploded the principal magazine in the citadel. Whish had been with the rocket troop at Hatrass, when the great magazine had been blown up there, and now he wrote that the sight of the Mooltan explosion was "awfully grand, and precisely similar to that at the siege of Hatrass, on the 1st of March, 1817." He added:

> I hope that the consequence may be the same; in which case the enemy would abandon the fort tonight; otherwise I contemplate assaulting the city tomorrow.

The batteries at this time in operation, as reported in the general's letter, were six 8-inch mortars, three 10-inch *ditto*, four 5½-inch *ditto* (opened on the 28th), six 18-pounders (opened on the Kooneeh-Boorj), two 8-inch mortars, two 10-inch *ditto*, and two 24-pounders (with the mortars in the first line, opened on the 29th). Five more 8-inch mortars were then laid down.

Seldom or never in any part of the world has a city been exposed to such a terrific shelling as the doomed city of Mooltan. The well served ordnance did tremendous execution upon both houses and inhabitants; and soon the ruined streets were choked with the mutilated bodies of the dead. The effect was highly creditable to the skill of both artillery and engineers. On the first day of the new year (1849) the breaches in the city walls appeared to be practicable, and the assault was fixed for the following day. It was on the 2nd of January that the city of Mooltan was carried by the British troops. The gallantry of the infantry column, on this occasion, will never be overlooked by the general historian; but it does not come within the scope of this memoir to record it. Mooltan was carried at the point of the bayonet, but the citadel still remained in the hands of Moolraj.

The batteries now, therefore, opened again, with tremendous effect, on the fortress. The possession of the city had enabled Whish to advance his guns, and he had erected new batteries of heavy ordnance to bear upon the citadel. On the 7th a battery of seven 18-pounders was completed and armed, and a mortar battery for three 10-inch howitzers. On the 8th a battery for six 24-pounders and six 18-pounders was commenced. The general wrote:

> The object of this battery, is to keep down the fire of the citadel opposite to it, and eventually to breach at the north-east angle.

On the following day a shell from the enemy's position ignited the seven 18-pounder battery, which was constructed of fascines and sand-bags, and burnt it down, in spite of every effort to extinguish the flames. The engineers in the meantime were sapping up to the foot of the glacis; and the enemy, alarmed by our near approach, were thinking of making terms for themselves. The interior of the citadel had become a ruin; and further resistance was, indeed, hopeless.

The garrison declared that they could no longer hold out against the terrible shelling, which was destroying them. Moolraj was at the last gasp. All his efforts to rally his followers were in vain. They told him that he must either sally out at the head of his men and cut his way through the besiegers, or abandon his post and trust himself to the clemency of the victors. So, the *dewan* began to sue for terms. The answer of the British general was, that nothing would satisfy him but an unconditional surrender. So, on the morning of the 22nd of January the garrison laid down their arms, and Moolraj came into the British camp.

The operations had lasted nearly four weeks, throughout which time the artillery were continually engaged—keeping up an incessant fire of shot and shell, from guns, howitzers, and mortars—first upon the city, and then upon the citadel of Mooltan. The practice is admitted to have been excellent. It was, said General Whish, with the enthusiasm of an old artillery officer, "the theme of admiration with all."

✶✶✶✶✶✶

The following remarks by Major Siddons on the artillery practice at Mooltan, taken from his admirable report of the siege, will be read with interest:—"The artillery practice was most excellent, and the exertions of officers and men indefatigable. It is impossible to over-rate the service rendered by the 8-inch and 10-inch howitzers. The walls are mostly of mud, or brick and mud; and it so happened that the part selected for the breach was very defective—a mere facing over the old wall. In this the 24-pounder shot brought down large masses; but where the wall was sound the shot buried themselves, whereas the shells penetrated and then acted as small mines. Against a mud fort, an howitzer must therefore be considered far preferable to a gun, though of course the latter would be more effective against a well-built stone wall. The inconvenience to howitzers is the difficulty of preserving the cheeks of the embrasures. The iron howitzer might, perhaps, with advantage be lengthened."

✶✶✶✶✶✶

The officers of the Bengal division especially named in his official despatch were Majors Garbett and Day; Captains Daniel, Anderson, Master, and Mackenzie; Lieutenant Mill (brigade-major), and Lieutenant Peter Christie (commissary of ordnance).

The following officers were present at the siege of Mooltan:—

Majors—H. Garbett, E. F. Day; *Captains*—J. H. Daniell, J. Anderson, E. V. Master, M. Mackenzie; *Lieutenants*—W. Hay, G. Moir, F. W. Swinhoe, F. Alexander, H. Francis, R. Mecham, D. J. Newall, A. Bunny, W. Miller, J. F. Raper, J. Thompson, H. T. Bishop; *2nd Lieutenants*—F. R. Debudé, J. Hunter, C. T. Graham, F. C. Simons, M. C. Sankey, J. G. Worthington, W. F. Quayles, E. W. Day;—Lieutenant John Mill, brigade-major; Lieutenant P. Christie, commissary of ordnance; Lieutenant W. K. Footes, brigade quarter-master.

In the course of the operations, the casualties in the Bengal artillery amounted to 1 European officer (Lieutenant James Thompson), 2 *havildars*, and 10 rank and file, *killed*; with 4 European officers (Lieutenants Bunny, Hunter, Sankey, and Graham), 3 *havildars*, and 62 rank and file, *wounded*. These include all the casualties since the raising of the siege. Lieutenant Bunny was wounded in September, and Lieutenant Sankey in November, 1848; the other two officers in the course of the January siege.

Before quitting the subject of these memorable operations, we must insert the following memorandum of the artillery practice at Mooltan, by Lieutenant Newall, which affords much interesting information relative to the details of the siege:—

> During the siege of Mooltan, the Bengal artillerymen were so few, that it was found impossible to afford a relief in the batteries without withdrawing gunners from the troops of horse-artillery. A relief, however, was thus effected daily between 3 and 4 p.m., which was found the most convenient hour, as it afforded time to the relieving officer to ascertain his range, &c. before nightfall, and to prepare and fix his ammunition for expenditure during the night. It was convenient, also, for the men in other respects.
>
> In the howitzer batteries, it was the practice to receive the charge ready weighed out from the magazine; but in the mortar batteries the charges were invariably weighed out in battery. The bursting charges of all shells were received in battery ready weighed out in small bags, and the shells were always filled by means of a funnel, and fuses prepared and set by means of a fuse-bench in the battery. Live shells were never sent down to battery from the magazine, as no advantage in point of time was to be gained thereby, the preparing of shells being found in the hands of expert men to fully keep pace with the working of the ordnance.
>
> The practice was thus rendered very much more satisfactory, as the length of the fuse could be altered according to circumstances; such as the variation of strength of powder, which was found to be most dependent on the state of the weather, and even of the ordnance, which as the day advanced would gradually warm, contracting the dampness of the powder, and rendering necessary an alteration in the length of fuse.
>
> The effects of the howitzers employed in breaching was a subject of satisfaction and astonishment to all; indeed, it is doubtful whether the natural mounds of the fort would have been practically breached without their aid. Even against the brickwork

their effects were conspicuous. These shells, made to burst at the moment of contact with the walls, afterwards during their passage through the *revêtement*, and ultimately with a longer fuse in the earth beyond it, would probably (against such masonry) have alone effected practicable breaches without the assistance of heavy guns.

At a distance of 150 yards, both the 8-inch and 10-inch howitzers were employed in breaching a scarp wall, part of which was invisible from the battery, and only reached by a plunging fire, obtained by very small charges, and succeeded admirably. At a distance of thirty-five yards, 8-inch howitzers were similarly employed with a charge of 8 oz., a very low velocity being requisite to prevent the shell from burying itself too far in the soft earth. Of the effects of the vertical fire, nothing could have afforded a clearer proof than the ruinous appearance presented by the interior of the fort on its surrender; and the explosion of the great magazine, which took place within one hour of its site being indicated to the batteries, was a subject of congratulation to the Bengal artillery employed, bearing testimony as it did to the accuracy of their practice.

On the 9th January, 600 shells were fired from an 8–inch mortar battery of six pieces in twenty-four hours, and the mortars did not suffer. No new feature, however, presented itself from the employment of these pieces, nor from that of the heavy guns, which, however, vied with the mortars and howitzers in utility. Doubtless it is by a judicious combination of the three that such powerful effects are produced,—but it may be worth inquiring whether, in the siege-trains employed against fortresses in the East, built as they generally are of old and often crazy materials, a greater proportion of howitzers might not be used with advantage, in cases where no particular object exists to curtail the transport of the shells, which is doubtless great.

In addition to what has been above stated of the effects of these most useful pieces in mining the defences and in counter-battery, which was conspicuous throughout the siege, it may be remarked that one shell was often found sufficient to silence the fire from an embrasure of the enemy for a whole day. Rack-lashing platforms were used by the Bengal Artillery throughout the siege for the guns and howitzers, and were found to answer most satisfactorily, and the small Bengal mortar platforms, consisting of three sleepers, upon which seven strong planks, each four feet long, were pegged transversely, were made up in the park, and thus taken down to the batteries, where they were expeditiously laid, and stood the firing both of the 8-inch and 10-inch mortars without renewal during the siege; the only difference being, that from the 10-inch mortars other sleepers were laid transversely beneath, to prevent the platforms sinking.

Having now reduced Mooltan, and captured the *dewan*, General Whish determined to move forward, with all possible despatch, to reinforce the commander-in-chief. Leaving, therefore, a British garrison in Mooltan, he commenced his march, with the headquarters, on the 29th January; an advanced brigade, with a troop of horse-artillery, having broken ground two days before. The main body of the Bengal division was accompanied by a siege-train of twelve pieces. The march which he then accomplished, though it has been unaccountably slurred over in the published papers, is one of the most memorable upon record. It was not only distinguished by the energy and rapidity which marked the general's movements, but by its effect upon the issue of the entire campaign. Had not Whish, with his leading column, reached Ramnuggur, as he did, on the 13th of February, Shere Singh would have ravaged the Rechna Doab, and the campaign would have been a long and desultory one.

******

As another opportunity is not likely to occur, it may be mentioned here that General Whish was instrumental in introducing some important improvements in the internal organization of the artillery. He was the first, when in temporary command of the horse-artillery (April, 1821), to establish regimental libraries for the use of the men. In 1836, he so far reformed the horse-artillery system, as to render it unnecessary that the guns should be accompanied into action by their waggons—a change, however, which was reversed in 1845. He was also, in 1841, instrumental in the abolition of winkers, as a portion of the harness of the horses.

******

Whilst the troops under the commander-in-chief were patiently awaiting the coming of General Whish, which would enable them to resume the offensive, the enemy seemed at one time inclined to become the assailant, but by some unaccountable freak of madness chose to abandon his strong position, and take to the open country. His probable object was more readily to procure food. In the second week of February, about half the Sikh Army changed ground to its left, and took possession of the Khuri defile, running through the sand-ridge. His advanced parties held Noor Jumal and Dingee, and occasionally even the villages of Burra and Chota Omrao, between our camp and Dingee. They were now on both sides of us; but as our camp was now formed, we were well prepared for an attack.

On the 11th, the signal-guns were fired, and our whole army turned out. The enemy was threatening us on both sides; but to our rear, his line had advanced from Khuri, even beyond the villages of Omrao, and could be plainly seen at the edge of the jungle from Mojawalla. Cavalry and horse-artillery were sent out to meet him on this side. The former threw out a chain of videttes, which the Sikhs did not attempt to break. It was not Shere Singh's object to attack us in camp, but to draw us out into the jungle. After a demonstration of about four hours, the Sikhs withdrew into their camps.

Early on the morning of the 12th, it was discovered, to our surprise, that the enemy had abandoned his position at Russool. His rear-guard was then quickly leaving the sand-ridge. On the 13th, he withdrew also from Khuri. At first, we were rather perplexed to ascertain in what direction he had proceeded, but it was soon ascertained that his march was towards Goojerat. Thus he had completely turned our right flank, and our remaining at Chillianwallah was consequently no longer prudent; but, on the contrary, there was the utmost need that we should make a corresponding movement, as it seemed to be the design of the enemy to cross the Chenab, and march straight upon Lahore. Luckily this was frustrated.

On the 15th, the army marched to Lussooria, which we had so fruitlessly quitted only a month before. From this it had been intended to cross the river at Ramnuggur, and endeavour to outstrip the enemy in the race to Lahore. But, fortunately, General Whish had now reached Ramnuggur, and, seeing the danger, should the enemy be able to cross the Chenab, he pushed forward the 53rd foot (which had come out from Lahore), with two guns of No. 6 field-battery, and some other troops, to guard the fords near Wuzeerabad, and Markham's brigade, with two guns of 4th troop 3rd brigade horse-artillery,—those lower down. Thus, Shere Singh was foiled, and his army remained encamped near the town of Goojrat, the centre of a richly-cultivated province.

From Lussooria our army moved towards the enemy, slowly, to

enable the Mooltan troops to join. On the 16th, they marched to Sadoolapore; on the 17th, to Kunjur; and after a halt, they reached Shahdiwaol on the 20th. By this time all Whish's force had joined, except Markham's brigade, and two guns—4th troop 3rd brigade—watching the fords. The brigade, however, crossed before the action.

The accession of strength in artillery which Whish brought us, was as follows:—4th troop 1st brigade horse-artillery, under Captain M. Mackenzie; 4th troop 3rd brigade horse-artillery (2 guns absent), under Captain J. Anderson; a troop of horse-artillery of the Bombay army (the horse field-battery of Bombay was on rear-guard duty), and four 18-pounders, and four 10-inch howitzers, under Major Day.

Our march from Lussooria had been through most beautiful cultivation. We had marched in a line of contiguous columns, encamping in the same order.

On the 21st, our artillery was thus disposed:—On the extreme right, under Lieutenant-Colonel Grant, Warner's troop, 1st troop 3rd brigade (attached to Lockwood's cavalry brigade), with Whish's division; Mackenzie's and Anderson's troops, under Major H. Garbett, with Gilbert's division; Fordyce's troop, and Dawes's battery.

In the centre, Major Horsford; four 18-pounders and two 8-inch howitzers, under Major Sir R. Shakespear; two 18-pounders, and two 8-inch howitzers, under Captain J. D. Shakespear.

Major Day; two 18-pounders and two 8-inch howitzers, under Captain Master; two 18-pounders, and two 8-inch howitzers under Captain Austin.

On their left, under Lieutenant-Colonel Brind, Kinleside's and Lane's troops, with Campbell's division—No. 5 (Major Ludlow's), and 10 (under Lieutenant Robertson), horse field-battery, commanded by Major Mowatt, with the cavalry on the extreme left—Huish's and Duncan's troops.

This time we had everything in our favour—a beautiful, level, open country, with no obstructions, a richly-cultivated plain, dotted with a few villages and trees. It was a bright sunny day: before nine the action was commenced. The enemy's camp was close to Goojrat, but he moved out about a mile to oppose us, occupying the villages of Burra and Chota Kalrha, in front of his centre and left. But we were not aware at first that he had any troops in them. As soon as he perceived our line, he fired three signal-guns. Our line then halted, while the commander-in-chief reconnoitred and made his dispositions. But little delay was, however, necessary—all was so clear—and we had marched from camp in battle order. The action soon commenced. The commander-in-chief, in his official despatch says:

> At half-past seven o'clock, the army advanced with the precision of a parade movement. The enemy opened their fire at a very long distance, which exposed to my artillery both the position and range of their guns. I halted the infantry just out of fire, and advanced the whole of my artillery, covered by skirmishers. The cannonade now opened upon the enemy was the most magnificent I ever witnessed. The Sikh guns were served with their accustomed rapidity; and the enemy well and resolutely maintained its position. But the terrific force of our fire obliged them, after an obstinate resistance, to fall back.

******

> *N.B.* The batteries engaged in action by those attached to the 1st and 2nd divisions, advancing to within about six hundred yards; and the heavy guns within eight hundred or one thousand yards of the enemy's artillery, on which they opened their fire about nine o'clock a.m.—*Brigadier-General Tennant's Despatch to the Commander-in-Chief.*

******

In his despatch to the commander-in-chief, General Gilbert says:—

> Having received orders to push forward my light troops, to force the enemy to show their position, I immediately advanced a troop of horse-artillery (Fordyce's), and Dawes's field-battery, which constantly drew a very heavy and well-directed fire from two large batteries which the enemy had established on either side of the village of Kalrha, by which they were nearly screened from the fire of our guns, which, with the light companies, were still further pushed forward. The heavy guns on our centre at this time opened a very destructive fire.

Of the artillery with his division, General Whish observes:—

> Both troops (Anderson's and Mackenzie's) began a spirited cannonade, and continued it for about three hours, at the rate of forty rounds per gun per hour, until the enemy's guns in our front were silenced.

Nos. 5 and 10, light field-batteries, were attached to the infantry division, under General Campbell. Of these, the general writes:—

I cannot find language to express my sense of the calm, steady, and admirable manner in which these two batteries were commanded and worked by Major Mowatt, the commanding officer, and by Major Ludlow, and Lieutenant Robertson. The infantry of the 3rd division had not occasion to fire a shot. The enemy were driven from their different positions, and from the field, by the fire of these two field-batteries, aided by that of the Bombay troop.

In the meanwhile, Huish's and Duncan's troops on the left, and Warner's on the right, acted in conjunction with the cavalry on our flanks. Of the former, General Thackwell thus writes:—

> To oppose the enemy's guns, I ordered Captain Duncan to move his troop of horse-artillery to the front, which he did in good style, and opened his fire within 500 or 600 yards. This movement was followed by the advance of Captain Huish's troop, and both did considerable execution upon the enemy. These troops (the Scinde Horse and a squadron of the 9th Lancers) made a most brilliant charge upon the enemy. At the same time, I advanced the guns and cavalry towards the enemy's line. The fire of the guns soon put the Gowcherras to retreat, and the glorious charge of the troops on the right, caused their whole force to seek safety in flight.

Brigadier Lockwood says:—

> At the commencement of the action, I directed Captain Warner to open his fire upon a large body of the enemy near a village in our front. But as they returned a heavy fire within accurate range, I changed position, left back, and the horse-artillery ceased firing. The enemy's horsemen now appeared in great force on our right, threatening to turn our flank. So, I changed front to the right. Captain Warner's guns opened with great effect upon the horsemen, and turned them; but they only retired a short distance, and then a regiment of their regular cavalry moved round by a circuitous route and got completely into our rear. I immediately detached towards them three guns, with a squadron of the 16th Dragoons, who, in conjunction with Major Christie's corps of irregular cavalry, drove them off. About this time a large *gole* of horse came on towards me, but as they turned at once from the fire of the guns, I refrained from ad-

vancing after them.

The two troops of horse-artillery under Lieut.-Colonel Brind were in reserve at the commencement of the action, but soon afterwards were brought to the front, for the purpose of enfilading one of the enemy's batteries.

After detailing the attacks on the villages of Burra and Chota Kalrha, which were taken in the most spirited manner by Brigadiers Penney and Hervey, Lord Gough continues, in his published despatch:

> The heavy artillery continued to advance with extraordinary celerity, taking up successive forward positions, driving the enemy from those they had retired to, whilst the rapid advance and beautiful fire of the horse-artillery and light field-batteries, which I strengthened, by bringing to the front the two reserved troops of horse-artillery under Lieutenant-Colonel Brind (Brigadier Brooke having the general superintendence of the whole of the horse-artillery), broke the ranks of the enemy at all points.

The battle was now over, and the pursuit commenced, the whole of the horse-artillery accompanying. The action was almost entirely an artillery fight. For about two hours and a half that arm alone was engaged. It was before the terrible fire of eighty-eight guns that the Sikh Army abandoned the field.

In his official despatch, the commander-in-chief thus writes:—

> To Brigadier-General Tennant, commanding that splendid arm, the artillery, to whose irresistible power I am mainly indebted for the glorious victory of Goojrat, I am indeed most grateful. Conspicuous as the artillery has ever proved itself, never was its superiority over the enemy, its irresistible and annihilating power, more truthfully shown than in this battle. The heavy batteries manoeuvred with the celerity of light guns; and the rapid advance, the scientific and judicious selection of points of attack, the effective and well-directed fire of the troops of horse-artillery and light field-batteries merit my warmest praise.

At the two villages alone were the infantry seriously engaged. Penney's (late Godby's) and Hervey's brigades were sent to take them, and were somewhat surprised to find them occupied by some considerable parties. Our left wing scarcely fired a shot. The cavalry was hardly engaged at all. The Scinde horse made one charge. All the horse-artillery suffered severely, especially the 4th troop 1st brigade, the 2nd troop 2nd brigade, and the 4th troop 3rd brigade. Captain Anderson, of the last-mentioned troop, was killed, as was also Lieutenant Day, of No. 10 horse field-battery.

The artillery loss was greater than that of any other branch in proportion to its numbers.

The artillery division lost in *killed*, 2 officers, 1 sergeant, 20 rank and file, 2 *lascars*, 1 *syce*-driver, and 3 *syces*; *wounded*, 1 European officer (Sir Richard Shakespear), 1 native officer, 4 sergeants, two trumpeters, 50 rank and file, 10 *lascars*, 8 *syce*-drivers, and 7 *syces*: *total*, killed and wounded, 111.

The enemy did not attempt to rally at the town of Goojrat, as it was supposed they would, but fled precipitately at once, leaving camp, baggage, and a vast quantity of material and artillery in the hands of the victors. It was almost to be regretted that they did not wait on their ground a little longer; their loss, except in the two villages, was from the artillery alone, and they suffered but little that afternoon in the pursuit.

The broken Sikh Army fled across the Jhelum, with a few hundred Afghan cavalry, who had left their mountains, hoping for some opportunity to avenge themselves on their old enemies. Sir W. Gilbert, with two divisions of infantry, and cavalry, and artillery, was ordered in pursuit.

The artillery branch consisted of the 2nd troop 2nd brigade and the 4th troop 2nd brigade horse-artillery, Blood's troop horse-artillery, Dawes's horse-battery, the Bombay horse brigade, and four reserve companies, with a well-equipped train, adapted to elephant-draught, the whole under Brigadier Huthwaite, C.B., with Brigade-Major Kaye as his staff officer. The brilliant success which attended Gilbert's rapid pursuit is well known. No further opportunity was given to our troops to gain distinction in the field. The march was an arduous one, the country most difficult, especially for heavy ordnance; but perseverance overcame all. The Sikhs soon saw the futility of further opposition; the *sirdars* surrendered—their army was disarmed, and disbanded at Hoormuch and Rawul-pindee,—and Gilbert drove the Afghans across the Attock, and into the rugged mountains of the Khyber; and thus ended the second Sikh war.

The under-named artillery officers were mentioned in general orders:—

Major-General Whish, C.B.; Brigadier-General Tennant; Lieutenant Olpherts, A.D.C.; Captain Abercrombie, D.A.A.G.A.; Brigadiers Brooke, C.B., and Huthwaite, C.B.; Brigade Majors Kaye and Cox; Captain Hogge, commissary, and Lieutenant Christie, deputy-commissary of ordnance; Lieutenant-Colonel Grant; Majors Garbett, Horsford, Day; Lieutenant-Colonel Brind; Major Mowatt; Lieutenant-Colonel Lane, C.B.; Majors Ludlow, Fordyce; Captains J. D. Shakespear, F. K. Duncan, L. P. Master, R. R. Kinleside, A. Huish, Major Sir R. Shakespear; Captains E. G. Austen, M. Mackenzie, W. K. Warner, M. Dawes; Lieutenants A. Robertson, H. Tombs (deputy assistant quartermaster-general), E. B. Johnson (deputy judge-advocate-general).

The following honorary distinctions were conferred:—

To be a Knight-Commander of the Bath.—Major-General Whish.

To be Commanders of the Bath.—Colonel Tennant, Lieutenant-Colonels Grant, Brind.

To be Lieutenant-Colonels.—Majors Garbett, Horsford, Day, Mowatt, Ludlow, Fordyce, Sir R. Shakespear.

To be Majors.—Captains J. D. Shakespear, Duncan, Master, Kinleside, Huish, Austen, Mackenzie, Warner, Dawes, Hogge, Abercrombie.

Also to be Majors on promotion to Captains regimentally.—Lieutenant E. Kaye, C. V. Cox, A. Robertson, P. Christie, H. A. Olpherts, H. Tombs, E. B. Johnson.

Brigadier-General Tennant was subsequently created a K.C.B.

In commemoration of the victories of the Punjab, a medal was struck, of which the following is a transcript:—

A vote of thanks was passed by both Houses of Parliament and by the Court of Proprietors to the armies engaged in these operations, and the eminent services of General Whish and Brigadier Tennant, of the artillery, were especially named. To the splendid working of the artillery the highest military authorities in the country mainly attributed the brilliant termination of the war: and we know not how this record of the services of the corps can be more fitly brought to a close than with the following well-merited tribute paid to the artillery by Lord Hardinge in the House of Lords, on the 24th of April, 1849:—

> It was, it appeared, to the skilful employment of the artillery that they were indebted for this victory; and great as the result had been with so small a loss of men, he (Viscount Hardinge) felt that that arm of the service was most admirably conducted on that occasion. This argued most admirable conduct on the part of the artillery; and it would appear, by most of the accounts received, that so effectually had this arm of the service been employed, that the Sikh artillery, though managed as usual with great bravery, was, notwithstanding all their efforts, perfectly silenced; so that it was not necessary for the British infantry to fire in line, with the exception of two regiments of Europeans and four regiments of Native Infantry.
> With the exception of those regiments, not a regiment of their infantry fired a musket-shot, so considerable was the service rendered by the Indian artillery. That force was certainly a most splendid one, and second he would say to none; and it had been mainly instrumental in obtaining for Lord Gough one of his best and most splendid triumphs. The statement made by his Lordship, in his despatch, was, that the heavy artillery—eighteen-pounders—were actually manoeuvred and handled with the facility of field-guns. He (Viscount Hardinge) had seen the same thing done with those eighteen-pounders during the campaign of the Sutlej. Two elephants were harnessed to each eighteen-pounder, and they carried the guns with the greatest facility over every sort of ground without any assistance and without causing any delay or impediment to the infantry.
> That practice was first resorted to in the campaign of 1846, when the heavy guns were brought up from Delhi, a distance of 300 miles, and were carried on every occasion without any trouble, and he believed that had never before been seen in

India. The able officer who commanded the artillery in the late battle had been mentioned,—he referred to Brigadier-General Tennant, who had been so much praised by Lord Gough; and he (Viscount Hardinge) wished to say that he had the honour of knowing him, and he was ably seconded by another excellent officer. Seeing the great importance of artillery in modern warfare, and seeing, also, that its value had been so signally manifested in India, he would remind their lordships at the same time that a committee was sitting elsewhere to investigate the state of the Ordnance Department; and he trusted that their lordships would not allow that valuable arm of the service, which took so much time to create, and which when created was so valuable, to be reduced below a scale of proper strength and efficiency.

In Bengal alone, the regular army had 200 pieces of artillery ready to be moved, comprising 120 nine-pounders, and the remainder three and six-pounders, and that was exclusive of all the artillery that belonged to local and irregular corps. Besides that, there was during the campaign more than 100 pieces of heavy artillery, of eighteen and twenty-four pounders, actually on the Sutlej, with 1,000 rounds of ammunition per gun. They were all complete and ready for action, and all that was required was the actual necessity for their movement. That was a state of readiness that was very much to be admired, and he hoped they would never consent to cripple that noble arm of their service.

★★★★★★

Note to Chapter 8.—It is stated in chapter 8, page 238, that a monumental column was raised (at Dum-Dum) to the memory of Captain Nicholl and the officers and men of the 1st troop 1st brigade, who perished so gloriously on the retreat from Caubul. As this sheet is going through the press, I learn that the column has been blown down during a *typhaun*, and that it is the intention of the regiment not to restore it, but to place, in its stead, a monumental slab in the Dum-Dum church. I trust that I shall be pardoned for saying that I believe such a resolution, if carried into effect, will be greatly regretted by many of the relatives of the brave men to whom the column was dedicated, and by some, at least, of the original promoters of the testimonial.

★★★★★★

ALSO FROM LEONAUR
AVAILABLE IN SOFTCOVER OR HARDCOVER WITH DUST JACKET

THE FALL OF THE MOGHUL EMPIRE OF HINDUSTAN *by H. G. Keene*—By the beginning of the nineteenth century, as British and Indian armies under Lake and Wellesley dominated the scene, a little over half a century of conflict brought the Moghul Empire to its knees.

LADY SALE'S AFGHANISTAN *by Florentia Sale*—An Indomitable Victorian Lady's Account of the Retreat from Kabul During the First Afghan War.

THE CAMPAIGN OF MAGENTA AND SOLFERINO 1859 *by Harold Carmichael Wylly*—The Decisive Conflict for the Unification of Italy.

FRENCH'S CAVALRY CAMPAIGN *by J. G. Maydon*—A Special Correspondent's View of British Army Mounted Troops During the Boer War.

CAVALRY AT WATERLOO *by Sir Evelyn Wood*—British Mounted Troops During the Campaign of 1815.

THE SUBALTERN *by George Robert Gleig*—The Experiences of an Officer of the 85th Light Infantry During the Peninsular War.

NAPOLEON AT BAY, 1814 *by F. Loraine Petre*—The Campaigns to the Fall of the First Empire.

NAPOLEON AND THE CAMPAIGN OF 1806 *by Colonel Vachée*—The Napoleonic Method of Organisation and Command to the Battles of Jena & Auerstädt.

THE COMPLETE ADVENTURES IN THE CONNAUGHT RANGERS *by William Grattan*—The 88th Regiment during the Napoleonic Wars by a Serving Officer.

BUGLER AND OFFICER OF THE RIFLES *by William Green & Harry Smith*—With the 95th (Rifles) during the Peninsular & Waterloo Campaigns of the Napoleonic Wars.

NAPOLEONIC WAR STORIES *by Sir Arthur Quiller-Couch*—Tales of soldiers, spies, battles & sieges from the Peninsular & Waterloo campaingns.

CAPTAIN OF THE 95TH (RIFLES) *by Jonathan Leach*—An officer of Wellington's sharpshooters during the Peninsular, South of France and Waterloo campaigns of the Napoleonic wars.

RIFLEMAN COSTELLO *by Edward Costello*—The adventures of a soldier of the 95th (Rifles) in the Peninsular & Waterloo Campaigns of the Napoleonic wars.

AVAILABLE ONLINE AT **www.leonaur.com**
AND FROM ALL GOOD BOOK STORES

ALSO FROM LEONAUR
AVAILABLE IN SOFTCOVER OR HARDCOVER WITH DUST JACKET

OFFICERS & GENTLEMEN by *Peter Hawker & William Graham*—Two Accounts of British Officers During the Peninsula War: Officer of Light Dragoons by Peter Hawker & Campaign in Portugal and Spain by William Graham .

THE WALCHEREN EXPEDITION by *Anonymous*—The Experiences of a British Officer of the 81st Regt. During the Campaign in the Low Countries of 1809.

LADIES OF WATERLOO by *Charlotte A. Eaton, Magdalene de Lancey & Juana Smith*—The Experiences of Three Women During the Campaign of 1815: Waterloo Days by Charlotte A. Eaton, A Week at Waterloo by Magdalene de Lancey & Juana's Story by Juana Smith.

JOURNAL OF AN OFFICER IN THE KING'S GERMAN LEGION by *John Frederick Hering*—Recollections of Campaigning During the Napoleonic Wars.

JOURNAL OF AN ARMY SURGEON IN THE PENINSULAR WAR by *Charles Boutflower*—The Recollections of a British Army Medical Man on Campaign During the Napoleonic Wars.

ON CAMPAIGN WITH MOORE AND WELLINGTON by *Anthony Hamilton*—The Experiences of a Soldier of the 43rd Regiment During the Peninsular War.

THE ROAD TO AUSTERLITZ by *R. G. Burton*—Napoleon's Campaign of 1805.

SOLDIERS OF NAPOLEON by *A. J. Doisy De Villargennes & Arthur Chuquet*—The Experiences of the Men of the French First Empire: Under the Eagles by A. J. Doisy De Villargennes & Voices of 1812 by Arthur Chuquet .

INVASION OF FRANCE, 1814 by *F. W. O. Maycock*—The Final Battles of the Napoleonic First Empire.

LEIPZIG—A CONFLICT OF TITANS by *Frederic Shoberl*—A Personal Experience of the 'Battle of the Nations' During the Napoleonic Wars, October 14th-19th, 1813.

SLASHERS by *Charles Cadell*—The Campaigns of the 28th Regiment of Foot During the Napoleonic Wars by a Serving Officer.

BATTLE IMPERIAL by *Charles William Vane*—The Campaigns in Germany & France for the Defeat of Napoleon 1813-1814.

SWIFT & BOLD by *Gibbes Rigaud*—The 60th Rifles During the Peninsula War.

AVAILABLE ONLINE AT **www.leonaur.com**
AND FROM ALL GOOD BOOK STORES

ALSO FROM LEONAUR
AVAILABLE IN SOFTCOVER OR HARDCOVER WITH DUST JACKET

ESCAPE FROM THE FRENCH *by Edward Boys*—A Young Royal Navy Midshipman's Adventures During the Napoleonic War.

THE VOYAGE OF H.M.S. PANDORA *by Edward Edwards R. N. & George Hamilton, edited by Basil Thomson*—In Pursuit of the Mutineers of the Bounty in the South Seas—1790-1791.

MEDUSA *by J. B. Henry Savigny and Alexander Correard and Charlotte-Adélaïde Dard*—Narrative of a Voyage to Senegal in 1816 & The Sufferings of the Picard Family After the Shipwreck of the Medusa.

THE SEA WAR OF 1812 VOLUME 1 *by A. T. Mahan*—A History of the Maritime Conflict.

THE SEA WAR OF 1812 VOLUME 2 *by A. T. Mahan*—A History of the Maritime Conflict.

WETHERELL OF H. M. S. HUSSAR *by John Wetherell*—The Recollections of an Ordinary Seaman of the Royal Navy During the Napoleonic Wars.

THE NAVAL BRIGADE IN NATAL *by C. R. N. Burne*—With the Guns of H. M. S. Terrible & H. M. S. Tartar during the Boer War 1899-1900.

THE VOYAGE OF H. M. S. BOUNTY *by William Bligh*—The True Story of an 18th Century Voyage of Exploration and Mutiny.

SHIPWRECK! *by William Gilly*—The Royal Navy's Disasters at Sea 1793-1849.

KING'S CUTTERS AND SMUGGLERS: 1700-1855 *by E. Keble Chatterton*—A unique period of maritime history-from the beginning of the eighteenth to the middle of the nineteenth century when British seamen risked all to smuggle valuable goods from wool to tea and spirits from and to the Continent.

CONFEDERATE BLOCKADE RUNNER *by John Wilkinson*—The Personal Recollections of an Officer of the Confederate Navy.

NAVAL BATTLES OF THE NAPOLEONIC WARS *by W. H. Fitchett*—Cape St. Vincent, the Nile, Cadiz, Copenhagen, Trafalgar & Others.

PRISONERS OF THE RED DESERT *by R. S. Gwatkin-Williams*—The Adventures of the Crew of the Tara During the First World War.

U-BOAT WAR 1914-1918 *by James B. Connolly/Karl von Schenk*—Two Contrasting Accounts from Both Sides of the Conflict at Sea During the Great War.

AVAILABLE ONLINE AT **www.leonaur.com**
AND FROM ALL GOOD BOOK STORES

www.ingramcontent.com/pod-product-compliance
Lightning Source LLC
Chambersburg PA
CBHW031616160426
43196CB00006B/161